LYAUTEY IN MOROCCO

LYAUTEY IN MOROCCO

Protectorate Administration, 1912–1925

ALAN SCHAM

UNIVERSITY OF CALIFORNIA PRESS

BERKELEY, LOS ANGELES, LONDON

1970

University of California Press
Berkeley and Los Angeles, California
University of California Press, Ltd.
London, England
Copyright © 1970, by
The Regents of the University of California
International Standard Book Number: 0-520-01602-5
Library of Congress Catalog Card Number: 74-92680
Printed in the United States of America

To My Mother and Father

CONTENTS

ILLUSTRATIONS

ABBREVIATIONS

AF   *Bulletin du Comité de l'Afrique Française*
AG   *Annales de Géographie*
AHES   *Annales d'Histoire Économique et Sociale*
AIEO   *Annales de l'Institut d'Études Orientales*
AM   *Archives Marocaines*
BO   *Bulletin Officiel du Protectorat de la République Française au Maroc*
CAIU   *Cahiers de l'Alliance Israélite Universelle*
CEA   *Cuadernos de Estudios Africanos*
CL   *Choix de Lettres* (by Lyautey)
CSMS   *Convegno di Scienzi Morali e Storiche*
DDF   *Documents Diplomatiques Français*
EI   *Encyclopaedia of Islam*
F-M   *France-Maroc*
IBLA   *Revue de l'Institut des Belles Lettres Arabes*
LA   *Lyautey l'Africain—Textes et Lettres du Maréchal Lyautey*
PA   *Paroles d'Action* (by Lyautey)
RC   *Renseignements Coloniaux*
REI   *Revue des Études Islamiques*
RJPUF   *Revue Juridique et Politique de l'Union Française*
RMM   *Revue du Monde Musulman*
RP   *La Revue de Paris*
VM   *Vers le Maroc. Lettres du Sud-Oranais (1903–1906)* (by Lyautey)

PREFACE

The purpose of this book is to outline the main institutional changes made in Morocco during the early phase of the French Protectorate, when a very remarkable man, Marshal Lyautey, held office as the first French Resident General (1912–1925). I have not attempted to discuss Lyautey's military achievement in pacifying and uniting Morocco, partly at a time when the First World War was in progress; nor to survey the economic developments and social changes that took place. I have limited the scope of the book to developments in the governmental apparatus, land and property administration, the educational system, and judicial organization.

Perhaps the most vexing problem encountered in a study of this nature is that of transliteration. Ordinarily there is the problem of whether to put Arabic words in academic or popular transliteration. Instead of choosing between these systems I have used the French system of transliteration. I have referred to Moroccan proper nouns according to the French spelling, with the exception of a few names of cities known commonly in English, such as Tangier, Fez, and Marrakesh.

In addition a glossary of Arabic terms has been included at the end of the book.

Maps 1 and 2 were redrawn from maps published in 1916 and 1922, respectively, by the Résidence Générale, Rabat.

I should like to acknowledge with gratitude the help given me by Professor André Adam of the Université d'Aix, F. R. C. Bagley of the School of Oriental Studies of the University of Durham, Nevill Barbour, Professor David M. Hart, cartographer Robert L. Williams of the Yale University Map Laboratory, and Juliana.

ALAN SCHAM

Southern Connecticut State College
New Haven
1969

xi

Tangier

ᵒArzila

ᵒLarache

RHARB

Cercle du

M. bel Ksiri   ● El Had Koure

REGION

▲Mehdia   Sebou   A. de
         Dar bel Hamri   □Petit

Rabat   de RABAT   C.
         ᵒMonod   ● Meknes
                    C. des
              Tiflet   Mek

Nkreila   Bataille
□   Moaziz Khemisset   Agourai
         C. de Zaer   Zemmour
Casablanca   Boul   Merzaga   ● Tedders
         □ Haut   C.
              ●   d'Oulmes   C.
Sidi Ali   Marchand
▲Azzemour   Bér Rechid   Christian   Territoire de
Mazagan ᵒ   My. bou Azza Zaïan   ●Ait Lias
□   ● Kreney ed Defa
         C H A O U I A
         Cercle des   ▲Settat ▲Kasba ben   Territoire   C. de
                          Ahmed   □
Doukkala   △   Oued Zem   de Tadla Khenifra
         Oulad Said   Khenifra
Rhal Mtal ᵒ   M. ben   Guisser   de MEKNES
         Abbou
C. des   A. d'El Boroudj
                                   □Kasba Tadla
Safi □ El Arba ᵒ   □El Boroudj
Abda
         ● Ben Guerir   ● Dar Ould Zidouh
         Cercle les Rehamna-Sraghna
              ● Kelaa
         ᵒ Sidi bou Othmane

Marrakech

Mogador ●

REGION de MARRAKECH

C. des Haha Chiadma

Cercle de Marrakech-Banlieue

□ Agadir Ighir

SOUS

Controle Civil territory

INTRODUCTION: ESTABLISHMENT OF THE PROTECTORATE

Of the possessions of France in North Africa, Morocco was the last to be acquired. The acquisition occurred as the result of the Treaty of Fez, signed on March 30, 1912,[1] when, after years of frustration and international wrangling, the other four European nations with similar interests in North Africa—England, Germany, Italy, and Spain—gave their approval.

The French took over Morocco for several reasons: (1) from a military point of view, to protect the Algerian border and French North African dominance and to ensure that no other European power controlled the southern shore of Morocco opposite the Straits of Gibraltar; (2) to maintain security for Europeans and Christians living in Morocco, this in conjunction with the *mission civilisatrice;* (3) to find new markets and economic opportunities for colonists, industrialists, and financiers; and (4) to introduce major reforms in the government.

The legal acquisition of the Sherifian Empire—if only as a protectorate,[2] and not as a full-fledged colony and permanent dependency—now gave France control of three North African countries, Morocco, Algeria, and Tunisia, which were governed by three separate administrations. General Hubert Lyautey was selected by the French Premier, Raymond Poincaré, and his Cabinet and Parliament, to be the first Resident General.

General (later Marshal) Lyautey found himself in a singular situa-

[1] See Appendix 1.
[2] Technically speaking, Spain controlled the Protectorate jointly with France, the Spanish Zone extending north of Fez and the Rif Mountains; it was, however, only a small portion of the whole country.

1

tion. Apart from his responsibility to the French Foreign Minister, he was given practically autocratic powers in the civil administration and military organization of the country. He set up the institutions of the country and appointed the men to fill the key posts in those institutions. When he wanted his way, he often got it. He was a determined man with definite, even dogmatic views, yet at the same time he was flexible and considered the opinions of subordinates. The new Protectorate required a man of decision. Lyautey brought the twentieth century to a medieval Morocco; he was to change that country during his thirteen-year rule more radically than it had been done before, since the first Islamic invasion in the late seventh century.

When the French officially entered Morocco after the signing of the Treaty of Fez, French troops were already located in that country, both along the Casablanca coast and on the Moroccan side of the Algero-Moroccan border, where they had been stationed since 1907. In the spring of 1912 these troops began the systematic military pacification of Morocco.

Since 1904 Frenchmen had been in Moroccan ports as members of the Moroccan Debt Administration, and had occasionally served as military advisers to the Sultan, but Frenchmen held no other official positions in the country prior to the establishment of the Protectorate other than the usual consular posts. Thus when the French entered Morocco in the spring of 1912, they were not total strangers to this beautifully strange and confused land, but they had many obstacles to overcome to restore order and introduce their panaceas.

1

LYAUTEY: THE SOLDIER-ADMINISTRATOR

I. *Early Career,* 1854–1911

. . . how I enjoy this kind of life! It is as though I had been put on the earth just for this. After twenty years of a routine career in France, after the anguish of being overlooked by fate so often, during the past three years I feel that I have finally been forging ahead, confident in what I am doing, leading my type of life, people, and affairs. I always felt as though I had been born to create, and now I am creating, to command and now I am commanding, to mull over new ideas, projects, and works, and now I am doing just that, and by the bucketful.

LYAUTEY TO HIS SISTER,
November 25, 1897

Indeed there is only one opinion about you [Lyautey]: that you are doing an excellent piece of work and are one of our finest hopes. No doubt you cause jealousy in some circles, but precisely because you are what you are!

JONNART TO LYAUTEY,
December 16, 1904

Louis-Hubert-Gonzalve Lyautey was born in Nancy on November 17, 1854. Laurence de Grimoult de Villemotte, his mother, came from an aristocratic family, being the daughter of a viscount from Normandy and a noblewoman from Lorraine. His paternal grandfather, Hubert, after whom he was named, and two of his great-uncles reached the rank of general; another great-uncle was killed as a young officer in Spain. His father, Just Lyautey, was a civil engineer. From his mother's family he inherited his interest in the fine arts, and from his father's, a longing for a life of action and duty. Both families bequeathed to Hubert Lyautey royalist sympathies.

When Hubert was a child, his family divided their time between their town house in Nancy and the family estate, Crévic (also in Lorraine). Thus he was brought up in the aristocratic and intellectual society of Nancy as well as in the simplicity of country life, where he came into contact with the family's tenants and peasant children with whom he played and who, upon his return to the charred ruins of Crévic many years later, were to greet a saddened General with a touching, "Bonjour, M'sieur Hubert."

When he was eighteen months old Hubert slipped from a balcony of the family house in Nancy to the street below. The spinal injury that resulted was to cause him pain and embarrassment for many years. He underwent major surgery two years later and was in bed until the age of six, when he was first able to hobble about with the aid of crutches. It was not until 1864, when he was ten, that he could begin a fairly normal life, with the aid of a steel brace (which he wore for two years). During this long period of enforced inactivity, Lyautey read a great deal.[1]

In his teens he attended several schools including the Lycée in Nancy and the École Polytechnique, and at the age of eighteen he was accepted for the French military academy, Saint-Cyr, which he entered in October, 1873. This had been his great childhood aim and was a considerable achievement in view of his early spinal injury.

A salient feature of Lyautey's character was always his great zest for life, and he was disillusioned when he discovered that this enthusiasm was not shared by the staff of Saint-Cyr. An important event in his life at this time was his introduction by one of the priests at the École de la Rue des Postes to the writings of Albert de Mun. During his first year at Saint-Cyr Lyautey succeeded in meeting de Mun at the Rue des Postes; as Maurois put it, Lyautey left the first meeting "conquered." From his boyhood Hubert Lyautey needed someone to look up to and respect, and sought a worthwhile meaning to life, and de Mun, who was then aide-de-camp to the Military Governor General of Paris, helped to provide this meaning. Captain de Mun was deeply interested in Catholicism and social reform, interests which captured young Lyautey's imagination, and as Maurois writes, "finally an officer, an elder, gave him a reason for living, one more exalted than the mere bearing of arms." Lyautey and three fellow cadets went up to de Mun's house, rang his bell and announced: "Our life is yours. What do you want us to do? Command. We shall obey." [2] This enthusiasm and desire for duty of his youth remained with Lyautey

---

[1] For the injury see Andre Maurois, *Lyautey* (Paris, 1931), p. 3. Much of the material in these first several paragraphs is drawn from Maurois, and from Général Yves de Boisboissel, *Dans l'ombre de Lyautey* (Paris, 1954), esp. pp. 333–334.

[2] See Maurois, p. 21.

throughout his professional career, both as soldier and administrator.

Lyautey completed his studies at Saint-Cyr at the end of 1875 and entered the Military Staff School in January 1876. Again, he was disillusioned and bored, and in the spring of 1880 he joined a cavalry regiment that was posted to Orléansville, Algeria, the same year. For the next two years he learned something of Islam, North Africa, and colonial administration, and he began studying Arabic, though for the last six months in Algeria, in an isolated outpost in the south, "again it seemed to him that his life was lacking in purpose and his need for devotion going unfulfilled." [3] This restlessness was manifested in what appeared to be a religious crisis.

He was promoted to the rank of captain in September, 1882, and ordered to join the IVth Regiment of the Chasseurs Légers at Épinal. Back in France early in 1883 he was ordered on a two months' mission to Italy, and afterward presented a report on the Italian cavalry to the Ministry of War, for which he was warmly praised by General Villemot, then Chief of the General Staff, for the Minister of War.[4] The trip to Italy indeed meant much more than work to Lyautey, twenty-seven years old and in the throes of understanding his maturing personality, for en route he stopped in Austria to meet the Comte de Chambord, in exile at Goritz. The meeting was profoundly moving to the young Lyautey. Immediately following the interview he wrote: "I have just left Him. The emotion from this is such, the soaring feeling so strong, that I cannot regain consciousness of my own personality, which has abdicated, been lost in Him during those hours of grace. The King of France!—I have seen Him, touched Him, heard Him." [5] Later, when he reached Rome, Lyautey again underwent an intensely emotional period when he had an audience with Pope Leo XIII, on March 31, 1883, and discovered to his dismay that the Pope was a republican, not a royalist. The impact of this event, closely following the earlier meeting with the Comte de Chambord, cannot be underestimated; it resulted in a climactic clash of values, hopes, and dreams with realities. Lyautey had always been deeply religious, and he felt now that his religion was failing him when he most needed it. All that month in Rome, Lyautey's mind was in turmoil, further aggravated by the hostility toward France in the Italian capital as a result of France's occupation of Tunisia. When he returned to his regiment at Épinal in May, his state of mind was totally different from what it had been two months earlier.

For a time, beginning in the autumn of 1883, Lyautey was A.D.C. to General L'Hotte, then Inspector General of Cavalry, at Commercy.

---

[3] *Ibid.*, pp. 24–32.
[4] The official notification is quoted in *Dans l'ombre*, p. 343.
[5] Maurois, pp. 28–29.

Back with his regiment at Épinal, he again had an opportunity to think and to read—especially the works of Herbert Spencer, Auguste Comte, Strachey, and various religious thinkers—and to do some writing. According to Maurois, it was not until after the death of the Comte de Chambord, sometime in the years between 1887 and 1891, that Lyautey accepted the Republic, and then only de facto, not ideologically, for he remained fundamentally a royalist.[6]

In September, 1887, Lyautey was given command of a cavalry squadron at Saint-Germain, where he began to develop certain definite ideas about the army and army life, especially as it concerned the enlisted men. He wanted to improve the soldiers' life, by providing recreation rooms for them where they could read and play billiards in the evening, and in fact the first recreation rooms were set up according to his ideas.

At thirty-three, however, Lyautey still felt bored and even stifled, and craved action. It was at this time that he came under another influence, which gave a new dimension to his existence. At the home of an old family friend, M. de Guerle, he became acquainted with a literary circle that included T. d'Haussonville, Eugène-Melchior de Vogüé, the Baignères, and Coppée. Lyautey and Vogüé soon became firm friends. At the home of the Baignères Lyautey met de Régnier, Jacques-Émile Blanche, and Marcel Proust.[7] These social and literary contacts were a source of great happiness for Lyautey, for he was one of those rather rare men who enjoyed both sword and pen.

One day while discussing his proposed army reforms with de Vogüé, Vogüé asked him to prepare some notes on his ideas for an article he intended to write for the *Revue des Deux Mondes*. Vogüé was so unexpectedly pleased with the notes Lyautey submitted to him that instead of using them in an article of his own, he had them published alone—anonymously, because officers in active service were forbidden to publish—under the title, "On the Social Role of the Officer in Universal Military Service." Lyautey's article, which appeared in the *Revue* in March, 1891, came to the attention of several prominent persons, and not long thereafter brought about a change in his career.

In March, 1893, Lyautey was promoted to the rank of major, and the following October he was made Chief of Staff of the VIIth Cavalry Division at Meaux. He still complained of boredom, however, and seemed disgusted, as Maurois says, "with the comfortable sterility" of the life he was leading.[8] But again, fortune intervened. In August, 1894, while on maneuvers in Brie, Lyautey was notified by the Ministry of War that he was to be sent to Indochina. The transfer was in fact a

[6] *Ibid.*, p. 35.
[7] *Ibid.*, pp. 36–37.
[8] *Ibid.*, p. 49.

reprimand, not a favor, for the article in the *Revue des Deux Mondes* had aroused considerable resentment and hostility among certain officers, and the Chief of the General Staff, General Boisdeffre, felt it advisable to remove Lyautey from the scene; but for Lyautey himself it was a welcome change.

Among Lyautey's fellow passengers on the voyage from Marseilles were colonial officers and administrators. It was a new experience for him, and he at once felt much happier. "In these talks with men of action," he wrote, "I feel far from the falsity of the *salons de lettres* and dinners of Paris, and just as far from the mummification of our moribund, idle, routine-plagued army. It is a resurrection." [9]

He arrived at Saigon in November, 1894, where he met the Governor General of Indochina, M. de Lanessan. The two men took an immediate liking to each other, and on the journey to Hanoi, Lanessan gave Lyautey some advice on colonial administration that was to prove invaluable in later years:

In every country there is a social framework. The great error of the Europeans who come as conquerors is to destroy these frameworks. The country so deprived falls into anarchy. One must govern with the mandarin, and not against him. The European, not being superior in numbers, cannot take his place, but only supervise. Therefore do not offend local traditions; do not change customs. There is in every society a leadership class, born to direct the affairs of the people, without which one is powerless. Use that class in our best interests.[10]

As a staff officer in Indochina Lyautey was soon given enough responsibility and action to satisfy even his energetic character, and he learned a great deal about the army and colonial administration. He had been in Indochina only a few weeks when he met the man who was to wield a particularly strong influence in his life, Colonel—later Marshal—Joseph Gallieni.[11] Lyautey was struck by Gallieni's unusual qualities, and Gallieni was likewise impressed by Lyautey and obtained his appointment as his Chief of Staff.[12] The two officers used to spend the evenings together talking, often over a game of whist, to the accompaniment of Chinese musicians. Lyautey always entered into the spirit of his surroundings and enjoyed drenching himself now in the spirit of the East, just as he was later to do in things Moorish; and various native objects were to be found in his home at Tonkin, including miniature pagodas and opium pipes.

[9] *Ibid.*, p. 52.
[10] *Ibid.*, p. 54.
[11] Marshal Joseph Gallieni (1849–1916) had an impressive career in the French Sudan and Indochina, and also in the pacification and reorganization of Madagascar (1887–1905), though it reached an unhappy culmination as Minister of War (1915–1916). He was made a marshal posthumously in 1921.
[12] Maurois, p. 64.

During this period Lyautey began learning the means of taking, securing, administering, and developing areas presently in enemy hands, or subject to enemy attack, and he later followed the basic principles involved in Madagascar, Algeria, and Morocco. Essentially, these principles concentrated on the well-being of the natives, providing them with security in their everyday life, and administering their affairs with understanding, respect, and generosity.

The relationship between Lyautey and Gallieni was so close that when late in 1896 Lyautey, then aged forty-one, heard that General Gallieni was being sent to Madagascar, he wrote to a friend that he was even considering leaving the army, to return to France, perhaps to marry and even to run for office, with the ultimate hope of becoming a colonial governor.[13] To another friend he revealed his frustration:

I am most definitely a creature of action. I have always believed this very much, and facts have finally confirmed it. After twenty years of being held down, I at last believed that I had reached that goal of action. I believed that favorable circumstances would put me in the saddle to do a bit of "Cecil Rhodism" and that, perhaps, I would leave behind my mark on a rich and lasting work. I believed that I was going to be one of those in whom men believe, in whose eyes thousands seek command, with whose voice and pen roads are reopened, countries repopulated and built. I hoped for all that, and if that escapes me, it will be a harsh blow. For, more than ever, I feel that without being able to accomplish productive, imperative, and immediate action, I shall become corroded and corrupted, and my abilities will remain unused. I am the antithesis of the anonymous and indirect agent, of the bureaucrat. I conceived of command only as the direct and personal form, of being present at the place, of always making the rounds [in person], of setting to work by talk, by personal charm, by the visual and oral transmission of one's faith, of one's enthusiam . . . And now the messenger brings us news of Gallieni's departure for Madagascar. Why did not the Havas Agency telegraph it to us? I cabled him that I was ready [to join him] and the devil with all this. Today, he is gone. Too late. What a shame! I have a terrible thirst for finding again an intense life, one of personal responsibility, and command, where I could work to my heart's content.[14]

What happened was not difficult to foresee. Gallieni, as the first Resident General of Madagascar, asked the Colonial Minister to let him have Lyautey; Lyautey was ordered to join his chief in March, 1897, and five months later was promoted to the rank of lieutenant colonel.[15] At long last his energies and abilities had the outlet for which he had so long hoped: "The essential thing is to know what one wants and where one is going. Now, I know what that is: to make social duty predominate over all other duties, the duty of freeing this

[13] Ibid., p. 70.
[14] Lyautey to A. de Margerie, Aug. 15, 1896, CL, pp. 112–113.
[15] Boisboissel, p. 334. Madagascar had been annexed by France in 1896.

country [Madagascar] from decay and ruin." [16] Like Bugeaud earlier in the century, he was now a *soldat-administrateur*, a position for which he had longed, and he worked enthusiastically under a man he greatly admired: "What a joy to give oneself to a task and to see it accomplished. What a reason to live for; while in France one always works at that which is never achieved." [17]

In the winter of 1897–1898 a dream of Lyautey's became a reality; he created his first city, and concerning this *"coup de collier créateur"*, as he called it, he said: I had the joy of the *urbs condita* in building this small city of Ankazobé, the plan for which I had myself sketched out on the ground and from which I saw it rise up with fatherly interest, house by house, street by street, tree by tree." [18]

During the years in Madagascar, Lyautey was to come into his own, with a new assurance, pride, and happiness. He asked his sister, the Comtesse de Ponton d'Amécourt, to have made for him a special ring, engraved with a short quotation, in English, from Shelley: "The soul's joy lies in doing." [19] Few mottoes could have been more appropriate for Lyautey. That his political and military ideas had matured is shown in the article he had written for the *Revue des Deux Mondes* a few years earlier. There he said, "The military and territorial commands must be brought together in the same hands. When the military chief is also the administrator of the area and takes a pocket of resistance, he thinks about the market place he will establish there after the fighting is over and he therefore does not take that area in the same way." [20]

Lyautey returned to France in 1899 on leave, and he was promoted to a full colonel in February, 1900. In February, 1902, he returned to France as commander of the XIVth Hussars, at Alençon, a position which, although not especially pleasing to Lyautey at the time, was to prove very eventful, for during the summer of 1903 at a luncheon with a close friend, M. Jules Charles-Roux, he met the newly appointed Governor General of Algeria, M. Jonnart.[21] Jonnart spoke to Lyautey of his difficulties in Algeria, especially the increasing number of

[16] Maurois, p. 75.
[17] Lyautey to Max Leclerc, Sept. 21, 1897, *CL*, p. 161. Marshal Thomas Bugeaud de la Piconnerie (later the Duc d'Isly; 1784–1849), was famous for his defeat of Abd el-Kader and conquest of Algeria where he was Governor from 1840 to 1847.
[18] Maurois, p. 80.
[19] Lyautey to his sister, Nov. 25, 1897, *CL*, p. 164.
[20] Republished in Maréchal Lyautey, *Du rôle social de l'officier* (Paris, 1946), pp. 31–60.
[21] Maurois, p. 96. Célestin-Auguste-Charles Jonnart (1857–1927) was a member of the Chamber of Deputies from 1889 to 1914, and of the Senate after 1914; he was Minister of Public Works, 1893–1894, and Governor General of Algeria, 1903–1911, 1918. During the World War he was the French High Commissioner in Greece, and from 1921 to 1924, Ambassador to the Vatican.

frontier incidents, and he seems to have been impressed by the remarks of the forty-eight-year-old colonel, especially when Lyautey spoke of Gallieni's methods of pacification. Late that summer more incidents occurred along the Algero-Moroccan frontier and Jonnart requested the Minister of War, General Louis André, to send him Colonel Lyautey. In September, 1903, Lyautey was on his way, to command the subdivision of Aïn Sefra, a desert post in southwestern Algeria, part of the Oran command, and a month later he was promoted to the rank of brigadier general. At Lyautey's request Aïn Sefra was made his own independent command. Algeria was to be the final proving grounds for Lyautey, for it was there that Jonnart taught him how to deal with politicians and ministers.

If Lyautey believed that a course of action was right, nothing could prevent him from pursuing it. Though he was forbidden to pass over the Moroccan frontier in pursuit of raiding tribal bands, he occupied Béchar across the frontier. When the Minister of War rebuked him, Jonnart came to Lyautey's rescue, giving him his full support, and informed the Minister that Lyautey was not even at Béchar, but at Colomb—a name Lyautey had just given to Béchar, which soon became known as Colomb-Béchar.[22] This town was in the heart of an area terrorized by the outlaws of Bou Amama and El Rogui. Lyautey ordered his men to occupy Ras el Aïn and Berguent, in order to protect the Moroccans living there. The Sultan, however, complained to the Quai d'Orsay, and the Minister of War ordered Lyautey to withdraw. Lyautey refused, and telegraphed a strong reply to Paris. His reasons were clear, as he later explained to his superior:

As I had the honor to inform you [previously], my personal word has been given to the [Moroccan] populations who are gathered around us and to whom I thought I was able to guarantee protection from France. Although I might have acted wrongly, facts proved the necessity of the action, but I must bear the responsibility for it. If I ought, as a soldier, to assure the execution and transmission of the first orders [from Paris ordering evacuation], I should be unable—not only without tarnishing my honor, but even without seriously compromising the word and prestige of French authority—to proceed myself with the evacuation of Ras el Aïn, that is, to abandon populations to whom I have solemnly guaranteed the protection of the French Republic. I therefore have the honor of addressing to you the enclosed, to be sent to the Minister

---

[22] See VM, pp. 75 et seq. In fact Jonnart was in Holland at this time and only heard about Lyautey's actions two days later, when he immediately sent off a telegram to the Premier stating: "1. General Lyautey has acted under my orders [which was not so]. 2. I approve of everything he has done. 3. If the order for evacuation is maintained, I shall leave to join him at his post myself." PA, p. 77. (Colomb-Béchar is situated just southwest of Figuig and is today a part of Algeria.)

of War, which is my request to be relieved of my command and put on half-pay.[23]

Lyautey believed that Moroccan terrorism could only be stopped by taking definite action; he also knew that the Moroccans wanted security and if given it would prove useful allies later. Furthermore, he had guaranteed the protection of the French Republic to the Moroccans, and French prestige would suffer if France declined this responsibility; and of course by committing the French to protect Morocco, he had at the same time committed himself and did not intend to go back on his word. Lyautey was a proud man, and his pride nearly brought his career to an abrupt end at several junctures. He believed that what he was doing now was not only morally right for him but also morally right for France; several months after this frontier operation Lyautey himself admitted: "This *pénétration discrète* of Morocco which I began clandestinely and which has scarcely begun, is so passionate a feeling that to leave would truly be a cruel disappointment for me." [24]

Lyautey was always a man of action, and he needed action, as bankers need money. He was a soldier who loved soldiering and camp life and camaraderie. "Lyautey, in this land of sunshine and great desert chieftains, was happy. . . . his love of fine uniforms and horses and brilliant escorts matched that of the Arabs; and like them he wore a large black burnous, to which were attached silver stars [indicating his rank of general]." [25] Lyautey, enraptured with life, described one of his encampments:

It is ten P.M. My lamp is lit on my camp table, in the large tent of the *bach-agha*, Si-Eddin, of the Ouled Sidi Cheikh. He sent it from Géryville with three others for me. It is as large as an apartment, lined in broadcloth and silk, and a layer of carpets covers the ground. The entrance is wide open and my flag is flapping. A tall red Spahi is on guard; my officers are smoking their last pipe around a glowing fire. A horse is whinnying, tugging at his rope. The servants are removing the leftovers from dinner under the supervision of the *caïd* from the neighboring tribe, who is dressed in a purple burnous . . . and the moon makes this night so refreshing after the hot day . . .[26]

Jonnart was more than happy with Lyautey, who in December, 1906, was promoted to General of Division and appointed to take over the Oran command.[27]

[23] *VM*, pp. 90–91. Lyautey quotes this in a letter to Major Henrys, Aug. 7, 1904.
[24] Maurois, p. 136.
[25] Général Henri-Joseph-Eugène Gouraud, *Lyautey* (Paris, 1938), p. 35.
[26] Maurois, p. 138.
[27] Appointed by *Décision ministérielle* of Dec. 9, 1906. See *VM*, p. 345n.

In Morocco, incidents were on the increase. In March, 1907, Dr. Émile Mauchamp, a French government doctor residing in Marrakesh, whose practice was made up largely of Moroccans and included Moulay Hafid, the heir to the Sultanate, was killed by a crowd of Muslims at the instigation of the German colony, reflecting both a growing anti-French attitude by German diplomats and personal enmity and jealousy on the part of local German nationals. That summer some French workers were also killed by a Moroccan mob in Casablanca. Thus, in March, 1907, Lyautey received orders to occupy Oujda, and in September General Drude was sent with a force to occupy Casablanca.[28] Meanwhile the Quai d'Orsay was slowly laying the foundations for a French take-over of Morocco, planned since 1900. Lyautey knew little or nothing about the secret treaties which the Quai d'Orsay was drawing up, but he realized that something had to be done, as he pointed out to de Vogüé:

Regardless of what one might want, Morocco is a danger to the flanks of Algeria, and unless we evacuate from the latter, it will be necessary to intervene with force in Morocco, for its anarchy has a direct repercussion on our authority and our Algerian interests . . . But (and the crux of the problem lies here) the unfortunate part of it is that our military and civil authorities conceive of this intervention [at Oujda] only as an "expedition," which is indeed frightening. Now, it is this idea that enrages me, that hurts me, to think that after four years, after what I have written and done here and elsewhere, no one yet understands anything about my method . . . When at the first incident or massacre I am given *carte blanche* in my choice of means and persons and complete latitude in time, I shall press on to Fez in a definitive fashion, without regrets *and at minimal expense.* But then I shall make use simultaneously and constantly of political and military means, based on my intelligence reports and dealings within the tribes, to break them up, to create in advance a favorable party for me there, to make a snowball . . . in a word, to practice my formula for the "mobile organization." What a fine and original task I would have! What a pity . . . I guarantee you that I suffer as a Frenchman, far more than as a man.[29]

In September, 1907, M. Eugène Regnault, the French Minister to Fez, was sent on a special mission to Sultan Abd el-Aziz, accompanied by Lyautey. Regnault was able to come to agreement with the Sultan over police organization on the Algero-Moroccan frontier.[30]

Upon Lyautey's return to Oran, news came of more trouble with a Moroccan tribe, the Beni Snassen, who only capitulated on New Year's Day, 1908. By now Lyautey's stock was going up, and the unknown junior staff officer of Indochina was now a well-known general

[28] Général Georges Catroux, *Lyautey le Marocain* (Paris, 1952), pp. 16 *et seq.* Catroux, who was an officer under Lyautey at this time, discusses these events.
[29] Lyautey to E. M. de Vogüé, Sept. 27, 1907; *CL*, p. 263.
[30] Maurois, p. 164.

in Algeria. He was summoned to Paris by Premier Clemenceau in February, 1908. General Albert d'Amade had replaced General Drude in Casablanca, and now Clemenceau asked Lyautey to replace d'Amade. It was a game of political musical chairs, a game that few professional soldiers like. Lyautey refused the post, saying that he must first study the situation, for he did not want to humiliate d'Amade, whom he respected as a soldier and as a man. Instead he got permission to go to the Chaouïa, the region running parallel to the coast behind Casablanca, in the spring of 1908 to study the situation on the spot. His report to Clemenceau supported d'Amade completely. At the end of 1908 Lyautey sent the government another report on the Algero-Moroccan frontier problem, in which he made this statement: "We must, when it involves the policing of natives, always keep this formula in mind: *make a show of strength in order to avoid having to use it.*" [31]

Toward the end of December, 1910, General Lyautey was appointed commander of the Xth Army Corps in France. Before leaving Algeria he married Mme Fortoul, the widow of an army colonel by whom she had had a son. Lyautey took command at Rennes in April, 1911.[32]

On the international scene, tension between Germany and France increased in July, 1911, when the German gunboat *Panther* appeared off Agadir. This proved the catalyst the Germans had hoped for, and in November of that year a Convention was signed by the two countries finally giving France a completely free hand in Morocco while Germany in turn received 100,000 square miles of equatorial Africa. On March 30, 1912, the Treaty of Fez, establishing the French Protectorate of Morocco, was signed.[33]

II. *Resident General, 1912–1925*

The French Third Republic in the second and third decades of its existence produced a type of military officer who found in the pacification and administration of France's overseas possessions the opportunity to practice an art not suited to the European battlefield. Organization and administration were the activities in which he showed his skill, not in military strategy. In such endeavors Gallieni and Lyautey were the outstanding figures.

RAYMOND F. BETTS,
Assimilation and Association in French Colonial Theory, 1890–1914.

[31] *Ibid.*, p. 176.
[32] *PA*, p. 63.
[33] François Charles-Roux and Jacques Caillé, *Missions diplomatiques françaises à Fès* (Paris, 1955), ch. 8.

The pacification of Morocco is a huge task requiring a long period of time, and do not deceive yourselves about it.

> LYAUTEY,
> *December 21, 1912*

This country must not be ruled by force alone. The rational method, and the only effective one—the one, moreover, for which I have been sent to carry out here, and no one else—is the continued and combined game of political preparation and military strength.

> LYAUTEY TO ALBERT DE MUN,
> *October 10, 1912*

Morocco represents the end achievement of French colonization and, with Lyautey, its triumph.

> RENÉ GALLISSOT,
> *Le patronat européen au Maroc—action*
> *sociale, action politique (1931–1942).*

I once read somewhere that no really great human work has ever been achieved, without its having been a labor of love.

> LYAUTEY, QUOTED BY BOISBOISSEL,
> *Dans l'ombre de Lyautey.*

A work rises only in the hand of its master.

> A MOROCCAN PROVERB

Regnault, the French Minister to Fez, was designated as the first Resident General of the new Protectorate, in April, 1912. That same month, however, serious riots broke out in Fez in which French officers were killed and the Sultan's life was threatened. Regnault immediately realized that Morocco needed a soldier-administrator at its helm and not merely a diplomat. The Minister of War, Alexandre Millerand, and Premier Poincaré considered three men—all generals —for the post: Gallieni,[34] d'Amade, and Lyautey, and following a Cabinet meeting at Rambouillet on April 27 General Lyautey was appointed first Resident General of Morocco.[35] On May 8, after a consultation with Millerand, Lyautey left for Morocco, by way of Marseilles on the cruiser *Jules-Ferry*. After a brief stop in Mers el-Kebir, Algeria, to discuss the Algero-Moroccan situation with various military commanders, and a brief visit to Tangier, he proceeded to Casablanca, where he landed on May 13.[36]

[34] Gallieni, when approached, stated that he was too old for the post and recommended Lyautey instead. Amédée Britsch, *Le maréchal Lyautey: le soldat, l'écrivain, le politique* (Paris, 1921), p. 129.

[35] Maurois, p. 186. See appendix 3 for a list of Residents General, 1912–1956.

[36] British, pp. 131–132. Lyautey summed up his first two years' work in Morocco in his Preface to his *Rapport général sur la situation du Protectorate au Maroc*

After a three-day stay at Casablanca where he spoke optimistically to the French community, Lyautey, with Colonel Henri Gouraud,[37] left on horseback for Fez, by way of Rabat and Meknes. A few hours before they reached Fez, an intelligence officer rode up with the news that the situation in Fez was very serious. A short time after, General Charles-Émile Moinier, the commander of the occupation troops, appeared on horseback with even graver news. From a military point of view, he reported, it was all over.[38]

Regnault himself met Lyautey at the gates of Fez and placed himself at the disposal of the new Resident General. Lyautey moved into the Dar Menehbi in Fez and had not even unpacked before General Brulard called upon him: it was too late, he said, to do anything—the situation was hopeless. Formalities proceeded. The following day Regnault, still officially the Minister of France, presented Lyautey to the Sultan, Moulay Hafid, and that evening the French community gave a small dance in honor of the new Resident General.[39]

The military situation was indeed as serious as Moinier had said, for Moroccan troops had massacred their French officers the month before and this had excited the local population.[40] In a city with a native population of 90,000 Muslims, Lyautey had only 4,000 French troops.[41] He called a meeting with the *oulama* and *chorfa*—who represented the upper and middle classes of Fez—in order to gain some support, from within the city at least, pointing out to them that they, as property owners, had as much to lose from a siege, if not

---

au 31 juillet 1914 (Rabat, 1916); this is reproduced in appendix 4. See also, Général Bernard, "La conquête et l'organisation du Maroc, 1912–1919; l'oeuvre du Général Lyautey," *La Géographie*, XXXIV (June–Dec., 1920), 337–360, 458–478.

[37] General Henri-Joseph-Eugène Gouraud (1867–1946) worked under Lyautey in 1912. In 1915 he became commander of the French Eastern Forces, and then of the IVth Army Corps; he later pacified Syria and ultimately became Governor of Paris (1923–1937).

[38] Maurois, p. 191.

[39] Britsch, p. 133.

[40] The first investment of Fez had lasted from March 1 to May 21, 1911, when General Moinier arrived with a relief column; this was followed by rumors of discontent among Moroccan troops. A second siege of Fez began on April 12, 1912 (just after the signing of the Treaty of Fez), followed by a mutiny and massacre on April 17. The second siege was over by April 21, though a series of courts-martial for the mutineers (lasting from April 25 to May 25) increased the fanatical anger of tribes surrounding Fez and led to the third siege of that city (May 12–31) during which Lyautey arrived on the scene. See G. H. Selous, *Appointment to Fez* (London, 1956), pp. 123–125, and 135 *et seq.* for the mutiny. Selous served in Morocco as a British consular official from 1910 to 1928 and was a personal friend of Lyautey, whom he first met in May, 1912, at Fez. Morocco was pacified in four stages: (1) 1912–1914, submission of the Bled el-Makhzen; (2) conquest of the Middle Atlas, 1912–1920; (3) Rif War, 1921–1926; (4) submission of the High Atlas and the Anti Atlas and the edge of the Sahara.

[41] Lyautey left the military command of Fez in Moinier's hands, so as not to embarrass him. Lyautey gives these figures in *LA*, I, 10.

more, than anyone else.[42] One evening after all preparations had been
made and there was nothing more that General Lyautey could do,
he summoned one of his officers who was also a poet and asked him
to read him some of his latest poems and some of de Vigny's. (Gallieni
would have smiled had he seen this.) The attack came on May 25,
at eleven o'clock at night. Tribesmen broke into the city and heavy
house-to-house fighting ensued. On the 26th Lyautey wrote to his
sister, ". . . this is neither a sinecure nor an enviable post that I
have here; just a lot of troubles, and what risks!" [43]—but of course
he liked nothing better. On May 31 reinforcements arrived from
Meknes, and the next morning Lyautey awoke to find that the attack
was over, the tribes having been forced to retreat under the French
artillery barrage.[44]

A few weeks later, in a letter to de Mun, Lyautey described the
situation generally as still "very bad":

Now the South, the Haouz and Marrakesh worry me greatly. I have not a
man I can spare to send there. If I had two extra months, I would go and
see the important feudal lords there myself—El Glaoui, Si Aïssa Ben Omar,
Anflous, Mtougui—to win them over to our side or to play them off against
one another. For the time being, however, I must complete and cement my
building of Fez, which is the key to the whole situation.

There were five particular elements involved, Lyautey explained.
First of all, Sultan Moulay Hafid had decided to abdicate, an event
which Lyautey hoped could be postponed: "Because of the obstacles
with which each day he impedes our collaboration, I should indeed
prefer his abdication, but I believe we must delay this at any price
because of its effect on the international scene." [45] Second, because
the population was so agitated, he feared that a Muslim "holy war,"
or *jihad*, might be declared, and that another Abd el-Kader might
appear and receive widespread backing. Third, there was the problem
of foreigners and *protégés*, "and the open hostility from everything
and everyone German or Spanish, the constant anxiety of having to
come up against foreign cover as soon as we find ourselves faced with
a case of insubordination, an offense or protest—all that holds up
everything." The fourth problem was the lack of competent commanding officers, apart from Gouraud and Brulard, and although he was

[42] *Ibid. Oulama* (sing. *alim*) are learned doctors of the law; *chorfa* (sing. *cherif*)
are Muslim nobles.

[43] *CL*, p. 288.

[44] Maurois discusses the siege, pp. 191 *et seq.*

[45] Earlier, on May 20, Lyautey had also expressed fears that Moulay Hafid's
abdication would further incite the tribes around Fez (*LA*, I, 5). On May 26 the
Sultan forcefully announced his desire to abandon Fez for Rabat. *Ibid.*, p. 7.

quite content with the quality of his younger officers, he needed at least "five or six *seigneurs*" in the upper ranks. Lastly, several more battalions were necessary to relieve his strained and overworked men, "but I am not asking for them yet, as I must first put everything in order so as to see what I need, and then where I need them." [46]

Gradually Lyautey built up his administration. Fortunately for a man of his direct way of working, he did not have to confer with the metropolitan government over such decisions as the creation of offices and appointment of officials, although he was obliged to go to Paris at least once a year to arrange for the funds he needed. He made laws and drew up projects for public works and was eventually able to realize his plans for the effective organization of Morocco. As Maurois has pointed out, Lyautey believed that "a colony should be administered for itself, not for metropolitan France," and that it would thereby "become a source of strength for France only by its own prosperity." "The two fundamental institutions of a colony," Lyautey said, "are free exchange [mental and physical] and no *gendarmes*." [47] The next thirteen years were to prove that freedom and confidence breed far more success than restrictions and suspicion.

Lyautey had qualities that appealed to the Moroccans, Berber or Arab. He was a man of decision, integrity, and justice; he liked a good show; he was a superb horseman, and a born leader. One of his greatest qualities was that he could adapt himself to new situations without restricting himself to any specific formula in his administration of Morocco: "Everything depends upon the time and place. You tried one method in Indochina and it succeeded; that does not mean it is going to work in Madagascar or Morocco. What is suitable for some is not necessarily suitable for others: climate, religion, race, history—so many elements can change the problem." [48] Whatever he did, he believed in doing well; in his own words: "It is as important to place a picture in a good position on a wall, as a [new] city in the countryside." [49] His flexibility of mind often made him the foe of rigid and unadaptable regulations, as Guillaume de Tarde related:

I remember General Lyautey's anger once. He had just visited a small out-post in Morocco, and the young official who had shown him about on his visit had struck him by his intelligence, energy, and ability to get things done. Getting into his car the General said to his *chef de cabinet*: "There is a remarkable boy; make him a *contrôleur* [civil intelligence officer]." "Im-possible, General, he hasn't been in the service long enough; the regulations

[46] Letter of June 16, 1912, *CL*, p. 290.
[47] Maurois, p. 213.
[48] Robert Garric, *Le message de Lyautey* (Paris, 1935), p. 177.
[49] Maurois, p. 214.

state . . ." "Then do I have to let a force that is really alive rot in these unimportant outposts; do I have to condemn this gentleman to mediocre tasks, under the pretext that he is not old enough? What nonsense! As if we had too many good men . . . And where does this regulation of yours come from in the first place? From France, naturally . . . but what is valid over there, perhaps, for drowsy ministries is detestable here where we have still to create everything . . . Now go and find the means for me. That boy must be made a *contrôleur* immediately.[50]

This incident was typical. When Lyautey reached a decision, he wished it to be carried out immediately, without having first to consult regulations, or having it typed in triplicate and sent out through various clerical channels. He had a tendency to make snap judgments of people and obviously believed his judgments were sound —and they usually were.

Maurois relates that one day Lyautey was asked about a technical matter, to which he replied: "I have my technicians for that sort of thing." "And you?" the question was put to him, "What do you do?" "Why, I am the technician of general ideas." [51] Needless to say, a man of Lyautey's temperament immediately attracted men, or repelled them, and those who were attracted were usually men who shared his values and outlook; to them he was simply *"le patron."*

On August 1, 1912, General Lyautey went to Rabat in order to see that Moulay Hafid would indeed abdicate, as he now thought advisable. The Sultan was now proving reluctant, but he finally yielded to Lyautey's persuasion and gave up the Sultanate, on August 12, in favor of his younger brother Moulay Youssef.[52] Six days later a pretender, El Hiba, had himself proclaimed sultan in Marrakesh, which his forces had just taken; and he now menaced the entire Chaouïa region.[53] Colonel Mangin, however, freed Marrakesh from El Hiba's bands on September 8, with the support of the *grands caïds,* so that Moulay Youssef was able to make his first official entry into that city a week later, to be proclaimed sultan by that city's oulama, according to Moroccan custom.[54] On October 20 the new sultan entered Rabat for the first time.[55] The Resident General intended that Moulay Youssef should travel to the various cities of his empire in order to be officially received and recognized by them, for Lyautey wanted the people to accept the sultan as their sovereign and not as a puppet of

[50] Quoted by Maurois, p. 215.
[51] Maurois, p. 216.
[52] Britsch, pp. 136–137; *PA,* p. 67. Moulay Hafid retired to Tangier on a pension of 375,000 francs.
[53] Britsch, p. 138; *LA,* I, 28.
[54] *LA,* I, 38. See appendix 5 for a chronology of Sultans from 1873 to 1969.
[55] *PA,* p. 70.

the French. He even went so far as to keep French troops and officials out of sight as the sultan approached the major cities.

The staff of the Resident General at this time was still only skeletal in structure, consisting of a Directeur Général des Finances, a Directeur Général des Travaux Publics, Lyautey's Délégué, a Secrétaire Général du Gouvernement Chérifien, and a Secrétaire Général du Protectorat.[56] Lyautey chose his chief administrators personally and expected a great deal from them: "In order to assist in the birth of this country, I don't want to see any Molière-type doctors gadding about in pointed caps and speaking Latin, but instead sturdy practitioners rolling up their sleeves and getting down to their work." [57]

In the middle of August, 1912, Lyautey addressed the French colony of Rabat for the first time. Throughout his Moroccan career he kept in contact as much as possible with the French immigrants, in order to coordinate their joint efforts, as well as to explain his own program and aims. This coordination was increased when he created local professional organizations whose members met periodically, and later through the Conseil du Gouvernement. At this meeting with the French *colons,* he wanted them to understand that all would not be easy, or as he put it, "Every time you harvest a field of corn just remember that not an ear of it could have grown without our troops being willing to die in order to protect you." [58]

The period from June to September of that first year was a critical one; although one sultan and one pretender to the throne were now out of the way, Lyautey still had much to contend with: "religious fanaticism, a strong attachment to medieval Islam, the ferocious fight for independence, anarchy, and xenophobia." [59] As he had learned

[56] The full development of the administration is discussed in ch. 2. During Lyautey's thirteen years in Morocco, the following officials held the key administrative posts: The Comte de Saint-Aulaire was the first Délégué des Affaires Étrangères à la Résidence (till May, 1916), followed by Lallier du Coudray, who held an interim appointment to this office until Urbain Blanc was appointed to it permanently; the Secrétaire Général du Protectorat was Paul Tirard, then Lallier du Coudray, and finally Pierre de Sorbier; the Secrétaire Général du Gouvernement Chérifien (on the abolition of this office in May, 1917, it was known as Conseiller du Gouvernement Chérifien) was M. Gaillard; M. Marc was Conseiller du Gouvernement Chérifien; the Directeur Général des Finances was first M. Gallut and then M. Piétri; Travaux Publics was headed by M. Delure and later by M. Delpit; the Direction de l'Enseignement (which became the Direction de l'Instruction Publique, des Beaux-Arts et des Antiquités in December, 1920) was headed by M. Georges Hardy; M. Malet was Directeur Général de l'Agriculture, du Commerce et de la Colonisation; Postes, Télégraphes et Téléphones were the responsibility of M. Walter; and Guillaume de Tarde was Directeur des Affaires Civiles (abolished in May, 1922). Boisboissel, *Dans l'ombre de Lyautey,* pp. 122–123.
[57] Réginald Kann, *Le Protectorat marocain* (Paris, 1921), pp. 76–77.
[58] *PA,* p. 70.
[59] *Ibid.,* p. 73.

in Indochina under Gallieni—"le maître des maîtres coloniaux"—it was necessary to give conquered peoples something that they could understand—military and economic security. Thus he planned to develop commerce, and to build railways, schools, hospitals, roads, and ports; for, as he said, it is "certain that military force alone does not suffice and that—in order to double [our progress]—we must speed up action as much as possible for economic and civilizing penetration." [60] Discussing this period of the Protectorate with students in Paris in December, 1912, he explained what he called the *"bonne méthode,"* which included "the unceasing combination of military and pacific action" and demanded a high degree of "firmness and foresight, energy and generosity, a method requiring vast stores of patience, during which time one must never let go or be discouraged." [61]

As often as not Frenchmen raised as many difficulties for the Resident General as Moroccans, and especially French politicians. For instance, the government had recommended, in July, 1912, that the Residency General should be a roving post only, having no permanent office, permitting Lyautey to move from one trouble spot to another. Lyautey, on the contrary, thought it essential to have a permanent base at the center of economic, military, and civil activity. Not only was there a physical necessity of having to channel governmental business—a process that would be confused if he were obliged to travel about with an army of administrators (and their inevitable files)—but also, from a psychological point of view, a permanent headquarters would represent stability and permanency in the eyes of both colons and Moroccans. Lyautey won his point and sufficient funds were allocated to build temporary barracks-like structures for himself and his administration, although he did not have permanent administrative quarters for another nine years.[62]

In October, 1912, an event took place without Lyautey's knowledge and without solicitation on his behalf—namely, his election to the Académie Française—but he was not able to deliver the traditional reception speech until eight years later.[63]

In December, 1912, Lyautey returned to Paris to report to the government on the situation in Morocco and to present his plans for the organization of that country to the Commission des Affaires Ex-

[60] *Ibid.*, p. 74.
[61] *Ibid.*, p. 79.
[62] Lyautey had asked for fifteen million francs for the buildings needed for the judicial and administrative services; he was only given 2,350,000 for setting up the courts and a mere 500,000 francs for administrative buildings. Owing to the peripatetic nature of his office, Lyautey had three branch headquarters in addition to the principal administrative headquarters at Rabat: at Casablanca, Fez, and Marrakesh.
[63] Maurois, p. 227.

térieures et Coloniales, and to ask for funds for his first credit.[64] When he returned to Morocco three months later, it was with the satisfaction of having money to spend on badly needed basic facilities. At once, he sent a report to the Foreign Minister containing a draft of a tentative reorganization of French, Muslim, and Jewish judicial administration, along with a request that a commission of jurists be drawn up to examine and elaborate on this outline.[65]

Even bureaucracies can move quickly when prodded, and in August, 1913, the new judicial organization was officially set up, and by October the Cour d'Appel was opened in Rabat.[66] That same month Lyautey accompanied President Poincaré to Madrid to meet Alfonso XIII and his ministers. The following spring the President of the Chamber of Deputies toured various Moroccan cities and military fronts and was present on May 16–17 at the meeting of the columns of Gouraud and Baumgarten in their march on Taza in a successful attempt to open the corridor between eastern and western Morocco.[67]

In the early part of 1914 Lyautey began to realize what a menace uncontrolled immigration into Morocco could be. Though he welcomed colons who were willing to contribute something to the country, he knew that mass immigration would lead to difficulties. Furthermore, Lyautey did not believe it was the mission or duty of Europeans to force their civilization and religions upon the natives of colonized countries. Rather, the Europeans should help the colonies. Ideally, as Georges Hardy has so aptly put it, colonization, "undertakes to respect the original talents and contributions of colonial populations, their moral personality, and everything that constitutes their personal being and maintains in them the *goût de vivre*. It improves their existence without disorientating them, without forcing them to break with their past. It raises the level of existence without sacrificing their own variety of life, which is the privilege of our species and no doubt their best guarantee of remaining a vigorous people." [68]

[64] *La*, I, 170–179; *PA*, p. 71.

[65] For this report, see appendix 6. Lyautey was not always satisfied with the first drafts of laws and one day when handed some he said to the officials, "One should be able to read and understand a law as clearly and as easily as one can a newspaper article. The text you are drawing up here is too complicated; that's how it seems to me anyway." Boisboissel, p. 123.

[66] *PA*, p. 94.

[67] *LA*, II, 170. The Fez-Taza corridor was sufficiently cleared and secured to permit rail and highway traffic by the end of 1916. The first military railway from Casablanca (via Rabat, Salé, Kénitra, Meknes) reached Taza on February 5, 1915, and the first military railway between Oujda and Taza was completed on July 14, 1915.

[68] Georges Hardy, *Portrait de Lyautey* (10th ed.; Mayenne, 1949), p. 371, and also p. 216. Hardy became Directeur Général de l'Instruction Publique under Lyautey, and years later Directeur de l'École Coloniale, in Paris. See also Wladimir d'Ormesson, *Auprès de Lyautey* (Paris, 1963), pp. 152–153. D'Ormesson worked directly under Lyautey from December, 1916, to December, 1917.

To be sure, Lyautey believed that Europeans did have certain very specific civilizing tasks. They could introduce into the country modern forms of transport and communication and manufacturing which would produce equipment and provide employment. They could introduce modern medicine and hygiene, new languages and knowledge—or what Lyautey termed his *"arsenal pacifique."* [69] Hardy's attitude to colonization was similar to that of many enlightened Frenchmen, including Lyautey:

> . . . one of the greatest privileges of colonization is that it is in fact capable of enriching the greatest number of people without impoverishing anyone in return. It develops unused property; it makes productive land that is unoccupied or is still being cultivated by primitive methods; it develops and uses virgin forests and valuable mines have been abandoned. It introduces industrial methods in areas still familiar only with handicrafts. In sum, it develops dormant wealth to the greatest benefit of humanity. If it sometimes causes spoliation, that is because it has been misused, for it provides enough to satisfy both the colonizers and the colonized. There is no need to use inhuman methods in order to attain its purpose, and it can—if done properly—produce only benefits to everyone. [70]

By July, 1914, several thousand immigrants were entering Morocco every month. They needed accommodations, land to lease or purchase, and work; and to add to these problems the cost of living was rising all the time. One partial solution was to carry out the programs for public works which would both create employment and enrich the country. The Resident General had in mind vast projects: the development of the ports of Casablanca, Mogador (Essaouira), Mazagan (El Djadida), Rabat, and Kenitra (or Port Lyautey, now Port Hassan II); the building of roads (he had 1,500 kilometers of roads on the drawing boards), including a coastal road from Mazagan in the south to Kenitra in the north, roads from Mogador to Marrakesh, from Mazagan to Marrakesh, from Casablanca to Marrakesh, from Kenitra to Fez, and a road bridging the corridor, from Oujda to Taza. [71] Because of the anarchy and lack of security prior to the Protectorate, no roads had yet been built in Morocco. [72] The task was gigantic enough to humble the dreams of even an ambitious civil engineer, and Lyautey's public works' program did not stop at roads and ports: commercial railways, too, were an absolute necessity. All public works had to be carried out by international tenders and, in the case of the

[69] *VM*, p. 68.
[70] Hardy, pp. 362–363.
[71] *PA*, pp. 109–112.
[72] It was ironic that the sultans never had an opportunity to ride in their splendid carriages imported from Europe.

Tangier-Fez railway,[73] had to be authorized by both the French Parliament and the Spanish Cortes. Bids were accepted for the first railway, from Tangier to Fez, in the summer of 1914. Lyautey realized that such works took time and patience. He told his fellow Frenchmen that summer:

Ports, roads, and railways are long-term projects. They can only advance slowly; and in this huge country one tends not to recognize the imperative technical needs involved in works of this nature, and thus ready to mistake slowness for inertia.

I therefore ask you to be realistic and honest and as a result of your own practical experience not to accept promises and dreams, but instead works in progress, and to give us credit for what we are doing and have to cope with, and try to understand how essential it is not to bungle things, or cause ruinous improvisations which our resources cannot permit us to risk.[74]

Although commercial railways could not be built before the Tangier–Fez railway was completed, narrow-gauge military railways were built and in December, 1911, the first railway line was laid down in Morocco, from Casablanca to Rabat. The 1911 Treaty also stipulated that the narrow-gauge lines should not be used for commercial traffic, but they were in fact opened to commercial traffic later during the war.[75]

During this period Lyautey also had to deal with the complex problem of property and property registration. Property registration was initiated in August, 1913, and in October, 1914, the first requests for property registration were received by the Administration.[76] (These, once accepted, gave a guaranteed title of ownership to the property which thereafter could only be dealt with in French courts, if litigation arose.)

Lyautey needed a great deal of money to carry out his projects and he frequently complained that he never had sufficient funds. On March 16, 1914, he finally obtained from the French government a long-term loan which permitted the beginning of the various projects outlined for the Protectorate.[77]

[73] The Franco-German Treaty of 1911 stipulated that no railways for commercial use (i.e., normal gauge) could be built before the completion of the Tangier–Fez line.

[74] PA, pp. 112–113.

[75] Charles F. Stewart, The Economy of Morocco, 1912–1962 (Cambridge, Mass., 1964), pp. 148, 149.

[76] PA, p. 118.

[77] The Law of March 16, 1914, authorized the French government to lend 170,250,000 francs to the Protectorate, repayable in seventy-five years, the first installment of which, 70,250,000 francs, was made available on June 1, 1914. The Law of March 25, 1916, however, increased that loan to a total of 242,000,000 francs.

On July 27, 1914, the Quai d'Orsay informed Lyautey that war was imminent, shortly thereafter he was further advised by the Minister of War that he would probably have to send back to France almost his entire military force.[78] When war was declared on August 3, Lyautey was asked to send home thirty-five battalions and to withdraw the remainder of his men to coastal regions. Lyautey informed the metropolitan government that he did not feel it necessary to withdraw to the coast (thereby evacuating most of Morocco), but that he was sending to France thirty-seven battalions of infantry, one cavalry brigade, six battalions of artillery, three companies of engineers, and two companies of telegraphists.[79] As Georges Hardy put it, "The gov-

---

J. Goulven, *Traité d'économie et de législation marocaines* (Paris, 1921), II, 178–181. This was broken down as follows:

(1)	Payement des dettes contractées par le Makhzen; dettes diverses	F. 25,000,000
(2)	Indemnités aux victimes des événements de Fez, de Marrakech, etc.	5,000,000
(3)	Travaux du port de Casablanca	50,000,000
(4)	Travaux de routes aux Maroc	71,750,000
(5)	Installation de services publics: (a) Aménagement provisoire de la Résidence générale et des services administratifs à Rabat	3,000,000
	(b) Installation des services administratifs dans les villes autres que Rabat	2,000,000
	(c) Installation des services judiciaires et pénitentiaires....	2,000,000
(6)	Construction, aménagement, installation : (d) D'hôpitaux, d'ambalances, de bâtiments divers pour l'assistance médicale	10,000,000
	(b) D'écoles, de collèges, de bâtiments divers pour l'instruction publique	10,000,000
	(c) Installation de lignes et de postes télégraphiques et téléphoniques, de bureaux postaux ou télégraphiques	12,000,000
(7)	(a) Premières dépenses nécessitées par la mise en valeur des fôrets du Maroc	4,500,000
	(b) Irrigation, champs d'essais, dessèchement et marais et autres travaux d'intérêt agricole	4,000,000
	(c) Exécution de la carte du Maroc	500,000
	(d) Premiers travaux d'exécution du cadastre	1,500,000
(8)	Subvention aux villes du Maroc pour travaux municipaux	27,050,000
(9)	Études de lignes de chemins de fer	1,500,000
(10)	Conservation des monuments historiques	2,500,000
(11)	Reconstitution du patrimoine immobilier du Makhzen: (a) Travaux de première mise en valeur du patrimoine makhzen; achats d'immeubles nécessités par l'exécution des plans d'extension des villes et la création de lotissements urbains et ruraux	3,000,000
	(b) Rachat de droits immobiliers de l'ancien sultan Moulay-Hafid	2,500,000
(12)	Apurement des deux comptes spéciaux ouverts dans écritures du Trésorier général du Protectorat: Installations provisoires de la Résidence actuelle et des service centraux et achats et ventes d'immeubles domainiaux à Rabat	4,200,000
	Total des Dettes:	F.242,000,000

[78] *LA*, II, 228, 229–230.
[79] *Ibid.*, pp. 266–267, 233–257; *PA*, p. 128.

ernment could scarcely reject such a proposition, which, at the same time satisfied its own basic requirements." [80] Despite the decrease of the number of effectives, Lyautey not only kept every foot of land he held on August 3, 1914, but even increased French gains during the war years. In September, the Minister of War bolstered Lyautey's forces by sending him sixteen battalions of infantry consisting of territorials and older men.[81] Lyautey's forces were still greatly under their former strength, but Lyautey found these reinforcements satisfactory: "They brought not only the indispensable material contribution needed, but also a solid moral backing as well. They consisted of older men, whose manly bearing strongly impressed the natives. They also supplied skills in many fields—public works, agriculture, sanitation, and rendered inestimable service to us." [82]

Morocco had been at war off and on for centuries, and casualties and fighting were nothing new to the empire, but in this war there were new elements. German propaganda and German agents were at work in the Sherifian Empire, and German submarines were in the Atlantic. Propaganda, and fear, began penetrating many areas, and German agents stirred up some fighting in areas that had been considered secure,[83] while the presence of German submarines led to talk of bombardment of various Atlantic ports.

Another element Lyautey had to contend with, a very important one, yet one that seems to have been little noted, was the change in his mental attitude. A mood of pessimism or negativism, perhaps mingled with a degree of bitterness, began to supplant his self-confidence of recent years. In May, 1912, he had written to his sister: "The situation is becoming more and more serious and difficult but I am surrounded by so much confidence and devotion by all my men, such a boon in itself, that I find in this incomparable strength." [84] And in October that same year he had written to Albert de Mun in a happy vein:

I have been living in a fairy-tale land for the last ten days; there is no oriental picture which could portray what I have seen since my arrival at Marrakesh, on that sunny morning. The Arab multitudes, the colorful horsemen, the large military standards, the continuous parades, the joyous fanfares of our troops, the perfume and liveliness of victory, the backdrop of the

[80] Hardy, p. 213.
[81] *LA*, II, 335. In July, 1914, Lyautey had 61 battalions and by June, 1915, only 19. See also *PA*, p. 129.
[82] *PA*, p. 129.
[83] E.g., Khenifra where 33 officers and 650 men were killed toward the end of 1914. See Lyautey's letter to his sister, Dec. 5, 1914, *CL*, pp. 310–311. On German interference in Morocco see, e.g., *LA*, III, 34–45.
[84] Letter to the Comtesse de Ponton d'Amécourt, May 12, 1912, *CL*, p. 287.

snow-covered High Atlas Mountains, and the encampment of the victorious column in the Sultan's large gardens; the reception of the officers in a palace drowned in verdure.[85]

By the end of April, 1913, when the military situation in Morocco was easing, he still remained optimistic.

In October, 1914, however, in a letter to de Mun, he complained for the first time about his men, who were angry because he was keeping them in Morocco away from the Great War, and who, in consequence, no longer rallied round their chief as in the past. Lyautey added how useless he felt to his country, although he realized that he was doing something of value, which his country required:

That suffices then for my conscience, but not for my heart, because I feel that our country will not understand it [i.e., his not fighting at the Front], and that here even the officers (with the exception of a small elite) do not understand it. Our race is above all too undisciplined and argumentative, and it is not easy to command them. My command is henceforth stripped of any consolation it might have had for me. For too many years I had rejoiced in the feeling of being loved and understood, and now that is no longer so. . . . My sacrifice has been complete, and I shall hold on to the very end; except that when a man has exercised such a command under such conditions, he is finished and has only to disappear.[86]

Lyautey had not been given a command on the Western Front (though Gouraud and Brulard had), and he was now left with only Henrys, Poëymirau, and a few others, the last of those with whom he really liked to work. To add to his depression, his family estate, Crévic, with all his possessions and manuscripts, had been burned to the ground by the Germans, and, he remarked to de Mun, "a worse disaster could not have happened to me." [87] In a letter to his sister seven weeks later he said: "Really, the older I become, the more I feel how, for people with deep roots like ourselves, houses and people are identified with each other; it is in the traditional houses that one relives best and most easily with one's memories." [88] So great a disaster was the destruction of Crévic to Lyautey that he could never bring himself to have the ancestral house rebuilt after the war.

A few weeks later, writing again to his sister, Lyautey explained why

[85] Letter of Oct. 10, 1912, *CL*, p. 299.

[86] Letter of Oct. 6, 1914, *CL*, p. 309. De Tarde also attests to the attitude of the soldiers, and how deeply it hurt Lyautey. Guillaume de Tarde, *Lyautey—le chef en action* (5th ed.; Paris, 1959), pp. 192–193. De Tarde served under Lyautey for several years. He was Secrétaire Général Adjoint du Protectorat (Feb.–Aug., 1914), interim Secrétaire Général (Aug., 1914–July, 1915), Chef Adjoint du Cabinet Civil at the War Ministry (Dec., 1916–Mar., 1917), and finally Directeur des Affaires Civiles (June, 1917–Dec., 1920).

[87] Letter of Oct. 6, 1914, *CL*, p. 310.

[88] Letter of Nov. 24, 1914, *CL*, p. 310.

he felt so bad about being kept in Morocco instead of going to the Front where the fighting was:

You are aware just how much I suffer from being kept here, realizing only too well that those who have not participated in the war in France will [afterward] be disqualified [in the eyes of the public] and will then have only to be buried, knowing only too well that, though people throw flowers over me, crying from the rooftops that I have "saved Morocco," deep down, they have been only too happy to keep me out of the war, annihilating my strength and authority for the future.[89]

The mood continued into the following year. In August, 1915, he wrote to his sister: "Here I must appear smiling and in good spirits to keep the others going, but I always feel so tempted just to let myself go and lose myself in despair, for there are so many things I want to cry out to the world, things which I feel are irremediable, which will leave me crushed after the war, but I stop myself from thinking about them." [90] After the spring of 1917, the mood was even intensified. Indeed, the war had a profound effect on Lyautey, and his fears of being crushed were only too well justified. By January, 1918, he was writing that he was "on the razor's edge." [91]

Another depressing factor, which intensified his growing feeling of isolation, was the death of close friends. Vicomte E.-M. de Vogüé had died a few years before the war, in 1910: Comte Albert de Mun died in 1914, and General Gallieni in 1916. Three of Lyautey's favorite officers who had served under him since 1903 at Aïn Sefra also died in the war years or soon after—Berriau in 1918, Colonel Delmas in 1921, and General Poëymirau in 1924—and another favorite officer and friend, General Henrys, was sent to France in 1916.

For Morocco, however, and for Lyautey's plans for that country, the war did allow a measure of freedom of administration that he had not previously had. Not only was there less control and interest in Morocco by metropolitan politicians, but also immigration declined, so that Lyautey could concentrate on building roads, cities, hospitals, dispensaries, and schools, for both Europeans and Moroccans.[92]

In 1915, in addition to continued military and political action, Lyautey found another front to fight on, that of morale and economics. On May 9, 1915, he opened a Horticultural Exhibition at Casablanca.[93] Two months later he went to France to see government officials and toured the Western Front, also managing to spend some

[89] Letter of Dec. 5, 1914, *CL*, p. 311.
[90] Letter of Aug. 27, 1915, *CL*, p. 312. Other letters reflect the same mood.
[91] Letter to his sister, Jan. 12, 1918, *CL*, p. 315.
[92] De Tarde, p. 132.
[93] *LA*, III, 46–51; *PA*, p. 137.

time with his sister and her family.[94] August again found him in
Casablanca, preparing for the first "real offensive" of the new front,
the Casablanca Exhibition, which opened on September 5, 1915.[95]
This trade fair displayed the principal import and export products
of Morocco and France, and was the first of three such fairs held in
Morocco during the war, in pursuance of Lyautey's *"politique du
sourire";* he considered them to be an essential part of the war effort.
Their purpose was twofold: to show France the economic value of
Morocco, and to give the Moroccans a feeling of stability, strength,
and prosperity, so as to keep their confidence. In Lyautey's words,
"this double objective was fully achieved." [96] The first Casablanca fair
was a splendid success, politically and economically. Several metropolitan officials came from France to see it, and were doubly impressed
when Lyautey's estimate of its psychological effect on the Moroccans
quite unexpectedly proved correct. A rebellious tribal chief fighting
General Henrys along the northern front in Morocco, hearing amazing
things about the fair, asked for a truce in order to see it for himself.
He was granted permission to go to Casablanca with complete im-
munity against arrest and was so delighted with all that he saw that
he returned to his men and surrendered with them to the French.[97]

In October, 1915, the French Minister of Education, Albert Sarrault,
came to Morocco to bestow on Lyautey the Médaille Militaire and the
Croix de Guerre.[98] That same month, King George V of Great Britain
made Lyautey an Honorary Knight Grand Cross of the Order of
St. Michael and St. George.[99]

At the end of 1915 General Lyautey left for France to take up again
with the government the tricky problem of finance, and also the
problems of troops, transport, and supplies for Morocco. In the New
Year spirits were not very high anywhere in Paris and in February
came the disaster of Verdun. Lyautey toured the Western Front, and
on February 29 he spoke to the Chamber of Commerce of Lyon on
some of the problems of colonial government.[100]

"Of these difficulties," he said, "the greatest and most inextricable, at
least initially—for it only becomes untangled gradually—is to conciliate, in a country where one has just arrived, the legitimate interests
of the natives and those of newly arrived Europeans. This is perhaps
the most delicate problem for colonial governments." But however
delicate, conciliation was necessary. "The duty of the government is

[94] *PA,* p. 164.
[95] *Ibid.,* p, 143.
[96] *Ibid.,* pp. 143, 199.
[97] *Ibid.*
[98] *Ibid.,* p. 155.
[99] Selous, *Appointment to Fez,* p. 190.
[100] For the text of this speech see *PA,* pp. 165–174.

precisely just that, to conciliate these interests. It is neither easy nor pleasant, because whoever says conciliation has to make compromises and reciprocal concessions, and, consequently, dissatisfaction arises from all quarters." The problem, he noted, was aggravated in Morocco by the uncontrolled influx of European immigration: "Throughout the entire [Atlantic] coastal region of Morocco, there was a veritable invasion, while nothing was yet ready to receive it, and my poor and very limited administrative personnel which I then had at my disposal has been literally inundated ever since. Before settlers could come to Morocco, he pointed out, a complete study of the land and its resources must be made and maps—until then nonexistent—must be drawn up, and a full program of colonization must await the searching out of property that was both reasonable in price and held in clear, legitimate title of ownership.

Lyautey always emphasized that Morocco, unlike Algeria, was not a colony but a protectorate, a distinction that was "no mere formality." He was deeply attached to Morocco and her people and he wanted Frenchmen to respect Moroccans as much as he himself did, as can be seen in this passage from his speech at Lyon:

. . . there you have an industrious, really hard-working, intelligent race, a race open to progress, and from whom much can be achieved, provided that what they want to have respected is scrupulously respected. Therefore we shall find in that country the most favorable conditions in which to accomplish the finest and best achievement, in cooperation with the natives, if we only leave behind at the port when we first enter the country, something that has elsewhere countered the effect of our original action, and can be summed up by the expression of *sale bicot* [dirty Arab] applied uniformly to every native, an expression so deeply shocking and dangerous that those to whom it is addressed cannot but understand it immediately and all the scorn and menace that it includes, as a result of which they nurture a bitterness which nothing can erase, as I have seen only too often.

No country better suits a protectorate type of regime, *one that is not transitory but definite,* the essential characteristic of which is close association and cooperation between the autochthonous race and the protecting race, joined in mutual respect, and the scrupulous safeguarding of traditional institutions. No system of administration permits so well the utilization to our benefit of the local institutions and the development of their resources. . . . Just remember that in Morocco there exists a number of persons of rank who, until just six years ago, were Ambassadors of independent Morocco to Saint Petersburg, London, Berlin, Madrid, and Paris, accompanied by their secretaries and attachés, cultured men who dealt as equals with European statesmen, who are skilled politicians and diplomats; nothing similar exists in either Algeria or Tunisia.[101]

[101] Lyautey's attitude to Morocco can be described as paternal. Rom Landau characterizes it as being one of "a benevolent autocracy and conscientious feudalism." Rom Landau, *Moroccan Drama, 1900–1955* (London, 1956), p. 93.

The Resident General left for Morocco in March, stopping again
at Madrid to see the King of Spain, as well as some of the Spanish
ministers, about affairs concerning the dual Protectorate. After a
short stay in Tangier he reached Casablanca on March 24.[102]

In the spring of 1916 General Lyautey appeared to be his old self
again, though late in June his troops were engaged on all fronts (except
around Marrakesh) and he had to deal with a general increase in military resistance.[103] Another trade fair (officially called a Samples Fair
this time) held in Fez in October resulted in an increase of commerce
and had a psychologically reassuring effect on the Moroccans.[104]

German agents in Morocco and submarines off the coast, which had
been a constant worry to Lyautey since war broke out, became especially menacing during this period, in which intercepted German
messages led to the expectation of attacks on shipping and the ports
of Casablanca and Rabat. Lyautey, without sufficient artillery to protect the ports, and fearful of the effect of such attacks on the Moroccans' confidence in the French, could only await events.

Unexpectedly, late in 1916, General Lyautey received a telegram
from Premier Aristide Briand asking whether he would accept the
post of Minister of War if it were offered to him.[105] Morocco was in a
particularly difficult position at this time, and Lyautey was taken
aback, but at the same time he realized that one of the great problems
in France during the war was the lack of coordination and unified
control and authority, which he believed he could change for the
better. His answer to Briand was hence a qualified no: the situation in
Morocco was touchy, and he did not feel that he could leave, but all
really depended upon whom they could find to replace him, for there
was no one in Morocco who could do so.[106] When General Gouraud,
in command of the IVth Army in Champagne, was suggested, the
Resident General acquiesced. But he still had grave doubts, and they
were not eased by events. The news of his replacement was published
by the Havas Agency before he himself had been officially notified,
and the article omitted to say that Gouraud's appointment as Resident

[102] *PA*, pp. 164, 177.

[103] *CL*, p. 314.

[104] *PA*, pp. 193–207.

[105] *Ibid*. Unfortunately, M. Pierre Lyautey has omitted the period December,
1916–March, 1917, in his otherwise valuable edition, *Lyautey l'Africain*. Aristide
Briand (1862–1932) was Premier from 1909 to 1911 and again in 1913. He was
Minister of Justice in Viviani's cabinet (1914–1915), headed a coalition government
from 1915 to 1917, was Premier again in 1921–1922, Minister of Foreign Affairs,
1925–1932, and Premier, 1925–1926. In 1926 he was awarded the Nobel Peace
Prize jointly with Gustav Stresemann. He was Premier for the last time in 1929,
from July to October.

[106] *PA*, p. 208.

General was only an interim one, until Lyautey returned. Other events proved even more disconcerting. Days before Lyautey's appointment, without consulting the future Minister of War, the Cabinet chose General Robert Nivelle to replace Joffre as Commander-in-chief. Lyautey did not hear the news until he arrived in Paris on December 22, and he felt, with reason, that it was an insult.[107] Furthermore, the Cabinet took it upon themselves to split up the powers of the Minister of War by creating a War Committee, which removed both Transport and Armament from the authority of the Ministry of War. Lyautey, who believed in the necessity of centralization, was unaware of the reduction in the powers of the office he was about to accept. On December 13 he received the official announcement of the make-up of the Cabinet, with his own name as War Minister, and the new ministries of Transport and Armament. He at once sent Briand a telegram:

It is with great surprise that I read about the constitution of the Ministry in the communiqué.

I see there that Armement and Fabrication de Guerre, on the one hand, Transports and Ravitaillements Militaire on the other—that is, the fundamental and vital organs of modern warfare—have been removed from the Minister of War, to which they should be subordinate, and now form two distinct ministries.

Now, it is the Ministry of War which I have been offered and it seems to me that it would only have been right to have informed me that it was to be reduced in authority, and that in consequence will no longer be capable of an efficacious role.

In the period of extreme crisis which our country now faces, there is one basic necessity which is obvious to everyone, to intensify the unity of direction of the war, and yet this unity is being diluted even more.

I thus formally reserve my acceptance of the Ministry of War, under the new and unforeseen conditions, until I am able to see for myself whether or not I am actually being given both the Ministry of War and the powers and means of action which circumstances render indispensable.

I shall hand over my office to Gouraud, on Monday, at Gibraltar.[108]

The Resident General took official leave of his officers and officials at Rabat on December 16, 1916,[109] and that same evening Sultan Moulay Youssef came to the Residency to say good-bye to the Lyauteys. Lyautey left on a submarine for Gibraltar, where he met Gouraud as scheduled and briefed him on the situation in Morocco. He stopped

[107] D'Ormesson, *Auprès de Lyautey*, p. 38. D'Ormesson, now a member of the Académie Française, served on Lyautey's staff throughout his brief career in Paris and discusses the events from December, 1916, to March, 1917, in great detail.
[108] *Ibid.*, p. 280.
[109] *PA*, p. 208.

at Madrid to confer with King Alfonso, and arrived in Paris on December 22.[110]

Once there, he still delayed his acceptance of the post, for he wished to examine the position closely and to ask the advice of various friends in high position. He did not like what he learned, but after due deliberation he decided on acceptance. One of his first acts was to dissuade Joffre, humiliated by his demotion, from resigning his commission altogether.[111]

In truth, however, Lyautey was not cut out to be a cabinet minister. In the words of Maurois:

> Everything irritated him. As a technician of general ideas he naturally had a great horror of useless details and would have preferred to give his time to creative work. Instead, however, he had to receive senators and deputies who came to ask special favors of him, and to report to him about generals who were then hostile to politicians. He could not complain about either Albert Thomas, or Herriot, for both were very loyal to him. But he needed to work in an atmosphere full of enthusiasm, and in this coalition of 1917, all was cabal, intrigue, and suspicion.[112]

Lyautey received no cooperation from the difficult Nivelle nor from Nivelle's General Headquarters. In order to increase over-all unification and coordination of inter-Allied command, he traveled to Rome and later to London. As early as January, 1917, on his return to Paris, following the Rome Conference (January 4–9), he was reported to have told one of his officers, speaking of the War Ministry, "Really, I don't know what more I can do there." [113] Shortly afterward he prepared a note addressed to the President of the Republic and Briand, stating that he might as well step down, for both the Rome Conference and the War Committee had been quite ineffective; unfortunately, he decided not to send it.[114] At this time General Lyautey received Nivelle's plan for a new offensive against the Germans. In Lyautey's view, the plan was clearly mad. Nivelle sent Colonel Georges Renouard, who had been a captain under Lyautey in Algeria several years before, to explain the plan to the Minister. As Maurois tells the story, Renouard placed various papers before the Minister and began explaining everything in a cold, aloof manner which puzzled Lyautey,

[110] D'Ormesson, pp. 18–19, 38. Lyautey and Alfonso XIII got along very well. D'Ormesson (pp. 18–19) quotes a typical remark made by Lyautey to the King (back in October, 1913): "If Your Majesty were not King of Spain, how I should like to have him on my general staff!" See also Maurois, *Lyautey*, p. 282.

[111] Maurois, p. 282. It was on Lyautey's initiative, and despite much political hostility, that Joffre was promoted to the rank of marshal. Britsch, *Le maréchal Lyautey*, p. 201.

[112] Maurois, pp. 286–287.

[113] *Ibid.*, p. 292.

[114] D'Ormesson, pp. 63–67.

because of their former friendly relationship. Lyautey turned in surprise to Renouard asking him what he thought of Nivelle's plan, but Renouard refused to comment:

"Renouard, I am asking you [*te*] to answer me; I am no longer the Minister of War and you are no longer Colonel Renouard; we are two Frenchmen standing face to face and dealing with the well-being of France . . . What do you personally think about the plan you have brought me?" "I have no right to judge my chief." Lyautey then took him by the shoulders and shook him: "All right, let's see, *mon petit Georges*," he said emotionally, "look at me straight in the eyes . . . For one minute put yourself back into the skin of my officer in Aïn Sefra whom I held in confidence and tell me the truth . . . What do you think of it?" Then, for a few seconds the mask fell from the Colonel's face. Tears came to his eyes. "General, I feel the same way you do about it . . . it's crazy." [115]

The remaining weeks of Lyautey's career as minister were none too happy. He tried unsuccessfully to have Nivelle's plan dropped, and even to have Nivelle replaced, and the disastrous results of this plan when it went into effect on April 16, resulting in 50,000 casualties, completely substantiated Lyautey's gloomiest forebodings. His career ended abruptly, not so much because of Nivelle, but because of politicians and political fickleness and dishonesty and because he always felt "ill at ease in his relationship with Briand, Joffre, and Parliament." [116]

In March, 1917, Lyautey attended an inter-Allied meeting in London. Since he also wanted to attend an open session on aviation in the Chamber of Deputies on March 14, he traveled all night from London in order to reach Paris on time, and he went directly from the railway station to the Cabinet, only to discover that Briand, despite his promise, and contrary to Lyautey's wishes, had decided to have this session held in secret. The subject of the interpellation was the newly created air force and its intended program. Lyautey had opposed this hearing because it would not only question his abilities and powers but would also release information to the enemy. Lyautey sat in silence throughout the morning session, only going to the tribune in the afternoon when an open session was held in the Chamber of Deputies. He had barely begun speaking before he was interrupted so abruptly and violently by members of the Left—who were furious with a man who challenged their authority and field of competence—that he had to stop and the session was adjourned. He tendered his resignation immediately afterward and Briand's government fell two days later, mainly as a result of the Nivelle controversy.[117]

[115] Maurois, pp. 296–297.
[116] De Tarde, p. 137.
[117] *PA*, pp. 213–214. Lyautey's speech is in *PA*, pp. 214–221. See also Britsch, pp. 213–220.

On March 25, five days after forming a new government, Ribot contacted Lyautey and asked him to return to Morocco to his old post as Resident General, and the General willingly agreed to do so.[118] In late May, after a visit to Vichy for treatment of a liver ailment, and conferences in Paris to settle various matters pertaining to finance, public works, and the army, he left for Morocco. Gouraud, with whom he conferred briefly in Madrid, returned to his old command of the IVth Army on the Western Front.

Back in Morocco on May 29 Lyautey was faced with disaffection in three large zones,[119] while at the same time the international situation was complicated by Russia's internal disorders. One of the major tasks was simply to boost morale—not an easy undertaking for a man who himself felt defeated. He had lost faith in mankind, no longer only because, as in August, 1914, his men were attracted to other poles, but because his own personal attraction was diminished; he had failed. Much worse than that, he had lost faith in himself.[120] The tenth anniversary celebration in August, 1917, of the arrival of the first French troops in Casablanca can hardly have been a happy event for a vanquished general.

At Rabat in September the Resident General opened the third trade fair since the beginning of the war, an occasion which he called a *"geste de guerre, foire de combat."* In his speech opening the fair, Lyautey gave his views on colonization, contrasting the destruction of war with the constructive work of the colonial army in Morocco:

> While the terrible European War is heaping up ruins and daily destroying the work of centuries, *the grandeur and beauty of the colonial war—which our troops are engaged in here—is that soon, on the very day following the cessation of fighting, it begins to create life,* and instead of leaving the earth dead behind it wherever it goes, it makes it productive, and cities and harvests arise, thus making available all sorts of possibilities for the future in regions until now bogged down in inertia.[121]

The year 1918 was a difficult one. As Lyautey himself described it:

> Losses accumulated; the restrictions and privations of daily life, aggravated in Morocco by distances and difficulty of communications, increased daily.
>
> It was above all necessary to be with the troops whose efforts became every day more difficult, and I spent almost all my time along the various fronts in Morocco, only returning to Rabat for brief stays when circumstances made it necessary.[122]

[118] D'Ormesson, p. 112.
[119] *Ibid.,* p. 156.
[120] De Tarde, pp. 200–201.
[121] *PA,* p. 239.
[122] *Ibid.,* p. 245.

Both the Allies and Axis were preparing for one last offensive; in Morocco, German agents were still at work, and rebel forces were successful in closing the Taza corridor again, for a few days, although General Poëymirau and the Foreign Legion soon reopened it permanently.

Ironically, the signing of the Armistice on November 11 meant further problems for Lyautey, not the least of which were those caused by the exhaustion of French troops and the immediate demobilization of the territorials. In December, his trusted assistant, Colonel Berriau, died, and in January General Poëymirau was seriously wounded in southern Morocco. Lyautey himself had to assume the command for several weeks until Poëymirau was well. [123] To add to the difficulties in this period of demobilization and lack of replacements, Lyautey was faced with serious resistance around the Moulouya River in the northeast, which obliged him to make frequent visits to military fronts and administrative posts,[124] and at the same time he was faced with numerous administrative problems, including the sudden postwar influx of colonists.

In April, 1919, a *dahir* (decree) was promulgated which was to have far-reaching and permanent consequences for tribal society and property. On April 27 the Protectorate permitted tribal property to be broken up. Although ownership of tribal land could only be transferred between members of the tribe or the State, land thus acquired by the State might be reserved for the creation of "colonization perimeters." [125] Plans for an official colonization program had been begun during the war and were now being put into effect, although unofficial colonization had long preceded this. By permitting the alienation of tribal property, Lyautey was paving the way for the break-up of many tribes and the loss of allegiance and values of their traditional way of life; in a word, it was the beginning of detribalization. These things were a side-effect and an inevitable result of the colonization program, but were not its purpose.

Lyautey went to France in September, 1919—the first time since his resignation—to discuss the serious problems caused by the dwindling numbers of his troops (due in part to the French and international monetary crisis). During his absence a grave economic and political crisis arose which reached such proportions as to result almost in a radical change in the Moroccan administrative structure. Inflation set in, silver was hoarded, and the Banque d'État almost failed. In October the metropolitan government took action to overcome the financial crisis which had led to a complete standstill in everyday business

---

[123] *Ibid.*, p. 284; and Britsch, p. 238.
[124] *PA*, p. 284.
[125] See Dahir of April 27, 1919, discussed in ch. 3, § V.

transactions. Despite the attempt of Urbain Blanc, Lyautey's Délégué and second-in-command, to restore confidence in the government, the press and public furiously attacked the Administration, demanding the resignation of the Directeur des Finances, M. Piétri, and the creation of a Moroccan Parliament, with members being elected by the colons, to assist a Résident Civil who would replace the Resident General. On October 29, 1919, Clemenceau issued a decree giving complete support to Lyautey and thereby thwarting any plans the colons might have had for the administrative reorganization of Morocco.[126] After this business gradually picked up and life returned to normal.

When Lyautey returned to Morocco in late November, he had at last received authorization to plan the first commercial railway in Morocco (apart from the Tangier–Fez line), from Petitjean (now Sidi-Kacem) via Kenitra and Rabat down to Casablanca.[127] At last his plans for a complete Transport System could be put in motion (see map 2).

Although the postwar agitation among the colons for more direct French rule of Morocco, as illustrated by the outbreak of public opinion in October, threatened to put an end to Lyautey's colonial principle of close collaboration with the Moroccans, Lyautey prevailed and on December 7, 1919, he informed the Sultan at Rabat that the principle of the Protectorate remained in force and that there was no danger of direct administration.[128]

In March, 1920, another step was taken to alleviate the monetary situation in Morocco when it was decreed that the franc would be the sole legal tender in Morocco (and not also the peseta hassani), though Lyautey felt it a mistake to call this tender the franc rather than the hassani.[129]

The postwar period brought about changes in the entire way of life in Morocco, of which Lyautey was fully aware. As he said, ". . . all proportions have changed. Even the same words no longer convey the same meaning. The old formulas have become meaningless, simply hiding the void that has been created." [130] The world of either-or no longer existed; it was no longer a case of either being at peace or at war, for in Morocco one always had to contend with war, and the new rapid means of communication only made this all the more vivid. Lyautey commented in January, 1920:

[126] *LA*, IV, 50–59; Britsch, pp. 243–245.
[127] *PA*, p. 295.
[128] *Ibid.*, p. 302.
[129] *LA*, IV, 58–59; Britsch, pp. 247–248. The franc notes issued by the Banque d'État gradually replaced the notes of the Banque de France and those of the Banque d'Algérie.
[130] *PA*, 306.

It is a situation without precedent and almost paradoxical, seeing a country, a third of which is resisting us and still remains to be conquered, where means of communication push ahead, where railways advance daily, where the *oeuvre colonisatrice* is developing with an intensity and rapidity which has never been seen anywhere else, under the protection of an Occupation Corps in full combat, whose mobile front traces out the borders of the areas thus far submitted to us, and whose casualty lists which reach me each evening, record the tragic but glorious statistics, while in our coastal cities life goes on apace quite normally.[131]

But there were hopeful signs, too. On June 1, 1920, General Poëymirau received the submission of the large Zaian (Berber) Confederation, and in October French forces finally occupied Ouezzan.[132]

Lyautey had gone far in his career, and had worked hard in his civilian-military capacity. One man who knew him well, a former British consular official, G. H. Selous, has commented, "All waking hours were working hours for him." Selous has described a typical working day in Lyautey's life at this time, explaining first of all that because of his old back trouble and the liver ailment contracted in Madagascar, he had to spend a great deal of time in bed during the last few years:

And so his large bedroom became his morning study or workroom and there, propped almost bolt upright in his bed by many pillows, he would begin promptly at 8 a.m. seeing the chief of his military cabinet in order to learn the latest reports from all military posts along the frontiers which were ever being pushed further into dissident territory; discussing with directors-general of the various Residency departments questions of policy, etc.; and transacting any other business offering until around 11.45 a.m.; when he would attend to the tiresome but unavoidable task of getting up. At about 12.30 he would appear in the reception saloons ready for lunch which, in his presence, was always a gay affair. Thereafter and, with but the dinner break, till 1 a.m. he never ceased to deal with business. Never was there a great chief more constantly available for the transaction of affairs of State, big or small, than Lyautey. He was most accessible, although well defended by his excellent staff against undeserving callers. Whenever he travelled about the Protectorate, as he constantly was doing, his car was always followed by several others full of secretaries and typists. No sooner had the day's final destination been reached, scarcely had the convoy of cars come to a halt, than the Resident-General's chancery was in the throes of being set up, ready within a quarter of an hour or so to despatch the business of the moment.[133]

---

[131] *Ibid.*, p. 308.

[132] Boisboissel, *Dans l'ombre de Lyautey*, pp. 131–132.

[133] Selous, *Appointment to Fez* (London: The Richards Press [now Unicorn Press]), p. 180. For a picture of Lyautey in the first years of the Protectorate, see Britsch, pp. 140–142. Britsch quotes P. Azan (from Azan's *Souvenirs de Casablanca* [Paris: 1911]) showing Lyautey's indefatigability and the demands he made on his closest officers: " 'Often I heard in camp—while everyone else was asleep—whether at 11

In May, 1920, the Resident General went again to France for the necessary business of defending his budget before Parliament. While he was in Paris, on May 21, a special decree was issued (confirming one of the previous October) to the effect that Lyautey could remain at his post indefinitely, thus waiving the usual age restrictions, though Lyautey himself had publicly made it known that he was more in a mood to give up his office than to continue.[134] On July 8 he was finally able to attend the official reception given in his honor at the Académie Française.

When he returned to Casablanca in September after a five-month absence, he brought another loan for Morocco and final authorization to begin work on the commercial railways, which in addition to those already mentioned, included connections between Fez and Oujda, Kenitra and Souk el-Arba, Casablanca and Marrakesh.[135]

Lyautey revisited France the following year and upon landing at Marseilles on February 19, 1921, was informed that he had just been promoted to the rank of Maréchal de France, the nation's highest military rank.[136] He was then sixty-six years old. The decision to promote him had been reached that very morning by the Cabinet, on the recommendation of Louis Barthou, and countless receptions awaited the new Marshal in Paris. Lyautey recorded his feelings in March while addressing the Ligue Maritime et Coloniale:

First let me tell you of my complete surprise, and how moved I was. I certainly had not expected such an honor. I can of course understand how such a thing could be done for our great war leaders, for those who on the Marne, Somme, and Rhine, saved France, civilization, and the world. But when one thinks of my military accomplishments alongside theirs, without any false modesty, I find it entirely unexpected that, after the little I have done, I am in such a place today before such an assembly.[137]

Lyautey was as surprised as he had been when elected a member of the Académie Française without warning eight years before. He had always expected to be given fairly good commands, just as he had probably always expected to reach the rank of general—as others in his family had done—for he always recognized his own merits; but to be made a member of the Académie Française or a Maréchal de France was another matter.

---

p.m. or at 4 a.m., the General's voice suddenly calling out: "Poëymirau!" and immediately the faithful echo: "Voilà, mon général!" Poëymirau presented himself two minutes later before the *"patron"* and we could hear the sound of their voices dictating and rereading orders.'"

[134] Britsch, pp. 248–250.

[135] *PA*, p. 313; Britsch, p. 251; *LA*, IV, 59. The signing of contracts for work on the railways was provided for by the Law of August 21, 1920.

[136] *PA*, p. 319.

[137] *Ibid.*, p. 320.

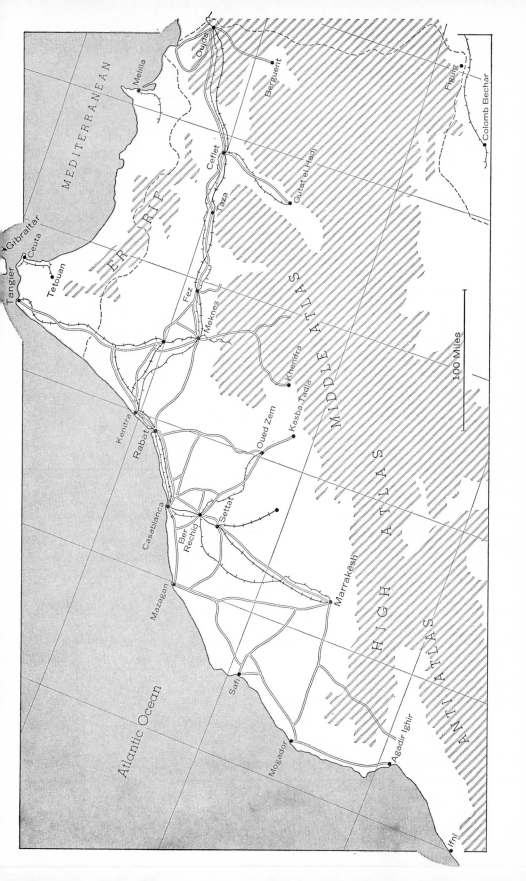

This trip to Paris was also satisfactory in that the government agreed
to give Lyautey the necessary resources (starting in 1922) to pacify
most of the remaining rebellious areas of Morocco within a period
of "three or four years." At that time Lyautey's troops were facing
three "veritable Kabylies" in Morocco:

If you leave me what I already have in troops and resources, then I ask of
you [France] not one man or one sou more. With intense effort and great
sacrifices by our men, thanks to the even greater energy of our generals,
officers, and men, I affirm that—within three or four years—you will have
been relieved of these three Kabylies whose continual confrontation we
cannot afford. If, on the contrary, you reduce our resources by even a few
hundred men or a few thousand francs, then it is impossible for me to
envisage just how long it will take to pacify Morocco, because it will be
necessary to fall back and maintain the status quo.[138]

During the remaining four and a half years of his administration,
however, Lyautey was to suffer humiliating setbacks—personal, political, and military—none of which was due to his own actions.

The newly promoted Marshal returned to Morocco in April, 1921.
He afterward made several speeches at Casablanca and received visitors
from the Continent, including (from October 8 to 13) the King and
Queen of Belgium, whom he had to leave for a tour of the fronts
along the Zaïan and the Beni Ouaraïn, south of Taza. The Chief of
Staff, Colonel Delmas, died in December, but the peripatetic Resident
General again had to leave for France early in January, 1922, on government business and to receive instructions for the intended visit
to Morocco in April of President Millerand.[139] While in the capital
Marshal Lyautey was asked to lecture to the Institut Colonial in the
risks involved in rushing the development of Morocco.

Nothing in the world is more dangerous than to believe in El Dorados, and I
have always feared this "enthusiasm" over Morocco. Morocco is obviously at
the present time "in the public eye," if I may say so. Everyone is being most
kind to me. It is à la mode to be so, but I do not know how long that will
last. For the time being, however, that is very useful to us in the matters with
which we have to deal; only that always makes me apprehensive, because,
in our country, which is so fickle, enthusiastic outbursts are often followed
closely by deceptions. That is why I say: "Be careful." Morocco is what she is;
she is not any more than that. I believe that she has admirable possibilities for
the future; a great deal is being done there; if I am but a small part of it, I
have had the good fortune to have a team of admirable collaborators whom
you have seen at work and who have been going at full steam since the
very beginning. But, from the economic point of view, from the point of

---

[138] *Ibid.*, pp. 330–332. Kabylies were mountainous Berber strongholds in Algeria.
[139] *Ibid.*, pp. 348, 354, 356. Millerand (1859–1943) a radical socialist, was President
of the Republic from 1920 to 1924

view of organization, Morocco is still in her infancy. Like all children, we must let her grow up; and we must let her achieve full growth in every sense. That is why I never stop saying: do not ask too much of Morocco, too soon.

But he defended the colonial policy in Morocco:

Despite many imperfections and many modifications still to be made in our methods of colonial policy, there is nevertheless one thing we have achieved: that is the knowledge of how to win the sympathy of the native. We do not have vis-à-vis him that arrogance, that aloofness which he in fact least forgives. . . . we have often been behind other colonial countries in the machinery and equipment built up in our colonies and in putting them into operation, but, despite everything, these races have remained faithful to us, for they have always felt that our heart is with them, and have therefore never felt an arrogance, coldness, and scorn between us. The results of this policy were the steady backing we received from them during the war, and which we shall find tomorrow.[140]

Lyautey thought it of the utmost importance that the French should be able to understand Islam and the values of a Muslim world, for as he put it, "It is above all on the *sympathies* which we find in it [Islam] that our establishment in North Africa rests, and which has become such an important factor in our national destiny." [141]

Marshal Lyautey returned to Morocco at the end of March. President Millerand's ten-day visit began on April 5. The President arrived in Casablanca and worked his way across Morocco, ending it at Oujda when on April 15 he was greeted by Algeria's Governor General and Lyautey's future successor, Théodore Steeg, who was to be Millerand's host on the next stage of his North African tour.[142]

Lyautey spent most of May and June with his troops at Tadla and on the Moulouya. He left again for Paris on June 24, stopping at Marseilles to see the Moroccan Pavilion at the Colonial Exhibition there. On July 7, just after he had reached Paris, he suffered a serious and painful liver attack. These attacks, which had plagued him for years, usually occurred without warning, and this time he was forced to stay in bed for several weeks, getting up only briefly to accept his Marshal's baton from President Millerand on July 14 at a review at Vincennes. He spent several weeks in convalescing in Lorraine, and by mid-October he was well enough to attend the inauguration of the Mihrab of the mosque in Paris. He returned to Morocco at the beginning of November.[143]

A month later, speaking before the second annual Congrès des

[140] *Ibid.*, pp. 357–358, 359.
[141] *Ibid.*, p. 361.
[142] *Ibid.*
[143] *Ibid.*, pp. 369–370, 375.

Hautes-Études Marocaines at Rabat, the Resident General took the opportunity of emphasizing to the Franco-Muslim audience the importance of close collaboration. He cautioned them not to destroy the rich culture of Islam or Morocco, for "the more I am with the natives, and the longer I live in this country, the more I am convinced of the greatness of this nation." "One can make a good and fine Morocco by remaining both Moroccan and Muslim." [144]

One result of President Millerand's visit to North Africa was his decision to coordinate French action in the Maghrib through permanent liaison of the three administrators of Morocco, Algeria, and Tunisia. The first annual Conférence Nord-Africaine was held in Algeria on February 6, 1923.[145]

On February 11, while motoring back to Rabat, Lyautey suddenly had another sharp liver attack.[146] He was taken to Taza and then Fez. Fearing that his life was in danger, the doctors at Fez told the Resident General that he must go to Paris as soon as possible for the removal of his gallbladder. Lyautey was in excruciating pain and his condition was aggravated by the intense spring heat. The local *oulama* and *imams* crowded into the courtyard near Lyautey's quarters and said the Ia el-Affif prayer for him, which, in the words of G. H. Selous was "as unprecedented as unexpected." [147] A few days later he was sufficiently well to be driven to the coast, and Maurois has recorded how, as he was about to leave, the imams asked him to enter one of their mosques—a singular honor for a non-Muslim. Lyautey's reply was typical: "I have always forbidden Europeans to enter your mosques; don't ask me to violate the very regulation that I myself established." [148]

Lyautey reached Rabat on March 27, somewhat recovered but still forced to remain in bed most of the time. Nonetheless, he spoke at the ceremonies opening the Port of Casablanca[149] and then the opening of the first section of the Rabat–Fez railway, when he had to meet several French parliamentarians and attend a large banquet at the Residency.[150] At the port ceremony he discussed not only the stages in the development of the port but also the general problem

[144] *Ibid.*, p. 378.
[145] *Ibid.*, p. 382.
[146] *Ibid.*, p. 385.
[147] Selous, p. 205.
[148] Maurois, pp. 310–312.
[149] Britsch, p. 154. Permission to begin this project had been granted by the Commission Internationale des Adjudications and the French Government on March 25, 1913.
[150] *PA*, p. 386. The Petitjean–Kenitra, Kenitra–Rabat, and Petitjean–Meknes sections of the Tangier–Fez line were opened in June, 1923, and the Meknes–Fez section was opened the following October. The line from Casablanca to Khouribga was inaugurated in September, 1923 (and extended to Oued Zem in 1926). The Rabat–Casablanca line was opened in 1925. The Tangier–Fez line was not fully completed until January, 1927, however.

of colonization, and again stressed that France must not violate her treaties with Morocco by switching over to direct administration. "I should like to add," he said, "that, thanks to this method [i.e., his own], I have never seen here, at least so far, any uprooted groups [in Moroccan society], any *déclassés,* or any 'Young Turks'." [151] He went on to enumerate the lessons he had learned in Indochina which he had applied in Morocco:

> I believe, with all my heart, soul, and experience, that the best method of serving France in this country is to assure the solidity of the establishment here, and that is the way to obtain the full support of this people.
>
> It is in material well-being that we have the best guarantee, that which will in the near future alleviate our burdens, for a confidence acquired as a result of our care and welfare for their moral and material interests will be for us a far more efficacious support than the protection of bayonets.
>
> It is in the moral sphere, the most noble, the highest and purest one, that the most worthy work of France and her traditions is associated with the destiny of the Moroccans—not as a subjected people—but as a people who are benefiting, thanks to our Protectorate, from the fullness of their natural rights and the satisfaction of all their moral needs.
>
> That, then, is the real essence of this native policy, of the policy of the Protectorate, to which I so firmly adhere through patriotism and conviction. For my country's sake, I hope that my successors will be as firmly attached to it as I am.[152]

Lyautey's health continued to deteriorate and on May 16 he left for Paris where he entered a clinic and was operated on. Following his operation, President Millerand visited him and he took advantage of his visit to ask the President to find a successor for him, because "If I return to Morocco, I shall end up by dying there [*y claquer*]." Millerand is reported to have replied: "Fine, leave your hide in Morocco, that will be *très chic*." [153] This was the Marshal's first attempt to resign from the Residency. He stayed in the clinic for two months and left for a long period of convalescence in Lorraine.[154] In his absence, his Délégué, Urbain Blanc, took over control, while General Calmel became acting Commander-in-chief.

Guillaume de Tarde relates how Lyautey's character changed in his last few years in the Residency, after his short stay at the Ministry of War. "In this daily struggle which he fought against his moral and physical weakening, and against political opposition, Lyautey's two greatest enemies took possession of him more and more: doubt in himself and suspicion of others." [155]

[151] *PA.,* p. 394.
[152] *Ibid.,* p. 395.
[153] Maurois, p. 312.
[154] *PA,* p. 395.
[155] De Tarde, p. 149.

Marshal Lyautey returned to Paris at the end of 1923 and went
back to Morocco with a new program, but only after much persuasion
by Millerand and because he felt it his absolute duty to do so.[156]
The second annual Conférence Nord-Africaine was held in Rabat in
April, 1924; Governor General Steeg represented Algeria and Resident
General Lucien Saint the Tunisian Protectorate.[157] Immediately following the Conference, Lyautey had to return to Paris for a second
operation, but he was back in Morocco on June 18, intending this
time to stay only temporarily, for as he said, "I felt even more than
during the previous year that I had the right to rest and that the
moment had come to pass on my work to a younger, stronger successor." [158] When, however, the Resident General toured the northern
front, on the Ouergha, he found that the withdrawal of Spanish troops
from the Rif on the other side of the Protectorate Zone had increased
the success of Abd el-Krim. As Lyautey later said, "From that time on,
I realized I could no longer—at least for the time being—plan on
leaving, duty compelling me not to flee before a situation which seemed
so menacing." [159] In August he returned to France to discuss with
the government the growing threat of Abd el-Krim:

I spent my stay communicating my fears to the ministers who were involved
with Morocco and doing my utmost to have the means made ready to deal
with the situation, that is during the first few months of 1925. The Foreign
Minister, the Premier, and the Minister of War listened to me with all the
attention and seriousness necessitated by the gravity of the situation, which
they clearly realized. But, in my conferences at the Ministry of War, the
Minister and I realized the impossibility of finding sufficient amounts [of
troops and equipment] that would be necessary, all the means then available
being—as represented to us at least—required in the occupation of the
Rhineland and the Levant.[160]

Marshal Lyautey returned to Morocco in November, 1924, filled
with anxiety but still outwardly cheerful in order to give his soldiers
and the Moroccans the confidence they needed. On December 11 he
sent a telegram to Paris describing the military situation and the
measures to be taken. Premier Herriot authorized Lyautey's measures,
and on December 21 Lyautey sent a detailed memorandum to Paris

[156] *PA*, 404. Unfortunately, Millerand, who always supported Lyautey, was out
of office the following year; had he remained in office, Lyautey's last year in
Morocco would have been far different.
[157] *PA*, 406; *LA*, IV, 233.
[158] *PA*, p. 409.
[159] *Ibid.; LA*, IV, 244–272. Abd el-Krim had inflicted a disastrous defeat on the
Spanish army in July, 1921, and as a result the Rif rebels had obtained almost
unlimited military supplies, including 166 pieces of artillery and the necessary
ammunition. See Selous, p. 205.
[160] *PA*, p. 413.

specifying the required military reinforcements, including five battalions and two engineer companies to be sent to him forthwith, in addition to the following by April 1, 1925: four more infantry battalions, two spahi squadrons, two mountain batteries, one signals half-company, and two air squadrons. At the same time he requested a special credit of 5,000,000 francs for the extension of road communications. (It should be noted that Paris had reduced his troops from ninety-five thousand in 1921 to sixty-five thousand in 1923.) His requests were, he emphasized, urgent: "I take the liberty of stating that *this minimum* must be forthcoming in entirety—otherwise, and at an early date, much more will be required; and it must be forthcoming by the indicated dates—i.e., *in time,* a factor which of itself will constitute the *greatest economy*." [161]

The outcome was tragically different. In the words of G. H. Selous, "the French Government signally failed to play up and execute his minimum requirements, modest as they were and clearly as, with studied insistence upon and re-iteration of essential points, he had specified them in language and with a lucidity of expression worthy equally of a highly experienced general and a member of the Academy." [162] On December 29 Lyautey was informed that only two battalions were on their way and that by the middle of February three more battalions and two sapper companies would be available. The four battalions requested for April, 1925, however, would be made available only on the Cabinet's decision following another specific request by Lyautey at that time. Unfortunately for Lyautey's policies, he was not at all popular in the socialist governmental circles then ruling French destinies.[163]

The first five or six months of 1925 taken up with direction of military operations against Abd el-Krim taxed Lyautey's energies to the utmost.[164] By mid-July the critical period had passed and reinforcements were finally arriving.[165] The unrelenting military demands on him made him realize that he could not be everywhere at once, especially in his state of health, and he asked for what he termed a military *"ad latus,"* who would relieve him of at least some part of his heavy burden. General Naulin was therefore appointed to take over the Moroccan military command, under Lyautey's over-all responsibility, and he arrived at the end of July. Lyautey said of this period: "I began to envisage the end of the crisis in the not too distant

[161] *LA*, IV, 227, 252, 264–272.

[162] Selous, pp. 207–208.

[163] *Ibid.* It should be noted that when Pétain took over as Commander-in-chief in August, 1925, he immediately requested an additional 28 battalions and got them! Catroux, *Lyautey le Marocain*, p. 243.

[164] Abd el-Krim surrendered on May 27, 1926.

[165] *LA*, IV, 372–376.

future, provided that my methods of political and military action—
which had for such a long period proved themselves—would be continued." [166]

But meanwhile, Painlevé had sent Marshal Pétain to Morocco,
against the latter's own wishes.[167] Lyautey did not know exactly why
Pétain had been sent but received him cordially,[168] though they were in
character and spirit total opposites. Pétain toured the fronts between
July 17 and 27 and telegraphed a report to Paris stating that vast
reinforcements were indeed needed and immediately. It was during
this period that the great rift between Lyautey and Pétain occurred,
and according to the faithful Catroux[169] it was the result of a stinging
accusation made by Pétain against Lyautey during a dinner given by
the latter in Pétain's honor, when Pétain stated that Lyautey had lost
some of his finest officers not on the battlefield but as a result of over-
work and Lyautey's own thoughtlessness. Needless to say, relations
between the two men were never the same again. Before returning to
Paris Pétain traveled to the Spanish Zone of the Protectorate, to Ceuta
and Tetouan, in order to see the Spanish High Commissioner, Primo de
Rivera, with whom he made plans for future collaboration against
Abd el-Krim. How much of this was known to Lyautey is not clear.
Pétain proceeded to Paris to see Painlevé, Briand, and Caillaux, when
apparently the final plans were made to hand over the military command of Morocco to Marshal Pétain, and on August 18 Lyautey
received a curt telegram informing him that he had been relieved of
the entire military command of Morocco: "Marshal Pétain will take
over the general direction of the troops and military services of
Morocco. Marshal Lyautey will place at Marshal Pétain's disposal all
the personnel and material he requests for the accomplishment of his
mission." [170] Pétain returned to Morocco on August 27 and the following day Lyautey left on a hurried trip to Paris, where he remained
until September 15.[171] During his absence Pétain began new operations in the Rif.

On September 24, 1925, the seventy-year-old colonial veteran asked

[166] Catroux, p. 225; *PA*, pp. 417, 419.

[167] Pétain objected to this task on two counts, saying that (1) at sixty-nine he
was too old, and (2) he had never led a colonial operation before. Georges
Blondel, *Pétain, 1856–1951* (Paris, 1966), p. 151.

[168] Catroux reports that Lyautey not only cooperated with Pétain, but did so
aimiably, Lyautey believing that Pétain "had not come as an investigator, that his
purpose was not to weaken but to strengthen his authority." Catroux, p. 224.

[169] *Ibid.*, pp. 225 *et seq.*

[170] *Ibid.*, p. 244. Paul Painlevé's government was in office from April 17 until
November 23, 1925. For French political background at this time see Jacques
Chastenet's *Histoire de la Troisième Rèpublique*, Vol. V: *Les années d'illusions,
1918–1931* (Paris, 1960), pp. 135 *et seq.*

[171] Blondel, p. 152.

to be relieved of the supreme command in Morocco, for the third and last time, and five days later he received a telegram from Foreign Minister Briand, on behalf of the Premier and the Cabinet, accepting his resignation.[172] The Resident General bade farewell to the Sultan in Rabat on October 10, and before a huge crowd gathered on the quayside left Morocco for the last time as its *patron*.[173]

On his arrival at Marseilles no senior officials, miltary or civilian, were on hand to greet him. In fact, he had been obliged to return to France on a small commercial ship, rather than on a French naval vessel, and it was only the British who, in his honor, provided him with an escort of two destroyers through the Straits of Gibraltar.

Lyautey spent most of his remaining years at Thorey, in his beloved Lorraine, preparing a few volumes of letters for publication. He died on July 27, 1934, at the age of seventy-nine, and in October, 1935, his ashes were conveyed by a French naval squadron, accompanied by fourteen ships of the British Second Battle Cruiser Squadron, to his mausoleum in Rabat.[174]

[172] *PA*, pp. 420, 426. For Lyautey's letters of resignation, see appendix 7.

[173] *Ibid.*, pp. 427, 429. He was officially replaced by Théodore Stéeg by a Decree of October 11, 1925, *BO*, 679 (Oct. 27, 1925), 1705.

[174] Selous, p. 211. Several honors came to Lyautey during his retirement, including the Gold Medal of the Royal African Society on December 4, 1928, in London, the first time it had ever been given to a foreigner. Selous, p. 193.

2

GOVERNMENT

I. PROBLEMS FACED BY THE FRENCH

Establishing new forms of government in Morocco on three different levels—central, municipal, and tribal—led to many problems, some of which were to plague French administrators to the end of the Protectorate.

The first task was to set up an all-encompassing French government on a central level in a country where nothing similar had ever before been known. It was a Christian and European government and alien in its strangeness, modernity, and efficiency, forcing itself upon Moroccan society. Under the best of circumstances the psychological atmosphere would be tense if not openly hostile, as the French were to find in other colonial conquests. The Moroccans had to be convinced that the French were there as their friends—a difficulty that Lyautey and his successors were never to overcome.

Lyautey first had to decide how much de jure and de facto power was to be granted Moroccans in the newly reorganized government. He decided to follow a system similar to that used in Tunisia, placing all modern and technical aspects of government in French hands only. There was to be a sharp division between French and Moroccan ministries, for Lyautey, despite his emphasis on cooperation, did not want Moroccans in his government. At this stage, Moroccans were not considered trustworthy, and owing to their lack of education in the modern European sense they were not regarded as capable of taking part in the French administrative mainstream. In a few instances, for example in Muslim education, Moroccans were, however, appointed to responsible posts.

Thus Lyautey had to find suitably qualified French officials—military and civil—for his government. He did not want men imbued with the

Algerian tradition of direct administration nor did he want stolid bureaucrats, but rather thinking men with imagination and initiative. The problem of finding such men, never easy, became more acute after the outbreak of the World War, as former departments of the government expanded and new ones were added, while at the same time many experienced officials left Morocco for war duty.

Another delicate problem, which was never solved satisfactorily, was that of trying to bring about cooperation between colons and the administrators of the Protectorate. As with the Moroccans, the Resident General did not intend to give the colons any influence in government policy, but realizing that they must have some way of expressing their views, he established the Conseil de Gouvernement, Comités d'Études Économiques, Chambers of Commerce, and so on.

Finally, since Lyautey was never in great favor with the politicians in Paris, he constantly had to battle for funds. As an avowed legitimist who had only reluctantly come to terms with the republic, he was an easy target in metropolitan political circles. Some parliamentarians, like the colons, criticized his policy of indirect administration of Morocco; they wanted Morocco treated as a conquered colony, as an Algeria, and not as a temporary protectorate. And there were other parliamentarians who wanted to shed their colonial possessions altogether.

II. CENTRAL ADMINISTRATION

A. BEFORE 1912

As a result of [recent] events, Morocco has been returning to a state of internal chaos. At present the State survives only because of the resistance of the Makhzen, that is to say, by the only element of cohesion still capable of imposing itself over national anarchy.

EUGÈNE AUBIN,
Le Maroc d'aujourd'hui, 1904

The administration of the Sherifian Empire has varied throughout the centuries.[1] During the reign of Sultan Moulay el-Hassan (1873–1894) the administration of Morocco was reshaped for the last time before the establishment of the Protectorate.[2] The salient feature of this sultan's government was the lack of any real delegation of power to the vizirs. The function of the vizirs or ministers was, in the main, restricted to seeing that the Sultan's decisions were executed; no

[1] See J. F. P. Hopkins' work, *Medieval Muslim Government in Barbary, until the Sixth Century of the Hijra* (London, 1958).
[2] René Maudit, "Le makhzen marocain," *RC*, No. 3 (1903), p. 297.

vizirial decrees were issued until after 1912 when they were introduced by the French.

1. The Sultanate[3]

The Sultan came to power by one of three means: through a power struggle; through nomination as heir presumptive by the previous Sultan; through selection from among the members of the royal family by the College of Oulama of the empire, those of Fez taking predominance in the decision.[4]

The Sultan was both secular and ecclesiastical ruler. His powers (at least in the effectively governed parts of the empire) were vast, undefined, and unquestioned. As the religious leader of his people, he was the Imam and the Caliph and Amir el-Moumenin (Commander of the Faithful). In an Islamic state religion was so inextricably a part of everyday life that there was no separation between the temporal and the ecclesiastical, no more than there was separation in classical Hebraic society. The people of Morocco, unlike those of Algeria or Tunisia, mentioned the name of their own ruler in their Friday prayers, whereas the Algerian and Tunisians repeated the name of the Ottoman Sultan. Domestic and foreign policy was initiated by the Sultan, and in the legal field he was the Islamic equivalent of a Supreme Court.

2. The Vizirates

Although the Sultan could and did delegate powers to vizirs, their main task was to help him examine affairs of state and to execute his decisions. Mohamed Lahbabi points out in an interesting work that Moulay Hassan introduced two innovations in his reorganization of the Makhzen, or government.[5] He defined the duties and powers of his ministers, and regularized the hours and work of government officials; thereafter vizirs and secretaries were to appear at their *beniqas* (ministries) at specific hours (a most unoriental innovation)[6] and the Council of Vizirs was to meet daily. Under Moulay Hassan there were five vizirs (see fig. 1).

The *Ouzir el-A'dham,* known also as *Essadr el-A'dham,* or simply, *el-A'dham,* was in effect the Grand Vizir. This title was of fairly recent creation, this official having previously been known simply as the

[3] For a general study of the court and Makhzen see Augustin Bernard, *Le Maroc* (Paris, 1913), Book III, ch. 5; and Eugène Aubin, *Le Maroc d'aujourd'hui* (Paris, 1904), chs. 10–12.

[4] André de Laubadère, "Les réformes des pouvoirs publics au Maroc," *RJPUF,* II (1948), 15.

[5] Mohamed Lahbabi, *Le gouvernement marocain à l'aube du XXe siècle* (Rabat, 1958), pp. 136–137.

[6] E.g., from 6–10 A.M. and from 3 P.M. to sundown. On vizirial reform see also Jean-Louis Miège, *Le Maroc et l'Europe (1830–1894),* Vol. IV: *Vers la crise* (Paris, 1963), pp. 130–135; and also Eugène Aubin, chs. 10–12.

FIGURE I
MAKHZEN BEFORE 1912

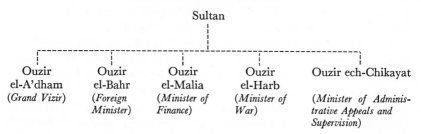

Ouzir. El-A'dham was now restricted to domestic affairs, but as Minister of the Interior and Counsellor of the Sultan[7] he was a most important minister and a person to be reckoned with, working more closely with the Sultan than almost any of the other vizirs.

El-A'dham was the direct intermediary between the Sultan and the Moroccan people, on both the tribal and municipal levels in political matters.[8] He arranged for all franchises and concessions involving the tribes; he kept an eye on religious fraternities to ensure that they were not undermining the Sultan's authority, and he also supervised matters involving military contingents and mobilization, besides supervising the imposition of taxes and the nomination of administrators.

The Ouzir el-A'dham nominated each new *caïd* (governor or mayor of a city), *cadi* (religious judge), *mohtaseb* (market inspector), *khatib* (leader of prayers), and *m'dris* or professor of the Qaraouiyne University, and examined each one's background.[9] He was assisted by two administrative secretaries, one for the North and one for the South.

The *Ouzir el-Bahr* acted as Foreign Minister for the Sultan, and he and the Ouzir el-A'dham were the two most powerful vizirs. The Ouzir el-Bahr often acted in the Sultan's name outside the empire on political and commercial missions to Europe, just as he did in Morocco in matters pertaining to international frontiers (such as border incidents, or surveying of undelimited areas). For instance, he represented Morocco in the meeting with the ministers of Spain and France in Rabat late in 1907.[10]

The Ouzir el-Bahr dealt with certain specific matters involving Europeans living within the empire: (1) claims submitted to the

---

[7] Lahbabi, p. 140.

[8] *Ibid.*, pp. 140–144.

[9] *Ibid.*, pp. 144–146.

[10] *Ibid.*, pp. 147–148. Other officials could, however, be sent as government representatives abroad, as when Moulay Hassan sent the Governor of Ribât el-Feth to Spain. See Aḥmed ben Khâled Ennâṣiri Esslâoui, *Kitâb Elistiqsa Li-Akhbâri Doual Elmagrib Elaqsâ* (trans. Eugène Fumey), *AM*, X, No. 2 (1907), 319.

government for indemnities, (2) questions arising from the protection of favored individuals (which were brought to his attention usually by a *caïd* or *amel*), (3) disputes concerning commerce, trade, imports and exports, and customs, and (4) acquisitions of real estate.[11]

The Makhzen had already realized in the nineteenth century the danger of foreign commercial and political penetration of Morocco; and following the Convention of Madrid in 1880 it tried to limit the "protection" offered by foreign governments to Moroccans. Thereafter the foreign consuls in Morocco had to submit to the Ouzir el-Bahr an annual list containing the names of proposed *protégés*. Indemnities, a painful aspect of the Ouzir's duties, involved the multifarious claims put forward to the Moroccan government by the foreign legations for payment of debts and reparations. An example of this was a claim made for compensation when a foreign ship was wrecked off the Moroccan coast in the late nineteenth century.[12] The acquisition of real estate, which was greatly restricted, was dealt with through his office only.[13]

There was only one exception to the rule that cases in these four categories had to be submitted to the office of the Ouzir el-Bahr, and that was when they originated in Tangier where most of the foreign delegations were located. There the Sultan dealt directly with the foreign diplomatic corps through his *Naïb,* usually bypassing the Ouzir el-Bahr.[14]

The office of the *Ouzir el-Malia,* or Minister of Finance, was created by Sultan Moulay Hassan. Before his reign, no single official had supervised the various components of State finances. There had been an *amin ed-dakhl,*[15] or administrator of revenues, an *amin el-kharadj,* administrator of expenditures, and an *amin el-oumana,* supervisor of administrators, the latter having under his control the *oumana* of the customs departments of the ports and the *oumana el-moustafad* of the cities of the realm.[16]

Under Moulay Hassan, the office of amin el-oumana was raised to that of Ouzir el-Malia and important administrative reforms were

---

[11] Lahbabi, pp. 149, 151.

[12] Eugène Fumey, *Choix de correspondances marocaine* (Paris, 1903), Part 1, pp. 1–2 (Official Documents). The great harm caused by the insidious pervasion of such claims in Egypt is described in David S. Landes's *Bankers and Pashas* (London, 1958).

[13] The complexities of property acquisition by foreigners in Morocco are discussed in ch. 3.

[14] Morocco had occasionally sent ambassadors to Europe, but it had never established permanent embassies there, although foreign legations had existed in Morocco for a long time; the diplomatic corps was only created in 1906 by the Act of Algeciras.

[15] *Amin* = administrator; pl. *oumana.*

[16] The city tax collector (i.e., taxes from the gates and markets).

carried through.[17] These included raising the salaries of all officials in
the Ministry of Finance, including those of the oumana of the ports,
bringing the various oumana under the Sultan's personal supervision,
and attaching to each local caïd well-paid oumana whose duty it was
to take the census, impose taxes, and so on.

FIGURE 2

MINISTRY OF FINANCE BEFORE 1912

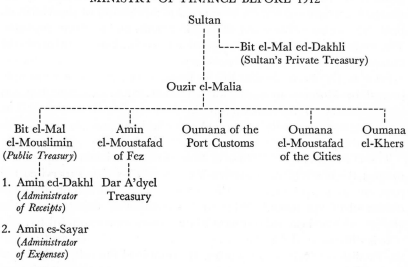

The Ouzir el-Malia (see fig. 2) was in charge of all State finances and
held extensive powers, though he was not empowered to contract
State loans.[18] He had to compile an annual list of businessmen living
in the four commercial cities of the empire—Tetuan, Salé, Rabat, and
Fez—who might be capable of holding the office of amin in the
customs departments. He supervised all the oumana of the country, that
is to say, the oumana of the customs, the *oumana el-moustafad,* and the
oumana el-khers.[19] The amin el-moustafad of Fez, also under the
Ouzir el-Malia, was the administrator of the Dar A'dyel Treasury,
which provided for the expenses of the Royal House.[20] The Ouzir

[17] Lahbabi, pp. 157–163. See also E. Michaux-Bellaire, "L'organisation des finances
au Maroc," *AM*, XI, No. 2 (1907), 171–251; and Michaux-Bellaire's other excellent
study, "Les impôts marocains," *AM*, I (1904), 56–96.

[18] Lahbabi, p. 158.

[19] These officials evaluated the *achour,* estimated the harvests for tax purposes,
and had those taxes collected.

[20] Lahbabi, p. 160.

el-Malia personally administered the Bit el-Mal el-Mouslimin or
Public Treasury, which received the *zekkat* and *achour,* the customs duties, the market and gate taxes, and the revenues from
Makhzen properties. The Sultan's Private Treasury, the Bit el-Mal
ed-Dakhli, however, was administered by the Sultan himself.

The Ouzir el-Malia had three important officials in his *beniqa:*
the *amin ed-dakhl,* the *amin es-sayar,* and the *amin el-hassab.*[21] The
amin ed-dakhl was the administrator of all funds received by the
Bit el-Mal, whereas the amin es-sayar, or administrator of expenditures,
paid the salaries of the vizirs, the *guich* troops, and all State expenses.
The amin el-hassab was in charge of all accounts of the Ministry of
Finance, and was the senior book-keeper.

Prior to the establishment of the Protectorate, the large loans contracted by Morocco in 1904 and 1910 had led to the establishment
of the Moroccan Administration du Contrôle de la Dette and its
administrator effectively controlled the Sherifian ports, since 60 percent of the port duties went to the Contrôle de la Dette.[22]

The *Ouzir el-Harb,* Minister of War, was another official appointed
to meet the needs of the nineteenth century. This vizir supervised the
payment and equipment of the army and at times took personal
command of the army.[23] Prior to the creation of this ministry the
allaf el-kebir had carried out most of the functions of this minister.

It is difficult to define the powers of the *Ouzir ech-Chikayat* or find
the English equivalent to his office. He combined the roles as Minister
of Administrative Appeals and Inspector General, having a variety of
functions and powers that overlapped those of the Ouzir el-A'dham or
Grand Vizir.[24] In addition he was a special Counsellor to the Sultan,
advising him on the management of Makhzen and Treasury property.
He examined the granting of privileges and concessions for the
moustafadats, as well as the renewal of exemptions from taxes, and he
recorded the *dahirs,* or imperial decrees, concerning such matters and
saw that they were put into effect.[25] He also decided on the suitability
of officials (e.g., *nadirs, khatibs, mouariths*) and confirmed them in
their posts—a function of his powers that seemed to overlap those of
the Ouzir el-A'dham, who examined the suitability and proposed the

[21] *Ibid.*

[22] The Contrôle de la Dette was established in June, 1904, as a result of the
French loan of 62,500,000 francs to Morocco. A further loan of 101,124,000 francs
was authorized in 1910. The Franco-Spanish Treaty of November 26, 1912, forbade
the Contrôle de la Dette to collect duties at any of the ports of the Spanish Zone
of Morocco; normal collections continued in the French Zone. Comte de La
Revelière, *Les énergies françaises au Maroc: études économiques et sociales* (2d ed;
Paris, 1917), pp. 373, 375, 377.

[23] Lahbabi, pp. 165–166.

[24] The French refer to him as the Ouzir des Réclamations.

[25] Lahbabi, p. 177.

nomination of municipal officials such as *caïds, mohtasebs,* and *cadis.*

The most important work of the Ouzir ech-Chikayat was in the field of appeals and supervision. He was a "veritable guardian of the lower administrative authorities" of the realm, examining complaints by local officials or complaints against them, including abuses such as unlawful imprisonment by local authorities, or the inability of the local authorities to carry out their task, or any known abuse of power by these officials.[26] If the Vizir considered the complaint justified, he submitted it to the Sultan, who then issued a dahir calling the delinquent official to order, or ordering an individual to obey the local authority. If there was a dispute between two officials, one stating that the other was acting in his jurisdiction, the aggrieved official could appeal to the Ouzir ech-Chikayat, who could order that the division of powers between the two offices be respected.

In none of the above mentioned procedures and cases did the Ouzir ech-Chikayat have punitive powers, however. He could not, for example, remove an erring official from his post or imprison him; he could only "invite" the guilty official to make immediate amends. But the Sultan could mete out a punishment (such as imprisonment and confiscation of property) if the Vizir's warning was not heeded.

B. CENTRAL ADMINISTRATION, 1912–1925 [27]

The task was singularly vexatious, for at the time of the establishment of the Protectorate, in 1912, we found ourselves before an absolute void. The Sultan was reigning over only that part of the Empire which was kept under control by our bayonets. The old edifice of the Moroccan State, which had been threatened by ruin for such a long time, had collapsed. The first thing we had to do was to revive the fallen government.

> RÉGINALD KANN,
> *Le Protectorat marocain, 1921*

The duty of the [French] Government and public opinion is to provide them [i.e., Lyautey's administration] with the means of carrying out their difficult task and to leave them complete freedom [of action] along with full responsibility. In practice, moreover, the Protectorate will be inspired by the circumstances and the development

---

[26] *Ibid.,* p. 178–179.

[27] For the general organization of the Spanish zone of the Protectorate see the following: Tomás García Figueras, *España y su protectorado en Marruecos (1912–1956)* (Madrid, 1957); García Figueras and Fernández Llebrés, *Manuales del Africa española* (Madrid, 1955); José-Maria Cordero Torres, *Organización del protectorado español en Marruecos,* 2 vols. (Madrid, 1943). Nevill Barbour briefly discusses it in his *Survey of North West Africa (The Maghrib)* (London, 1959). The Spanish government's official publication in Morocco was the *Boletín Oficial de la Zona,* which was published as of 1913.

of Morocco. On paper everything looks simple enough, but reality is
less accommodating; difficulties crop up day by day and it is only as
they occur that they can be tackled. This, however, does not prevent
one from first coming there prepared with an over-all plan, with
a set purpose already laid out. This goal should not be merely the
various forms of development of Morocco, to the greatest benefit of
France, without injuring in any way the interests of other European
Powers in that which rightfully concerns them.

The political program of the French Protectorate may be defined
in a few words. It is, above all, a matter of reestablishing law, order,
and security, conditions which are essential for a normal life in the
country, and which have always been lacking until now.

AUGUSTIN BERNARD,
Le Maroc, 1913

The administration established by the French government in Morocco
was legally defined as a protectorate. Unlike a colony, a protectorate
implies only temporary intervention in the affairs of another nation, by
common consent of both parties through an international agreement.
Some interpret this to mean that the protected country can no longer
be considered to have the character or status of a state, whereas others
believe that the country is still a state, though deprived of any
sovereignty whatsoever over its own territory. Still others believe that
sovereignty is indivisible and that the protected country therefore
remains a sovereign state, over whose territory the protecting country
has no claim. To Frédéric Brémard, however, there exists an intermediary stage, "that of the duality of sovereignties, of the association
of sovereignties." This was the French policy followed in Morocco.

According to it, the sovereignty of the protector country and that of the
protected country are exercised concurrently over the same territory, each
operating in the particular domain reserved to it. The Protectorate is a
contractual tie between two states, the weaker of which transfers—in favor of
the stronger one—*a part* of its rights of sovereignty, in return for the material
and moral support which the stronger supplies; but it maintains a part of
its own sovereignty.

Thus there is no *division*, but an *association* of sovereignties. Over
Moroccan territory, two sovereignties are exercised concurrently, French
sovereignty and Sherifian sovereignty; or if one prefers another formula, one
can say that there is in Morocco, French participation in Sherifian sovereignty.[28]

The French are thorough administrators and have developed
bureaucracy into a fine art. This must be borne in mind when considering the innovations that they introduced into the government of
the Sherifian Empire. Indeed, they did more than innovate: they

[28] Frédéric Brémard, *Les droits publics et politiques des français au Maroc*
(Paris, 1950), pp. 23, 24.

swept away almost the entire administrative structure of the empire, at least at the ministerial level.

Of the five ministries existing before 1912, all but the Grand Vizirate were abolished, and it was greatly altered. The French divided the central administration of their Protectorate into two sections: (1) the Makhzen or Sherifian departments, headed by Muslim officials; and (2) the Residential and Neo-Sherifian departments, which were primarily technical ministries, administered by Frenchmen (see fig. 3).

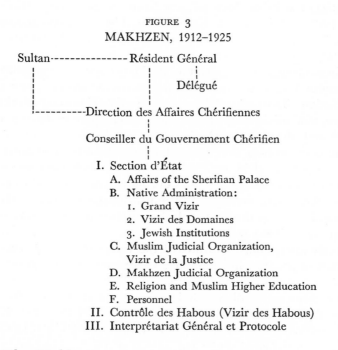

FIGURE 3

MAKHZEN, 1912–1925

Sultan -------------- Résident Général

Délégué

Direction des Affaires Chérifiennes

Conseiller du Gouvernement Chérifien

I. Section d'État
   A. Affairs of the Sherifian Palace
   B. Native Administration:
      1. Grand Vizir
      2. Vizir des Domaines
      3. Jewish Institutions
   C. Muslim Judicial Organization,
      Vizir de la Justice
   D. Makhzen Judicial Organization
   E. Religion and Muslim Higher Education
   F. Personnel
II. Contrôle des Habous (Vizir des Habous)
III. Interprétariat Général et Protocole

1. The Makhzen

The Makhzen or Sherifian ministries were modified in structure during the first years of the Protectorate; some ministries were abolished and new ones were set up.[29]

a) The Sultanate—Legally, the Sultan stood at the head of the government, but although the monarchy was maintained, the Sultan

[29] For a brief study of the Protectorate, see Réginald Kann, *Le protectorat marocain* (Paris, 1921), chs. 5–11; see also E. Durand, "La réforme politique et administrative du gouvernement chérifien depuis 1912," *RJPUF*, IX (1955), 83–122; and Pierre Lyautey, "La politique du protectorat en Afrique marocaine. Ses origines de 1905 à 1918," *CSMS*, II (1938), 987–1002. F. Brémard's study of the theory of the Protectorate, the Sultan's sovereignty, and the idea of association— *Les droits publics et politiques des français au Maroc*, Titre Ier, chs. 2–3— is especially interesting.

was now more or less a figurehead, the real ruler of the country being the Resident General. The Sultan remained the supreme religious leader of the Moroccan Muslim population, while in the temporal sphere his powers were limited to signing the dahirs placed before him by the Resident General, and to investing and dismissing his officials,[30] but he had no power to appoint officials without the approval of the Resident General, and no say in foreign affairs.

b) Ministerial Reorganization—The Makhzen was first reorganized by the French in October 1912, when four Sherifian ministries were set up: (1) the Prime Minister, the Grand Vizir, (2) the Minister of War, (3) the Minister of Finance, (4) The Minister of [Muslim] Justice.[31] The functions of the Minister of War, however, were immediately tranferred to the Commander-in-chief of the French troops, who in Lyautey's time was the Resident General himself.[32] The Ministry of War under the French Protectorate was no more than a legal fiction. Two years later, in 1914, the Moroccan Ministry of Finance was officially abolished, its powers passing to the Grand Vizir,[33] and ultimately to the French.

Two new vizirates were created by the French. The Vizirat des Habous was created in 1912[34] the Vizirat des Domaines, or of State (Private) Domain in 1919.[35] Thus during Lyautey's period of administration there were four Sherifian ministries: (1) the Prime Minister, the Grand Vizir, (2) the Vizir de la Justice, (3) the Vizir des Domaines, and (4) the Vizir des Habous.

Lyautey always liked to think of the Protectorate as a benevolent protector of the Sherifian Empire, its institutions and government, and his policy was that the French should govern Morocco by supervision rather than by direct administration.[36] Therefore the Makhzen, that is, these four ministries, were to come under the supervision of the Protectorate administration and in 1920 all Makhzen affairs and ministries were placed under the Direction des Affaires Chérifiennes, which was directed by a Frenchman, the Conseiller du Gouvernement Chérifien, acting as intermediary between the Makhzen and the

---

[30] Albert Ayache, *Le Maroc—bilan d'une colonisation* (Paris, 1956), p. 82. Lyautey realized that the Sultan was merely a puppet and tried to alter this.

[31] Sherifian Firman of Oct. 31, 1912, *BO*, 3 (Nov. 15, 1912), 17, and Art. 1; see also Général Lyautey (ed.), *Rapport général sur la situation du Protectorat au Maroc au 31 juillet 1914* (Rabat, 1916), Part 2, ch. 1.

[32] Sherifian Firman, Oct. 31, 1912, Arts. 1 & 3.

[33] Dahir of Aug. 5, 1914, *BO*, 96 (Aug. 21, 1914), 690.

[34] Dahir of Oct. 31, 1912, *BO*, 3 (Nov. 15, 1912), 17.

[35] Dahir of April 27, 1919, *BO*, 342 (May 12, 1919), 421. This vizirate also had a brief existence; it was suppressed shortly after Lyautey's retirement (i.e., in 1927).

[36] Résidence Générale, *Renaissance du Maroc: dix ans du Protectorat, 1912–1922* (Rabat; n.d. [1922]), p. 113.

French.[37] The French maintained a close liaison with the Secrétaire Générale du Protectorat. The four ministries, convening as the Conseil des Vizirs, met every Saturday at the Palace, presided over by the Conseiller du Gouvernement Chérifien.[38]

2. *The Direction des Affaires Chérifiennes*

The Direction des Affaires Chérifiennes, which now encompassed the Makhazen, was created in 1920.[39] The Conseiller du Gouvernement[40] was in charge of Muslim affairs, that is, relations with the Makhzen, the administration of native justice, and the supervision of Muslim education and institutions.[41] He took part in the Conseil des Vizirs where he was the permanent and direct agent of French supervision. He had a double role: to present to the Sultan and the Makhzen the measures to be taken by the French administration (and explain the reasons for them to the Moroccans), and to report to the French authorities the effect which the French measures had in Moroccan circles and all the means necessary to bring about complete understanding on both sides.[42]

The Direction des Affaires Chérifiennes was divided into three sections: the Section d'État, the Contrôle des Habous, and the Interprétariat Général et Protocole.

The Section d'État consisted of six subsections. The first of these dealt with matters concerning the Sherifian Palace. Subsection two handled native administration, including the Grand Vizirate, the Vizirat des Domaines, and Jewish institutions (described in ch. 5). Theoretically, the Grand Vizir, who sat on several important committees, was given wide powers, but in fact he was limited to presenting projects drawn up in his office in the form of dahirs for the Sultan's signature. His pre-Protectorate powers of acting as a sort of Minister of the Interior and supervising the municipal administration run by the pachas and caïds were transferred to French officials. The Vizir des

[37] Dahir of July 24, 1920, Arts. 1 & 2. The office of Conseiller du Gouvernement (Counsellor of the Sherifian Government) had taken over the powers of the Secrétaire Général du Gouvernement Chérifien; the Secrétariat was abolished by the Decree of May 19, 1917, *BO*, 241 (June 4, 1917), 611.

[38] A. de Laubadère, "Les réformes des pouvoirs publics," p. 2. An equivalent Conseil des Directeurs of the Residential and Neo-Sherifan Directions was set up in 1929. Cf. Residential Circular of Mar. 19, 1929. Although Lyautey was very much opposed to the idea of joining these two councils, they were eventually united as the Conseil des Vizirs et des Directeurs, under Resident General Juin by Vizirial Decree of Sept. 15, 1947. See also Laubadère, p. 25.

[39] Dahir of July 20, 1920, *BO*, 408 (Aug. 17, 1920), 1407.

[40] The Conseiller du Gouvernement Chérifien was created by Art. 4. of the Decree of May 19, 1917.

[41] Général Lyautey, *Principes fondamentaux de l'organisation gouvernementale du Protectorat marocain* (Rabat, 1918), p. 6.

[42] J. Goulven, *Traité d'économie et de législation marocaines* (Paris, 1921), I, 134.

Domaines was in charge of the Service des Domaines which was directly administered by a lower official. The Vizir's main task was to present all dahirs concerning State Domain to the Sultan for his signature, and relevant vizirial decrees to the Grand Vizir for his signature. The Vizir signed all important leases, documents, and contracts,[43] studied all reports made each week by his *chef du service* concerning management of State Domain, and received claims from Moroccan citizens. (For a detailed account of this Service, see ch. 3.) In 1920 the Service des Domaines was transferred to the Direction des Finances.[44]

The third subsection was headed by a Vizir de la Justice who supervised cadis and their courts and appeals against sentences given by cadis, and heard lawsuits by natives against the Protectorate authorities.[45] Makhzen justice and judicial organization, including the secular courts of the pachas and caïds, the Haut Tribunal Chérifien, and matters involving representation of the Makhzen before French courts were all handled by the fourth subsection of the Section d'État. Religion and higher Muslim education were the responsibility of a special Deputy of the Grand Vizir, and a sixth subsection handled all matters concerning the personnel of the native judicial and administrative services of higher education and religion.

Besides these six subsections, a Vizir des Habous (property constituted as a special religious trust) was responsible for the study and preparation of Habous legislation. This intricate subject will be discussed in chapter 3. In addition, the Interprétariat provided translations of official documents and it was also the Chancellery of the Sherifian Orders and handled all matters of protocol concerning the Sherifian Palace.[46]

3. Central Administration of the Protectorate

Morocco was administered de facto by three important individuals: the Resident General,[47] the Délégué to the Residency, and the Secrétaire Général du Protectorat (see fig. 4). They were assisted by the individual *directeurs* of the various Residential and Neo-Sherifian departments (to be discussed in the last section of this chapter).

a) *Commissaire Résident Général*—The first Commissaire Résident

[43] Dahir of Apr. 27, 1919, Arts. 3 & 4.
[44] Dahir of July 6, 1920, *BO*, 404 (July 20, 1920), 1203.
[45] Dahir of July 24, 1920, Art. 3., *BO*, 407 (Aug. 10, 1920), 1366.
[46] *Ibid.*
[47] The Comte de La Revelière believed that the success and prosperity of a protectorate depended upon four factors: (1) the type of man selected to head the protectorate; (2) respect for the Moroccans; (3) French colons with the right mental attitude, prepared to work hard, and to take the initiative in agriculture, industry, commerce, and finance; and (4) the "pioneers having sufficient capital, or credit made available for the development of the Protectorate." De La Revelière, *Les énergies françaises*, pp. 10–47.

Général, or Resident General as he will be referred to, took office in April, 1912, as a result of the Treaty of Fez of March 30, 1912.[48] The Resident General, as the chief administrator of the Protectorate, possessed great authority and was responsible only to the French Foreign Minister.[49]

He had four main duties.[50] He directed the over-all administration of the Protectorate;[51] he was the intermediary between the Sultan and foreigners, thus acting as Morocco's Foreign Minister; as Minister of War, he was the Commander-in-chief of the land and sea forces of Morocco; and he drew up and approved all the decrees and laws required for the administration and reform of the Protectorate.[52] Four cabinets—Civil, Diplomatic, Political, and Military—assisted him in these tasks. In addition he had the two Residential Directions—the Direction des Affaires Chérifiennes and the Direction des Affaires Indigènes et du Service des Renseignements—also responsible to him.

Lyautey's powers were quasi-dictatorial, in as much as no one in Morocco could prevent him from acting, and though later there were consultative assemblies of both Moroccans and Frenchmen, they had no voting or veto power against the Resident General. The most effective check over Lyautey was the Commission des Finances of the Chamber of Deputies in Paris, which decided on the amount of credit to be given the Protectorate.[53]

b) *Délégué à la Résidence Générale*—The Délégué à la Résidence Général, or Délégué as he will be referred to, was the Minister Plenipotentiary and second-in-command to the Resident General. His task was twofold: to act in place of the Resident General when necessary;[54] and to supervise the civil administration of the empire, in addition to handling diplomatic questions.[55]

c) *Secrétaire Général du Protectorat*—After the Resident General

[48] Art. 5 of the Treaty stated: "The French Government will be represented at the Court of His Sherifian Majesty by a Resident Commissioner General, as the depository of all the powers of the Republic in Morocco, and who will ensure the execution of the present agreement." For a study of the government in the early days, see Général Lyautey (ed.), *Rapport général sur la situation du Protectorat du Maroc au 31 juillet 1914*, Part 2, ch. 2, "La Résidence générale et les services centraux." See also René Pourquier and Roger Changneau, *Cours élémentaire d'organisation administrative marocaine* (Rabat, 1949–1951).

[49] Decree of June 11, 1912, Art. 1, *BO*, 1 (Nov. 1, 1912), 2; and also Arts. 5 & 6 of the Treaty of Fez. The Decree of June 11, 1912, announced the powers of the Resident General and is quoted in appendix 8.

[50] See on this, Résidence Générale, *Renaissance du Maroc*, pp. 124–125.

[51] Decree of June 11, 1912, Art. 2. See appendix 9 for a more general breakdown of the administrative structure, including the French courts, than is shown in fig. 4.

[52] *Ibid.*

[53] *PA*, p. 100.

[54] Decree of June 11, 1912, Art. 4.

[55] Decrees of May 19, 1917, Art. 2, and July 20, 1920, Art. 1.

FIGURE 4

RESIDENTIAL* AND NEO-SHERIFIAN DIRECTIONS, 1912–1925

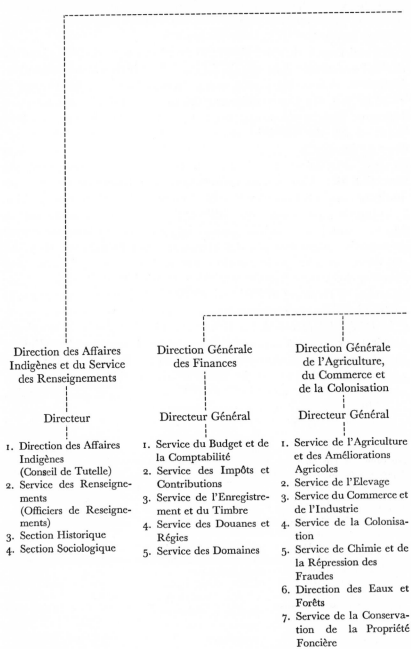

Direction des Affaires Indigènes et du Service des Renseignements

Directeur

1. Direction des Affaires Indigènes (Conseil de Tutelle)
2. Service des Renseignements (Officiers de Reseignements)
3. Section Historique
4. Section Sociologique

Direction Générale des Finances

Directeur Général

1. Service du Budget et de la Comptabilité
2. Service des Impôts et Contributions
3. Service de l'Enregistrement et du Timbre
4. Service des Douanes et Régies
5. Service des Domaines

Direction Générale de l'Agriculture, du Commerce et de la Colonisation

Directeur Général

1. Service de l'Agriculture et des Améliorations Agricoles
2. Service de l'Elevage
3. Service du Commerce et de l'Industrie
4. Service de la Colonisation
5. Service de Chimie et de la Répression des Fraudes
6. Direction des Eaux et Forêts
7. Service de la Conservation de la Propriété Foncière

* The Direction des Affaires Indigènes et du Service des Renseignements is the only Residential Direction listed here; the other Residential Direction was the Direction des Affaires Chérifiennes, shown in Fig. 3.

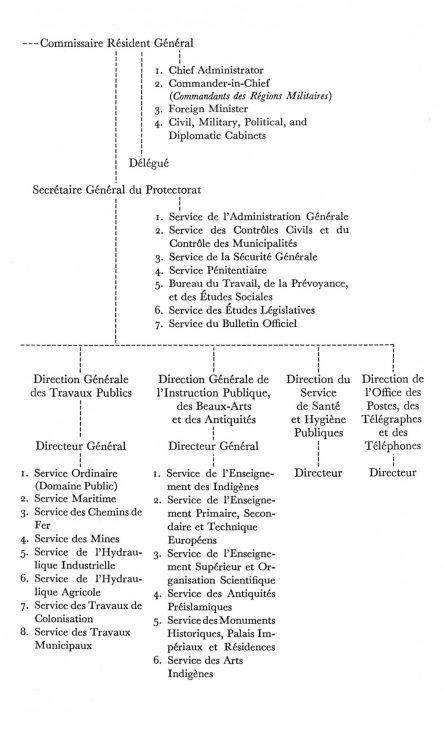

--- Commissaire Résident Général

    1. Chief Administrator
    2. Commander-in-Chief
      (*Commandants des Régions Militaires*)
    3. Foreign Minister
    4. Civil, Military, Political, and
      Diplomatic Cabinets

Délégué

Secrétaire Général du Protectorat

    1. Service de l'Administration Générale
    2. Service des Contrôles Civils et du
      Contrôle des Municipalités
    3. Service de la Sécurité Générale
    4. Service Pénitentiaire
    5. Bureau du Travail, de la Prévoyance,
      et des Études Sociales
    6. Service des Études Législatives
    7. Service du Bulletin Officiel

Direction Générale des Travaux Publics	Direction Générale de l'Instruction Publique, des Beaux-Arts et des Antiquités	Direction du Service de Santé et Hygiène Publiques	Direction de l'Office des Postes, des Télégraphes et des Téléphones
Directeur Général	Directeur Général		
1. Service Ordinaire (Domaine Public)	1. Service de l'Enseignement des Indigènes	Directeur	Directeur
2. Service Maritime	2. Service de l'Enseignement Primaire, Secondaire et Technique Européens		
3. Service des Chemins de Fer	3. Service de l'Enseignement Supérieur et Organisation Scientifique		
4. Service des Mines	4. Service des Antiquités Préislamiques		
5. Service de l'Hydraulique Industrielle	5. Service des Monuments Historiques, Palais Impériaux et Résidences		
6. Service de l'Hydraulique Agricole	6. Service des Arts Indigènes		
7. Service des Travaux de Colonisation			
8. Service des Travaux Municipaux			

the Secrétaire Général du Protectorat was the most important official of the Protectorate, and in Lyautey's own words it was he "who truly put the administrative organization of the Protectorate on a sound footing." [56] He assisted the Délégué and deputized for him when he was absent, and had the general task of maintaining central control of civil and administrative matters over the Neo-Sherifian Directions.[57] The real importance of his office gradually grew, and its authority was greatly increased after the abolition of the Direction des Affaires Civiles in May, 1922,[58] and transfer of its powers to the Secrétaire Général.[59] He was in charge of the Service des Études Législatives and the Service du Bulletin Officiel.[60] He headed the very important Service des Contrôles Civils et du Contrôle des Municipalités, through which he was placed in charge of the entire program of civil supervision in the French Zone.[61] The Service de la Sécurité Générale[62] was also under him, and he directed and supervised the police of Morocco, and in connection with this, also the Service Pénitentiaire, or prisons. He furthermore directed the Service de l'Administration Générale. A Residential Decree of May, 1922, attached the Bureau du Travail, de la Prévoyance et des Études Sociales to the already mentioned Service des Études Législatives. He was also responsible for the Civil Cabinet of the Resident General, while the Secrétaire Général Adjoint was the Chef du Cabinet Diplomatique, and as such directly responsible to Lyautey.[63]

d) *Residential and Neo-Sherifian Departments*—The Residential and Neo-Sherifian departments, or Directions, were under direct

---

[56] *PA*, p. 83. Lyautey's first civil administration was embryonic, consisting of five chief officers, with Paul Tirard as Secrétaire Général du Protectorat, M. de Sainte-Aulaire as Délégué, M. Gaillard as Secrétaire Général du Gouvernement Chérifien, M. Delure as Directeur Général des Travaux Publics, and M. Gallut as Directeur Général des Finances.

[57] Decree of July 20, 1920, Art. 1, and A. de Laubadère, "Les réformes des pouvoirs publics," p. 20; see also E. Durand, "La réforme politique et administrative," pp. 83 *et seq; Renaissance du Maroc*, pp. 126 *et seq.*

[58] Residential Decree of May 15, 1922, *BO*, 499 (May 16, 1922), 800, and another Residential Decree of the same date.

[59] Another Residential Decree of May 15, 1922, Art. 1.

[60] The first of these examined legislative or regulatory questions and then prepared the resultant Sherifian legislation (*Renaissance du Maroc*, p. 126). The *Bulletin Officiel* (or simply *BO*) was the official publication of the Protectorate.

[61] Residential Decree of May 15, 1922, Art 1. A Corps du Contrôle Civil was established by the Decree of July 31, 1913 (*BO*, 25 [Sept. 5, 1913], 343) responsible to Lyautey. When the Direction des Affaires Civiles was created in 1920, the Corps du Contrôle Civil was transferred to it, and when this latter Direction (Affaires Civiles) was abolished in 1922 the Service des Contrôles Civils was attached to the Secrétaire Général du Protectorat and became known as the Service des Contrôles Civils et du Contrôle des Municipalités (by Residential Decree of July 21, 1920, *BO*, 406 [Aug. 3, 1920], 1318, Art. 1).

[62] Residential Decree of May 15, 1922, Arts. 2–4.

[63] Général Lyautey, *Principes fondamentaux*, p. 4.

French administration and included the modern, technical branches of the government, in addition to those concerned with native affairs. At the beginning of the Protectorate, there were only two main departments: the Direction des Finances, responsible for the budget, treasury, property, and postal, telephone, and telegraph services; and the Direction des Travaux Publics, responsible for public works, agriculture, forestry, and historical monuments.[64] As the Protectorate expanded territorially and developed, these two departments grew so much that additional Directions were set up until by 1925 there were eight in all.[65]

The Direction des Affaires Indigènes was created in 1917; the Direction du Service des Renseignements was attached to it and became the *Direction des Affaires Indigènes et du Service des Renseignements* shortly thereafter.[66] This was a Residential Direction and thus under Lyautey. It dealt with most of the political matters involving the Moroccans and consisted of a Service des Renseignements, a Section Historique, and a Section Sociologique.[67] It was administered by a *directeur*, and one of its most important tasks was to handle tribal affairs, especially tribal property (the Directeur des Affaires Indigènes being also president of the Conseil de Tutelle which managed tribal affairs),[68] and it was the guardian of the native *collectivités* (tribes), managing tribal property and regulating their Sociétés de Prévoyance (Provident Societies).[69] The Service des Renseignements, the work of which is described later under "Regional Administration," was especially important. The directeur was the senior officer in charge of native police; he was the chief of the intelligence officers, and supervised all administrative action taken by them.[70]

[64] Victor Piquet, *Le Maroc: géographie et histoire—mise en valeur* (Paris, 1917), p. 267.

[65] In this total I am excluding the short-lived Direction des Affaires Civiles, the duties and offices of which were transferred to the Secrétaire Général du Protectorat. It was created by Dahir of Oct. 23, 1920 (*BO*, 418 [Oct. 26, 1920], 1818) and was abolished by Dahir of May 15, 1922, *BO*, 499 (May 16, 1922), 800. Under the Secrétaire Général, the five Services of the Direction des Affaires Civiles, for general administration, police, prisons, municipal government, and public works, were sometimes changed in title, but they more or less had the same duties. For example, the Service de l'Administration Municipale was joined with the Service du Contrôle Civil, taking the new name of Service du Contrôle Civil et du Contrôle des Municipalités.

[66] Dahir of June 2, 1917, Arts. 1 & 3, *BO*, 242 (June 11, 1917), 631. In 1936, after further development, this department became the Direction des Affaires Politiques, and then, in 1946, the Direction de l'Intérieur. See Laubadère, p. 21; and Frédéric Brémard, *L'organisation régionale du Maroc* (Paris, 1949), p. 101.

[67] Created, respectively, by Vizirial Decrees of Sept. 13, 1919, *BO*, 378 (Jan. 19, 1920), 106, and Oct. 14, 1919, *BO*, 366 (Oct. 27, 1919), 1215, and by Dahir of June 2, 1917, Art. 3.

[68] Discussed in detail in ch. 3 under "Collective Property."

[69] *Renaissance du Maroc*, p. 134.

[70] Lyautey, *Principes fondamentaux*, p. 5.

The *Direction Générale des Finances* was created in the first year of the Protectorate, but it was not completely organized in its final form until 1920.[71] It consisted of five Services: the Service du Budget et de la Comptabilité, the Service des Impôts et Contributions, the Service de l'Enregistrement et du Timbre, the Service des Douanes et Régies, and the Service des Domaines.

The Service du Budget et de la Comptabilité drew up the budget, kept the accounts of the government's revenues and expenditures,[72] floated loans, handled the movement of funds and monetary questions in general, dealt with relations with the Banque d'État, administered the Moroccan Debt and the tobacco monopoly, and made all necessary financial studies. It also managed the Caisse de Prévoyance for government employees and had charge of municipal tax collections and receipts, and direct taxes, and it inspected the accounts of the various Services, the municipalities, public establishments, and societies under state supervision.

The Service des Impôts et Contributions was in charge of the urban tax and the *tertib* (the principal agricultural tax), even in military regions, and also managed the native Sociétés de Prévoyance, and the liquidation of loans.[73]

The Service des Douanes et Régies was in charge of the collection of customs duties, the supervision of the coast and frontiers, the suppression of contraband, and most matters having to do with exports and imports.[74]

The Service de l'Enregistrement et du Timbre drew up and collected the registration duties and stamp duties, and assessed real estate values for official purposes.

The Service des Domaines collected financial proceeds from the State Domains, preserved and managed existing and newly acquired State Domain, including properties acquired by the state because of lack of heirs or through default. It also had the important task of preparing plans for colonization, including the demarcation, sale, and establishment of colonization parcels.[75] This Service was transferred to the Direction des Finances in July, 1920.

The *Direction Général de l'Agriculture, du Commerce et de la Colonisation* also evolved into a fully independent department in 1920.[76] Like the Direction Général des Finances, it was one of the key

---

[71] Dahir of July 24, 1920, Art. 2.

[72] *Ibid.*, Art. 3.

[73] *Ibid.*

[74] *Ibid.*

[75] *Ibid.* For a detailed account of the activities involved, see ch. 3, under "Public and State Domain."

[76] Dahir of July 24, 1920, *BO*, 409 (Aug. 24, 1920), 1433, and modified by Dahir of Feb. 28, 1921, *BO*, 437 (Mar. 8, 1921), 395, Arts. 2 & 3.

instruments of the Protectorate; its work was divided among seven separate Services.

The Service de l'Agriculture et des Améliorations Agricoles was very important to both European and Moroccan farmers, for it provided all kinds of technical information on agriculture; it carried out agricultural experiments, sought to combat diseases affecting crops, drew up rural legislation, and provided mutual credits and agricultural cooperative aid.

The Service de l'Elevage supplied information concerning livestock and methods of improving breeds. It also conducted zoological experiments, fought animal diseases, and maintained veterinary and health inspectors.

The Service du Commerce et de l'Industrie was set up to inform the public of new commerce and industry opportunities; it studied the economy, encouraged industry and commerce, immigration, labor, and tourism, and protected industrial, literary, and artistic property.

The work of the Service de la Colonisation was to seek lands that could be made available for colonization. It drew up annual programs for official colonization, supplied information to immigrants, and studied the economic uses of colonization centers. It also made studies of rural colonization sectors in cooperation with the Service des Domaines.

The Service de Chimie et de la Répression des Fraudes prepared and applied legislation against any type of adulteration of drinks, foods, and agricultural products, and carried out technical and scientific research. It also set up farm stations, drew up soil maps in collaboration with the Service Géologique, and carried out research on the industrial use of products of the soil.

The Direction des Eaux et Forêts and the Service de la Conservation de la Propriété Foncière were also attached to the Direction de l'Agriculture. The Service de la Conservation de la Propriété Foncière played a particularly important role in the Protectorate. (Both these last two categories are discussed in ch. 3.)

The *Direction Générale des Travaux Publics,* one of the oldest departments of the Protectorate, was reorganized in 1920.[77] Four Services were directly responsible to the administrator, the Directeur Général, who was codirector of several other bureaus. The Service Ordinaire saw to the upkeep of highways and the management of Public Domain (see ch. 3) and supervised insalubrious areas, freshwater navigation, and power and light distribution.[78] The Service Maritime built and maintained ports, lighthouses, beacons, buoys,

---

[77] Dahir of July 24, 1920, *BO,* 409 (Aug. 24, 1920), 1436. The above study includes the modifications made by the Dahir of Apr. 23, 1924, *BO,* 606 (June 3, 1924), 861.

[78] Dahir of July 24, 1920, Art. 3.

managed all Public Domain in the ports, administered the Service de
l'Aconage, and supervised maritime commerce, navigation, and fishing
(under the Service du Commerce, de la Navigation et de la Pêche
Maritimes). A ship mortgage office was also set up. The Service des
Chemins de Fer constructed the railway lines planned by the state and
supervised the construction and use of all railways and tramways. The
Contrôle des Transports also worked through this office. The Service
des Mines dealt with all aspects of mining, including geological
surveys and maps. (Public and Private Domain including highways,
harbors, lighthouses, etc. are discussed in ch. 3.).[79]

Three other Services—the Service de l'Hydraulique Industrielle,
that of the Hydraulique Agricole, and that of Travaux de Colonisation
—were codirected by the Directeur Général des Travaux Publics and
the Directeur Général de l'Agriculture.[80] The Service des Travaux
Municipaux came under the codirection of the Directeur Général des
Travaux Publics and the Chef du Service des Contrôles Civils et du
Contrôle des Muncipalités. The initiative concerning projects involving any of the last four Services, however, did not lie with the
Directeur Général des Travaux Publics, but with the other codirector.
The Directeur Général also had the task of constructing all necessary
civilian public buildings,[81] which in the past had been the responsi-
bility of the oumana el-moustafad and the Makhzen.

The *Direction Générale de l'Instruction Publique, des Beaux-Arts
et des Antiquités* had undergone several changes by the time it was
reorganized in 1920 and 1921.[82] At the beginning of the Protectorate
there was a single Direction de l'Enseignement, headed by a Muslim,
in charge of both religious (Muslim) and secular education. In 1914,
however, when religious and secular education were separated, religious education became the responsibility of the Vizir de la Justice
and secular education was transferred to the French.[83] The new
Direction de l'Enseignement was created in December, 1915.[84] A Service
des Antiquités, Beaux-Arts et Monuments Historiques had been
created as early as 1912,[85] and in 1918 the Office des Industries d'Art
Indigène was set up;[86] the latter was attached to the Direction de
l'Enseignement in March, 1920.[87]

In February, 1921, the Direction Général de l'Instruction Publique

[79] See Dahir of July 1, 1914, Art. 6.
[80] Dahir of July 24, 1920, Art. 5.
[81] *Ibid.*, Art. 6, added by Dahir of Apr. 23, 1924.
[82] Dahir of Feb. 28, 1921, modified the Dahir of July 26, 1920, *BO*, 408 (Aug. 17, 1920), 1393.
[83] Dahir of Aug. 5, 1914, *BO*, 96 (Aug. 21, 1914), 690, and Dahir of Mar. 9, 1915.
[84] Dahir of Dec. 23, 1915.
[85] Residential Decree of Nov. 28, 1912, *BO*, 5 (Nov. 29, 1912), 26.
[86] Residential Décision of Jan. 12, 1918, *BO*, 274 (Jan. 21, 1918), 50.
[87] Vizirial Decree of Mar. 9, 1920, *BO*, 386 (Mar. 16, 1920), 454.

des Beaux-Arts et des Antiquités was set up, consisting of six Services.[88] The Service de l'Enseignement des Indigènes dealt with the organization and administration of native schools.[89] The Service de l'Enseignement Primaire, Secondaire et Technique Européens was concerned with all European schools. The Service de l'Enseignement Supérieur et Organisation Scientifique administered and supervised higher education, institutes of scientific research, and libraries and archives. The Service des Antiquités Préislamiques was responsible for the supervision and preservation of antiquities, and the direction and inspection of excavations. The Service des Monuments Historiques, Palais Inpériaux et Résidences was concerned with the preservation of historical monuments, and with the construction and maintenance of imperial palaces and museums.[90] The Service des Arts Indigènes organized, administered, and supervised apprenticeship to professions in the native arts, and maintained museums of native art.[91]

The two remaining Directions need be mentioned only briefly. A Direction du Service de Santé et Hygiène Publiques was first organized in March, 1915, and served both civilians and military personnel, Moroccans and Europeans.[92] The Direction de l'Office des Postes, des Télégraphes et des Téléphones became an independent department in January, 1916.[93] In addition, two other sections should be mentioned here. An Office du Transport was created in February, 1920 (but, unlike any of the above Directions, was under the direct authority of the Délégué), and an Office Chérifien des Phosphates was created in August, 1920.[94]

e) Regional Administration. The Sherifian Empire, unlike the Ottoman Empire, had never possessed a system of provincial administration, primarily because of the weakness of the Sultanate. The only institutions that could be called regional were those of the tribes, which were in most cases independent of Makhzen control.

The French established a system of regional administration in an effort to control the country more effectively. They set up two types of regional administration in Morocco: military and civil, the country being divided up into a series of *régions, territoires, cercles, circon-*

---

[88] This Direction was created by Dahir of July 26, 1920, *BO*, 408 (Aug. 17, 1920), 1393, its official title being altered to the above by Dahir of Feb. 28, 1921. The *service* structure was reorganized by Dahir of Dec. 17, 1920, *BO*, 426 (Dec. 21, 1920), Art. 3.

[89] Dahir of Dec. 17, 1920, Art. 3.

[90] In 1924 the name of this *service* was changed to that of Beaux-Arts et Monuments Historiques (Dahir of Apr. 1, 1924).

[91] Dahir of Dec. 17, 1920, Art. 3.

[92] See Residential Decrees of Mar. 20, 1915, Jan. 3, 1916, Mar. 9, 1918, June 21, 1919, and Jan. 21, 1920.

[93] Dahir of Jan. 21, 1916.

[94] Ordre of Feb. 8, 1920, and Dahir of Aug. 7, 1920.

scriptions, annexes, and *postes,* in that order (see Map 1). Every region was first under military control, and then, after being gradually pacified, passed to a civil administration. The regional military areas began functioning in 1912, but the first officially designated civil regions were not set up until 1919 and 1920, consisting of Rabat, Casablanca, Oujda, and the Rharb.[95]

In December, 1923, a Residential Decree announced a completely revised regional organization set up in the following manner:[96]

A. Civil Zone
    1. Régions Civiles of: (a) Rabat; (b) Chaouïa (*chef-lieu,* Casablanca); (c) Rharb; (d) Oujda.
    2. Contrôles Civils of: (a) Mazagan; (b) Safi; (c) Mogador.
B. Military Zone
    Régions Militaires of: (a) Fez (including Taza); (b) Meknes; (c) Marrakesh.

This regional organization was flexible and was revised on several occasions under later Residents General.[97]

Each region had its *chef de région,* who in the military areas was the military commander, under whom were *officers de renseignements,* who were responsible to the Directeur des Services des Renseignements in the Direction des Affaires Indigènes et des Services des Renseignements.[98] Lyautey had direct control over these officials, of whom there were at first a great many. By 1927 the number had been reduced to 220 for the whole of Morocco, whereas in the summer of 1914 there were 120 in the Chaouïa alone.[99]

The officier de renseignements had three main duties: military, political, and administrative, the order of priority varying with the extent to which each region had been pacified. He collected all important military and political information from his area in order to facilitate military action in it if necessary. He also advised on the systematic

[95] Instruction of Aug. 4, 1912, *BO, 2* (Nov. 8, 1912), 10. The Régions Civiles of Rabat and Casablanca were created by Residential Decree of Mar. 27, 1919, *BO, 336* (Mar. 31, 1919), 289. Oujda was created by Residential Decree of Dec. 22, 1919, *BO, 377* (Jan. 12, 1920), 59. The Rharb was created by Residential Decree of Nov. 6, 1920, *BO, 422* (Nov. 23, 1920), 1981.

[96] Residential Decree of Dec. 11, 1923, *BO, 585* (Jan. 8, 1924), 25.

[97] In 1926, 1935, and 1940, to wit: the Residential Decree (of Théodore Steeg) of Nov. 26, 1926, *BO, 737* (Dec. 7, 1926), 2303 (as a result of the ending of the Rif War); Residential Decree (of Henri Ponsot) of Sept. 29, 1935, *BO, 1196* (Oct. 11, 1935), 1182, and also Residential Decree of Dec. 20, 1935, *BO, 1211* (Jan. 10, 1936), 34 (following the general pacification and unification of Morocco); and Residential Decree (of General Noguès) of Sept. 19, 1940, *BO, 1456 bis* (Sept. 23, 1940), 911.

[98] Marshal Bugeaud in the nineteenth century first created Bureaux Arabes in Algeria which later became the Service des Affaires Indigènes, and the Service des Renseignements in Tunisia.

[99] Arthur Girault, *Principes de colonisation et de législation coloniale,* Vol. V (5th ed.; Paris; 1928), p. 252. Lyautey gave the figure of 120 officials in July, 1914; *PA,* p. 118.

pacification of the area, and on the preparation of the administrative and political groundwork in the light of the native tribal structure. He had Moroccan auxiliary forces at his disposal to aid him when necessary.[100] The second stage of this work was chiefly administrative, and he had to supervise all the details of the functioning of the administration and judicial organization of the Moroccans, which included examining cases, penalties, and fines, and ensuring that justice was meted out; he also had to supervise the collecting of taxes.[101] Thus he generally supervised and advised the local native authorities, but at all stages he had to prepare and channel all questions regarding native policy to the Residency.[102]

Once the Région Militaire had been pacified and organized by the officiers de renseignements, it was then transferred to civilian responsibility, becoming a Région Civile.[103]

The *contrôleurs civils,* as civil supervisory agents, were put in charge of a Région Civile, under the authority of the Secrétaire Général du Protectorat, and were in the Service des Contrôles Civils et du Contrôle des Municipalités. The Contrôle Civil was instituted by a Decree of July, 1913, and was further regulated by Residential Circulars of August, 1917, and April, 1919, and a Residential Decree of April, 1920.[104] During Lyautey's administration, the powers and competence

[100] Girault, V, 252; also André Colliez, *Notre Protectorat marocain: la Ière étape, 1912–1930* (Paris, 1930), p. 180.

[101] Goulven, *Traité d'économie,* I, 193.

[102] Girault, V, 253.

[103] Britsch briefly described what occurred when on April 1, 1913, the Chaouïa was converted, unofficially, to a civil region. Amédée Britsch, *Le maréchal Lyautey: le soldat, l'écrivain, le politique* (Paris, 1921), pp. 152–153.

[104] Residential Decree of July 31, 1913; Residential Circulars of Aug. 27, 1917, and Apr. 25, 1919; Residential Decree of Apr. 3, 1920. Lyautey sent out this letter to the Chefs des Services Municipaux concerning the post of contrôleur civil, on May 4, 1914:

"The *contrôleur civil* cannot himself administer anything personally; but he is, at the same time, representative of the Government of the Protectorate with the local native authorities, and guide, counsellor, and supervisor of these authorities. They are not, in fact, prepared for our stage of development or our methods of administration; they receive instructions from a higher authority, the Makhzen, but these instructions, prepared upon the advice and initiative of officials of the Protectorate, are not always well received by the local native authority. It is up to the agents in charge of supervising them to explain the meaning of such instructions, to guide the native authority, and to supervise the execution of the instructions.

"I cannot recommend too highly, as regards this part of your powers, to keep in close contact with the native leaders, to send for them any time you feel it necessary, but without your summons sounding imperative or compulsory; finally and especially, to go to them personally every time you can spare the time, and this, even *without any specific purpose in mind,* in order to win their confidence, to get to know them and to make them know you, to hear their *desiderata* or their complaints, to obtain their criticisms of the administrative or judicial organizations and reforms which may have repercussions on their functions, to make them know and appreciate our methods and the purpose we are pursuing, etc.

of the contrôleurs civils were purely supervisory, though during later stages of the Protectorate they became administrative and were increased significantly.[105]

J. Goulven has best described the eight categories of tasks of the contrôleur civil:

1. The principal mission of the contrôleurs is the *supervision of native authorities,* whose place they must never take themselves, because their role is not to administer. This mission is a most important one, and the manner of exercising it is as important as the formula of the Protectorate itself. It is through the personal influence which the contrôleurs civils gain over the native leaders, with whom they are placed, that the development of the *oeuvre civilisatrice* of France in Morocco will depend. In fact, not only must they play the part of censor with the representatives of the Makhzen, but they must also serve as their educators. The means of action of the contrôleurs civils available for accomplishing their task are powerful, because nothing which concerns the native authorities of their *circonscription* can escape them. No nomination, no sanction, no dismissal may be made without their advice and consent. No administrative *service* may correspond with the native authorities without going through the obligatory intermediary of the contrôleurs civils.

On the other hand, the contrôleurs civils have to intervene in some matters, often difficult, such as the preparation of the lists [of taxpayers] and the collection of taxes which are the tasks of the *caïd;* these are seconded by commissions presided over by the representative of the *autorité de contrôle locale.* Moveover, the Sherifian government, for the purpose of giving protection, has created Sociétés de Prévoyance Agricole. It has entrusted the chairmanship of them to the caïds, but the representative of the contrôle has been placed beside them. The contrôleurs civils may even receive a delegation of some powers from the chairman of these societies.

2. But it is the supervision of the *cadis* which represents one of the most delicate tasks, and at the same time one of the most demanding which fall

---

Finally, to consider various questions which have arisen or which might have come to your knowledge through complaints by individuals or through communications from the Resident General.

"Learn quickly of the importance in not dealing with the natives through written correspondence only; a verbal message followed, when it is such, by a succinct note to record the agreement reached, will render you far more service than a mere exchange of letters which often are not understood. This procedure may also be used efficiently even for the municipal decrees or other acts of municipal administration, the meaning of which is so often not realized by the *pachas* who sanction them with their signatures.

"I do not need to insist on the necessity of maintaining with regard to the native leaders an attitude of courtesy and deference which they never fail to notice, and of never giving them advice of any kind before witnesses other than your immediate collaborators." Quoted in J. Goulven, *Traité l'économie,* I, 195. See also LA, III, 273–279.

[105] See Decree of Oct. 3, 1926, Residential Decree of Sept. 19, 1940, etc. Frédéric Brémard discusses these later developments clearly and in detail: *L'organisation régionale du Maroc,* pp. 53 *et seq.* This treatise is probably the most valuable one of its kind on regional organization, although J. Goulven's *Traité d'économie et de législation marocaines* is excellent for the early period of the Protectorate.

upon the shoulders of the contrôleurs civils. A delicate task because the cadi is a religious personage; a difficult task, because it is he who handles all real estate matters, and because the recognition of real property rights is surrounded in Muslim countries by considerable difficulties which colonists, as newcomers on African soil, must always come up against. The cadis must hold a certain number of registers recording the acts which they draw up. These registers must all be submitted for the inspection and then initialing of the contrôleurs civils.

3. The contrôleurs civils must also handle *municipal matters,* either directly or indirectly. As a general rule, they only do this indirectly, because the municipalities are all situated in important areas and possess a specialized personnel. In this case, the correspondence of the Chefs des Services Municipaux passes entirely through the hands of contrôleurs civils of the area, whether incoming or outgoing. These officials must then express opinions without entering into the details of these administrations. In exceptional cases, the Services Municipaux are directed by the contrôleur civil of the area, when the importance of these services does not necessitate a division; that is what is found, for example, in Settat, Salé, and Kenitra.

4. The contrôleurs civils have no judicial powers, but the Dahir of August 12, 1913, on the judicial organization of the French Protectorate in Morocco has made them *officiers de police judiciaire,* as auxiliaries of the *commissaire du gouvernement* with the courts. A Dahir of March 24, 1914, has also, provisionally and temporarily, authorized that the French judicial organization, when required to proceed with an inquiry or a visit to places, or an interrogation in civil matters, at a distance from the seat of the competent jurisdiction, may be placed in the hands of the contrôleurs civils. The latter must naturally second the French judicial organization in every search into crimes and offenses in their areas. They must facilitate its task with the native authorities, but they must scrupulously abstain from intervening in the procedure itself. They are recommended, when a European is involved in a penal matter, to work in liaison with French judges.

5. The contrôleurs civils have, naturally, an important role to play *with regard to colonization,* the development of which they must ensure. They [must] seek lands suitable for colonists. A Residential Circular of April 25, 1919, charged the contrôleurs civils to intervene actively in the real estate disputes during registration procedures, to try to conciliate the parties involved and thus to help the colonists who are looking for the security indispensable in appraising property which they have purchased. The contrôleurs civils preside over the commissions in charge of distributing the subsidies for stock farms. They must supervise the execution of proper measures to be taken to avoid the outbreak and spread of cattle diseases. During locust invasions they have an active role to play in getting the native leaders to set in the struggle for protection. The contrôleurs civils preside over the commissions in charge of drawing up the electoral lists of natives for the Chambres d'Agriculture et de Commerce, and in supervising the election of members of these Chambres.

6. The contrôleurs civils are consulted about the execution of large-scale *public utility works:* roads, bridges, etc., located in their areas. They have to sponsor the construction and maintenance of tracks and obtain secondary agents to help them with this. The expenses involved in these works come from the general budget. In the Chaouïa, a special fund-raising group has been instituted in order to provide these works, and there the Administration

des Travaux Publics fulfills this role, which moreover devolves upon the contrôleurs. The contrôleurs civils must also work in liaison with the Service Hydraulique Agricole to provide water holes, wells, drinking troughs, irrigation works, etc. . .

7. The contrôleurs civils are consulted in everything having to do with *education* in their areas. Their assistance is especially useful in the organization of native education.

8. *To ensure public health and hygiene,* to fight epidemics, to provide hygiene facilities in native quarters are the tasks of contrôleurs civils who have two categories of doctors attached to them to ensure the measures of hygiene necessary for the preservation of public health: the *médecins-chefs* of mobile sanitation groups, and the colonization doctors.[106]

f) The Conseil du Gouvernement, and the Chambres d'Industrie, de Commerce et d'Agriculture—The Chambres Consultatives de Commerce, d'Industrie et d'Agriculture were created in 1913 at Rabat and Casablanca, their members being appointed by the Resident General[107] to give the colonists a means of defending their interests. By the end of 1917 the Chambres were permitted to elect their own presidents.[108] In June, 1919, permission was given for the election of these bodies by the French farmers, individuals, and businessmen themselves, and in the same year a Moroccan section was added, whose members, however, were nominated by vizirial decree.[109]

There were three types of Chambres: (1) Chambres Consultatives de Commerce et d'Industrie, (2) Chambres Consultatives d'Agriculture, and (3) Chambres Consultatives Mixtes d'Agriculture, de Commerce et d'Industrie. By 1927 there were Chambres de Commerce et d'Industrie at Rabat, Casablanca, Kenitra, and Mogador;[110] Chambres d'Agriculture at Casablanca and Rabat: and six Chambres Mixtes d'Agriculture, de Commerce et d'Industrie at Meknes, Fez, Oujda, Mazagan, Safi, and Marrakesh. The primary role of all of these Chambres, which were purely consultative, was to provide a means of liaison with the Residency by expressing the views and wishes of the professional classes concerned. A Conseil Supérieur de l'Agriculture and a Conseil Supérieur du Commerce et de l'Industrie were set up in 1921 to work with these Chambres.[111]

[106] J. Goulven, *Traité d'économie,* I, 197–201. Goulven bases this study on the Residential Circular of Aug. 27, 1917. See also Girault, *Principes,* V, 250–251, and Colliez, *Notre Protectorate marocain,* pp. 182 *et seq;* and for the ultimate regional organization, Stéphane Bernard's *Le conflit franco-marocain, 1943–1956,* Vol. III: *Institutions et groupes sociaux, annexes* (Brussels, 1963), pp. 44–45.

[107] By Residential Decree of June 29, 1913, *BO,* 37 (July 11, 1913), 236. See also Laubadère, "Les réformes des pouvoirs publics," p. 139, and Girault, V, 216 *et seq.*

[108] Residential Decree of Dec. 28, 1917, *BO,* 271 (Dec. 31, 1917), 1412.

[109] Two Residential Decrees of June 1, 1919, *BO,* June 30, 1919, pp. 654, 660; Dahir of Jan. 20, 1919, *BO,* 327 (Jan. 27, 1919), 71.

[110] Girault, V, 262.

[111] Two Dahirs of Jan. 15, 1921, *BO,* 433 (Feb. 8, 1921), 206.

In March, 1919, Lyautey created a new Residential institution, the Conseil du Gouvernement.[112] At first it met monthly and consisted of the presidents and vice-presidents of the various Chambres, and of the Comités d'Études Économiques; later it also included delegates from the Commissions Municipales.[113] The chief purpose of this Conseil was to discuss budgetary and economic matters; it had no official voice in the government, which did not have to act on its suggestions. In June, 1919, the delegates to the Chambres Françaises Consultatives were permitted to be elected by the colonists, industrialists, and businessmen of the various Chambres.[114]

In May, 1923, a second college (to use the French term) of members was added to the Conseil made up of Moroccans: the presidents and vice-presidents of the Chambres Marocaines Consultatives. At the same time the French representatives were limited to the presidents and vice-presidents of the Chambres Françaises Consultatives d'Agriculture, de Commerce et d'Industrie and of the Chambres Mixtes.[115]

In 1926 Resident General Steeg added a third and final college to the Conseil du Gouvernement, in which French citizens in Morocco, other than the farmers, businessmen, and industrialists already represented, now gained a voice.[116]

III. MUNICIPAL ADMINISTRATON

A. BEFORE 1912

In the Sherifian Empire, municipal administration usually meant the possession by a few men of almost dictatorial powers, something not necessarily to be condemned since not all societies work efficiently under a democratic regime. Unfortunately, however, a keen interest in public welfare was not one of the characteristics of Oriental administrators. In order to describe government at the local or municipal level, I shall take Rabat as my example, although municipal government often varied from city to city in consequence of numerous

[112] Residential Decision of Mar. 18, 1919.

[113] Laubadère, p. 138; Brémard, *Les droits publics*, pp. 84 *et seq.* Lyautey established the *Comités d'Études Economiques* (composed of colons) in order to provide a further means of liaison between his administration and the economic needs of the colons.

[114] Residential Decree of June 1, 1919.

[115] This was done by two Residential Décisions of May 10, 1923, *BO,* 553 (May 29, 1923), 663–664.

[116] Residential Décision of Oct. 13, 1926, *BO,* 730 (Oct. 19, 1926), 979. The Conseil was not altered again until the Residential Décision of Dec. 20, 1947 (*BO,* 1835 [Dec. 26, 1947], 1334), when Moroccan representation was increased, and a representative of Moroccan Jewish interests was added.

factors, such as whether the city was closely under the Sultan's authority or not, whether it was a port or inland city, whether it was in close contact with Europeans or in a remote region.

1. Pach or Caïd

Most towns or cities were headed by a *pacha* or *caïd* (see fig. 5). In Tangier the city's chief administrator was known as pacha: in Rabat his title was caïd. In small towns, however, an *amel* (governor) might be in charge of the over-all administration of perhaps three different towns, having appointed a *khalifa* (lieutenant governor) to administer each town directly. A khalifa administered El Kçar El Kebir in just this way, although in reality he was the amel's puppet and powerless.[117] The caïd or pacha was appointed by the Sultan, and often the post was held by the same family for generations.[118] Such posts were usually obtained by the individual who spent his money most wisely at the Sultan's court. In cities which were free from direct interference by the Sultan, though still under his over-all authority, such as Rabat (but not Tangier), the caïd's powers were sweeping. He was the administrative head of the city, the senior police official, the judge in all cases not involving Chrâa (Muslim religious) courts, the commander of the local military forces, the senior religious official (*imam*),[119] and also a tax collector.

The caïd or pacha had furthermore to handle matters involving Europeans, such as claims for indemnities or protection, although in such cases all decisions were made at the ministerial level by the Ouzir el-Bahr (Foreign Minister). In Tangier, however, where the diplomatic corps resided, the Sultan was represented directly by a special official, his *naïb* (agent).[120]

One of the most important administrative tasks of the caïd or pacha was that of periodically sending locally collected taxes to the amin el-oumana at the Ministry of Finance in Fez.[121] Because of the insecur-

---

[117] E. Michaux-Bellaire and Georges Salmon, "El Qçar El Kebir: une ville de province au Maroc septentrional," *AM*, II, No. 2 (1904), 37. For a sketchy history and study of the administrative changes of Tittāwŭn or Tetuan, see A. Joly, in collaboration with MM. Xigluna and L. Mercier, "Tétouan. Deuxième partie: historique," *AM*, V, Nos. 2 & 3 (1905), 161–264 and 311–430. This article is primarily historical, rather than being a systematic administrative survey.

[118] This was the case in Rabat.

[119] L. Mercier, "L'administration marocaine à Rabat," *AM*, VII (1906), 350 *et seq.* Cf. the position in Fez in Roger Le Tourneau's interesting work, *Fès avant le Protectorat: étude économique et social d'une ville de l'occident musulman* (Casablanca, 1949).

[120] Lahbabi, *Le gouvernement marocain*, pp. 149–150. The office of naïb was only created under Sultan Moulay el-Hassan in the last quarter of the nineteenth century. See note 14 above.

[121] Mercier, p. 355. In Tangier, however, the local oumana of the customs department sent their taxes directly to Fez.

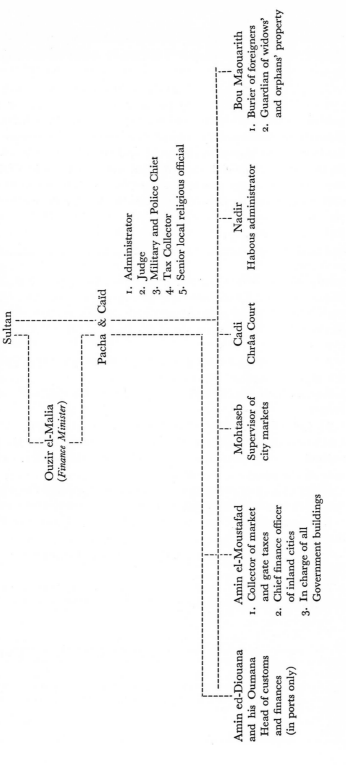

FIGURE 5
MUNICIPAL ADMINISTRATION BEFORE 1912

Sultan

Ouzir el-Malia
(*Finance Minister*)

Pacha & Caïd

1. Administrator
2. Judge
3. Military and Police Chief
4. Tax Collector
5. Senior local religious official

Amin ed-Diouana
and his Oumana
Head of customs
and finances
(in ports only)

Amin el-Moustafad
1. Collector of market
   and gate taxes
2. Chief finance officer
   of inland cities
3. In charge of all
   Government buildings

Mohtaseb
Supervisor of
city markets

Cadi
Chrâa Court

Nadir
Habous administrator

Bou Maouarith
1. Burier of foreigners
2. Guardian of widows'
   and orphans' property

ity of the Bled el-Makhzen, (or the land under direct governmental control) an elaborate convoy was usually required to accompany the taxes.

The caïd's or pacha's primary role in certain cities, such as Rabat, was to head the troops and police force.[122] The caïd of Rabat, for instance, had nearly 2,000 soldiers (all but 50 of them infantry) under him, although only about 250 of them were regular troops; they were used mainly for guarding the *qasba* and manning the city's batteries.[123] As senior police official, the caïd had forty men at his service, and of these, seven or eight supervised the Customs. The name *makhzen* was also applied to the police who were headed by their chief constable (or *mechâoury*), who took his orders from the caïd. The mechâoury and his policemen (*mekhazenya*) received no official salary and hence had to fend for themselves; they were usually recruited from special tribes around Rabat. They kept order in the city and were responsible to the *mohtaseb* (market inspector) when he required them to arrest persons guilty of fraud and the like in the city markets. Apart from the mohtaseb, they arrested or freed all persons only on the orders of the caïd or cadi. They were also used as official couriers by local officials.

As a local religious leader (*imam*), the caïd of Rabat used to go to the Djama' Moulay Sliman, escorted there and back by regular infantrymen preceded by musicians, and lead the Sabbath prayers every Friday.

As judge in commercial and criminal cases (that is, all cases not subject to the Chrâa), the caïd held his audiences in his *mahakma*, assisted by his deputy (*khalifa*). These audiences were usually held at nine in the morning, and in the afternoon from two to five. The caïd also had to convey the Sultan's messages to the people and usually did this by means of a town crier.

In Rabat the caïd was in charge of collecting the *hedya*, the only direct tax paid by the citizens, and the *frida*, a type of arbitrary tax levied by the government on the rural populations whenever it was short of funds.

The pacha or caïd received a monthly salary, from the oumana of the Customs.

2. *Customs*

The *amin ed-diouana*, or Délégué du Contrôle des Douanes pour

---

[122] In El Qçar El Kebir the local administrator had no real power. See Michaux-Bellaire and Salmon, "El Qçar El Kebir," p. 37. In Tangier the pacha had strong administrative powers and was also a judge, but he had no direct command over military units, see G. Salmon, "L'administration marocaine à Tanger," *AM*, I (1904), 2.

[123] Mercier, pp. 353, 355-358.

les Service de la Dette Marocaine,[124] and two native oumana,[125] headed the customs' department and managed most of the city's finances. They levied the 10 per cent *ad valorem* duty on imported merchandise,[126] confiscated contraband, received the market taxes (*mekous*) collected by the amin el-moustafad and sent them to the caïd for shipment to Fez; they paid the salaries of the Makhzen officials, including the caïd (except for officials such as the cadi, mufti, and lesser employees, who were paid by the Habous), farmed out to the highest bidders the right to collect the various mekous, and auctioned fruit and other produce from Habous property, in accordance with the directions of the *nadir* or administrator. The responsibility of the oumana was considerable and their work was vital to the life of the city.

3. Amin el-Moustafad

The *amin el-moustafad* was responsible for all the market and gate taxes in the city. As has been seen, the amin ed-diouana auctioned off the privilege of collecting the market and gate taxes each year to tax-farmers. Those tax-farmers used their own employees to collect the market and gate taxes in the city, who in turn gave the funds to the amin el-moustafad, who in turn delivered them to the amin ed-diouana. Surprisingly, the amin el-moustafad was also responsible for removing the trash and refuse of the city, although M. Mercier describing the situation in Rabat as he saw it in 1906, wrote:

If the *amin el-moustafad* were at all conscientious, he could maintain the city in excellent condition. But this [i.e., the collection of refuse] is done very irregularly, being suspended altogether during rainy weather until the mud has dried up; and the city is then horribly filthy when it rains, for there is a bed of liquid mud at least ten centimeters deep in which all the animals splash about, in the middle of the street, splattering the pedestrians.[127]

The amin el-moustafad was chosen for his post by the Makhzen with the caïd's approval from among the honorable businessmen of the city and appointed by the Sultan.[128] In inland cities, the amin el-moustafad was of more importance than in coastal cities such as Rabat.[129] In the inland cities he was the chief of the city's financial services (whereas in Rabat this position was held by the amin ed-

---

[124] This official was only created in 1904.
[125] *Oumana,* pl. of *amin.*
[126] Mercier, pp. 379, 391.
[127] *Ibid.,* p. 391.
[128] Michaux-Bellaire and Salmon, "El Qçar El Kebir," p. 41.
[129] Lahbabi, p. 159.

diouana).[130] In all cities, however, the amin el-moustafad was in charge of the collection of gate and market taxes and also responsible for the upkeep of all Makhzen buildings and the Sultan's palaces. In addition he was in charge of the official Makhzen postal services, and paid city officials such as the caïd or pacha when there was no amin eddiouana or customs department in the city.[131] Taxes were collected on every camel- or donkey-load entering and leaving the city,[132] the amount depending upon the load capacity of the animals as well as the type of load or material being carried. A camel, for instance, carrying a load of barley was charged more than a donkey carrying the same grain, but in lesser quantity. There were also slaughterhouse fees, levies on most animals sold in the city's markets, and levies on hides, rugs, and almost everything sold in the city.[133]

4. Mohtaseb

The mohtaseb was chosen for his post from among the wealthiest and most honest businessmen of the city, and was appointed by the Sultan. He was the chief of the market police, or market inspector, and was thus very powerful in the world of commerce; he inspected all products for standards of work (e.g. the quality of the dyes), including food products, set the price each day for the staple food products sold in the markets, and sampled the main food products. As chief of the market police he could have businessmen arrested by the police (assigned to the market by the caïd) if they had committed fraud or sold products at prices other than those fixed by himself daily.[134] Mohtasebs in Morocco at the turn of the century had a high reputation for honesty.

5. Cadi, Mufti, Adoul

The cadi, mufti, and adoul all had to do with the judicial system and are discussed under that heading in Chapter 5.

The cadi of Rabat, as head of the Chrâa judicial organization, was appointed by the Sultan, whereas in Tangier the pacha proposed the nominee to the High Cadi of Fez, the Cadi 'l-Coudat, who then made the appointment.[135] The cadi in turn selected the adoul (notaries) from among the faqihs of that city, the mufti, and the bou maoua-

---

[130] The amin el-moustafad of Fez, however, held a higher rank than those of the other cities of the empire, for he was also in charge of the Dar A'dyel Treasury to which all market and gate taxes of the empire were paid, and including the duties from tobacco, kief, and sulphur. Ibid., pp. 159–160.

[131] "El Qçar El Kebir," p. 41.

[132] Except when the person possessed a nefoula, or receipt, proving he had already paid.

[133] Mercier, pp. 388–389.

[134] Ibid., pp. 392–393.

[135] Salmon, "L'administration marocaine à Tanger," p. 3.

rith.[136] The cadi's competence was restricted to matters subject to the Chrâa and was only extended to criminal cases at the special request of the caïd or pacha. He neither gave written judgments nor held records of any type, and he was not entitled to any payment from parties involved in a litigation, his salary being paid by the nadir of the Habous.[137]

The mufti (jurisconsult) was also paid by the local nadir, and in addition he received fees from litigants requiring a *fetoua*,[138] or opinion or interpretation extracted from Muslim law, in support of their case before a cadi.

6. Nadir

The *nadir* was the administrator of a specific local group of properties belonging to the Habous, or pious foundations (known as *Waqf* in other Muslim countries). He was appointed by the Sultan[139] and was usually a fairly old and very honest individual. (For a detailed account of the nadir and the Habous, see ch. 3.) The nadir saw to the upkeep of Habous property, the harvesting and selling of its crops, the payment of salaries of public officials dependent on the Habous, and the leasing of Habous property.

7. Bou Maouarith

The *bou maouarith* had the task of burying all strangers who died in the city. He also managed the property of widows and of orphans (until they reached their majority).

B. MUNICIPAL ADMINISTRATION UNDER THE PROTECTORATE

Officially organized municipalities were created by the French in the spring of 1917, and in Lyautey's time were set up in the following cities: Casablanca, Rabat, Salé, Kenitra, Mazagan, Safi, Mogador, Ber-Rechid, Meknes, Marrakesh, Fez, Azemmour, Sefrou, Settat, Taza, Oujda.[140]

---

[136] Mercier, p. 394.

[137] At Tangier, however, the cadi was paid by the Customs' oumana. "L'administration marocaine à Tanger," p. 24.

[138] Mercier, pp. 399, 401.

[139] This means of appointment was relatively recent, having been started in the nineteenth century by Sultan Moulay Abd er-Rahman (1822–1859).

[140] Dahir of Apr. 8, 1917, *BO*, 236 (Apr. 30, 1917), 486. See also Brémard, *Les droits publics et politiques*, pp. 90–94, and Goulven, *Traité d'économie et de législation*, I, 210 *et seq.* All the cities except Oujda were named in the Vizirial Decree of Apr. 28, 1917, Art. 1, *BO*, 236 (Apr. 30, 1917), 489. Oujda was added by Vizirial Decree of Mar. 22, 1920, *BO*, 388 (Mar. 30, 1920), 524. After Lyautey's departure Ouezzan was added by Vizirial Decree of Dec. 18, 1926, *BO*, 740 (Dec. 28, 1926), 2485.

1. Pachas or Caïds

The pacha or caïd, helped by his khalifa, continued to be the titular head of the municipality (see fig. 6). His previous autocratic powers were naturally abolished, though, as we shall see, he remained the central municipal authority and the sole judge in legal matters brought before the Makhzen court.

The pacha or caïd was nominated by dahir, just as in the past. He was responsible for the administration and maintenance of municipal properties, and he represented the municipality when it was involved in a litigation.[141] The police powers formerly belonging to the pacha or caïd, or the mohtaseb in the markets, passed in 1924 to the French Police du Service Général.[142] The military powers of the pacha or caïd were also taken from him. He now administered the municipal finances in collaboration with the Chef des Services Municipaux, and after consultation with the Commission Municipale drew up the budget, executed the budget once approved, and handled the municipal administrative accounts.[143] The Chef des Services Municipaux, working also with the Commission Municipale, was now responsible for the supervision of municipal government; the pacha's or caïd's only remaining position of authority was as judge, and even his judicial powers were reduced considerably.

3. Chef des Services Municipaux

The Chef des Services Municipaux, to whom were delegated most of the pacha's powers, assisted and supervised the pacha or caïd in the municipal administration, and countersigned any decrees made by him.[144] His principal responsibility was to ensure that the Municipal Services functioned smoothly: municipal works, municipal police,[145]

[141] Dahir of Apr. 8, 1917, Art. 2. See also Goulven, I, 215–218.

[142] The pacha's original police powers had been stated in Art. 4. of Dahir of Apr. 8, 1917, but were rescinded by Art. 13 of Dahir of Mar. 1, 1924, *BO*, 596 (Mar. 25, 1924), 545.

[143] The municipal budget received funds primarily from the gate taxes, special duties, in addition to state taxes, various municipal taxes, revenue from municipal property and resources drawn from certain commercial and industrial sources (such as public utilities including water and electricity and public transport). On the other hand, municipalities were authorized to contract loans and to receive subsidies from the state. Muncipal expenses were the expenses incurred in administering the municipality (such as municipal salaries, equipment, the functioning of various services, public works and their maintenance), and various subsidies (given for certain public institutions and schools). See Brémard, *L'organisation régionale du Maroc*, p. 122.

[144] Dahir of Apr. 8, 1917, Art. 8. The Chef des Services Municipaux was nominated by Residential Decree.

[145] The Service de la Sécurité Générale was attached to the Secrétaire Général du Protectorat by Dahir of Mar. 1, 1924, and included the three main categories of police in the Protectorate (excluding the Police Mobile): (1) Police de Sûreté, (2) Police du Service Général, and (3) Police Spéciale. The Police du Service Général was responsible for police work in the municipalities.

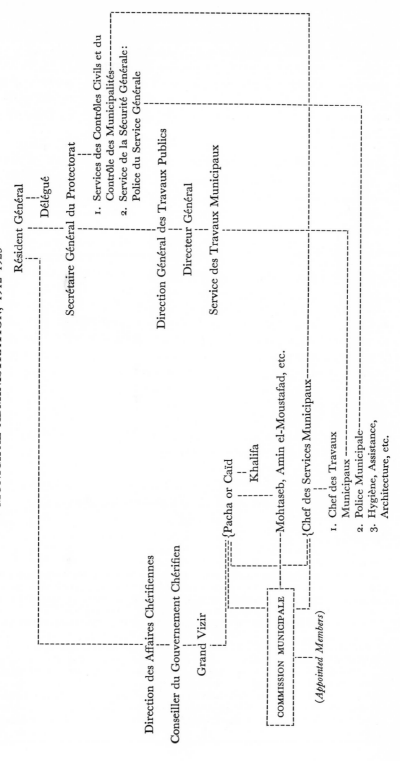

FIGURE 6

MUNICIPAL ADMINISTRATION, 1912–1925

public health, public assistance, and architecture.[146] He also worked
as a supervisor, liaison officer, and coordinator between the civil and
military services involved in the municipality. The Chef des Travaux
Municipaux, who was responsible for all engineering works and programs, was under the supervisory authority of the Chef des Services
Municipaux and the technical authority of the Directeur Général des
Travaux Publics.

3. Commissions Municipales

Two types of Commissions Municipales were created by the French:
the Commission Municipale Indigène and the Commission Municipale Mixte.[147] All the members of the Commission Municipale
Indigèe were Moroccans, with the exception of the Chef des Services
Municipaux.[148] This type of Commission could be divided, at the
pacha's suggestion, into two distinct sections, each functioning separately: a Muslim section, representing the interests of the Muslim
community in the city, and a Jewish section, representing the interests
of the Mellah. The Commission Municipale Mixte consisted of both
European and native sections, and the native section could likewise
be divided into Jewish and Muslim sections.[149]

Each Commission Municipale Mixte was set up by decree issued by
the Grand Vizir, which specified the number of European and native
notables to be appointed to it.[150] It is noteworthy that no one in the
municipal government, including members of Commissions, held an
elective post. The members of the Commissions were appointed for
one year only. The local pacha presided over the two types of Commissions, while the Chef des Services Municipaux served as vice-president. The native and European members voted, each in their separate
sections, on any proposal brought forward; the votes of both sections
were totaled separately, then added together, and the decision of the
majority prevailed. In addition to the voting members, the following
non-voting municipal officials took part in municipal deliberations:

[146] Dahir of Apr. 9, 1917, Art. 8.

[147] A third type of commission, totally unlike the others, being both deliberative
and elective, was created for Fez by the Dahir of Sept. 2, 1912. It was the only
one of its kind and it was abolished by Dahir of Mar. 23, 1944. See also
Laubadère, "Les reformes des pouvoirs publics," pp. 155–159.

[148] Art. 12, Dahir of Apr. 8, 1917. The only existing Commission Municipale
Indigène, that of Sefrou, was transformed into a Commission Municipale Mixte
on January 1, 1927. See also A. Girault, *Principes de colonisation*, V, 257.

[149] The Commission Mixte of Meknes, for instance, consisted of the pacha, who
was president; the Officier du Bureau des Renseignements, who was the Chef
des Services Municipaux, acting as vice-president; the Chef des Travaux Municipaux;
the amin el-moustafad; the mohtaseb; six Muslim notables; two Jewish notables;
and three French notables. See Piquet, *Le Maroc*, pp. 278 et seq.

[150] Dahir of Apr. 8, 1917, Arts. 15, 16, 18, and 20 (as modified by Vizirial Decree
of Jan. 27, 1923).

the mohtaseb, the Chef des Travaux Municipaux, the Directeur du Bureau Municipal d'Hygiène, and the Receveur Municipal. Not only was none of the municipal offices elective, which is not surprising at this early stage in the development of the Protectorate, but none of the meetings of the Commissions Municipales was open to the public. The members of the Commission were consulted by the pacha on the following matters: (1) acquisitions, exchanges, or alienations, or any other transaction having to do with municipal property; (2) acceptance by the city of gifts and legacies; (3) legal matters other than those involving confiscation; (4) the drawing up of the municipal budget and taxes, and the approval of municipal accounts and loans; (5) the authorization of contracts entered into by the municipality involving at least 5,000 francs annually; (6) programs of public municipal works; (7) the opening, closing, or changing of local markets; (8) fixing of the price list for staple food products sold in the markets; and (9) the granting of permits for the opening of permanent theatres.

These nine preceding points show some of the striking changes made by the French. Most property in cities not owned by the Habous or individuals was owned by the Makhzen and was now administered by the Commission Municipale and not by the amin el-moustafad. A city could now for the first time be involved in a legal action. Its public utilities, which had previously been administered by the Habous, were now transferred to the municipality, which also had to maintain them. Municipal budgets were introduced for the first time to regularize the city finances. Taxes were no longer imposed by the amin ed-diouana, the pacha, or the amin el-moustafad, but by the Commission Municipale. Public works which had been administered by the Habous or Makhzen, depending upon the type of project involved, became the responsibility of the Commission. The mohtaseb's traditional task of fixing price lists for staple food products was now done by the Commissions, which also saw to the opening, closing, and changing of markets.

The French, though maintaining some of the outward forms, swept away most of the traditional powers of the municipal officials and for the most part transferred them to the Chef des Services Municipaux and the Commissions Municipales. In cases of disagreement between the Commissions and the pacha, the matter was referred to the Grand Vizir, who had the authority to decide on the matter there and then.[151]

4. Judicial Organization

The judicial organization in the municipalities consisted of the religious courts and the civil and criminal courts. In criminal cases, the pacha or caïd could impose penalties of imprisonment for up to

[151] *Ibid.,* Art. 21.

two years only, and fines up to 2,000 P.H. only.[152] More important cases were tried in the Chambre Criminelle of the Haut Tribunal Chérifien. All civil and commercial cases were tried by the pacha except those involving persons within the jurisdiction of French courts, those concerning real estate, which were dealt with either by Tribunaux du Chrâa, or French courts when registered property was involved, and those concerning personal status or inheritance among Jewish subjects, which were settled by Tribunaux Rabbiniques. Thus the pacha's (caïd's) competence in his traditional role as judge was greatly restricted, though he remained the sole judge, just as in the past.

IV. TRIBAL ORGANIZATION

Since Morocco's society has always been largely based on tribal organization, no study of government in Morocco would be complete without a glance at tribal organization in the Sherifian Empire.

The Moroccan tribes could be classified as follows: (1) the *naïba,* or tax-paying tribes, which came under the authority of the Makhzen, (2) the *guich* tribes, which supplied troops for the Makhzen, in lieu of taxes, and (3) those tribes which usually managed to escape governmental authority.

Tribal organization consisted of four administrative levels: a confederation, a tribe, a *fraction* or *canton,* and a village. The confederation was made up of several tribes; the tribe of several fractions; the fraction in turn consisted of several villages, or *ksour;* and the village of a few clans. Of these four levels, the confederation was rarely formed, except in times of crisis.[153]

A. TRIBAL ADMINISTRATION BEFORE 1912

One caïd generally headed each tribe, although there were exceptions to this rule. He was aided by, or himself assisted, a *djemaa* (assembly of notables). The caïd—in naïba tribes—was usually chosen by the Makhzen (as for instance in the Rharb)[154]—in other words by the

---

[152] Dahir of Aug. 4, 1918, Art. 1, *BO,* 306 (Sept. 2, 1918), 838.

[153] A notable exception was the Aït Atta of the Sahara. See Georges Spillmann, *Les Aït Atta du Sahara et la pacification du Haut Dra* (Rabat, 1936). See also A. Bernard, *Le Maroc,* Book IV, ch. 4. There were approximately 600 tribes in Morocco, the average tribe consisting of 10,000–15,000 persons; each *fraction* consisted of 2,000–3,000 inhabitants in from four to twenty villages; each village, *ksar* (pl. *ksour*) or *douar,* consisted of from a few families to perhaps a thousand persons. Brémard, *L'organisation régionale du Maroc,* pp. 125–127.

[154] See E. Michaux-Bellaire's long article, *Le Gharb,* Vol. XX of *AM* (1913); see also by the same author, *Quelques tribus de montagnes de la région du Habt,* Vol. XVII of *AM* (1911), especially pp. 42 *et seq.*

Sultan. In the Bled el-Makhzen a djemaa sometimes held far less power than in the Bled es-Siba, beyond the Sultan's authority, for though the caïd had to treat the djemaa with respect, he could, if the need arose, request military aid from the Makhzen without consulting the djemaa. In a tribe totally free from interference from the Makhzen, the caïd—or sheikh, as the leader of each fraction—usually paid the greatest deference to the djemaa, being chosen by the djemaa and not by the Makhzen. If a caïd displeased his djemaa, he could expect imprisonment as well as confiscation of his property.[155] Among the tribes of the Rif, which were for the most part not under Makhzen control, differences between fractions or cantons supporting rival candidates for caïd often led to physical clashes, because it was the traditional right of the *arm'aren* (notables) of every fraction of the tribe to choose the caïd.[156] A caïd thus usually represented the interests of one or more fractions of the tribe and naturally showed deference to them, but the notables of other fractions had to submit to him.[157] Among the tribes of the Figuig area, however, the djemaa reigned supreme.

In mountainous areas of southern Morocco, there were tribes whose chiefs ruled almost dictatorially, backed by personal power and prestige; that was not always the case there and tribal societies were often even more complex in the south. In the Oued Dra' area, the town of Nesrat was governed by two assemblies, the Upper Assembly (Djemaa el-Kebira) and a Lower Assembly (Djemaa el-Amma).[158] The

[155] In the Bled el-Makhzen tribes could only seize the chattels of a man, for the Sultan alone had the right to seize any real property. Among the tribes of Figuig, however, which were beyond the control of the Sultan, the djemaa could have a man's real property confiscated by the tribe, though in such a case the djemaa usually limited itself to one piece of property, not taking all that a man owned. See Roger Gromand, "La coutume de la 'Bezra' dans les ksour de Figuig," *REI*, V, No. 3 (1931), 277–312; and G. H. Bousquet, "Le droit coutumier des Aït Haddidou des Assit Melloul et Isselatena (Confédération des Aït Yafelmanes): notes et réflexions," §VI, *AIEO*, XII (1954), 158–169.

[156] See A. Rezzouk's interesting article, "Notes sur l'organisation politique et administrative du Rif," *AM*, V, No. 2 (1905), 265–275.

[157] *Ibid.*, pp. 268–270.

[158] Nesrat, though tribal in structure (the Nesarta and Aït Insrat), followed a sedentary existence within the immediate area of the town, with an embryonic form of urban life. It had its own permanent Tribal House (Dar el-Qbila), mosques, schools, cemeteries, irrigation works, and permanent officials to run these. See F. de La Chapelle, "Une cité de l'Oued Dra' sous le protectorat des nomades: Nesrat," *Hespéris*, IX, No. 1 (1929), 29–42. See also Robert Montagne, *Les Berbères et le makhzen dans le sud du Maroc* (Paris, 1930); and the same author's *Villages et kasbas berbères: tableau de la vie sociale des Berbères sédentaires dans le sud du Maroc* (Paris, 1930). Montagne stresses that the family organization was the basis of all social life among the Berbers of southern Morocco, and this was true of tribal societies throughout Morocco. Discussing the Berber "republics" of the High Atlas, he gives the following divisions in social life: One group of families, perhaps fifteen to twenty of them, which made up one clan, formed the *ikhs*. Each ikhs had its chief, who was both elderly and rich; the next social unit was the

Upper Assembly was composed of twelve to fifteen members, and was presided over by two of its members.[159] As indicated by its name, it was the senior of the two Assemblies, with a member from the important families of each fraction, who could not be removed from office unless he committed some very serious offense. They decided on the policies to be followed by the town and maintained relations with the neighboring tribes and with the suzerain nomads who acted as guardians of their town, to protect it from marauders. They were also responsible for maintaining a police force within the ksar, offering hospitality to strangers, selecting the outside tribe which would protect the town, declaring war, settling disputes over land or water, and trying crimes committed within the town. The Lower Assembly, or Assembly of the People, held an inferior position in the administration. It handled policing beyond the city walls and daily relations between the inhabitants and the protecting tribe, and it tried lesser breaches of the law. Its members, usually twenty in number, were selected by the Upper Assembly from the members of each fraction. In legal matters, jurisdiction was divided between the assemblies and the cadi.

Towns like Nesrat were, by their own choice, the vassals of other tribes. The protector tribe was ruled by a powerful chief or *amghar,* appointed to office for one year, who governed his tribe through an Assembly of Notables. A special official, called the *amghar l'ar,* handled daily relations between the tribe and its vassals.

Thus, although tribal structure was essentially the same throughout the empire, it varied according to the local needs of particular tribes. Nesrat's double assembly system was in contrast to the single assembly system that prevailed in most other areas of Morocco—the Rharb, Rif, Figuig, and the High Atlas—and its protector tribe

---

village, consisting of two or three ikhs, which centered around a mosque and irrigated fields held more or less in common. The next unit was the *canton,* or republic, which consisted of several villages; one council of notables administered each republic, its members being chiefs who represented each ikhs. The republic was roughly equivalent to a *fraction* and several cantons or fractions equaled one tribe, the cantonal administration being by far the most important. In the High Atlas, in the independent republics or cantons, the Council of Notables selected a *moqaddem* as president, who usually had great power and sometimes became uncontested master of not only his canton (especially in the High Dra and the Dadès), but even of the tribe. For a discussion of Berber tribal structure see Saïd Guennoun, *La montagne berbère—les Aït Oumalou et les pays Zaïan* (Rabat, 1933), e.g., pp. 139–171. See also F. de La Chapelle, "Les tribus de haute montagne de l'Atlas occidental: organisation sociale et évolution politique," *REI,* II, No. 3 (1938), 339–360. De La Chapelle shows the traditional basis of tribal organization, the purpose and structure of organization being similar, despite differences in nomenclature. For a valuable study of the physical structure of some Berber groups (as well as their tools), see André Adam, *La maison et le village dans quelques tribus de l'Anti-Atlas* (Paris, 1951).

[159] F. de La Chapelle, "Une cité de l'Oued Dra'," pp. 31–34, 37.

created a special officer to act as intermediary between vassal and tribe.

Guich tribes, on the other hand, did not possess a normal tribal structure,[160] having originally been based on Turkish military lines, each group having at its head a caïd, as commander. The caïd's command was divided into *rhas* of five hundred horses, each rha being commanded by a *caïd er-rha*. The rha in turn was subdivided into five *miyas,* each miya under one *caïd el-miya.* In all guich structures, regardless of their geographical location, this sort of organization was maintained.

B. TRIBAL ADMINISTRATION, 1912–1925

> They [the Moroccans] still do not know us well. We frighten them. They still remain rather withdrawn, but they are easy to win over when one shows them intelligent sympathy, especially when they feel that they are appreciated. For the secret is a welcoming hand, and not a condescending one, a loyal man-to-man handshake, made in order to understand one another. As Colonel Berriau said: "this race is not inferior to us, it is merely different." Let us learn their ways, just as they are learning ours. Let us both adapt.
>
> MARSHAL LYAUTEY,
> *Rabat, May 26, 1921*

In Morocco the French found it much more difficult to make changes at the grass roots level than at that of the central administration. Although sultans had come and gone, and methods had varied with them, tribal administration, with little essential variation throughout the centuries, was not so easily altered. The French realized that they could not sweep away institutions that were so much a part of the people, and a very conservative people; instead they brought about changes in the bases of power and authority within the tribes.

From the beginning, the French made a point of differentiating between Arab and Berber. This policy culminated in the famous Berber Dahir of 1930 which, in the words of Nevill Barbour, "was designed to encourage Berber separatism by perpetuating Berber customary law," [161] and which in turn acted as a catalyst in the embryonic nationalist groups throughout the country.[162]

---

[160] E. Michaux-Bellaire, *Le Gharb,* p. 145. See also Eugène Aubin, *Le Maroc d'aujourd'hui,* pp. 184 *et seq.*

[161] Nevill Barbour, *Morocco* (London, 1965), p. 176.

[162] In 1928 the French authorities published a tentative list of tribes officially recognized as following Berber customary law (see Vizirial Decree of Apr. 16, 1928, *BO,* 838 [Sept 2, 1928], 1273): Beni M'Tir, Gerrouan du Sud (Aït Yazem, Aït Ouikhelfen, and the two *douars* Aït Makchoum and Aït Krat of the Aït Lhassen), Beni M'Guild (Irchlaouen, Aït Arfa, Aït Ouahi, Aït Mouli, Aït Meghoual, Aït Mohand ou Lhassen, Aït Lias, Aït Bougueman, Aït Ougadir, Aït Messaoud), Aït Youssi (ex-

Apart from the cities, the administration of Morocco before the
Protectorate was largely in the hands of the tribes and their djemaas.
As the French gradually pacified more and more of the country, the
newly installed French overlapped the authority of the traditional
tribal djemaas. Most of the tribes which formerly lay beyond the control of the Makhzen, from 1912 were gradually drawn within it by the
French so as to link up and unite all parts of the empire.

As early as 1914, the French announced their intention of respecting Berber customs and laws, as distinct from Islamic law of the Arab
tribes; but it was not until 1916 that official reorganization of Moroccan tribes was first attempted.[163] The French acted on the presump-
tion that some of the traditional administration must be changed.
They therefore created official, legal djemaas to represent the tribes
and tribal units of the empire. At the tribal level, the djemaa was
presided over by the caïd, and at the fractional level by the sheikh.
At both levels, however, its members were no longer appointed by
the tribes or fractions, but by the French chef de région (military or
civil) discussed earlier in this chapter. The notables appointed to the
djemaa remained members of it for three years only. The djemaas
now also included French supervisory agents (autorités locales de
contrôle) who, in agreement with the president (caïd), fixed the agenda
of the meetings and the times when the djemaa was to be convoked;
furthermore, minutes of the proceedings were now recorded. The traditional authority of the djemaa was so greatly reduced that the original djemaa was scarcely recognizable; it was limited to giving advice
on matters involving its group, and to managing its tribal property,
and it could thus no longer summon troops, declare war, raise taxes,
and so on. The djemaas established by the Dahir of November, 1916,
may be termed Official or Administrative Djemaas; they never suc-

---

cept the fractions belonging to the Pachalik of Sefrou and the *fractions* Aït
Makhlouf, Aït Kaïas, and Haï Nadjen), Aït Seghrouchen of Immouzer, Aït
Seghrouchen of Sidi Ali, Aït Seghrouchen of Harira, Aït Seghrouchen du Sud
(Aït Bouchaouen, Aït Bou Meryem, Aït Mesrouh, Aït Khalifa, Aït Saïd, Fouanis,
Aït Ben Ouadfel, and Aït Bel Ihassen), Zemmour, Zaïan (Zaïan ou Aït Sgougou), Aït
Ali, Ida ou Tana, Aït Brihim, Ida ou Bakel, Ida ou Guersmouk, Aït Outferkal,
Aït Abbès, Aït Bou Guemmez, Irezrani, Beni Alaham, Aït Atta N'Oumalou, Aït
Bouzid, Aït Seri (Aït Oumel Bert, Aït Ouirra, Aït Mohand, Aït Abdelouli), Aït
Izdeg, Aït Ouafella, Aït Aïssa, Aït Ayache, Ichkern, Aït Ihand, Aït Ishaq, Beni
Ouarain, Marmoucha, Aït Sokhman (Aït Saïd ou Ali, Aït Dauod ou Ali, Aït Abdi,
and Aït Hamama), Aït Hassan, Aït Morrad, Aït Haddidou, Aït Atta, Kebala of
Guir and of Ziz, Aït M'Hamed, Aït Ougoudid, Demsira, Douirane, Seksaoua, Ida
ou Mahmoud, Gedmioua (*fractions,* Aït Gair, Imelouane, Iouensekten, Aït Oassa,
Aït Tiksit), Beni Youb, Beni Zehna, Beni Zeggout, Ahl Isiouant.
[163] Dahir of Sept. 11, 1914, *BO,* 100 (Sept 21, 1914), 742: ". . . the tribes of
Berber custom are and remain regulated and administered by their own laws and
customs, under the supervision of the [French] authorities." See also Laubadère,
"Réformes des pouvoirs," p. 160. Dahir of Nov. 21, 1916, *BO,* Arts. 1–4 (Dec. 18,
1916), 1170 (modified by Dahir of Mar. 11, 1924).

ceeded in taking on the appearance of a living tribal institution. One critic has gone so far as to call them "stillborn" institutions, and another thought that the so-called "protection" given to the tribes by the French was stifling the capabilities and responsibilities to which these assemblies had long been trained.[164]

Under the reorganized administration, tribal matters were handled by the Directeur des Affaires Indigènes, assisted by the Conseil de Tutelle which held important powers over tribal income and property (discussed in ch. 3).[165]

Theoretically, the first Administrative Djemaa created by the French also acted as a separate djemma in its management of the tribe's collective property. It was not until 1937 that management of such property was withdrawn from the competence of the Administrative Djemaas and handed over to djemaas specially created for that purpose.[166] Several other modifications of tribal administration occurred years after Lyautey's retirement. Judicial djemaas, limited to Berber tribes and functioning as Tribunals of Customary Law, were brought into being,[167] as well as special Berber djemaas to handle local (*douar*) matters. In 1946 more power was given to the djemaas at douar level when delegates from the Berber tribes were permitted to elect members to these djemaas.[168]

[164] Laubadère, p. 162; Louis Milliot, *Les terres collectives (blâd djemâ'a)—étude de législation marocaine* (Paris, 1922), pp. 113–114. Milliot (p. 113) says that "the most serious reproach with which the Protectorate could be accused, was the exaggerated prudence exercised in the legislation concerning management of collective property."

[165] Dahir of Apr. 27, 1919, Art. 3, *BO*, 340 (Apr. 28, 1919), 375. The composition of the Conseil was first stated in Art. 3 of the Dahir of Apr. 27, 1919, but was changed by Dahir of May 20, 1924, to include: the Directeur des Affaires Indigènes, as president, the Conseiller du Gouvernement Chérifien, the Directeur Général de l'Agriculture, du Commerce et de la Colonisation, the Chef du Service des Contrôles Civils et du Contrôle des Municipalités, and two Moroccan notables, appointed by the Grand Vizir. See also Girault, *Principes de colonisation*, V, 260. The composition of the Conseil de Tutelle was again altered by the Dahir of Oct. 9, 1937, and by that of July 28, 1956. See also Albert Guillaume, *La propriété collective au Maroc* (Paris, 1960), p. 26.

[166] Dahir of Oct. 19, 1937, *BO*, 1313 (Dec. 24, 1937), 1644.

[167] Dahirs of May 16, 1930, *BO*, 918 (May 30, 1930), and Apr. 8, 1934, *BO*, 1120 (Apr. 13, 1934), 306.

[168] Dahir of Feb. 14, 1946.

3

PROPERTY

I. PROBLEMS FACED BY THE FRENCH

In dealing with various aspects of property in the new Protectorate Resident General Lyautey was faced with at least two major problems: first, that of reducing Islamic jurisdiction over large amounts of land and property holdings in Morocco; second, that of announcing to the Moroccans that the French government would have to expropriate tens of thousands of acres from tribal and national patrimony.

If a Moroccan had tried to implement these two policies, it would have been difficult enough; for a European it was a mammoth task. Before either policy could be put into effect, a general survey of the entire country had to be begun. Maps had to be drawn which included not only geographic surveys, such as river beds and mountain chains, but also tribal property demarcations (a most touchy and complicated subject), and national, religious, and private property holdings. To do this Lyautey needed thousands of competent surveyors and officials, the majority of whom were to be Frenchmen, with Moroccans only at a lower level; needless to say, he was not provided with such numbers. He had to appoint commissions to define Muslim property rights and, most importantly, he had to introduce a land-property registration system into the country to establish ownership in order to secure permanent individual property rights before French courts, which were to have exclusive jurisdiction over all newly registered land.

The expropriation of tribal land was necessary if Lyautey was to find room for colonists, but it had long-term, serious effects for both the French and Moroccans. It meant breaking up and reducing much tribal property, destroying the essence of traditional society. The tribal womb was no longer safe—the Moroccan no longer had his traditional security of an immune society. Lyautey also had to find the land needed for colonists, which meant that he had to know how many colonists to plan for and how to regulate their flow of entry into the country. He was never able, however, to place curbs on immigration, nor did he ever know how many colonists to expect during a given year. This caused serious difficulties, for he had to arrange for all the facilities required by newly arriving Europeans—schools, housing, work, financial aid, protection, medical facilities, and so on. Thus the problems involved in property changes were at once vast, far-reaching, and subtle, for European as well as Moroccan.

II. INTRODUCTION

The concept of land holding and ownership varies according to the times, values, laws, and religions of a society. In Western Europe private ownership of land is more prevalent than public or State ownership, and even though public ownership of land or institutions, such as schools and hospitals, is fairly common, the financial means of maintaining them are often far different from those employed in Islamic lands—hence the frequent inability of the Western European to understand the bases of institutions in Islamic society.

Islam is a communal religion. In theory at least, during the developing periods of medieval Islam, newly conquered land became the property not of the individual warriors, their families, or tribes, but of the Muslim community as a whole; this was especially so in Morocco.[1] Every country has had its share of contradictions, however,

---

[1] See Louis Gardet, "La propriété en Islam," *IBLA*, XXXVIII, No. 2 (1947), 114; E. Michaux-Bellaire, "Le droit d'intervention du nadir des habous de l'amin el moustafad et du pacha, dans les transmissions d'immeubles," *RMM*, XIII, No. 3 (1911), 488; Michaux-Bellaire and Paul Aubin, "Le régime immobilier," *RMM*, XVIII, No. 1 (1912), 33. As the authors of this last article point out, the situation in Morocco, as regards Muslim conquest of land, tends to be confused; for historically speaking, Morocco cannot be considered as a land of Muslim conquest, except for El Qçar El Kebir, Tangier, Arzila, Larache, Mehedya, Casablanca, Azemmour, Mazagan, Safi, and Agadir—the ports that had been occupied by Christians and reoccupied by Muslims and thus considered as territories conquered by Muslims.
Territories have traditionally been divided into two theoretical categories, so far as the Chrâa was concerned, the Bled el-Islam (the land ruled by the Muslims) and the Bled el-Harb (the territory held by infidels, the territory of war, which had yet to be conquered). The Bled el-Islam was divided into territories conquered by force (*anouâ*) and territories of capitulation (*çolha*), whose inhabitants converted to Islam in order to retain their property. These categories are very important so far as the future structure and economy of the country are concerned, for conquered lands according to Muslim law were considered *Waqf*, or *Habous*, as they are called in Morocco, i.e., inalienable property belonging to the entire Muslim community, funds derived from which were used for a variety of public needs, to be discussed later in this chapter. E. Michaux-Bellaire, *Quelques tribus de montagnes de la région du Habt*, Vol. XVII of *AM* (1911), p. 161; also, by

and Morocco has certainly had hers, as will be seen later, for example, when customary property rights are discussed. Therefore, although in theory State land belonged to the Muslim community, exceptions have always been made, and in consequence various categories of property ownership arose.[2]

From the ethno-geographic point of view, Morocco was divided into three broad areas. These areas, which had existed for several centuries, may be said to have taken shape under the Saadian Sultan, El-Mansour, in the late sixteenth century, and in fact represented the degree to which the Sultan's authority was respected.[3]

The first of these three areas was known as the Bled el-Makhzen, or the area in which the Sultan's government ruled the people in both secular and spiritual aspects and where the Sultan was considered the supreme religious and secular authority, and actually appointed local government leaders and collected taxes.[4] This, the most Arabized area, consisted of less than one-third of the country. The tribes there were either the tax-paying *naïba,* or the *guich* who in return for military service were exempt from taxation.[5]

The Djebala region, stretching from the River Sebou up to the Mediterranean, consisted of Berber mountain tribes which, though they acknowledged the Sultan as the supreme religious authority (Amir el-Moumenin) and thus paid the two religious taxes, the *zekkat* and the *achour,* nevertheless kept their sovereignty over their land and did not pay the *djezya* and the *kharadj.*

The third area was the Bled es-Siba ("land of dissidence"), by far the largest area of Morocco, including most of the eastern and southern regions of the empire, where the Berber tribes only recognized the Sultan's authority as Imam (religious leader) and paid few taxes if any.

Property and property rights in the Sherifian Empire not only varied according to ethno-geographic divisions but also, varied, often

---

the same author, "Le droit d'intervention du nadir," p. 488, and "La propriété et les habous," *AM,* XX (1913), 94.

All land that had capitulated was of importance to the Sultanate because it was over its inhabitants alone that the Sultan could demand both the *djezya* and *kharadj* taxes. In Morocco, however, over the centuries the Sultanate began to consider all the lands as its own and tried to exercise the kharadj over everyone (except the Habous). This policy of all-embracing sovereignty was begun by the Almohades, under Abdelmmouen ben Ali toward the middle of the twelfth century A.D., and was continued until the twentieth century.

[2] Theoretically, however, private ownership of property was permitted. Gardet, pp. 111, 117, 120.

[3] Ch.-André Julien, *Histoire de l'Afrique du Nord—Tunisie, Algérie, Maroc,* Vol. II: *De la conquête arabe à 1830* (Paris, 1956), p. 212.

[4] The *djezya* (capitation tax) or the *kharadj* (property tax), and the *zekkat* (alms) and *achour* (harvest tax).

[5] Michaux-Bellaire, *Quelques tribus,* pp. 162–163.

considerably, within each division according to tribal custom and dictates.

The changes in land and property holdings in Morocco under the French Protectorate will be considered in their several categories after the general machinery installed by the French authorities to deal with property holdings and rights has been described. The chaos and corruption of previous regimes necessitated a thorough reform of the Moroccan property administration by the French. General Lyautey acted without delay. His tactic in this administrative field was very different from what it would have been in a military operation; he ordered a sharp frontal attack on the "enemy"—that is, on the administrative confusion remaining from the rule of past Sultans.

PROPERTY REGISTRATION

The key to the entire real property administration under Lyautey's regime was the system of land and property registration. This system was instituted in August, 1913, although the first requests for registration were not accepted by the government until October, 1914.[6] Its purpose was to register most of the real estate in the Sherifian Empire, and thereby to ensure that all property would be held under clear titles in the Protectorate, especially that of Frenchmen who, before the Protectorate, had felt little confidence in the Muslim attitude which was generally hostile toward them as far as acquisition of property was concerned.

All properties now registered were placed under the exclusive jurisdiction of French courts, although these courts—either Tribunaux de Première Instance or the Cour d'Appel—could call in Muslim consultants should the need arise.[7] Registration of property was for the most part optional, being obligatory only in the case of alienation or exchange of Domain properties, in the exchange of properties

[6] Dahir of Aug. 12, 1913, BO, 46 (Sept. 12, 1913), p. 206. This Dahir was modified by others of Oct. 27, 1916, May 2, 1917, Sept. 24, 1917, June 10, 1918, Mar. 10, 1921, and Feb. 23, 1924. See also J. Goulven's study of property registration, in Traité d'économie et de législation marocaines (Paris, 1921), II, 309 et seq., and PA, p. 118.

[7] Dahir of Aug. 12, 1913, Arts. 2 & 5. Article 2 refers to the French judicial organization discussed in another Dahir of Aug. 12, 1913 (in BO, 46 [Sept. 12, 1913], 9). Prior to the Protectorate all real property litigations were dealt with by the cadi; eight years after the establishment of the Protectorate, this situation was altered so that cadis, who were still competent to handle many categories involving real property, were now excluded from two important categories: (1) when a French national or assimilé was involved in a real property litigation (Dahir of Sept. 1, 1920, Art. 2); (2) when the real property concerned was registered with the Conservation, regardless of the nationality of the parties involved, even if they were all natives (Dahir of Aug. 12, 1913, Art. 3). See also Paul Marty, "La justice civile musulmane au Maroc," REI, V, No. 4 (1931), 289.

which had previously been, but which were no longer, part of the public Habous, or when so ordered by a judicial institution in the course of attachment proceedings.[8]

As has been seen in chapter 2, the Service de la Conservation de la Propriété Foncière or simply the Conservation, was one of the seven Services of the Direction Générale de l'Agriculture, du Commerce et de la Colonisation.[9] It was regulated by provisions outlined as early as the summer of 1915.[10] Other aspects of Muslim property came under the authority of several different Directions (See fig. 7), but it was through the Conservation that all property to be registered was channeled.

Offices of the Conservation were set up throughout the French Zone of the Sherifian Empire, and their number was gradually increased as new regions were pacified.

The officials of the Service de la Conservation de la Propriété Foncière were nominated by the Sherifian government, on the recommendation of the Resident General, and were directly responsible to the Chef du Service de la Conservation. These officials of the Conservation had the following duties: (1) registration of property; (2) registration of real estate rights; (3) registration and preservation of all maps and documents concerning registered property, including cadastral surveys; (4) communication to the public of information concerning the properties currently being dealt with by the Conservation; (5) collection of all fees necessary for the various formalities involved in registration.[11]

Offices of the Conservation, with jurisdiction in the respective cities, were opened at Casablanca in 1915, Oujda in 1917, Rabat and Marrakesh in 1919, and Meknes in 1923.[12] A Conservation Officer of

[8] Dahir of Aug. 12, 1913, Arts. 7 & 8. See also Arthur Girault, *Principes de colonisation et de législation coloniale,* Vol. V (Third Part) (5th ed; Paris, 1928), pp. 343 *et seq.,* 366; and Charles F. Stewart, *The Economy of Morocco, 1912–1962* (Cambridge, Mass., 1964), p. 72.

[9] The section on the Service de la Conservation de la Propriété Foncière in Art. 3 of Dahir of July 24, 1920, reads as follows: "The preparation and application of the legislation concerning the property registration system. Execution of the operations prescribed in order to apply legislation relative to the property system. Demarcation and the drawing up of a cadastral plan of the properties to be registered. A Cadastral survey. Application of the clauses with a view to the functioning of the Commission d'Arbitrage et de Conciliation in real property litigations."

[10] Vizirial Decree of June 4, 1915, *BO,* 137 (June 7, 1915), 336 (modified by others, e.g., Vizirial Decree of Mar. 11, 1917); the Dahir of June 2, 1915, *BO,* 137 (June 7, 1915), 319, regulated registration itself.

[11] Vizirial Decree of June 4, 1915, Arts. 3 & 4. The organization of the administrative personnel was dealt with in Vizirial Decree of Sept. 29, 1920, *BO,* 419–420 (Nov. 2 and 9, 1920), 1870.

[12] Dahirs of June 5, 1915, *BO,* 137 (June 7, 1915), 344; Mar. 11, 1917, *BO,* 233 (Apr. 9, 1917), 418; Oct. 25, 1919, *BO,* 368 (Nov. 10, 1919), 1285; and Sept. 25, 1923, *BO,* 572 (Oct. 9, 1923), 1225.

FIGURE 7

PROPERTY UNDER THE PROTECTORATE, 1912–1925

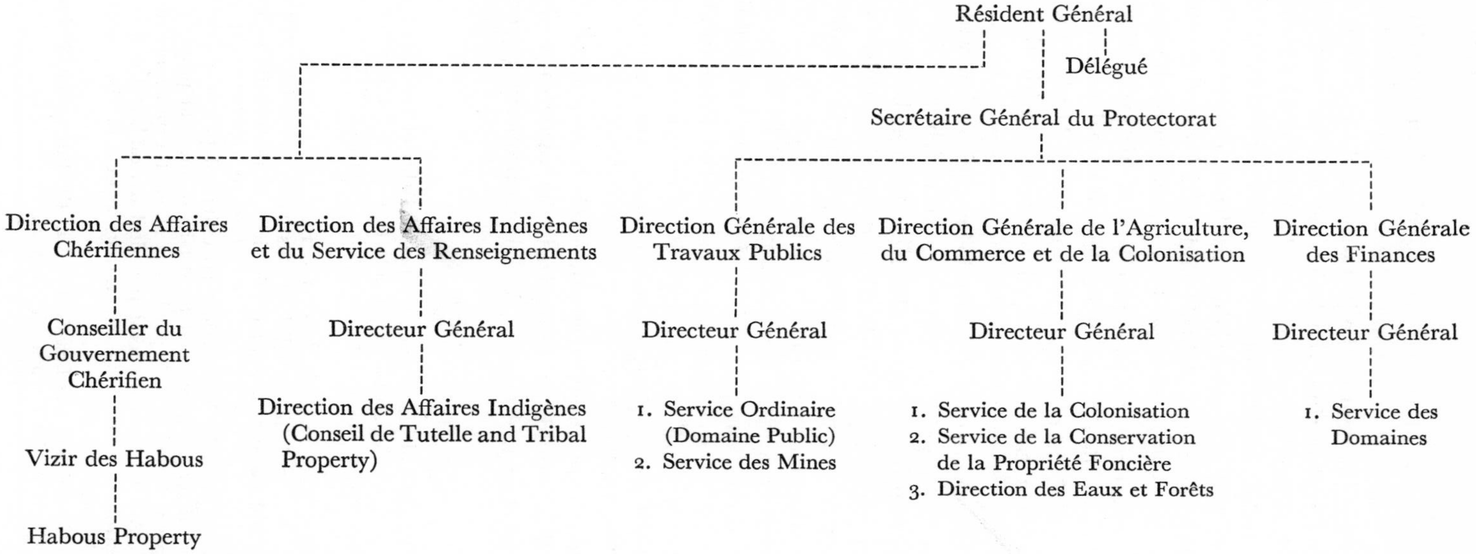

Résident Général

Délégué

Secrétaire Général du Protectorat

Direction des Affaires Chérifiennes

Conseiller du Gouvernement Chérifien

Vizir des Habous

Habous Property

Direction des Affaires Indigènes et du Service des Renseignements

Directeur Général

Direction des Affaires Indigènes (Conseil de Tutelle and Tribal Property)

Direction Générale des Travaux Publics

Directeur Général

1. Service Ordinaire (Domaine Public)
2. Service des Mines

Direction Générale de l'Agriculture, du Commerce et de la Colonisation

Directeur Général

1. Service de la Colonisation
2. Service de la Conservation de la Propriété Foncière
3. Direction des Eaux et Forêts

Direction Générale des Finances

Directeur Général

1. Service des Domaines

Real Estate and Mortgages was appointed in every town that was the seat of a Tribunal de Première Instance and had charge of registration in an area equivalent to the jurisdiction of the Tribunal.[13] Apart from obligatory registration, the following persons were allowed to apply for registration:[14] (1) owners of real estate; (2) a joint-owner of property subject to the *chefâa* right[15] of the other joint-owner; (3) holders of the following real property rights: usufruct, occupancy, long-term leases conferring mortgage rights,[16] and *antichrèse* (i.e., the contract permitting the creditor to enter into possession of the debtor's properties and to collect any and all profit from his properties until complete repayment of his debts); (4) holders of a real property right resulting from the division of property admitted by Muslim law; (5) holders of real property easements, or of mortgages, with the consent of the owner.

The mortgagor could also ask for registration when the mortgage had not been paid at maturity, in which case he could seize the property.[17] Property could also be registered by the legal guardian of an incapacitated person. Persons qualifying under one of these categories had to send a written declaration in French to the nearest Conservation office, giving all particulars pertinent to the property.[18] The pending registration was announced by town crier in the area concerned and was posted in public places, and published in Arabic and French in the official journal of the Protectorate, the *Bulletin Officiel*.[19] If there was any opposition or litigation, the matter was to be settled by a specially created Commission Permanente d'Arbitrage et de Conciliation.[20]

In June, 1915, the Protectorate officially announced the real property rights that would be recognized: (1) ownership of real property; (2) usufruct of real estate; (3) Habous property; (4) occupancy rights;

---

[13] Dahir of Aug. 12, 1913, Art. 9.

[14] *Ibid.*, Art. 10.

[15] *Chefâa*, right of preemption. See below, Dahir of June 2, 1915, *BO*, 137 (June 7, 1915), 319, fixing legislation applicable to registered properties—Arts. 22–24.

[16] Muslim canon law did not recognize "mortgages." L. Gardet, "La propriété en Islam," p. 121.

[17] Dahir of Aug. 12, 1913, Arts. 11 & 12.

[18] *Ibid.*, Art. 13. This included: (1) his name, profession, civil status, nationality, domicile, and name of spouse; (2) domicile in the locality of the Conservation in which jurisdiction the property was located; (3) full legal description of the property proposed for registration; (4) estimated purchase price and assessment of the value of the property; and (5) details of the real property rights existing on the property, including full particulars about the possessors of those rights.

[19] *Ibid.*, Art. 18. Even the local Juge de Paix, caïd, and cadi of each district were closely involved in carrying out various aspects of the registration. Arts. 14–61 deal with these details.

[20] This Commission was first discussed in the Instruction Résidentielle of Apr. 25, 1919. J. Goulven also discusses it (II, 312).

(5) long-term leases; (6) surface rights; (7) antichrèse; (8) claims of creditors and mortgages; (9) Muslim customary rights, such as, *gza, istidjar, guelsa, zina, houa;* and (10) acts and transactions carried out by the Conservation.[21] It is significant that the French authorities recognized and honored Muslim legal customary property rights. Before 1912 Muslim jurists had never agreed on the definition of these rights. The French immediately appointed a special commission to study these rights, and as a result of its work clear legislation was ultimately drafted.[22]

SUMMARY

The process of establishing real property registration was complicated and involved some of the most important rights of the Muslim population. Basically it meant that persons who held property or property rights which had been clearly established by the Conservation de la Propriété Foncière, and registered in the *Livre Foncier,* thereafter held titles which were definitive and unimpeachable in the eyes of the French judicial organization throughout the Empire.[23] Furthermore, the registration process gradually removed much property from the control of Moroccan courts, and also exposed to risks of damages or injustice many Moroccans who held their property titles through oral agreement, who were totally ignorant of the new French registration system, or who could not afford the costs involved in registration of property that was rightfully theirs.[24]   *148470*

Be that as it may, a system of ensuring property and property rights was very much needed. The system employed by the French was as good and as valid as any at the time, and so far as the Moroccans

[21] Dahir of June 2, 1915, Art. 8, *BO,* 137 (June 7, 1915), 336.

[22] See Louis Milliot, *Démembrement du habous—menfa'â, gzâ, zînâ, istighraq* (Paris, 1918).

[23] Dahir of Aug. 12, 1913, Title Two and Art. 62. By Dec. 31, 1925, 204, 943 ha. of property had been registered under this system. Girault (*Principes,* V, 371) gives the following breakdown of these statistics:

Number of Registrations			Value in Millions of Francs	Area in Hectares
URBAN PROPERTY	(French	3,388	247.5	1,761
	(Foreign	1,320	85.1	478
	(Moroccan	840	61.5	351
RURAL PROPERTY	(French	1,176	47.1	150,309
	(Foreign	210	4.1	3,854
	(Moroccan	581	9.7	48,188
		7,521	455.3	204,943

[24] Costs involved in registration were published in the Vizirial Decree of Feb. 25, 1920, *BO,* 384 (Mar. 2, 1920). Charles F. Stewart is critical of the registration system in relation to the Moroccan; see *Economy of Morocco,* p. 72.

were concerned, efforts were made to inform the public and to notify the interested parties, orally and in writing, in French and in Arabic.

Scholars have usually classified property in Morocco into four categories: *Melk*, Makhzen (State) Property, Habous, and Collective Property.[25] For purposes of elucidation, this classification can be further broken down as follows: (1) real estate held by foreigners; (2) Habous; (3) collective, or tribal property; (4) Public Domain; (5) Makhzen property, or State Domain; (6) colonization sectors; (7) Melk (private property); (8) property owned by Jews; and (9) the Sultan's personal property. Of these categories, the first six contained most of the property in the Sherifian Empire and will be discussed in this chapter.

III. ACQUISITION OF REAL PROPERTY BY FOREIGNERS

The right of foreigners to acquire real property in Morocco was established for the first time in 1880 by the Convention of Madrid,[26] Article XI of which stated:

> The right to own real property in Morocco is hereby recognized for all foreigners.
> The purchase of real property must be carried out with the prior consent of the [Moroccan] Government, and title deeds of these properties must follow the forms prescribed by the laws of [that] country.
> Any questions which arise concerning this right will be decided by these same laws, through appeal to the Minister of Foreign Affairs stipulated in the treaty.

It also stated (Art. XII) that all foreigners and foreign *protégés* who either owned or leased agricultural land must pay the local agricultural tax.

A detailed agreement on the property which foreigners could own was not, however, made until 1906 by Article LX of the Act of Algeciras:

[25] For an early study of property in Morocco see Émile Amar, *L'organisation de la propriété foncière au Maroc: étude théorique et pratique* (Paris, 1913).

[26] Convention of Madrid of July 3, 1880. In Turkey foreigners were permitted to own property from 1867; in Tunisia from 1857; in Egypt from 1864. It is interesting to note that a French Ordonnance of 1761 forbade Frenchmen to purchase land or property in Morocco (or any Muslim country), apart from absolute necessities, such as a house, shop, etc. Michaux-Bellaire and P. Aubin, "Le régime immobilier," p. 37. On this and other aspects of property rights of foreigners, see also Émile Amar's work.

In conformity with the right which has been granted them by Article XI of the Convention of Madrid, foreigners will be able to acquire real property throughout the entire Sherifian Empire and H.M. the Sultan will give necessary instructions to the administrative and judicial authorities in order that authorization for the drawing up of such acts shall not be refused without a legitimate reason. As for subsequent transfers by legal act between living persons, or after their demise, they will continue to be exercised without hindrance.

In the ports open to commerce and within a radius of ten kilometers around these ports,[27] H.M. the Sultan henceforth accords in general, permission to foreigners to purchase property, without the previous authorization required for each purchase by Article XI of the Convention of Madrid any longer being necessary.

The above-mentioned permission is also granted to foreigners in El Kçar El Kebir, Arzila, Azemmour, and ultimately in other coastal and inland areas, but only for acquisitions within a two-kilometer radius of these cities.

Wherever foreigners have acquired property, they will be able to construct buildings, in conformity with the regulations and customs [of the country].

Before authorizing the drawing up of real property conveyance acts, the *cadi* must ensure, conforming with Muslim law, that all the title deeds have been regularly established.

The Makhzen will appoint in each of the cities and jurisdictions indicated, *cadis* whose duty it will be to certify these titles.

Sultan Abd el-Aziz, however, could not, in spite of the Algeciras agreement, authorize the purchase of property everywhere in his empire, because his authority was not recognized by much of the Berber population outside the Bled el-Makhzen, as indeed the Sultan, himself, had admitted.[28] In the Figuig area, for instance, there was a special, nonreligious custom called the *bezra* which forbade the population to sell, give away, or transfer their real estate to "foreigners," meaning anyone not of their own tribe.[29] If any member of the tribe defied this custom, his property was subject to confiscation by the local *djemaa*. In some cases, however, Europeans did not act according to the letter of the law, for more than one property was purchased in the Bled el-Makhzen without Sherifian consent; indeed this was generally the case in the Chaouïa.[30]

Although Europeans were able to purchase real property in Morocco,

[27] These ports were Tangier, Casablanca, Rabat, Mazagan, Safi, Mogador, Larache, and Tetuan.

[28] See "Sherifian Letter," wherein the Sultan admitted this, in his instructions to his delegates at the Algeciras Conference. "Le régime immobilier," p. 39. It was the Ouzir el-Bahr (Foreign Minister) who directly controlled and authorized the acquisition of real estate by foreigners. Mohamed Lahbabi, *Le gouvernement marocaine à l'aube du XXe siècle* (Rabat, 1958), p. 151.

[29] See Roger Gromand's interesting article, "La coutume de la 'Bezra' dans les ksour de Figuig," *REI*, V, No. 3 (1931), 277 *et seq.*

[30] "Le régime immobilier," p. 40.

provided that they carried out such transactions through Muslim courts,[31] they disliked having to deal with the Moroccan judiciary. In consequence, Europeans generally went before their consular courts which then had to decide the question of competence and enforcement, and whether or not to send their nationals before a Moroccan court.[32] The French consular courts, for instance, asserted their competence in all property matters and applied the principles of the Code Civile to Frenchmen whenever such cases arose, thereby obviating the application of the *lex rei sitae.*

In Algeria much of the land and property owned by Frenchmen entirely escaped Muslim jurisdiction and was governed by the Code Civile, including properties purchased by Europeans, and properties belonging to Muslims, either when the owner was also a French citizen, or when he had been granted a deed of title by a French court.

As has been seen, the Act of Algeciras permitted foreigners to acquire property within ten kilometers of the eight ports open to commerce. Unfortunately, this arrangement was complicated later by the acceptance of a 101,124,000 franc loan in 1910 from France by Morocco, which pledged the revenue from the domain lands of the ten-kilometer areas around these ports as partial security for the loan.[33] Another difficulty was the fact that all the land within an area of two kilometers around El Kçar El Kebir was Habous property and therefore inalienable, and most of the land within an area of ten to twelve kilometers around most ports of the Sherifian Empire was Makhzen property, much of it in the hands of guich tribes.[34] Thus, what at first glance seemed a fairly clear-cut definition of properties available to foreigners was in fact far from defined or legally available.

IV. HABOUS

A. BEFORE 1912

In Morocco Habous properties belonged to the Muslim community and were consecrated in perpetuity for religious purposes.[35] The in-

---

[31] See Art. XI of the Convention of Madrid and Art. LX of the Act of Algeciras.

[32] "Le régime immobilier," pp. 42, 44.

[33] Loan of Mar. 21, 1910; see Section 4 of Art. III. The loan was to be amortized over a 75-year period, which meant that all security for the loan (and there were five sources of security) would be pledged for that period. This treaty is in P.-Louis Rivière, *Traités, codes et lois du Maroc,* Vol. I: *Accords internationaux* (Paris, 1924), p. 163.

[34] "Le régime immobilier," pp. 42–44.

[35] See J. Luccioni, *Le habous ou waqf (rites malékite et hanéfite)* (Casablanca, n.d.), pp. 13–15. For a general discussion of Habous property see pp. 76–78.

come from them went for the most part toward the upkeep of mosques and mosque officials, hospitals, schools and students, the payment of salaries of professors, judges, and special collectors of religious taxes, relief for the poor, and so on.[36] Habous property, or pious foundations, are said to have been first established by the Prophet in the seventh century and have since developed in every Islamic land.[37]

1. Habous Administration

Traditionally there had been one *nadir,* or Habous administrator, in each mosque or *zaouïa* (Muslim brotherhood). He was appointed by and from among the notables of the quarter of the town or city in which the mosque was situated. He paid the salaries of the mosque officials, kept the property in repair, and so on. Toward the middle of the last century, an important change was introduced by Sultan Moulay Abd er-Rahman (1822–1859).[38] In order to channel the vast funds of the various Habous into his own hands, if only indirectly, he did away with private nadirs (and all nadirs had hitherto been private, that is, not government officials) of each mosque and re-

---

[36] Al-Moutabassir, "Les habous de Tanger," *RMM,* I, No. 3 (1907), 329–330. This contains excellent detailed accounts of expenditures of Habous funds in Tangier.

[37] A building or piece of land became Habous property at the wish of the owner, who bequeathed it to the cities of Mecca or Medina, or to a pious foundation, a mosque, or a *zaouïa,* or for the creation of a school or hospital. Habous property probably reached its zenith in wealth and extent under the Almohades or Merinids.

El Boukhari related in his collection of Hadith that Omar ibn el-Khattab one day approached the Prophet, telling him he would consider it a great privilege to dedicate some of his land for a worthy cause, whereupon the Prophet told him to put it into Habous and distribute its revenues to the poor. E. Michaux-Bellaire, "Les biens habous et les biens du makhzen, au point de vue de leur location et de leur aliénation," *RMM,* V, No. 7 (1908), 438–439. See also Asaf A. A. A. Fyzee, *Outlines of Muhammadan Law* (London, 1955), p. 232.

Frede Løkkegaard, in *Islamic Taxation in the Classic Period* (Copenhagen, 1950), regards the date of creation of this institution and the name of its creator as untraceable (p. 53): "Probably the *waqf* came into existence in a conflux of ideas descended from the Byzantine institution of *piae causae,* charitable institutions, and the Iranian one of *ruvânakân,* legacies for the benefit of the souls of the deceased which no doubt carried on their existence in connection with the cult of *Mazdaism* under Islam. Probably the institution has even been influenced, in some way or other, by the Jewish *qârbân* system. In fact there exists between them some rather striking points of resemblance, and on the whole much speaks in favour of a strong Jewish influence upon the forming of the entire *fiqh* system."

For accounts of *waqf* development in Turkey, see: Muhammed Ahmed Simsar, *The Waqfiyah of 'Aḥmed Pāšā* (Philadelphia, 1940), Excursi I and II; H. A. R. Gibb and Harold Bowen, *Islamic Society and the West,* Vol. I, Part 2 (London, 1957), ch. 12; Fyzee, ch. 9, for India. Doreen Warringer discusses very briefly the position in Egypt, Syria, and Iraq in *Land Reform and Development in the Middle East* (London, 1962), ch. 2; Ann S. K. Lambton for Persia: *Landlord and Peasant in Persia* (London, 1953), ch. 11.

[38] Al-Moutabassir, pp. 332–333; Michaux-Bellaire, "Les biens habous et les biens du Makhzen," p. 443.

placed them with two nadirs for each city.[39] These two nadirs, appointed by the Sultan and virtually his agents, controlled the administration of the Habous of each city. The nadirs were subject to the general supervision of the Ouzir ech-Chikayat, a Minister of Administrative Appeals and Inspector General, whose task was to see that the Habous Administration functioned smoothly and that funds were used as intended by law.[40]

This system introduced by Moulay Abd er-Rahman remained in force until the Protectorate, although in practice the centralization was never so efficient as that which was later developed under the French. Under Sultan Moulay Abd er-Rahman the amount of Habous property and the resultant income were greatly reduced, because the new nadirs destroyed most of the former property registers which had been handed over to them by the private nadirs, so that they could usurp for themselves any Habous property that suited them, and transferred the title deeds of the remaining property into new registers.[41] As E. Michaux-Bellaire has pointed out, it was in Moulay Abd er-Rahman's time that alienation of Habous property began in earnest.[42]

2. Habous Property and Tenancy Rights

There were two general classifications of Habous property: (1) Habous constituted for a religious establishment directly, without intermediary parties or heirs, which was called *tahbis,* or Habous endowment, and (2) Habous constituted to bring profit to one or more private intermediary parties before payment of the remainder to a religious foundation, which was called *ta'qib,* or private Habous.[43] The private party might be either a family or a zaouïa.[44] Generally speaking, land was

[39] Rabat, however, had only one nadir; see, L. Mercier, "L'administration marocaine à Rabat," *AM,* VII (1906), 399–400.

[40] The extent of the Ouzir's power naturally ended with that of the Sultan, i.e., where the Bled el-Makhzen ended and the Bled es-Siba began. In the latter, nadirs were usually appointed by the local djemaas. Lahbabi, p. 176.

[41] Al-Moutabassir, p. 333.

[42] Michaux-Bellaire, "Les biens habous," pp. 443–444.

[43] *Ibid.,* p. 438; Al-Moutabassir, p. 327. In addition, Jews and Christians also were permitted to constitute property into *waqfs;* Gardet, "La propriété en Islam," p. 125.

[44] Goulven considers the zaouïa as a third category; see *Traité d'économie et de législation marocaines,* II, 296. The endowment could also take the form of a perpetual charity in favor of some or all of the founder's relatives and their descendants; Michaux-Bellaire, "Les biens habous," p. 439. Family Habous were established to act as trusts for family property, to ensure that it would not be confiscated by the government, or as Løkkegaard (p. 54) puts it, "for dodging the tax assessors and to safeguard personal property in other ways."

There were two types of zaouïa Habous in Morocco: the most well known were the private religious schools organized by *marabouts;* the others were for a particular saint's grave. The nadirs of this latter type of zaouïa Habous were usually appointed by the local village or tribal *djemaa.* A great many of these latter zaouïas did not

considered Habous property either through conquest or testamentary bequest.[45]

When property was constituted as Habous, three principal effects were produced: (1) the act of constitution was irrevocable; (2) the constituted property was inalienable; (3) the property could not be inherited (though rights to income from private Habous could be inherited).[46]

There were exceptions to the principle of inalienability of Habous property. According to Sidi Khalil, if a mosque needed to be enlarged and the sale of a piece of Habous property could provide the funds necessary for the enlargement, alienation of the property was permitted with the Sultan's authorization.[47] Or, if a person wished to acquire the ownership of some Habous property, he could arrange for an exchange of that particular property for another one of his own which he would give to the Habous in its stead, but the property given in exchange by the private individual had to be of greater value than the one ceded to him by the Habous; moreover, the transaction required the Sultan's authorization. Such an exchange was called *el-mou'aouadha*. Likewise, Habous property could be sold to enlarge streets, to build cemeteries, or to maintain Habous property.[48]

Habous property was often leased to private persons, through the local nadir, although such leases were not supposed to be of long duration. Sidi Khalil, for example, stated that the lease could be for two years; other jurists declared three to be the maximum, although the duration of the lease could be extended if the building was in

---

have any Habous at all and therefore did not have a nadir, but simply a *moqaddem* who collected the offerings which served to maintain the tomb. The Habous of mosques or saints in isolated areas usually consisted of fields, gardens, olive trees, vineyards, orchards, even flocks of sheep. The revenues received from a saint's Habous were divided up in three ways: one part of the revenues went to the descendants of the saint (perhaps half of the total amount), another part provided for the maintenance of the saint's tomb, and the third share went to the nadir of the local mosque toward mosque revenues. Mosque revenues (outside the Bled el-Makhzen) were used for maintenance of the mosque, etc., for hospitality of guests, and for a special fund in each village (e.g., in the Djebala) for buying arms and ammunition to defend the village. See Michaux-Bellaire's extremely interesting work on this subject, *Quelques tribus de montagnes de la région du Habt,* especially pp. 173 *et seq.*

[45] Gardet, p. 125.

[46] Sautayra and Eug. Cherbonneau, *Droit musulman—statut personnel et des successions,* Vol. II: *Des successions* (Paris, 1874), p. 395; W. Heffenig, "Wakf," *EI,* IV (1934), 1096. Some Moroccans have complained that strict observance of Malekite rulings over Habous caused much harm, and that a more realistic view, such as that of the Hanafi school, was needed. See Al-Moutabassir, p. 326.

[47] Michaux-Bellaire discusses Sidi Khalil in "Les biens habous et les biens du makhzen," p. 439.

[48] Michaux-Bellaire, *Les habous de Tanger—registre officiel d'actes et de documents,* Vol. XXII of *AM* (1914), p. 17. Vol. XXIII also deals with the subject.

need of repair.[49] In such a case the nadir could consent to a lease for the time judged necessary and the rent would be used instead entirely for reconstruction or repairs. The extension of leases in order to carry out repairs served as a legal loophole and led to serious distortions of the original intention of the Habous jurists.

When Sidi Khalil stated that ownership of Habous property was indefeasible, he meant that no one could claim ownership of Habous property on the grounds of the length of his residence on the property, not even when the rent had been paid over a very long period of time. There could be no *moulkiya* in Habous.[50]

In Morocco public Habous fell into two subcategories: land and property—mosques, schools, hospitals, charitable institutions, gardens, aqueducts, fountains, baths, shops, etc.—administered directly by Habous officials, or nadirs; and land and property leased by nadirs to private parties (as distinct from private or family Habous). The first of these was the simpler of the two. The revenues derived from such properties were not taxable[51] and were administered by the nadirs for the maintenance and further development of these properties, and after deduction of such expenses, to pay the mosque personnel, the nadir and his personnel, the cadi, the mufti, and so on.

Habous property that was leased by the nadirs (at auctions) consisted of fields, orchards, and such lands, as well as buildings, which private parties desired to use for farming, business, and habitation.[52] Among the tenancy rights involved were the following: *menfa'a, intifâ', gzâ, guelsa, haloua, zina, zerîba, ghibthâ, meftâh, istighrak,* and *hazaqa.*[53]

Within the category of tenancy rights of Habous property were to be found many contradictions as to legality or illegality, especially where there was a discrepancy between local custom and the prescriptions of the Chrâa. The position of the various jurists concerning what was or was not legal, with regard to property rights and customary practice, is fully analyzed by Louis Milliot in his valuable work, *Démembrement du habous.*

One of the main difficulties arising over leases of Habous property was the problem of length of tenancy. According to Islamic law, the length of tenancy of Habous property had to be specified in the original

---

[49] Les biens habous," p. 440.

[50] *Ibid.;* Michaux-Bellaire, "Le droit d'intervention du nadir des habous," pp. 489–490. *Moulkiya* refers to private ownership of property, though in Berber areas it often refers to perpetual possession of a piece of land though the person held no title to its ownership. Moulkiya was attested to before two adoul by twelve known witnesses supporting the possessor's claim and stating that the claimant had been living on the property for at least the past ten consecutive years.

[51] It was only under the French that they were first taxed: See Residential Circular of May 14, 1918, discussed later.

[52] Al-Moutabassir discusses many of these, pp. 336–342.

[53] *Hazaqa* was applicable only to Jewish tenancy of property owned by Muslims.

tenancy contract and could not be of long duration, whereas in fact
it was common to find tenancy agreements which not only failed to
specify the length of tenancy, but which even led to, and often implied,
perpetual tenancy. This virtual right of perpetual tenancy, which had
become very common over the centuries, led tenants to consider the
rent due to the Habous, not as a rent, but almost as a tax; and usually
the amount charged by the administration was so little that by the
twentieth century the Habous were financially ruined. Much of the
trouble was also due to the fact that Muslim jurists had never been
greatly concerned with defining the various types of tenancy and
tenancy rights.

In order that the difficulties between types of tenancies may be
understood, some of the main points are listed below.[54]

Menfa'a was the use and tenure of a property whether or not it
was accompanied by ownership of the property and entitled the holder
to the profit of the property. By its nature the menfa'a right could be
transferred to a third party; for Muslim jurists were opposed to *intifâ'*
—that is, untransferable tenure of the right of usufruct.[55] Consequently,
the menfa'a right could be detached from the property, ceded, and
acquired separately from the right of ownership. As will be seen later,
the power to sublet (tenancy rights) was the basis of most other tenancy
rights recognized by Islamic jurisprudence in Morocco. The menfa'a
right could be transferred or acquired separately from the ownership
right, and this could take place either in exchange for payment or free
of charge as a legacy or a donation. The transfer of the menfa'a right
was included as an intrinsic part of the rent paid for the use of the
property.[56] Furthermore the holder of the menfa'a right could lend
the use of the property, whereas the occupant of a *zaouïa, medersa,*
or *ribat*—being the holder of the right of *intifâ'*—could not cede his
right of occupancy to a third party. The difference between menfa'a
and intifâ' was a very important legal point.

In Morocco two other tenancy rights had been the subject of much
dispute over the past centuries; they were known as the *guelsa* and
the *gzâ* rights, and were both forms of menfa'a rights.[57]

In the case of the guelsa right the owner of the land sold the
guelsa right and at the same time leased the property to one and
the same person. The guelsa, more than any other tenancy right,
caused confusion and difficulty, and more than one jurist had condemned it on the grounds that it did not originate from the Chrâa,
and that the early oulama had never mentioned it, and that it could

[54] See also Luccioni, pp. 101–112.
[55] Milliot, *Démembrement,* p. 10; Løkkegaard, p. 53; Luccioni, p. 101.
[56] Milliot, *Démembrement,* pp. 9–10.
[57] Heffenig, pp. 1096, 1100.

not be justified by *qiyas* (analogy).[58] The only sanction for the guelsa was customary use, which was often in complete contradition with the Malekite exposition of the Chrâa.[59] The guelsa rights consisted of the right to occupy a piece of property, enjoy the use of it, and draw profit from it, but without being the owner of the property.[60] Difficulty arose from the fact that the guelsa rights, as customary rights, also presupposed perpetual tenure.[61] Both the guelsa and gzâ were remarkable in that though they did not emanate from the Chrâa but from custom (*orf*) and usage (*âda*),[62] they were nevertheless admitted by most of the Muslim jurisconsults.

Islamic law distinguishes between ownership and occupancy of property[63] and thus a person could occupy land, as in the case of the guelsa, without being its owner. The guelsa and gzâ were property rights leased by persons who, by custom, had obtained permanent occupancy, by virtue of their being the first occupants of the property.[64]

The gzâ rights, too, were rights to occupancy (without ownership) of property in return for rent; but these were applicable only to agricultural land, whereas the guelsa rights were applicable to houses and workshops. Both the gzâ and guelsa served to facilitate the perpetual use and tenure of Habous estates or properties, and as Louis Milliot has pointed out, so far as Muslim law and judicial sanction are concerned—in theory at least—they were both null and void.[65] Yet as Abderrahman al-Fâsî, the celebrated Moroccan jurist, stated apropos of customary practices of Fez, these two tenancy rights, although neither established nor recognized by the Chrâa, had become *amel,* that is, current practice with the force of law, and were based on the right of prior occupancy.[66]

Rent derived from property of the Muslim community was paid to the Bit el-Mal Treasury (discussed in ch. 2), and this was true of the rent received from the guelsa and gzâ of such property. It was paid

[58] Al Medjaci said: "The *guelsa* is among the evil things to which men are accustomed." Mohammed ben Al Hasan Al Medjaci, "Naouazil" (trans. E. Michaux-Bellaire), *RMM, XIII*, No. 2 (1911), 239–241. Milliot also comments on Al Fâsî's study of As-Sidjilmâsi, *Démembrement,* p. 14.

[59] There were four schools of legal thought in medieval Islam, and the Malekite school has been followed in Morocco.

[60] E. Michaux-Bellaire, "La guelsa et le gzâ," *RMM,* XIII, No. 2 (1911), 197.

[61] *Démembrement,* p. 64.

[62] "La guelsa et le gzâ," p. 197.

[63] Gardet, "La propriété en Islam," p. 112.

[64] "La guelsa et le gzâ," pp. 197, 202.

[65] *Démembrement,* p. 13.

[66] "Commentaire de Sidi Mohammed ben Qasim As-Sidjilmasi ar-Rabati" (trans. E. Michaux-Bellaire), *RMM,* XIII, No. 2 (1911), 217; "La guelsa et le gzâ," p. 202. The right of first occupancy was also the basis for the Jewish tenancy right, the *Hazaqa.*

nominally as a *kharadj* (property tax), which just before the Protectorate was known as *naïba*.[67]

The guelsa was exercised almost exclusively over improved, or built-up Habous and Makhzen property, but very rarely over private property.[68] It was a right of acquired possession, not derived from paying a sum to the owner of the property, but from the fact that the tenant had remained on a rented property for a certain time; and the tenant could rent or sell this right to a third party, on condition that the latter continued to reimburse him for the guelsa and the rent due to the owner of the property; thus it was a type of sublease. Another method of obtaining a guelsa right for a property was by an arrangement with the nadir of a mosque property. If a shop or house belonging to that particular Habous had remained empty and thus unproductive for a certain period,[69] a new lessee ready to pay the arrears from the period during which the property had remained unoccupied could obtain a guarantee of permanent occupancy from the nadir on condition that in the future he would continue to pay the same rent. The lessee thereby achieved the guelsa, or "key right," and with the sanction of the Habous administration itself, and could in turn sublet the property for a higher rent than he himself had been paying, or sell his guelsa right to a third party, who would then have to pay the rent arranged by the nadir with the original contracting party.[70] It is clear from the foregoing that the guelsa right to a property often brought appreciable profits to its holder while the rent stipulated for the Habous and the Bit el-Mal would perforce remain the same, even over a span of centuries. This was the situation in Morocco at the turn of the twentieth century.

A third way by which Makhzen and also Habous properties could be placed in the possession of an individual was by royal grant. This practice had been traditional throughout the Islamic world, for example in the Ottoman Empire, though with many variations. The administrator of all the property belonging to the Muslim community was in principle the Imam, who was also the Sultan. In compensation for services rendered, or for any other reason, the Sultan could issue a decree, called a *tenfida*, or concession,[71] granting to an individual the tenure of one or more properties belonging to the Makhzen, or also, in later times, belonging to the Habous. Payment of rent for

---

[67] E. Michaux-Bellaire, "L'impôt de la naïba et la loi musulmane," *RMM*, XI, No. 8 (1910), 396.

[68] "La guelsa et le gzâ," pp. 203–204.

[69] The regulations dealing with Habous properties made it mandatory that no Habous property should be unproductive for a long period.

[70] "La guelsa et le gzâ," p. 204.

[71] Al-Moutabassir, pp. 338 *et seq.*

such properties was generally demanded; but sometimes Makhzen properties were given to beneficiaries who were not required to pay rent and who thus gained virtually complete ownership. This type of grant was common in both medieval Europe as well as in medieval Islam.[72] In the case of Habous properties, however, similar gifts could only be made by the Sultan when accompanied by the revenue from the properties, which were not sent to the Bit el-Mal but to the local Habous.

After the establishment of the Protectorate, the French authorities soon became aware of the confusion surrounding Muslim property rights, and in 1913 appointed a commission to study them; it was called the Commission d'Étude des Droits de Gzâ, Guelsâ, Clé et d'Autres Droits, and consisted of high-ranking Muslim officials.[73] The commission drew up definitions of the various tenancy rights with the purpose of clarifying but not altering meanings.

Gzâ, or istidjar, was defined as a lease of unimproved land in order to raise buildings, or plant crops on it. The duration could either be determined—for twenty years, for example—by month and year, or could be left undetermined. The origin of the gzâ contract was as follows: when the Habous or Makhzen possessed land that was unproductive, the nadir, who could not obtain any return from it, rented it to a party who could use and develop it, for a specific duration.[74]

The guelsa right, as defined by the commission, was the usufruct of a property by virtue of a perpetual contract of lease. It was applicable to shops, workshops, and factories. This kind of contract had usually come into existence when the country was sparsely populated or lay in ruin. The nadir, being incapable of restoring the estates under his supervision, leased them to a party who could install himself there with the appropriate materials, paying a monthly sum, due forever, even if he later left the property.

Connected with the guelsa was the zina ("improvement")—that is, the lessee's title to improvements and accessories, such as windows, installed by him. When the holder of a guelsa found the property in-

---

[72] "La guelsa et le gza," pp. 204–205.

[73] The Sultan of Morocco appointed the following persons to take part in this Commission, along with the Directeur Général des Habous: The Grand Vizir, Fakih Si Mohammed Guebbas; the Minister of Justice, Fakih Si Bouchaïd Doukkali; the Minister of Finance, Fakih Si Abderrahman Bennis; the Second Secretary of Justice, Fakih Si Larbi Naciri; the Secretary of the Beniqa (Ministry) of the Habous, Si Larbi Djerrari; the two oulama of Fez, Si Mohammed Mani Senhadji and Si Abdelaziz Bennani; the two oulama of Rabat, Si Ahmed Bennani and Si Mohammed Rounda; the two oulama of Salé, Si Ahmed Aouad and Si Allal Taghraoui; MM. Caldéraro and the Sherif Omar, delegates of the Secrétariat Général du Gouvernement Chérifien. The definitions were made at the session of the Commission on Dec. 26, 1913. Milliot has printed these minutes in the fourth appendix of Démembrement, pp. 124–132.

[74] Ibid., pp. 126–128.

adequately equipped and himself incurred expenditure on necessary improvements, his ownership of these improvements was recognized. This was the position where Habous property was concerned. In Makhzen property the zina was equivalent to the gzâ of the Habous. The occupant built a house or construction on Domain land given to him for unlimited duration, for which he paid a specified sum.

The key right (sometimes called the *orf, ghibta, halous*) meant the transferee's right to obtain possession of the guelsa and to obtain the transferor's renunciation of future profits in his favor.

The *istighrak* right arose when a rent was paid to the Habous for a property in a dilapidated state. The lessee put the leased estate in order and then enjoyed the use of it for a small sum. Any deed or contract of this nature was usually for a long duration. The following example was given by the commission: when a Habous property was in a ruined or nearly ruined state, a party might propose to repair it. The cost of repairs was estimated by experts on the spot and was paid off by agreed deductions from the rent. The remainder of the rent went to the owner of the repaired property (i.e., the Habous). In the meantime, however, the lessee might carry out further repairs, thus obtaining an excuse for continuing to pay a reduced rent; and the Habous seldom succeeded in recovering its property.

The *menfa'a* rights included all the preceding ones, and as in the past permitted the beneficiary to dispose of them to a third party.[75] The *intifâ'*, on the other hand, restricted the tenancy of an estate to the original tenant, having been contracted for his benefit alone.[76]

B. HABOUS PROPERTY DURING LYAUTEY'S ADMINISTRATION

As stated previously, there were two types of Habous properties in Morocco: public and private (the latter including zaouïas). Both continued under the Protectorate to be governed by many of the original Muslim regulations and customs,[77] and were administered by a special office dealing solely with the Habous.

Since the Habous properties were so important in the daily life of Morocco, as in other Muslim countries, Lyautey quickly saw the urgency of tackling the problem of their administration. A series of dahirs and residential circulars on this subject was issued from 1912 almost up to the time of Lyautey's resignation, while the immediacy of the problem as judged by Lyautey is seen by the fact that most of the legislation concerning the Habous was dealt with between 1912 and 1918.

[75] *Ibid.*, p. 128; see also Heffenig, p. 1096.
[76] *Démembrement*, p. 128.
[77] Dahir of June 2, 1915, Art. 75, *BO*, 137 (June 7, 1915), 319.

1. Habous Administration

Habous property was defined by French legislation as being mort-
main, noncommercial, indefeasible, and inalienable, usually connected
with pious works. In the years immediately prior to the establishment
of the Protectorate many of the Habous properties had disappeared,
and many others had become unproductive through negligence or
dishonesty of Habous officials.

The Direction Générale des Habous was established in October,
1912.[78] Its Directeur Général was responsible to the Secrétaire Général
du Gouvernement Chérifien; throughout the first years of the Protectorate, however, there was much reshuffling of titles and offices
at nearly every level of government administration, and in 1915 the
Direction des Habous became the Vizirat des Habous, and its director
was made a vizir. In May, 1917, the office of Secrétaire Général du
Gouvernement Chérifien was replaced by that of the Conseiller du
Gouvernement Chérifien, and in July, 1920, the Conseiller was made
director of the newly created Direction des Affaires Chérifiennes housing the Makhzen ministries, the Habous thereby becoming one of the
three administrative groups placed under the Conseiller (see fig. 8).[79]

FIGURE 8

HABOUS ADMINISTRATION, 1912–1925

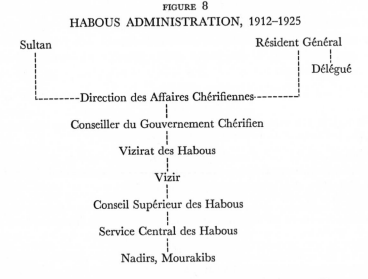

The powers and duties of the Habous Ministry (its director will
hereafter be referred to as vizir), as outlined in July, 1913, included
the centralization of the administration of the Habous (both public

[78] Dahir of Oct. 31, 1912, *BO*, 3 (Nov. 15, 1912), 17. See also Goulven, *Traité
d'économie*, II, 300 *et seq.*

[79] Decree of May 19, 1917, Art. 4, discussed in ch. 2., and Dahir of July 24, 1920, *BO*,
407 (Aug. 10, 1920), 1366. See also ch. 2, § IIB.

and private) and the ensuring of close supervision of the nadirs and mourakibs.[80] The Vizir des Habous thereby succeeded to the post held by the Ouzir ech-Chikayat in pre-Protectorate Morocco.

The Vizir des Habous was assisted by the Conseil Supérieur des Habous which had been set up in May, 1914.[81] Its main task was to supervise all actions of the Habous and to study all questions concerning the effective administration of Habous property. It was empowered to (1) verify accounts of completed transactions; (2) to examine general and supplementary budgets produced by the Vizir des Habous; (3) to create a reserve fund; (4) to deduct amounts for necessary expenses; and (5) to reinvest Habous funds, and the like. The decisions of the Conseil Supérieur des Habous were to be taken by majority vote and then submitted to the Sultan. The importance of the Conseil can be seen from its membership, which consisted of the Grand Vizir, as president; the Vizir de la Justice, as vice-president; the Conseiller du Gouvernement Chérifien, or his deputy; the Vizir des Habous; the Chef du Service de Contrôle des Habous; a senior official of the Direction Générale des Finances; a member of the Conseil Supérieur d'Ouléma;[82] and five Muslim notables.

2. Habous Property and Lease Revision

The first task of the Vizir des Habous was the appointment of commissions for every city and town to list and evaluate all Habous property, which was initiated in December, 1912.[83] These commissions drew up an inventory of all Habous assets throughout Morocco, which was to be the basis for future legislation concerning lease and rent revision in respect of Habous properties.[84]

---

[80] Dahir of July 13, 1913, BO, 47 (Sept. 19, 1913), 357. By tradition, the Habous such as zaouïas and mosques were in theory placed under the supervision of the cadis who had to see to it that they were kept in good repair, etc., whereas in reality zaouïas escaped the control of the cadis. Michaux-Bellaire, Les habous de Tanger—registre officiel d'actes et de documents, p. 10. The nadirs and mourakibs, as the local Habous administrators, were responsible for every local Habous transaction, which had to be duly recorded in one of the following registers: (1) one for the recording of all the Habous properties in that locality; (2) one for the annual adjustments of accounts; (3) one for all matters concerning guelsa and gzâ rights; (4) one for all requests for long-term leases; (5) one containing all requests made by individuals wishing to purchase Habous property; (6) one containing all transfers (alienating Habous property) for works of beneficence or for some general need; (7) one for the recording of correspondence received; and (8) one for registration of correspondence sent out.

[81] Created by Dahir of May 16, 1914, Arts. 1, 2, 5, BO, 83 (May 29, 1914), 384. It only met for the first time in August, 1917.

[82] See ch. 5, § III.

[83] Dahir of Dec. 11, 1912, BO, 14 (Jan. 31, 1913), 69. Each commission was presided over by a nadir and consisted of two experts in business affairs, an agricultural expert, a construction expert, a master joiner, and an architect or similar person.

[84] See Circular of the Direction Général des Habours of Jan. 24, 1913, BO, 14 (Jan. 31, 1913), 69.

In June, 1913, as a further step toward ending the traditional abuses at the expense of the Habous, *adoul* (notaries) were forbidden to draw up leases over Habous property comprising the guelsa, zina, and so on without the authorization of the local cadi.[85] Subsequently, when land or property rights were to be leased or sold, it was the local nadir's duty to make a full inquiry into the matter and trace back the legal ownership of such rights. In the past such care had not been taken, the ownership of property having been established merely by the testimony of witnesses before adoul, or by adoul alone, if the person involved was known to the adoul already.

Frenchmen, too, were guilty of abuses concerning Habous property, and in June, 1913, General Lyautey forbade all municipal and military authorities to occupy Habous property without authorization from the Habous Ministry:

> The Direction Générale des Habous informs me that, in certain regions of the Protectorate, municipal officers and military authorities have, in some cases, installed themselves in Habous properties.
>
> I should like to draw your attention to the inconveniences caused, so far as policy is concerned, by the occupation—even if temporary—of property of pious foundations: In the eyes of the natives it may be interpreted as spoliation if a rent—even a low one—is not determined by the local *nadir*. For foreigners, it creates unwelcome precedents which they do not fail to quote, and not without reason, when they have difficulties with the Habous.
>
> We must not lose sight of the fact that we are held responsible for discretion in matters of pious foundations, and that these properties may not be occupied on the strength of dubious claims, or be alienated without authorization by the administration concerned.
>
> In exceptional cases when the local authorities might be in absolute necessity of using a particular Habous property, the *nadir* responsible for it could seize it, as a preliminary step. These authorities will, at the same time, have to submit their request to the Secrétariat Général du Gouvernement Chérifien in order that the matter be adequately studied by the Direction. The principle of compensation or of rent to be paid will, however, always have to be respected, and the allocation of any property will only be permissible through the agency of the competent administration.[86]

As has been seen, Protectorate officials had immediately begun to supervise the activities of local Habous officials, with the object of eliminating negligence in the drawing up of deeds, leases, and property rights and in the handling of accounts. The antiquated rent system and lack of definition of the length of leases were dealt with in July, 1913.[87] The ludicrously low rents hitherto demanded for Habous

[85] See Dahir of June 26, 1913.

[86] Lyautey's Residential Circular of June 28, 1913. See also a similar Residential Circular issued on Sept. 10, 1913.

[87] The detailed Dahir of July 21, 1913, *BO*, 47 (Sept. 19, 1913), 358.

property were to be reassessed throughout the empire, and it was hoped that efficient and expeditious machinery could be created to deal with this and all other Habous business. Revenues derived from Habous property were dealt with in five categories: (1) current rents, (2) long-term leases, (3) cash payments for Habous property, (4) sale of fruit and harvested crops, and (5) transfer of Habous property and leases.

There were no longer to be leases of Habous property of an undetermined duration.[88] Shops, fondouks, heris, Moorish baths, and houses were to be let at public auction for a period of two years only, and unimproved agricultural land was to be let at public auction for a period of one year, all auctions being carried out in Arabic and French.[89] The long-term leases were to be leases of unimproved land or else land on which stood dilapidated buildings, which could be let for a period of ten years. New measures were introduced to adapt rents to the rise in the cost of living. Thus if a lessee chose to renew his lease for another ten years, he was required to pay 20 percent more rent than previously; this was increased by another 20 percent if the same party elected to renew his lease for a third period of ten years. After the third period, or after thirty years, the lease automatically expired and was not renewable.

Precise legal descriptions of all properties were to be recorded: dates of the contracts, names and professions of the contracting parties, etc. Adjudication Commissions were set up with power to give final decisions on leases and other matters pertaining to Habous properties. The decisions arrived at by such commissions were final and could not be appealed against.[90]

The sale of Habous properties was not permitted except in the case of unimproved land. A person wishing to purchase a parcel of such land was to apply the request to the local nadir, who forwarded this request to the Vizir des Habous who alone had the authority to dispose of such property. In the event of the latter agreeing to the sale, the parcel in question thereby ceased to be Habous and became *melk* (private property).

All fruits and crops harvested from Habous property were to be sold at public auction, as in the past; and, as in the case of real

---

[88] The procedure involved in auctioning leases on Habous property is set forth in Dahir of May 22, 1917.

[89] Dahir of July 21, 1913, § I. Tenures of Habous property encumbered by any of the menfa's rights (i.e., guelsa, gzâ, etc.) were still valid on a perpetual basis. They will be discussed later. Sect. II dealt with leases and rents.

[90] *Ibid.*, § II (clause 2 of the second part), and clause 3, §s III & IV. Each commission consisted of the local cadi (or his naïb), as president; the mourakib of the Habous; the nadir of the Habous; and the two adoul of the cadi.

property, the auctioning was to be carried out in both French and
Arabic.

The Census and Evaluation Commission recommended in August,
1913, that the nadirs immediately enforce payment of the present-day
rent due by occupants of Habous property, who were to be given a
three-month period in which to comply or vacate the property.[91]

As has been seen, the abuses practiced by the adoul in the drawing
up of Habous contracts and leases prompted the French authorities
to subject them to close supervision by the cadis and nadirs. This
still did not solve the problem of irregularities at the local level, because even some cadis were themselves responsible for gross irregularities, especially concerning private Habous of families and zaouïas.[92]
For instance, cadis were in some cases authorizing leases of up to
sixty years' duration, although this was no longer legal, and they were
even disposing of private Habous property, which should have reverted
to the public Habous when there were no longer any living heirs. To
curb such actions, as of December, 1913, cadis were no longer permitted
to sell Habous property on their own authority, and further were only
allowed to authorize leases of Habous property of up to two years'
duration.[93]

3. Verification and Revision of Leasehold Rights

Although a general revision of leases and rents of Habous properties
had been decreed in July, 1913, there remained one very important
group of Habous property that had escaped specific mention and
reevaluation: the gzâ, istidjar, zina, guelsa, and so on. As has been
shown in this chapter, the rents received by the Habous for the lease
of these rights were in most cases unrealistically low, having sometimes
been unchanged for hundreds of years. The rents received were so
low, indeed, that by the twentieth century they usually did not even
cover the cost of the repairs of the properties, although the original
holders had often sublet them at ten and even twenty times the unchanged original rent.

In February, 1914, these rights were revised and reapportioned. The
existing holders of such rights were confirmed as the rightful holders,
provided that they conformed to the new regulations. Of the revised
rent due the Habous for each property, 30 percent was to go to the

[91] Dahir of Aug. 13, 1913. (This commission had been created by Dahir of
Apr. 20, 1913.) It was not until 1916, however, that artisans renting Habous shops
were notified of the newly fixed rents recommended by the commission. Dahir of
June 4, 1916 (resulting from Dahir of July 21, 1913).

[92] A *zaouïa* or Muslim brotherhood was a combination of a private school and
monastery. Family Habous came under the supervision of the Vizir des Habous,
whose authorization was required for any lease exceeding two years.

[93] Dahir of Dec. 2, 1913, *BO*, 71 (Mar. 6, 1914).

Habous, but 70 percent was to be returned to the lessee, that is to say, was not to be paid. Furthermore, there was to be no immediate change in the amount of rent due for the first two years (that is, from February, 1914, to February, 1916), after which there was to be a progressive rise in rents in the following manner: 15 percent of the rent was to be paid in the six years after February, 1916, after which this was increased to 20 percent for the next six-year period; during a further six-year period 25 percent of the rent was due, and following the expiration of the last six-year period the full 30 percent of the newly stipulated rent was to be paid.[94]

Since this measure would not have sufficed to safeguard the interests of the Vizirat des Habous in the event of further rises in the cost of living and value of property, in July, 1916, it was agreed to set up a special commission to reevaluate Habous rents every three years.[95]

Income due the Habous from the various types of leases and rights encumbering Habous property had thus been ensured through a fair revision of rents over a graduated period; it still had not been established, however, who in fact legally held the tenures encumbering Habous property. The French authorities therefore proceeded in June, 1918, to bring about the establishment of two types of commissions for this purpose: Commissions d'Enquête and a Commission de Révision des Droits Réels Grévants les Biens Habous.

The Commissions d'Enquête was set up in June, 1918, in the principal cities of the empire with the purpose of registering the declarations of all persons purporting to hold any Habous leasehold rights.[96] Each commission was composed of local Habous officials, who registered all property rights encumbering Habous property and then made a full inquiry into the legality of each right, including a thorough examination or analysis of the titles involved. A dossier concerning each case was then sent by the presidents of the Commissions d'Enquête to the Commission de Révision des Droits Réels.

One Commission de Révision des Droits Réels Grévants les Biens Habous was set up in Rabat in June, 1918, and was composed of the following officials: The Vizir des Habous, as its president; the Vizir de la Justice; the Conseiller du Gouvernement Chérifien; the Chef du Cabinet Diplomatique; the Chef du Service du Contrôle des Habous; the Conseiller Judiciaire du Protectorat; two oulama; two Muslim

---

[94] Dahir of Feb. 27, 1914, Arts. 1–5, BO, 74 (Mar. 27, 1914), 183. Rent on such properties was based on 6 percent of the value of the particular property concerned, and thus, ultimately, only 30 percent of that 6 percent evaluation was to be paid.

[95] Dahir of July 8, 1916, BO, 196 (July 24, 1916), 758.

[96] Dahir of June 25, 1918, Arts. 1, 2, 7, 8, BO, 299 (July 15, 1918), 673. Each commission consisted of the mourakib of the local Habous district, as president; the nadir in whose jurisdiction the commission was held; two former nadirs, or naïbs of nadirs, or two adoul; and two adoul, one acting as secretary.

notables; and a secretary-interpreter.[97] The task of the Commission de
Révision was to hear and settle any cases or disputes involving Habous
property which had arisen in the Commissions d'Enquête. The Commission de Révision was empowered to order a further inquiry into
any particular case, and to uphold or reject any claim. Any person
failing to declare his titles, or to appear before either a Commission
d'Enquête or the Commission de Révision was presumed to hold an
irregular title to any rights he claimed and was given a three-month
period in which to present himself; if, however, he then failed to
appear, he automatically forfeited any rights to which he might have
been entitled. Decisions made by the Commission de Révision were
final and could not be appealed against.

4. Public Utilities of the Habous

Traditionally, the Habous had as a rule been responsible for the
maintenance of urban services, such as sewers, city gates and walls,
bridges, streets, watering troughs, and water supplies. These services
and utilities were handed over in August, 1914, to the Service des
Travaux Publics of the various municipalities.[98]

V. COLLECTIVE PROPERTY

> We are trying to convince them [the Moroccans], and we have already
> been able to make them understand that the only real form of property
> is individual private property. And thus, as we transform collective
> tribal property into private property, as we increase the value of the
> estate of each member of the tribe, we ask in return to have a part
> of the collective tribal property transferred to State ownership. It is on
> this same collective property that we are creating sectors to be made
> ready for French colonization.
>
> MARSHAL LYAUTEY,
> *Paris, December 5, 1923*

Until recently a map of Morocco would have shown a conglomeration
of tribal lands, forming a patchwork of irregular boundaries. The
larger territories were usually the lands of tribal confederations, each
of which included several tribes. There were perhaps six hundred
tribes in the empire. In a sense, the tribal confederation was to
Morocco what the state is to the United States, the country to England,
or the *département* to France. Most of Morocco was inhabited by
tribes that controlled the Bled es-Siba, that is, the very extensive

---

[97] Dahir of June 25, 1918, Arts. 1, 2, 4, 5, 7, *BO*, 299 (July 15, 1918), 674.
[98] Residential Circular of Aug. 20, 1914, Arts. 1 & 2. Muslim cemeteries were
still maintained under Habous administration, Residential Décision of Sept. 12, 1915.

territories where the Sultan's administrative authority was not recognized.

The Sultan considered himself the ultimate owner of all tribal lands throughout the Sherifian Empire, with the tribes as the perpetual occupants, which in turn could grant special subleases and thereby enable each family of a tribe to dispose of its property. Important decisions pertaining to the tribe were made generally by the *djemaa* (tribal council) consisting of the tribal notables and family heads; the nominal head of the tribe, the caïd, took orders from the djemaa.

Although the traditional names of offices and institutions were maintained by the French, tribal structure was fundamentally altered. The Directeur des Affaires Indigènes was the chief administrator of tribal affairs, along with the Conseil de Tutelle. At the local level officiers de renseignements or contrôleurs civils, depending whether the region were military or civil, worked directly with the tribes.

A. OFFICIAL DJEMAAS

The French created official tribal djemaas (see ch. 2) in November, 1916,[99] whose members consisted either of all the family heads, or else of the tribal notables, all of whom were nominated for a three-year period by vizirial decree upon the recommendation of the *chef de région* (to whom the *autorités locales de contrôle* were responsible).[100] The official djemaas had few real powers, these being limited to: advising the French autorité locale de contrôle of the interests of the tribe; administering collective property of the tribe or *fraction*;[101] and representing the tribe, with the assistance of the autorité locale de contrôle, in all legal matters.[102] The autorité locale de contrôle, generally a contrôleur civil, was always present at every meeting of the djemaa, and helped the caïd to prepare the agenda.[103]

B. TRIBAL PROPERTY, 1912–1925

The administration of tribal property was dealt with at length in April, 1919,[104] and will be considered in the following categories:

[99] Dahir of Nov. 21, 1916 (modified by Dahir of Mar. 11, 1924), *BO*, 217 (Dec. 18, 1916), 1170. Albert Guillaume discusses the full evolution of djemaas under the French in his legal treatise, *La propriété collective au Maroc* (Paris, 1960), especially pp. 19 *et seq.*
[100] Dahir of Nov. 21, 1916, Arts. 1 & 4.
[101] Submitted to the regulations of the Dahir of July 7, 1914 (Part One, Title I, clause 2), *BO*, 90 (July 17, 1914), 579, making tribal property inalienable, along with that of guich tribes.
[102] Apr. 27, 1919, Art. 5.
[103] Dahir of Mar. 11, 1924, Art. 3.
[104] Dahir of Apr. 27, 1919, Arts. 1–3, *BO*, 340 (Apr. 28, 1919), 375.

Administration, Ownership, and Alienation; Leases; Revenues from
Tribal Property; Delimitation of Collective Property (see fig. 9).

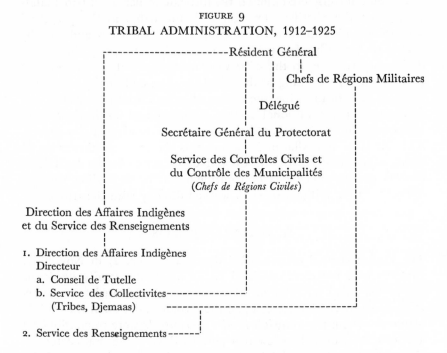

FIGURE 9
TRIBAL ADMINISTRATION, 1912–1925

1. Administration, Ownership, and Alienation

The djemaa managed the ownership rights of its collective property,
but only under the guardianship and supervision of the State, which
at the executive level was represented by the Directeur des Affaires
Indigène and the Conseil de Tutelle. This Conseil, established in
April, 1919,[105] was an important institution in tribal affairs, and its
membership, as altered in May, 1924, included: the Directeur des
Affaires Indigènes et du Service des Renseignements, as its president;
the Conseiller du Gouvernement Chérifien; the Directeur Général de
l'Agriculture, du Commerce et de la colonisation; the Chef du Service
des Contrôles Civils et du Contrôle des Municipalités; and two
Moroccan notables, appointed by the Grand Vizir.[106]

[105] *Ibid.*, Art. 3; this first Conseil consisted of: the Directeur des Affaires Indigènes,
as its president; the Conseiller du Gouvernement Chérifien; a French judge, appointed by the Premier Président of the Cour d'Appeal; and two Muslim notables,
appointed by the Grand Vizir. It also had a secretary and an interpreter (Art. 12).

[106] Dahir of May 20, 1924, *BO*, 607 (June 10, 1924), 881. In 1937 the Conseil was
again modified (by Dahir of Oct. 9, 1937). It was reorganized for the last time
by Dahir of July 28, 1956, and was made up of: the Ministre de l'Intérieur, as
president; the Ministre de l'Agriculture; the Directeur des Affaires Politiques du

Although, as a general rule, tribal property remained inalienable, exceptions were now permitted. No individual tribesman could sell his particular share of the land;[107] but if the majority of the members of the djemaa agreed to a division of tribal land by allocating a specific portion to each head of family of the tribe, that division might be authorized by the Conseil de Tutelle, and the parcels of land could then be alienated, or given in collateral security, or sold to foreigners, but only with the authorization of the Conseil, and following a ten-year waiting period, which in exceptional cases could be reduced to five years.[108] Yet ownership of collective property remained indefeasible except for members of the tribe, and then only for the

---

Ministère de l'Intérieur; the Directeur des Affaires Administratives du Ministère de l'Intérieur; and two members appointed by the Ministre de l'Intérieur. (The Directeur des Affaires Indigènes et des Renseignements had by this time become the Ministre de l'Intérieur.) See also Guillaume, *La propriété collective*, ch. 2.

[107] In Berber tribes individuals were permitted to part with *melk* (private) property, even to nontribal members or to foreigners (depending on the tribe). The djemaa's consent was required, however (Dahir of June 15, 1922, Arts. 1–3, *BO*, 505 [June 27, 1922], 1034). The autorité locale de contrôle then notified the Conservation de la Propriété Foncière of the alienation, and if the Berber had a clear title to the land its sale could be authorized, although it had to be registered immediately with the Conservation (*ibid.*, Art. 3 *et seq.*). In most other respects Berber tribes were reorganized in the same manner as any other naïba tribe. Cf. Dahir of Sept. 5, 1921, and Dahir of Nov. 28, 1921.

[108] Dahir of Apr. 27, 1919, Art. 4. This ten-year waiting period was introduced so as to put an end to speculation, for, as Louis Milliot wrote, if the native were "free to alienate his property immediately, he would be greatly tempted by the high prices offered him. And it is thus not the European speculator here whom he would have to worry about." Louis Milliot, *Les terres collectives (blâd djema'â)* —*étude de législation marocaine* (Paris, 1922), p. 118.

The position concerning division and alienation of tribal property was subsequently altered several times; for instance, the Dahir of May 28, 1938, confirmed that tribal land could be divided up and alienated, but only after a period of thirty years (which was reduced to ten years in exceptional cases). This was done in order to prevent an expected rush to buy land in the Boufekrane area. In 1945 (Vizirial Decree of Aug. 14, 1945), a right of perpetual tenancy was given in some tribes to each tribal member. By the Dahir of Mar. 19, 1951, alienation of tribal property (i.e., to private individuals) was authorized, with a view to ensuring a rational assessment of rural collective property and to encouraging urban construction. Such sales, however, were carefully regulated by the Protectorate. Finally, the Dahir of Jan. 22, 1952, simplified the means by which the State could acquire tribal property, if all parties agreed to the alienation, and permitted expropriation if the collectivities and the Conseil de Tutelle were unwilling.

The Circular (no. 2976) of Nov. 13, 1957, recognized an innovation begun by some tribes in 1950. It authorized the equal division of tribal lands among the families of the tribe, while keeping some land in reserve. The families paid no rent in cash but did give a part of their harvest to the tribe. This type of division was in effect a tribal lease; the lands were let for a ten-year period, and if the male head of the family died, a widow with children was permitted to keep the land till the children were married. This Circular was applied particularly in the Chaouïa, Rharb, and areas around Meknes and Fez. See also Guillaume, who discusses these latter events, pp. 27–30, 97–99.

parcels which they had personally inhabited and possessed at that time and with the consent of the other co-owners.[109]

Immediate alienation of tribal property could be arranged and acquired by the state alone, and then in two ways only. Collective land might be expropriated by the State by right of eminent domain for public works programs and the like, or when the Protectorate authorities wished to establish "colonization perimeters" on it.[110] In either case the collectivity (that is, the tribe) was indemnified for the loss of its property. Although the djemaas could not veto such expropriation, they were consulted, if only for the sake of form. Both the djemaa and the Conseil de Tutelle were consulted for their opinion of an intended expropriation, for as the guardians of tribal property it was their duty to see to the tribe's welfare. Thus, for instance, the Conseil was responsible for ensuring that each tribe possessed "lands sufficient for its normal development." [111] At the same time the Conseil de Tutelle also had to take "into account its estimate of the advantages which the natives would gain from European settlement of the region, or from the setting up of agricultural or industrial centers." [112] Be that as it may, and even if the Conseil objected to the proposed expropriation, the Directeur des Affaires Indigènes had the authority to overrule it.[113]

2. Leases

Three categories of leases were defined under French legislation: short-term, long-term, and perpetual leases.

A tribal djemaa was empowered to grant a lease for tribal property for a duration not exceeding three years, and such leases had to be recorded by written contract (as opposed to the traditional oral agreement); they could only be renewed to the same lessee with the authorization of the Conseil de Tutelle. Likewise the djemaas could authorize leases of one year for the grazing of livestock; these leases could be renewed twice for an additional year without the Conseil's authorization, but any extension beyond the first three-year period required authorization.

Only one form of long-term lease was now permitted, a lease for a

---

[109] Dahir of Apr. 27, 1919, Art. 10.

[110] Dahirs of Aug. 31, 1914, and Apr. 27, 1919, Arts. 10, 11, 14. In the latter case the application of the Chef du Service des Domaines was proceeded with, according to the view taken by the Directeur de l'Agriculture.

[111] Dahir of Apr. 27, 1919, Art. 13.

[112] Ibid. Today this may sound like out-and-out hypocrisy on the part of the French, and indeed there were certainly strong financial interests in the background applying pressure on the French government (e.g., cf. Albert Ayache's Le Maroc— bilan d'une colonisation (Paris, 1956); the ubiquitous French mission civilisatrice, however, was also sincerely believed in by many, including Lyautey.

[113] Ibid., Arts. 11 & 16. Cf. Art. 5.

period of ten years, which could only be granted by the djemaa with
the consent of the Conceil de Tutelle.[114]

The djemaa was also permitted, with the Conseil's consent, to
alienate some of its property in perpetuity (through a lease, not a
sale), under the following conditions: (1) the alienated property had
to be registered with the Conservation de la Propriété Foncière in the
name of the tribe; (2) the consent of the majority of the members of
the djemaa was necessary and had to be attested by an authentic
document; (3) alienation had to take place at public auction; and
(4) an annual and perpetual rent was to be paid the tribe.

3. Revenues from Collective Property

When tribal property was leased, expropriated by right of eminent
domain or for colonization, or alienated in any other way, it was the
Conseil de Tutelle that had to decide, in each case, how best to
reinvest the sums received, whether as compensation for alienated
property, or as rents.[115] Generaly speaking, all such amounts received
were either credited to the savings account for tribes with the
Trésorerie Générale du Protectorat (entitled "Collectivités, Leur
Compte de Fonds en Dépôt"), or went directly to the tribes.[116]

All capital credited to the tribal "savings account" was paid in by
the Directeur des Affaires Indigènes, and it was he alone who could
withdraw any of it. The account for tribes at the Trésorerie Générale
was "general," and all funds received from all tribes went into one
general account; whereas current accounts for each individual tribe
were held at the Direction des Affaires Indigène (Service des Collectivités).

The use of the sums received was decided by both the Conseil de
Tutelle and the djemaas. Proceeds received from expropriation, leases,
or alienation of the rights of perpetual tenure could not be used by
the Conseil for the construction of highways, wells, and watering
troughs, or for the improvement of sanitation, unless the djemaa
specifically requested this. Sums accruing from perpetual rents or from
long-term leases were to be distributed among the families of the tribe,
if this was feasible; otherwise the money, including sums received
from the alienation or expropriation of tribal property, was to be

[114] *Ibid.*, Arts. 7 & 8. This was done in the following manner: the djemaa requested authorization of the lease from the autorité locale de contrôle who in
turn submitted it, with a detailed report, to the Directeur des Affaires Indigènes,
who passed it on to the Conseil de Tutelle which would accept or reject it. If
the lease was approved by the Conseil, the autorité de contrôle formally drew up the
boundaries of the leased property in the presence of all parties concerned (members
of the djemaa, lessee, neighbors).

[115] *Ibid.*, Art. 8; Vizirial Decree of Dec. 26, 1920, Art. 4, *BO,* 430 (Jan. 18, 1921), 83.

[116] Vizirial Decree of Dec. 26, 1920, Arts. 1–4.

invested in real estate or to be applied generally to benefit the tribes, for instance for charity, tribal legal costs, improvement of land and buildings, cultivation of virgin land, construction of shelters for flocks, planting of crops and orchards, purchase of animals or agricultural materials, or irrigation projects.[117] In most cases sums received from the various categories went directly to the Trésorerie Générale and were later withdrawn as required; in the case of revenues received from leases and the like, they could be distributed among the tribal families, as shown above.[118]

When the djemaas wished to use funds from revenues and compensation moneys, they sent a written request to the Conseil de Tutelle stating the manner in which they wished to have the funds used. After studying the request of the djemaa, and hearing the views of the autorité locale de contrôle (and in some cases, of the local representatives of the Directeur de l'Agriculture, the Service d'Élevage, and the Service des Domaines), the Conseil would make its decision, which was conveyed to the Directeur des Affaires Indigènes who issued authorization for the withdrawal of the necessary funds. The Conseil thus had the key role in permitting the distribution of funds, and of living up to its paternalistic title, by ensuring that tribes did not squander their patrimony.

4. Delimitation and Registration of Collective Lands

In pursuit of the policy of defining all property and property rights within the Sherifian Empire the Directeur des Affaires Indigènes as the guardian (tuteur) of "collectivities," was empowered to request delimitation of the boundaries of collective properties, although the djemaas were also consulted.[119] The properties were then studied and surveyed by a special commission,[120] with the procedures involved in the survey of property borders being announced to the public in advance and news of the delimitation being posted in the cadi's mahakma, the Conservation de la Propriété Foncière, all French courts in the area, the office of the Direction des Forêts, the Service des Domaines, and the Direction des Affaires Chérifiennes. Any parties opposing a delimitation had the right to lodge their objections with the commission or the autorité locale de contrôle for hearing under a prescribed procedure.

[117] Dahir of Apr. 27, 1919, Art. 14, and Vizirial Decree of Dec. 26, 1920, Art. 4.
[118] Vizirial Decree of Dec. 26, 1920, Arts. 1, 2, 4.
[119] Delimitation of tribal property was first introduced by Dahir of Feb. 18, 1924, *BO*, 596 (Mar. 25, 1924), 542. See Art. 1.
[120] *Ibid.*, Arts 2, 4–6. Each commission consisted of the following: a representative of the Conseil de Tutelle; a representative of the autorité locale de contrôle, the djemaa of the area, the caïd, a surveyor, a representative of the Direction Générale des Travaux Publics (if necessary), an interpreter, and two adoul.

The purposes of such delimitations were generally to facilitate the alienation and expropriation of tribal land for public works or colonization settlements, or to halt unofficial alienation of tribal land by Moroccans. The Directeur des Affaires Indigènes was now empowered to have tribal properties registered with the Conservation de la Propriété Foncière,[121] which at the same time placed all collective properties in this category under the sole jurisdiction of French courts.

5. Alienation of Berber Property

In June, 1922, special provisions were made whereby Berber tribesmen adhering to customary law (as opposed to the Chrâa) were permitted to alienate melk property only.[122] In such a case the djemaa made a complete study of the property concerned (boundaries, etc.), notifying the autorité locale de contrôle of the intended sale, who in turn informed the local office of the Conservation de la Propriété Foncière.[123] If everything was in order immediate consent was given, and the property was registered with the Conservation.

[121] Ibid., Art. 10. Albert Guillaume, in his La propriété collective (p. 36), gives the following figures for surveyed and registered tribal property:

(1) Area of collective property registered by 1960:

Rabat	58,243 ha.
Casablanca	36,047
Fez	8,879
Meknes	4,935
Oujda	3,784
Mazagan	6,449
Oued-Zam	14,651
Agadir	25
Marrakesh	23,906
Total	156,919

(2) Area of collective property delimited by 1960:

Province of Oujda		481,100.97 ha.
" " Taza		458,617.43
" " Fez		48,510.96
" " Meknes		196,400.23
" " Tafilalt		117,033.20
" " Rabat		201,462.23
" " Casablanca		236,890.73
" " Tadla		147,845.27
" " Marrakesh		991,465.47
" " Ouarzazate		187,604.00
" " Agadir		82,313.67
Total		3,149,246

[122] Dahir of June 15, 1922, Art. 1, BO, 505 (June 27, 1922), p. 1034. Tribes classified as adhering to Berber customary law were listed in the Vizirial Decrees of May 5, 1923, Mar. 8, 1924, and Apr. 16, 1928; see ch. 2, n. 162 for a list of these tribes.

[123] Dahir of June 15, 1922, Arts. 3 & 4.

In all other respects, however, the regulations governing tribal property, issued in April, 1919, applied to Berber tribal property.[124]

VI. PUBLIC AND STATE DOMAIN

A. INTRODUCTION

Although Public Domain, State (Private) or Makhzen property, Habous, and collective property are all forms of public property in Morocco, the distinctions between them are important. Whereas Habous property is of a specifically religious nature, and collective property is purely tribal, Public Domain and State or Makhzen Domain are technically public property. Before 1912 no real distinction was made between Public Domain and State or Makhzen property,[125] and the confusion led to malpractices and alienations by Makhzen (i.e., government) officials. In 1895 the Sultan's regent tried to halt such abuses by having an inventory drawn up of existing Makhzen property, which consisted of government buildings throughout the empire, some natural resources, properties confiscated by the government or Makhzen from public officials or important persons who had fallen into disgrace, property which had reverted to the state when an individual died without leaving an heir, and guich lands.[126]

There were two general categories of Domain property in the Sherifian Empire—Public and Private (or State, Makhzen)—and three subclassifications.

Public Domain, which the Protectorate authorities declared to be inalienable, included the following:[127] (1) the seashore to the furthest limit of the tides, as well as a zone of six meters measured from that limit; (2) roadsteads, ports, harbors, and related installations; (3) Lighthouses, beacons, navigational works; (4) all waters above or beneath the ground, watercourses, and all sources of water;[128] (5) lakes, pools,

---

[124] Dahir of Sept. 5, 1921; see also Dahir of June 2, 1923.

[125] By Makhzen property I refer to Makhzen melk and private domain. Cf. Michaux-Bellaire and Aubin, "Le régime immobilier," pp. 22–24. This was also confused with the Sultan's private property.

[126] Dahir of Apr. 25, 1895. Lahbabi, *Le gouvernement marocain*, p. 159; Amar, *L'organisation de la propriété foncière au Maroc*, p. 27. At the time of the establishment of the Protectorate there were six groups of guich tribes and they were considered Makhzen tribes: the Ehl Sous (at Fez and Marrakesh), the Oudâïa (Marrakesh and Rabat), the Cherâga (between the Sebou and Fichtâia), the Oulad Djama (the Cherârda, on the left bank of the Sebou), the Bouakhor (Negroes, Meknes), and Er-Rifi (around Tangier). Cf. *Labour Survey of North Africa* (Geneva, 1960), p. 52; Amar, pp. 37–39.

[127] Dahir of July 1, 1914, Arts. 1 & 4, *BO*, 89 (July 10, 1914), 529.

[128] According to Muslim law, waters could not become private property. Gardet, "La propriété en Islam," pp. 112–113, 130,

lagoons, etc.; (6) navigation canals, irrigation canals, etc.; (7) artesian wells, public wells, and watering troughs; (8) dikes, barrages, aqueducts, and similar projects falling within the category of public works; (9) highways, roads, streets, railways, tramways, bridges, and generally all means of communication for public use; (10) telephone and telegraph lines; (11) defense and fortification works, military posts, etc. Although Public Domain had been declared inalienable, if there were portions which were of no use to the public, they could be classified as alienable, by the Directeur Général des Travaux Publics, who was the general administrator of all Public Domain.[129] By the same token, the authorities later consented to leasing Public Domain for temporary occupation to tribes or private persons, when this would not harm the public interest.[130] Applications to lease Public Domain were addressed to the Directeur Général des Travaux Publics, who could consult the Chef du Service des Domaines when assessing the rent to be paid. As in the case of Habous, leased Public Domain was closely supervised by the government. The lease could not exceed ten years in duration, and the rent was to be paid annually. All rents were subject to periodic revision, at least once every five years.

The three subclassifications of Private Domain were: mines and minerals; forest; and Makhzen melk (which could be alienated and used for colonization).

B. ADMINISTRATION

Domain properties were administered by four different departments of the Sherifian government (see fig. 10). Public Domain was administered by the Direction Générale des Travaux Publics, and all legal matters pertaining to it came under the exclusive jurisdiction of French courts.[131] Private Domain, however, even though it was classified in only three categories, was administered by four different authorities, as follows:

The Service des Mines, established in 1920, was subordinate to the Direction Générale des Travaux Publics.[132]

The Direction des Eaux et Forêts, which came under the authority of the Directeur Général de l'Agriculture, du Commerce et de la Colonisa-

[129] Dahir of July 1, 1914, Art. 5. The Directeur Général notified the Grand Vizir, who in turn issued a decree to that effect.

[130] Dahir of Nov. 30, 1918, Arts. 1–3, 5–7, BO, 326 (Jan. 20, 1919), 37.

[131] Dahir of July 1, 1914, Arts. 6 & 8. Any contract alienating, temporarily or permanently, Public Domain as concessions to third parties required the countersignature of the Directeur Général des Finances; the Dahir of Nov. 8, 1919 (Art. 2) gave the Directeur Général des Travaux Publics the right to immediate possession of any Public Domain, without the concurrence of any other authority.

[132] Dahir of July 24, 1920, Art. 3, BO, 409 (Aug. 24, 1920), 1436.

FIGURE 10

PUBLIC AND STATE (PRIVATE) DOMAIN, 1912–1925

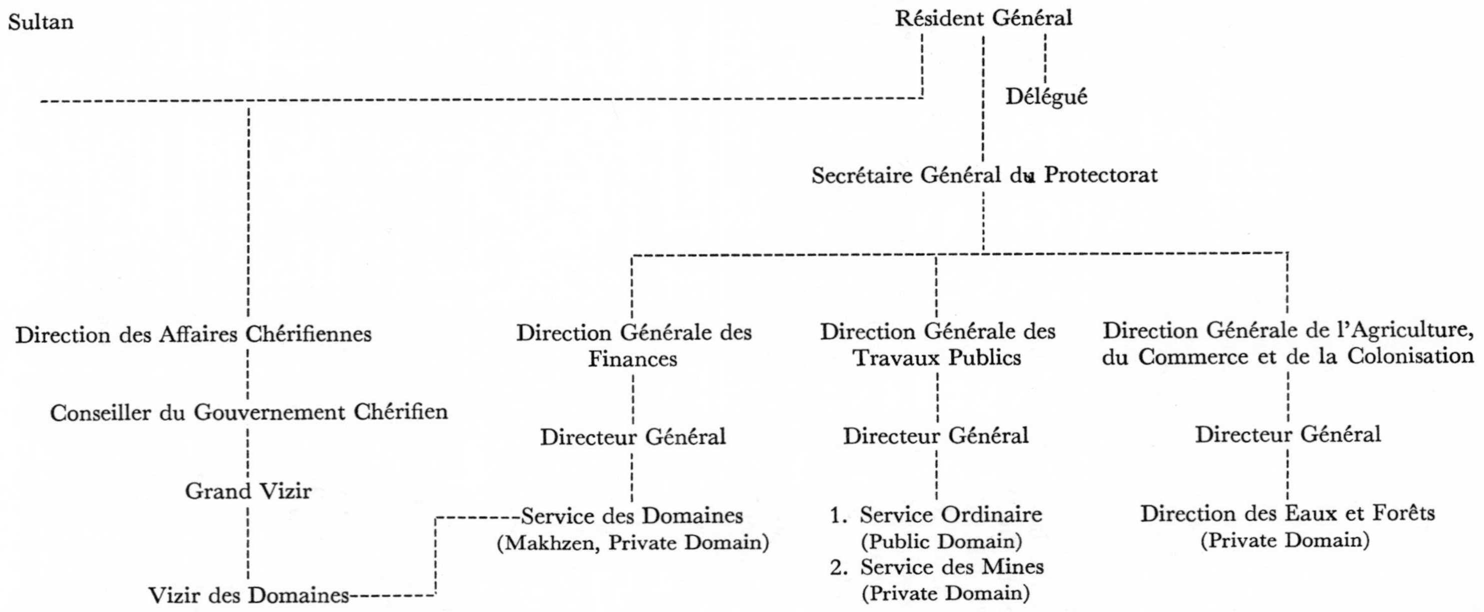

Sultan

Résident Général

Délégué

Secrétaire Général du Protectorat

Direction des Affaires Chérifiennes

Conseiller du Gouvernement Chérifien

Grand Vizir

Vizir des Domaines

Service des Domaines
(Makhzen, Private Domain)

Direction Générale des
Finances

Directeur Général

Direction Générale des
Travaux Publics

Directeur Général

1. Service Ordinaire
   (Public Domain)
2. Service des Mines
   (Private Domain)

Direction Générale de l'Agriculture,
du Commerce et de la Colonisation

Directeur Général

Direction des Eaux et Forêts
(Private Domain)

tion, prepared and applied forestry legislation, saw to the delimitation and upkeep of forests and the development of their resources, planted new forests, prevented the spread of sand dunes, and examined questions concerning hunting, freshwater fishing, and related subjects.[133]

The Service des Domaines was established in September, 1912, becoming the Vizirat des Domaines in April, 1919.[134] It was attached to the Direction Générale des Finances in July, 1920,[135] and thus passed under the dual supervision of the Vizir des Domaines and the Directeur Général des Finances, while continuing to be administered directly by the Chef du Service des Domaines. The Vizir had an executive rather than an administrative post, for he brought all dahirs concerning State Domain to the Sultan for his seal, presented all vizirial decrees concerning State Domain to the Grand Vizir for his signature,[136] received weekly reports from the Chef du Service des Domaines, and received complaints from Moroccan citizens. The chef du service administered all property belonging to the Makhzen, and he and the Vizir des Domaines together signed all leases and contracts relating to the use and development of State Domain.[137] As administrator of the State Domain, the chef du service was responsible for the disposal of products from Private, or State Domain, as well as for the upkeep and general management of its properties, which included properties reverting to the State because of lack of heirs as well as those reverting to the State through legal default. The Service des Domaines also drew up plans, maps, and documents pertaining to colonization (mainly of guich properties) derived from State Domain and included the demarcation and sale of colonization areas.[138] In November, 1912, a Commission Spéciale de Révision des Biens Makhzen was set up to study all rights, claims and titles to Makhzen property so as to define further Makhzen holdings.[139] The work of this commission soon came to a halt, mainly because several of its original members left it and were not replaced. In 1918 the commission was reconstituted so as to be able to resume its work, its new membership including: the Vizir des Domaines, as its president; the Chef du Cabinet Diplomatique, or his deputy; the Directeur des Affaires Chérifiennes, or his deputy; the Chef du Service de l'Interprétariat of the Cour d'Appel, at Rabat;

---

[133] *Ibid.*, Art. 2. This was previously a Service, but became a Direction by Dahir of Feb. 8, 1922, Art. 1, *BO*, 487 (Feb. 21, 1922), 306.

[134] Dahir of Apr. 27, 1919, *BO*, 342 (May 12, 1919), p. 421. This ministry was suppressed in 1927. See A. de Laubadère, 'Les réformes des pouvoirs publics au Maroc," *RJPUF*, II (1948), 18.

[135] By Dahirs of July 6, 1920, and July 24, 1920, Art. 2.

[136] Dahir of Apr. 27, 1919, Arts. 3, 5, 6.

[137] *Ibid.*, Art. 4; Dahir of July 24, 1920, Art. 3.

[138] Dahir of July 24, 1920, Art. 3, §5.

[139] Vizirial Decree of Nov. 9, 1912.

the Chef du Service des Domaines, or his deputy, acting as reporter; an
alem, appointed by the Vizir de la Justice Chérifienne; and an inter-
preter-secretary.[140] All cases and claims submitted to the Commission
were studied by it, and it had the authority to settle each case then
and there, without there being any right of appeal.[141]

Following the traditional Moroccan method of reward, it was decided
to grant parcels of State Domain not exceeding two *zouijas* to Moroccan
ex-soldiers,[142] and a special commission under the authority of the
Directeur des Affaires Indigènes was set up in Rabat to compile a list
of all Domain properties that could be used for this purpose.[143] These
plots were given to soldiers provisionally—during which period they
could not be transferred, attached, or encumbered in any way—and
later were granted in full ownership.[144]

C. DELIMITATION AND REGISTRATION OF DOMAIN PROPERTIES

In order to define properties classified as State Domain, delimitation
of this property was begun in January, 1916, the same was also done
for Public Domain.[145] By securing for the State clear titles of ownership, delimitation served to obviate unnecessary lawsuits, and in May,
1922, registration of Domain properties, already delimited, was
provided for automatically, thus permanently securing all such
titles.[146]

VII. EXPROPRIATION

In the Protectorate of Morocco the term expropriation meant either
(1) the mandatory seizure of property, by right of "eminent domain,"
for public welfare, or (2) the mandatory seizure of property for
colonization.

The ability to exercise a right of "eminent domain" is necessary for

---

[140] Dahir of Feb. 3, 1918, Art. 1 (as modified by Dahir of July 16, 1919), *BO,*
280 (Mar. 4, 1918), p. 218.

[141] Dahir of Feb. 3, 1918, Arts. 2 & 5.

[142] Dahir of Dec. 27, 1919. In Morocco the sultans had traditionally followed this
practice, remnants of which were still visible during the Protectorate, for the guich
tribes had been given their land in just such a manner.

[143] Vizirial Decree of Dec. 27, 1919, Art. 2. It consisted of: the Directeur des
Affaires Indigènes, as its president; the Directeur des Affaires Civiles (whose office
was suppressed by Dahir of May 15, 1922); the Directeur Général de l'Agriculture,
etc.; the Conseiller du Gouvernement Chérifien; the Chef de la Section Marocaine
à l'Etat-Major; and the Chef du Service des Domaines.

[144] Dahir of Dec. 27, 1919, Arts. 4 & 5.

[145] Dahirs of Jan. 3, 1916, Art. 1, *BO,* 168 (Jan. 10, 1916), 36, and July 1, 1914,
Art. 7, *BO,* 89 (July 10, 1914), 529.

[146] Dahir of May 24, 1922, *BO,* 502 (June 6, 1922), 919.

any civilized state. The French authorities laid down the basis for their program in Morocco in 1914.[147] Public and private property could now be claimed for the following: construction of highways, railways, or ports; urban works, military works, forestry management and development, redevelopment of mountain lands, and the preservation of historic sites or monuments, and the like. Several categories of property were specifically exempt from this right of eminent domain: mosques, sanctuaries, official cemeteries, Public Domain, and military property.

Nowhere in either the Dahir of August, 1914, or in any of those that subsequently modified it, was colonization mentioned as one of the reasons for which property could be expropriated. Indeed, expropriation for purposes of creating colonization "sectors" only occurred, indirectly, in legislation concerning tribal property and Makhzen melk, or State Domain, as seen previously.[148]

Most declarations of intended expropriation emanated from the Direction Générale des Travaux Publics, and all expropriations had to be cleared through French courts.[149] No construction—or whatever was the intended purpose of the expropriation—could be begun without the authorization of the Directeur Général des Travaux Publics. In every case of expropriation compensation was to be paid to the party concerned.[150]

Generally an expropriation occurred in the following way:[151] The Service des Travaux Publics issued a notification to the pacha or caïd of the locality stating the property required. The pacha or caïd then issued a draft decree to this effect, which was published in the *Bulletin Officiel* and local newspapers. It was the duty of the caïd and the autorité locale de contrôle to notify the owners of the property concerned. Within a month of that announcement the owner was required to report to the autorité locale de contrôle in order to agree upon the compensation for the property.[152] The case then went before the Tribunal de Première Instance of the locality where the expropriation was announced, and the compensation fixed.

The compensation to be awarded was based upon two considerations: (1) the value of the property prior to expropriation (including buildings and crops); and (2) the appreciation or depreciation of the

---

[147] Dahir of Aug. 31, 1914, Arts. 3 & 7, BO, 101 (Sept. 28, 1914), 755. This was modified by Dahirs of Nov. 8, 1914, May 3, 1919, Oct. 15, 1919, and Jan. 17, 1922.

[148] Large numbers of expropriations of collective property occurred in the 1925–1935 period. Guillaume, *La propriété collective*, p. 69. Expropriation of tribal property was first mentioned in Art. 10, Dahir of Apr. 27, 1919. An example of tribal property expropriated for future colonization is found in the Vizirial Decree of July 29, 1925, *BO*, 669 (Aug 18, 1925).

[149] Dahir of Aug. 31, 1914, Arts. 2, 4, 12.

[150] *Ibid.*, Art. 10 (modified by Dahir of Jan. 17, 1922).

[151] *Ibid.*, Art. 5 (modified by Dahir of May 3, 1919) & Art. 8.

[152] *Ibid.*, Art. 10 (modified by Dahir of Jan. 17, 1922), & Arts. 12, 13, 15, 17, 27.

remainder of the property that was not expropriated. If the party
affected was not satisfied with the amount awarded him, he had the
right to appeal, provided that the value of his property was more than
3,000 francs. When a piece of expropriated property was encumbered
by a right of usufruct, the owner of that property had to negotiate
the matter privately with the holder of the usufructory right, after the
court had fixed the compensation, in order to arrive at the share
that would result to the holder of the right. If a piece of unimproved
property (or property having only wooden buildings) was urgently
needed by the Service des Travaux Publics, it could be expropriated
immediately (with dispensation from the normal procedure), whereupon the party appeared without delay before the local Juge de Paix
who announced the amount of the compensation to be awarded,
although the party also had a right to state the amount he wished to
receive and could appeal if the value of his property amounted to more
than 500 francs. If property had to be occupied temporarily by the
Directeur Général des Travaux Publics for a public work's project—
such as any of those listed above—the party whose property was
being temporarily occupied was also compensated by the government.[153] Temporary occupancy, however, could not exceed a period of
five years; if a longer period was required, and the party affected did
not agree to a further extension, the government had to expropriate
his land. Temporary expropriation did not include the occupancy of
the courtyard, orchards, and gardens attached to dwelling houses and
surrounded by enclosures. Military authorities were also permitted to
expropriate property, or to occupy it temporarily, under certain
circumstances.[154]

VIII. COLONIZATION

What we from our [European] point of view call colonization, missions
to the heathen, the spreading of civilization, etc., has another face—
the face of a bird of prey seeking with cruel intentness for distant
quarry—a face worthy of a race of pirates and highwaymen.
C. G. JUNG,
Erinnerungen, Träume, Gedanken

Installing French colonists in Morocco conforms both with the framework of interests of the Protectorate and with that of the native
population. Sufficiently numerous French colonists are necessary in
order to constitute the armature upon which the action of the

[153] *Ibid.,* Arts. 30 & 35. Land or other matter might have to be extracted or
excavated, etc.
[154] Dahir of Nov. 8, 1914, *BO,* 108 (Nov. 16, 1914), 830; and Dahir of July 23,
1924, *BO,* 618 (Aug. 26, 1924), 1356.

Protectorate is based and to make French influence dominant in this country. On the other hand, not only do European agricultural works offer an advantageous outlet to native laborers seeking work, but, too, these works are necessary in order *to give the right example to the native landowners*, so that the superiority of European agricultural methods can be seen and appreciated. Yet this European colonization does not risk developing into an invasion. Thus, under such circumstances the native population has nothing to fear.

ARTHUR GIRAULT,
Principes de colonisation et de législation coloniales. Vol. V

What is bitter does not become sweet, even though it is in the bottom of a bee.

A MOROCCAN PROVERB

The conquest of a foreign land has often led to subsequent colonization, and perhaps no nation in modern history has colonized so thoroughly as has France, especially in Tunisia, Algeria, and Morocco. To be sure, most conquered countries have not been very attractive for European civilization. The climatic conditions of the Sudan or of the Indian subcontinent certainly discouraged any permanent mass colonization—but Morocco was a different story. The climate is generally like that of the Côte d'Azur or of Southern California.

France went into Morocco primarily for military and economic reasons, and colonization naturally played a big part. In Algeria, colonization had developed on a huge scale, and the colon lobbyists became very strong indeed. In Morocco, however, colonization never reached the proportions achieved in Algeria, or in Tunisia,[155] and one of the most important reasons for this was that though Lyautey supported colonization, he did not believe in colonizing the country to the detriment of the Moroccans, or in bringing in colonists who were not already prepared with the knowledge or capital needed for agricultural work. Another obstacle to massive colonization was that, unlike Algeria for instance, Morocco did not contain vast stretches of uninhabited, unclaimed land, because all land there was owned by the tribes, the Habous, the State, or individuals.

A. IMMIGRATION

There was no system of regulated immigration during Lyautey's administration, and this in itself was to prove a source of difficulty.

---

[155] Jean Poncet, *La colonisation et l'agriculture européennes en Tunisie depuis 1881—étude géographique, historique et économique* (Paris, 1962), p. 330. In Tunisia, which was territorially much smaller than Morocco, over 750,000 ha. had been colonized by 1950, whereas in Morocco, only 250,000 ha. over that figure were ultimately colonized. See also Jean Despois, *La Tunisie orientale—Sahel et basse steppe: étude géographique* (Paris, 1955), especially Part 4, chs. 4 and 5.

Some legislation governing the entrance of foreigners into Morocco was enacted but it had little or no effect on French immigration.

From November, 1914, any foreigner landing in a port in the French Zone of the empire had to prove his identity, his last address, his means of maintaining himself in Morocco, and too his reason for coming there; and in December, 1915, the French listed four categories of persons who were automatically denied entry into Morocco, including persons who had been expelled from, or forbidden entry into, France or French territories.[156] In addition, a Service de Surveillance de l'Immigration was created in June, 1915.[157]

FIGURE II

EUROPEAN IMMIGRATION INTO MOROCCO, 1912–1928 *

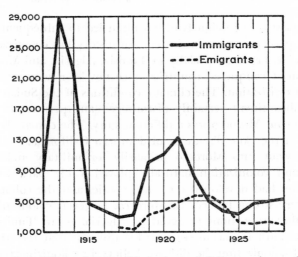

* From Jean Célérier, *Le Maroc* (Paris: Armand Colin, 1953), p. 216

The numbers of immigrants permitted to enter remained entirely unregulated, and in consequence Protectorate officials never knew how many immigrants to expect. In 1913, for instance, approximately 29,000 immigrants flooded into the ports of the empire, which led Lyautey to remark in 1914:

But when it is a question of such a numerous and rapid immigration as that which Morocco attracts, how does one discern, how can one distinguish at first glance—in this influx of arrivals in which the older established colonists are lost among the newcomers—when the adventurers are not distinguishable from the real workers?[158]

[156] Ordonnance of Nov. 13, 1914, and Dahir of Dec. 8, 1915. See also Goulven, *Traité d'économie*, II, 446.
[157] Created on June 8, 1915; it was under the authority of the Chef du Service de la Police Générale at Rabat.
[158] *PA*, p. 121.

By 1915 the number of immigrants had fallen to less than 5,000, but in 1921 it was again up to over 13,500, as seen in figure 11.

B. DEVELOPMENT OF COLONIZATION

Despite Lyautey's sometimes unsympathetic attitude, legislation and programing were developed to pave the way for colonization. A Comité de Colonisation was set up in 1916 to establish close liaison between the various Services involved in the preparation and execution of future colonization programs,[159] though the apparatus to deal with colonial development, the Service de la Colonisation, was not founded until July, 1920.[160] This Service came under the authority of the Direction de l'Agriculture, du Commerce et de la Colonisation, and its task, in collaboration with the Service des Domaines, was to locate lands that could be used for colonization (which included the study and development of rural parcels), to establish annual programs for colonization, and to supply information to interested immigrants.[161]

Land for official colonization came from two principal sources: tribal collective property and Private State Domain (chiefly Makhzen melk, including guich property).[162] In February, 1918, a Commission Spéciale de Révision des Biens Makhzen was set up to develop areas for colonization from the Private Domain of the state,[163] and in April, 1919, the way was officially paved for alienating tribal (naïba) land for colonization,[164] as discussed in sections IV and VI of this chapter.

Land made available for official colonization by the government was distributed in the following manner: 25 percent to recently arrived immigrants, 25 percent to Moroccan ex-soldiers, and 50 percent to immigrants who had already been in Morocco for at least two years but who had not yet purchased any agricultural land.[165] The government, however, in contrast to Algeria, did not give free concessions of land;

[159] Residential Decree of Nov. 9, 1916, BO, 214 (Nov. 27, 1916), 1108. It was presided over by the Délégué à la Résidence Générale and consisted of various chefs de services. See also G. Jacqueton, "La colonisation française au Maroc," AG, XXXIII (1924), 309; Girault, Principes, V, 382–384.

[160] Dahir of July 24, 1920, BO, 409 (Aug. 24, 1920), 1443. For a good discussion of colonization, see Stephen H. Roberts, The History of French Colonial Policy, 1870–1925 (London, 1963), pp. 582–587.

[161] Dahir of July 24, 1920, Art. 2, §4.

[162] Guillaume, p. 54; Ayache, Le Maroc, p. 151; Goulven, II, 465.

[163] Dahir of Feb. 3, 1918, BO, 280 (Mar. 4, 1918), 218. In 1923 the Directeur Général de l'Agriculture stated that 100,000 ha. of State Domain at the most were available. Jacqueton, p. 310. Cf. the situation in Tunisia where Habous property far exceeded State Domain. J. Despois, chs. 1, 4, 5 of Part 5.

[164] Dahir of Apr. 27, 1919, Art. 10, BO, 340 (Apr. 28, 1919), 375.

[165] Résidence Générale, Renaissance du Maroc: dix ans du Protectorat, 1912–1922 (Rabat, n.d. [1922]), p. 285.

all portions of land were sold, at reasonable prices and on accommodating payment terms. In December, 1921, colonists were officially permitted to have their property registered by the government with the
Conservation de la Propriété Foncière,[166] and in 1922 they were
permitted to request, on their own initiative, that their property be
registered in their own names, in order to facilitate the arrangement
of mortgages.[167]

Three categories of property were made available by the government
to colonists: (1) Small colonization lots, including lots for market
gardening, of two to five hectares, and lots for orchards and dairies of
twenty hectares; (2) medium-sized colonization lots, of 200 to 400
hectares; and (3) large-sized colonization lots, up to thousands of
hectares.[168] To help colons acquire land, special facilities for mortgages
were arranged by the government.[169] Lots falling within the first two
categories were sold at fixed prices (set by the Protectorate authorities)
to buyers singled out by public lottery from among the applicants.[170]
The medium-sized lots were by far the most popular; they were grouped
into rural settlements, located at Matmata, Bir Tam Tam, Boufekrane,

[166] Dahir of Dec. 5, 1921, *BO,* 482 (Jan. 17, 1922), 58. In Tunisia the same
property registration system was used (based on the Torrens Act); there, however,
the colons were very slow to register their property in the 1880's although at the
time the French openly admitted that the reason for registration was "to support
the right of ownership of the present master of the land [i.e., the French] while
at the same time breaking all former claims to this soil, not only by the *khammes*
[peasant laborers], but also by the traditional occupants and those holding it as
djeddari [perpetual lessees] and *enzélistes* [i.e., equivalent to the customary property
rights of Morocco, such as the *guelsa*]." Poncet, p. 150. See also Al-Moutabassir,
"Les habous de Tanger," p. 331.

Paul Cambon in 1885, then Resident General of Tunisia, in his report to the
government stated that the reason for establishing the Loi immobilière tunisienne
du 1er juillet 1885 (property registration) was that "in order to attract and hold
capital (necessary for the development of natural resources), it is important that
we protect the acquirers of property from their ignorance of the language, laws,
and customs of the country, as well as from any unforeseen claims, in a word, that
we ensure the facility and security of such transactions. Now, under the system of
Muslim legislation and local customs, such facilities and security did not exist."
Quoted by Poncet, p. 147.

[167] See Dahir of May 22, 1922, *BO,* 502 (June 6, 1922), 918. Prior to that, only the
government could request registration.

[168] Goulven, II, 288–295; Girault, p. 382. Two important conditions were attached
to anyone applying for medium-sized lots: (1) he was not permitted to possess
more than a total of 500 ha. in Morocco; (2) he had to live on and work the land
himself. Goulven (II, 289–294) quotes all requirements and procedures. In the
first years of the Protectorate, however, Lyautey envisaged medium-sized lots of
100–150 ha. only. *LA,* III, 198.

[169] E.g., Dahir of Dec. 22, 1919, modified by Dahir of May 14, 1920. Goulven, II,
216–217.

[170] To be paid in ten annual payments; Goulven, II, 291. A Commission
d'Expertise consisting of officials and colons was set up to establish the prices to be
asked.

Petitjean, Aïn el Aouda (Rabat), Boulhaut, Bir Djedid Chavan, Foucauld, Sidi Bennour, Ouedzem, and Marchand.[171]

Large-sized colonization lots were sold to colons at public auctions to the highest bidder. Of these, from 1918 to October, 1924, eighteen lots were sold, totaling some 14,000 hectares in addition to another 10,000 hectares held by the Compagnie du Sebou in the Rharb.[172] In 1923 Lyautey estimated that there were over 1,000 colons on 400,000 hectares.[173] In 1924, a little over a year before Lyautey retired, about 500,000 hectares had been acquired by colons, consisting of 1,274 lots—most of them cultivated for crops—the majority of which ranged from two to 500 hectares.[174] Yet by 1922 only 57,000 hectares had been allocated through the official colonization program, of which 30,000 hectares had been set aside from former tribal properties.[175] An intensified period of expansion followed between 1923 and 1932, when over 200,000 hectares were officially allocated by the Protectorate authorities.[176] The world economic crisis hit the colons especially hard between 1930 and 1932 and resulted in a sharply reduced official colonization program[177] as well as an equally sharp increase of bankruptcies among them; the last sales of official lots took place between 1933 and 1935. By 1935 a total of 271,000 hectares had been officially distributed by the Protectorate among 1,735 parties.[178]

Unofficial, private colonization was also taking place and indeed had begun before the establishment of the Protectorate. It far outstripped

[171] Ayache, p. 153.

[172] *Ibid.* The Compagnie du Sebou was controlled by the Banque de Paris et des Pays-Bas. René Passeron, *Les grandes sociétés et la colonisation dans l'Afrique du Nord* (Algiers, 1925), pp. 275 *et seq.*

[173] Lyautey's address before the Académie d'Agriculture, on Dec. 5, 1923, *PA,* p. 398. Charles Stewart (p. 77) states that 8,000 ha. were allocated by the Protectorate between 1916 and 1918 and that from 1918 to 1923 official colonization accounted for 71,500 ha., divided into 449 parcels.

[174] P.-L. Rivière, *Traités, codes et lois du Maroc,* III, 832.

[175] Louis Milliot, *Les terres collectives,* pp. 108–109. Most of this total was subdivided into six colonization lots: (1) 4,000 ha. from the Guernouan tribe (of the south) near Meknes; (2) 5,000 ha. in the Fez area; (3) 7,000 ha. from the Sfafa tribe and from the Oulad Yahia tribe in the Rharb (northeast of the Mamora forest); (4) 5,600 ha. near Kenitra; (5) 4,500 to 4,000 ha. from the Mazamza tribe (in the southern Chaouïa area); and (6) 1,800 ha. in the northern Chaouïa area, from the Ziaida tribe. Ayache (p. 153) gives a figure of 57,000 ha. by 1922, and Stewart (p. 77) a figure of 71,500 ha. divided up among 449 parcels, by 1923.

[176] René Gallissot, *Le patronat européen au Maroc—action sociale, action politique (1931–1942)* (Rabat, 1964), p. 18; Ayache, p. 153. Stewart (p. 77) says that the most active period lay between 1926 and 1933. The official colonization program was administered by the Service de la Colonisation. Private colonization was unofficial and unregulated, private parties purchasing property from other private parties.

[177] This occurred in the Tunisian Protectorate during the same period. Poncet, p. 290.

[178] Ayache, p. 153.

the official program. During the same 1923–1932 period, seen above for official colonization, 358,000 hectares were purchased privately from Moroccan owners, which in itself far surpassed the entire amount of official colonization achieved by the Protectorate authorities from its establishment until independence in 1956. By 1935 a total of 840,000 hectares had been acquired by colons, and by 1953, just under 200,000 hectares more had been added to the 1935 figure.[179] Of these, the largest holdings were in the areas of Casablanca, Rabat and the Rharb, Meknes, Fez, and Marrakesh, in that order.[180]

Incentives and aid were given the settlers by the government. During Lyautey's administration subsidies were given for clearing virgin land and for planting olive trees.[181] Most valuable of all was the provision of short-, medium-, and long-term agricultural credits, which were first distributed by the Caisses de Crédit Mutuel, established in 1923, and later by the Caisse Fédérale and the Caisse des Prêts Immobiliers. Most of the capital was supplied for these caisses by the State, which also provided two-thirds of the capital required to found Sociétés Coopératives, which numbered twenty-three by 1939 and seventy-three by 1954.[182]

C. RESULTS AND SUMMARY

> More than any other country, Morocco lends itself to fruitful development; it is a country with a future. It possesses great wealth, which for the most part has not yet been developed, and is thus capable of offering real hopes for our national activity. But let us not forget that it is definitely not a *bled* yet to be discovered. That has already been done; it has been inhabited and cultivated for many centuries, and we must not think that, on arriving there, we have only to set up a tent, purchase some land, and begin some sort of business or farm in order to realize appreciable profits.
>
> In reality it is quite different. The future *colon* will have to act cautiously, making a thorough study of the situation, as a necessary first step.
>
> COMTE DE LA REVELIÈRE,
Les énergies françaises au Maroc, 1917

Many Moroccans have naturally denounced the French rule of their country, and Albert Ayache has drawn up a very strong and well-documented case for the Moroccan point of view in his book *Le*

---

[179] *Ibid.*, p. 154; Gallissot, pp. 18–19; Stewart, p. 77. Of a total of 1,017,000 ha., 728,000 ha. had been acquired privately.

[180] Ayache, p. 154.

[181] These subsidies were suppressed in 1923 and in 1936, respectively. Ayache, p. 155. During the Second World War there were subsidies for the purchase of agricultural materials, and also reductions in fuel prices.

[182] Ayache, p. 155.

Maroc: bilan d'une colonisation. On the subject of French colonization he says:

The immediate preoccupation of the new regime [the Protectorate] was to
favor the appropriation of Moroccan land by foreigners and to give a
definitive character to this appropriation by surrounding the property with
incontestable judicial guarantees. This was the object of the Dahir of August
12, 1913, regulating the registration of property, and the establishment of
the Service de la Conservation Foncière in 1915.[183]

As is often the case with sweeping generalizations, aspects of truth
and fiction are interwoven in this statement. It is true that France
went into Morocco for, among other reasons, economic aggrandize-
ment, and to help toward this the French went to the tremendous
expense of colonizing Morocco. When Ayache states, however, that
the immediate preoccupation of the new regime was to favor and
develop colonization, he is wrong; for Lyautey, the master of the new
regime, was opposed to large-scale appropriation and colonization.
He feared especially that Morocco might experience the large-scale
speculative colonization carried out in Tunisia by strong companies
in the 1880's which had resulted in the first French colons being speculators or "an aristocracy of absentee owners and of large, indirect
developers" rather than farmers working their own land.[184] Indeed,
the program for official colonization was not put into effect until after
the First World War. Furthermore, the first official large-scale colonization did not begin in earnest until the mid-1920's, just as Lyautey
was resigning his post as Resident General. What is more, the per-
centage of land expropriated by the French for colonization, in contrast to that which was purchased privately from the Moroccans, was
certainly small.

Ayache claims that already by 1913 Europeans possessed more than
100,000 hectares, even though at that time no system of guarantees for
property had been established by the Protectorate; indeed, most of
these acquisitions had been made before the establishment of the
Protectorate.[185] He goes on to state that "during the course of 1912
and 1913, abuses reached such proportions [as regards colonization]
that a Dahir of July, 1914, declared 'the lands occupied collectively
by the tribes' to be inalienable." In fact the French authorities were

---

[183] *Ibid.*, p. 148. For a valuable and stimulating study of France's legacy in North
Africa see Eugène Guernier, *La Berbérie, l'Islam et la France*, Vol. II (Paris, 1950).
[184] Poncet, p. 141.
[185] Ayache, p. 149. Stewart (p. 75) quotes a figure of 73,000 ha. According to official
figures, there were about 5,400 French citizens in Morocco on January 1, 1911, but by
January 1, 1914, this figure had jumped to 26,000. Général Lyautey (ed.), *Rapport
général sur la situation du Protectorat au Maroc au 31 juillet 1914* (Rabat, 1916),
p. 482.

trying to stop the land-grabbing[186] which Ayache contends they were trying to encourage, and this Dahir was issued for the precise purpose of stopping alienation of tribal lands to speculators. Ayache fails to point out that "abuses" (that is, land-grabbing and speculation) were also practiced by Moroccans, especially between 1913 and 1919, and to such an extent that the economy was damaged and tribal holdings were reduced. Individual Moroccans benefited to the detriment of the tribes and of French colonization also.[187]

[186] Lyautey was under great pressure from colon lobbyists, such as the powerful M. Obert who, when addressing the Congrès de Marseille in 1922, asked that another million ha. be colonized by 1942; of this amount he anticipated that 755,000 ha. would be taken from tribal djemaas and another 155,000 ha. from Private State Domain! Jacqueton, "La colonisation française au Maroc," p. 311. The Directeur Général de l'Agriculture, du Commerce et de la Colonisation, M. Malet, stated in 1923 that only 100,000 ha. at the most could be colonized from Private Domain. See Jacqueton, p. 310. As has been shown, even by the 1950s less than 300,000 ha. had been officially colonized (i.e., from tribal and Domain property). G. Jacqueton was a fervent expansionist and defended further colonization of guich lands in Morocco, for as he put it (p. 312), "il n'y a pas de temps à perdre: toute heure perdue pour la colonisation rurale, pour le peuplement français du bled marocain, pourrait contribuer à la compromettre."

[187] Milliot, *Les terres collectives*, pp. 115–116. He points out (p. 120) that a great many Frenchmen—"thousands," he says—had to give up the idea of settling in Morocco for want of (inexpensive) land. Milliot gives an example of how Moroccans were threatening their own patrimony, in such a way that the French were afraid to stop them for fear of being accused of "spoliation":

"In 1913 all the land extending between Casablanca and Rabat, along the coast, was certainly collective [tribal] property. Apart from a few gardens or orchards, there were scarcely any crops there, except some basins of low-lying ground fertilized by alluvial deposits. Since 1919 the situation has been reversed; planted fields of a single native owner cover tens of kilometers, now replacing fallow land. The new occupants claim a right of private property over these lands held collectively by tribes, with the result that the Administration is afraid to contest the matter, since the inventory of collective lands available for colonization in the Chaouïa at the beginning of 1921 covered several thousand hectares.

"For those who doubt the accuracy of our facts, we point out in advance that the same phenomenon is taking place all along the highway between Fez and Taza.

. . . .

Are the natives going to be permitted to install themselves as private owners [over this tribal land] without our realizing that they are violating the land title by their occupation, without reserving for our colonization a part of this land, the peaceful possession of which France now assures to the natives?

"Until 1919 the Protectorate confined itself to stopping the alienation of tribal property, leaving it to the *cadis* and *caïds* to enforce this ruling. We now know only too well that this task has been betrayed [by the caïds and cadis]. In contempt of dahirs and custom, the cadis have applied Chrâa to tribal land. The caïds have closed their eyes to the whole matter. As for the French *autorités de contrôle*, we really cannot blame them for not having protected an institution which the legislator could not define. Had they indeed known about it they would not have been able to prevent the natives from unceasingly decreasing the amount of fallow land [to the detriment of the tribes]. On the contrary, it was their duty to encourage it by every possible means and they did not fail to do so. Now, this effort accomplished, the native is fully convinced that he is now the sole [legal]

Altruism is more theoretical than realistic, and the French did not incur the great expense of administering another country without the intention of ensuring that they would profit from it. At the same time the French claimed that the Moroccans would benefit from French colonial settlements and industrial installations,[188] and so they did, in the long run, just as they benefited from contact with European civilization and values, or French civilization as Frenchmen chose to call it. Gabriel Hanotaux gives this explanation:

> Races are great and powerful because of the importance and results of the tasks that have been assigned to them.
> Let me be clearly understood—this is not only a matter of a great number of conquests; it is not even a matter of increasing public and private wealth. It is a question of extending abroad to regions which only yesterday were still barbarian the principles of a civilization of which one of the oldest nations of the world has the right to be proud.[189]

Nevertheless, the Moroccan had to pay for these new benefits. He was placed under foreign rule and much of his richest land or most

---

owner of this land, and if he is denied this traditional right, he feels that he is being robbed [by the French]."

Milliot here refers to the fact that the Moroccan Muslim traditionally had the right of ownership of any fallow, virgin land. Herein lies the crux of Milliot's complaint, for, according to Islamic law, tribal property is not one of the three legally recognized categories of property (i.e., property owned by the Muslim community, *melk*, and Habous) and tribal land is not strictly speaking an Islamic institution, for there is no reference to it either in the Koran or in the *Hadith*. Nevertheless, it is in fact recognized by the Chrâa (see Guillaume, *La propriété collective*, pp. 12–14)—hence Milliot's objection to the Chrâa being applied to such property cases for according to the Chrâa, property of the Muslim community that has lain fallow for at least seven years can be *vivifiés* by the planting of crops on it, which in turn permits the new occupants to claim individual right of ownership over the land. However, Guillaume has pointed out, "It is impossible to contest the fact that the form of collective property has not come down to us from Muslim law, and yet it is in fact recognized by the Chrâa." A. Guillaume, p. 14, and also pp. 11–13. In other words, in collective or tribal property, we have a new classification of property which was created by custom and subsequently recognized by Islamic law. Milliot's complaint is that tribal land was being alienated to individual Moroccans even though the French specifically forbade the alienation of collective property except under certain strict conditions. See Vizirial Decree of 1912, of Mar. 6, 1914, and Dahir of April 27, 1919.

[188] E.g., see Dahir of Apr. 27, 1919, Art. 13, discussed earlier in this chapter.

[189] Gabriel Hanotaux, *L'énergie française* (Paris, 1902), p. 365. Many others expressed similar feelings regarding the French civilizing mission. In 1922 Charles Castre put it this way: "There lives in French hearts a spontaneous piety (in the nature of a spiritual instinct) for the civilizing mission to which France has ever dedicated herself." Charles Castre, *The Ideals of France* (New York, 1922), p. 34. A minority did not agree with this view, e.g. Alfred Fouillée: ". . . we are often naïve enough to believe that what makes us happy will make everyone happy, that all of humanity must think and feel as does France." Alfred Fouillée, *Psychologie du peuple français* (Paris, 1914), p. 181.

important pasture land was taken for colonization. Although he was compensated for its loss—a point that Ayache fails to make—the compensation could not in itself be adequate. Monetary payments could not compensate for the effects of the loss of pasture land which led to a reduction of the size of flocks kept by mountain tribes[190] and to loss of income that resulted from smaller harvests. Yet there were Frenchmen at that time who tried to look realistically at the situation and its effects. Louis Milliot, the jurist and author, saw the situation in 1922 as follows:

. . . a great deal of tribal land is fit only for the transhumance of flocks, and the land that is rich enough to grow crops should only be taken away by compulsory purchase after broad consideration of present and future needs on the basis of the needs of the present occupants. The Moroccan population is very prolific and the quelling of civil wars, together with the improvement in the general conditions of hygiene and the reduction of infant mortality, will rapidly raise the figure. Let us not uproot these people and by thoughtless measures congest the cities with a proletariat which will be ready to follow agitators or troublemakers. Besides, the Moroccan native will not allow large slices of his land to be taken away. Hard-working, intelligent, and open to modern ideas, he is jealous of his land, which he fears will be taken from him, as was that of the Algerian. It is not without great difficulty that we have succeeded in making him understand that the alienation of collective land will ultimately be to his own advantage. Any untimely or premature measure, such as a large distribution of small colonization parcels, will certainly convince him that he has been the victim of vast spoliation, from which serious trouble could result. It is better to see the situation the way it really is: Morocco is not a colony established for the settlement of immigrants, but Frenchmen can appear there in the form of large companies possessing large amounts of capital. Their role should be to educate the native and to introduce him to modern methods of production; to have associated him with their resultant fortune will represent their real profit.[191]

In fairness to the Protectorate authorities, it should be stated that out of approximately one million hectares colonized by 1953, less than one-third had been expropriated by the Protectorate for official colonization,[192] the remaining two-thirds having been purchased privately

---

[190] Jacques Berque illustrates this in *Le Maghreb entre deux guerres* (Paris, 1962); see especially pp. 117–125. He cites the Marmoucha tribe which in 1926 descended from the mountains with 120,000 sheep, as they did each winter, but which by 1931, because of French policies, had been reduced to 37,000 sheep—a reduction of more than two-thirds in five years' time. Professor Berque also quotes (p. 122) from a letter written by a French officer in 1921: " 'Cette colonisation, soit officielle, soit privée, a pris une telle ampleur qu'elle a réduit dans une proportion très appréciable les terrains dont disposaient les tribus du Nord.' "

[191] Milliot, *Les terres collectives*, p. 110.

[192] In 1960 Albert Guillaume estimated total tribal holdings (including desert areas) at about 6,000,000 ha. Guillaume, p. 36.

by Frenchmen from Moroccans. Ayache fails to make this point also.[193]

This is not to say that the French were altruistic missionaries, but rather that France has often been the home and birthplace of dreams and ideals and that men like Gallieni and Lyautey were products of such an environment. Lyautey was an idealist; he was not out for "all he could get," and his consideration and moderation often sheltered the Moroccans from the harshness of metropolitan French politicians and lobbyists, a harshness they were later to feel directly, once men like Lyautey were gone.

[193] Frenchmen complained about the great difficulty they had in purchasing land privately from Moroccans. As Milliot put it, during Lyautey's regime "the European encounters the greatest difficulties in surmounting the native's reluctance to sell him his land, whereas on the contrary the Moroccan speculator has no trouble at all." Milliot, Les terres collectives, p. 118.

4

FRANCO-MUSLIM EDUCATION

I. BEFORE THE PROTECTORATE

A gentleman without reading is like a dog without training.
A MOROCCAN PROVERB

A. INTRODUCTION

Before the Protectorate there was neither a centralized educational authority nor a central budget for education in the empire.[1] Primary and secondary schools were maintained for Muslim children in the cities, towns, and most villages. There were also Jewish and European schools. The teaching in the Muslim schools, and also Koranic instruction in the mosques, were financed by gifts from local people and funds from the Habous. The Jewish schools were maintained by the local Jewish communities. Traditionally, there were three levels of education in the Sherifian Empire: primary, secondary, and higher.

Education presented less of a problem to Lyautey and his advisers than might at first glance be expected. All education, with the exception of that of Jews and Christians, had been administered by Muslims alone. To have tried to alter this would have caused great antagonism among Moroccans, and the French wisely did not tamper with the schools existing before their arrival. Instead, they set up an entirely French school system for the Moroccans. Over a span of a few

---

[1] Unfortunately, very few books or articles have been published on the subject of education in Morocco; one of the best is by E. Michaux-Bellaire, "L'enseignement indigène au Maroc," *RMM*, XV, No. 10 (1911), 422–452. It is on this article that most of this section is based. For background on *zaouïas*, see Michaux-Bellaire's *Conférences*, which is the entire Vol. XXVII of the *Archives Marocaines* (1927), especially chs. 1–4.

years the French hoped to introduce at least one segment of Moroccan youth to a modern European education. In the schools for the elite young members of society, modern sciences, mathematics, languages, and history were taught by French, not Muslim, teachers and in French, Muslim teachers being restricted to the teaching of purely Muslim subjects, such as Arabic and Islamic law. Schools for Moroccan girls were even introduced on a minor scale, to the horror of orthodox Muslims.

Lyautey had two objectives: to overcome traditional Muslim antipathy toward all non-Muslim education, and to educate young Moroccans in the twentieth-century European tradition, building up a nucleus of persons who would spread the understanding of his ideas and government, and also training a body of educated Moroccans who could step into government posts at a later date. Education was to prove one of the few promising openings for Moroccans, for the greatest difficulty was finding enough educated Muslims and Frenchmen to instruct Moroccans, in French, Arabic, and Berber.

B. THE EDUCATIONAL SYSTEM

Primary education in Morocco—for boys only—was based on the Koran and was given in schools called *msid* in the cities and *djemaa* in the tribal areas. The pupils (*m'hadra;* sing. *m'hadri*) were taught by a *faqih* (theologian), who knew the Koran from memory. The Koran was the only text studied, and after the pupils had learned the alphabet, the faqih proceeded to dictate the Koran, *sura* by *sura,* and the pupils were supposed to commit it to memory, one *sura* at a time. The schoolboy who successfully memorized the Koran was called a *taleb* (pl. *tolba*). Boys who were unable to memorize the entire Koran eventually left school to learn a craft, or to become shepherds. By the beginning of the twentieth century, most boys were attending a Koranic school for at least a certain length of time.

Only a few of the primary pupils ever reached the secondary schools. Here they learned, also by memorization, classical Arabic grammar, the fundamental doctrines and practices of Islam, and some of the simpler aspects of Islamic law. Usually the curriculum consisted of Cenhadji's *El-Adjouroumiya* and Ibn Malik's *El-Alfiya,* two famous versified textbooks on grammar; Ibn Achir's work, *El-Mourchid El-Moïn ala Ed-Darouri min Oloum Ed-Din* and commentaries on it, for the fundamentals of Islam; and *Touhfat El-Houkam fi Nakat El-Oqoud ou El-Hakam,* a versified text on law (simpler than the standard textbook by Sidi Khali), and commentaries on it.

Although in former times there had been facilities for higher education in several cities of the empire, for a long time prior to the Protectorate they had survived only in Fez, at the Qaraouiyne Mosque. The students lived in *medersas* (colleges), only five of which remained by the twentieth century. The students were not taught in these buildings, but in the Great Quaraouiyne Mosque. The courses included grammar, law, theology, and rhetoric. Surprisingly, history had never been taught at the Qaraouiyne University and geography not for a long time past.

II. FRANCO-MUSLIM EDUCATION, 1912–1925

> Everyone knows what a difficult task it is to organize education in a [foreign] country that is open to European influences: if we are satisfied merely with transplanting our [French] academic institutions, then we risk falsifying the entire work, upsetting the natives, producing social refugees, malcontents, and firebrands of anarchy. Thus above all we must seek a means of adapting education to the needs of the country. The Protectorate, from the very beginning, has undertaken to accomplish this to the best of its ability.
>
> GEORGES HARDY,
> *Histoire des colonies françaises*
> *et de l'expansion de la France*
> *dans le monde*, III: *Le Maroc,*
> *la Tunisie, la Syrie.*

> We shall never be able to do anything without these intellectual bonds which are indeed the strength, honor, and grandeur of a society.
>
> LYAUTEY, *address to the*
> *"Congrès des Hautes Études Marocaines,"*
> *at Rabat, December 7, 1922*

A. INTRODUCTION

When the French established the Protectorate and began revamping the educational system, they made no effort to interfere with the Muslim and Jewish schools, which were mainly religious.[2] They did, however, completely change the educational emphasis in Morocco by creating a new type of primary school, known as the Franco-Muslim schools.

The traditional Islamic schools were brought under one central governmental authority, the Direction des Affaires Chérifiennes and the Grand Vizir (see fig. 12). In 1915 the Vizir de la Justice was put in charge of all Islamic education, including the traditional primary

---

[2] The exceptions were those established and administered by the Alliance Israélite Universelle, which established its first school in Morocco in 1862. Gérard Israël, *L'alliance israélite universelle: 1860–1960.* Numéro Spécial, *CAIU,* CXXVII (Feb., 1960), 77.

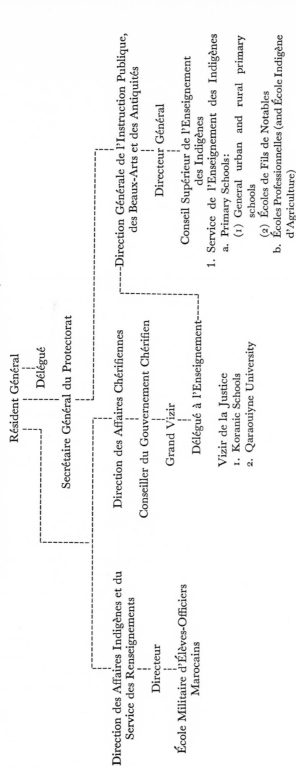

FIGURE 12

MUSLIM AND FRANCO-MUSLIM EDUCATION, 1912–1925

Résident Général

Délégué

Secrétaire Général du Protectorat

Direction des Affaires Chérifiennes

Conseiller du Gouvernement Chérifien

Grand Vizir

Délégué à l'Enseignement

Vizir de la Justice

1. Koranic Schools
2. Qaraouiyne University

Direction des Affaires Indigènes et du
Service des Renseignements

Directeur

École Militaire d'Élèves-Officiers
Marocains

Direction Générale de l'Instruction Publique,
des Beaux-Arts et des Antiquités

Directeur Général

Conseil Supérieur de l'Enseignement
des Indigènes

Service de l'Enseignement des Indigènes

1. Service de l'Enseignement des Indigènes
   a. Primary Schools:
      (1) General urban and rural primary
          schools
      (2) Écoles de Fils de Notables
   b. Écoles Professionnelles (and École Indigène
      d'Agriculture)
   c. Secondary Schools:
      Collèges Musulmans
2. Service de l'Enseignement Supérieur et
   Organisation Scientifique
   a. Institut des Hautes Études Marocaines
   b. Institut Scientifique Chérifien

and secondary Koranic schools, and the Qaraouiyne University which was supported entirely by Habous funds.[3] All these schools with some exceptions[4] remained much as they always had been, their purpose being to produce Muslim teachers, university lecturers, lawyers, judges, and notaries. The French did not assume the administrative power to supervise and inspect education in these schools.

B. FRANCO-MUSLIM EDUCATION [5]

The new educational system superimposed by the French was directed by the Direction Générale de l'Instruction Publique, des Beaux-Arts et des Antiquités.[6] Franco-Muslim education was administered by the Service de l'Enseignement des Indigènes on the primary and secondary level, and by the Service de l'Enseignement Supérieur et Organisation Scientifique, for higher education.[7]

The purpose of Franco-Muslim education was to supply an education system solely for Moroccans which would, at the primary school level, run parallel with the traditional Koranic schools by providing the rudiments of modern knowledge in addition to religious lore. For each school or group of schools the French set up Comités de Patronage, and a Conseil de Perfectionnement for the more important schools. An interesting feature of these local committees is that they were made up of both Frenchmen and Muslims who worked out their problems together.

Heading the whole program was the Conseil Supérieur de l'Enseignement des Indigènes, created in February, 1916, but reorganized

---

[3] Dahir of Mar. 9, 1915, *BO,* 129 (Apr. 12, 1915), 187. At first one official, Faqih Si Mohammed El Hadjoui, headed the Direction de l'Enseignement, as it was originally called; but this Direction was abolished in August, 1914 (by Dahir of Aug. 5, 1914, *BO,* 96 [Aug. 21, 1914], 690). Previously it had dealt with both religious education and modern education, including the sciences, arts, and foreign languages. In 1914 the French authorities, convinced that no Moroccan was yet capable of handling all these branches of study, abolished and reorganized the Direction. Religious education did remain under Moroccan control, but all other education was allocated to a newly created Direction directly under the French. See André Colliez's excellent book, *Notre Protectorat marocain: la Ière étape, 1912–1930* (Paris, 1930), p. 276.

[4] The modern Koranic schools, or *Écoles coraniques rénovées,* in which French was now taught.

[5] For a general discussion of Franco-Muslim education see Georges Hardy, "L'education française au Maroc," *RP,* No. 8 (Apr. 15, 1921), pp. 773–788. For a study of the first few years of the Protectorate, see Général Lyautey (ed.), *Rapport général sur la situation du Protectorat au Maroc au 31 juillet 1914* (Rabat, 1916), Part 2, ch. 9.

[6] Created by Dahir of Feb. 28, 1921, *BO,* 437 (Mar. 8, 1921), 395, which modified Art. 1 of Dahir of July 26, 1920, *BO,* 408 (Aug. 17, 1920), 1393. In 1915 (Dahir of Dec. 23, 1915) this had first been called the Direction de l'Enseignement.

[7] Dahir of July 26, 1920, Art. 3 (as modified by Dahir of Dec. 17, 1920, *BO,* 426 [Dec. 21, 1920], 2133).

in October, 1921, as follows: the Grand Vizir, as its president; the Directeur Général de l'Instruction Publique, as its vice-president; the Vizir de la Justice; the Grand Vizir's Délégué to the Direction Générale de l'Instruction Publique; the Directeur des Affaires Indigènes et du Service des Renseignements; the Chef du Service de l'Enseignement des Indigènes; the directors of Muslim schools of higher education; and three Muslim notables.[8] The Conseil was consulted on all general questions pertaining to the organization of native education.

The above Conseil was quite distinct from the Conseil de l'Enseignement established in 1919 and modified in 1925, which dealt with the supervision of all matters concerning private schools in Morocco, including the authorization of the opening of new private schools, as well as the texts to be used in them.[9] It was composed of the following members: the Directeur Général de l'Instruction Publique, as its president; the Premier Président of the Cour d'Appel, or his delegate; the Procureur Général of the Cour d'Appel, or his delegate; the Grand Vizir's Délégué to the Direction Générale de l'Instruction Publique; a representative of the Délégué à la Résidence Générale; a representative of the Secrétaire Général du Protectorat; a representative of the Cabinet Diplomatique; an inspector, a headmaster, and a teacher of secondary education (appointed by the Directeur Général de l'Instruction Publique); two teachers from private schools (also appointed by the Directeur Général de l'Instruction Publique); and a secretary.[10]

1. Primary Education

Two streams of education were established by the French for the Moroccans: one for the majority of the people, leading to apprenticeship in one of the crafts or building professions, the other for the elite of Moroccan society, who were to be trained for higher forms of education, leading to posts in the government and professional employment.

a) *Primary schools*—These schools, established in rural and urban districts, were intended to provide a skill or vocation for their pupils, as well as a special course in practical French.[11] Practical, manual work was especially stressed. The schools in the cities prepared their pupils for industrial apprenticeship and sometimes had small workshops, and the rural schools prepared the children for agricultural

[8] Dahir of Oct. 31, 1921, Art. 5, *BO*, 474 (Nov. 22, 1921), 1793; see Colliez, p. 269. For the original composition see Dahir of Feb. 17, 1916, Art. 6, *BO*, 175 (Feb. 28, 1916), 218.

[9] Dahirs of Oct. 15, 1919, Arts. 1–3, *BO*, 368 (Nov. 10, 1919), 1284, and June 26, 1925, *BO*, 666 (July 28, 1925), 1269.

[10] Dahir of June 26, 1925.

[11] The French generally called them *écoles de quartier*. See Dahir of Feb. 18, 1916, Arts. 9 & 10.

work;[12] children were thus trained in skills that would be useful in their particular areas. The vocational courses included basket weaving, the making of cases and moldings, joinery, metalwork, and general repair work.

Both the urban and the rural schools were headed by French head-masters, assisted by French and Moroccan staff.[13] In 1925 Fez had three such schools with a total of just over 100 students, and by 1929 the French had increased the number of primary schools to twenty-nine for boys with 5,462 pupils, and twelve schools for girls with 1,894 pupils.[14] Upon completion of their work in these schools, the pupils could then go on to an *école professionnelle*.

There were also other types of primary schools, termed by the French *écoles coraniques rénovées*, which were unofficial. They were set up by Moroccans as a first attempt to blend the East with the West. In addition to the traditional courses on the Koran and Arabic grammar, the pupils were also taught some elementary French.[15] These schools were fairly popular; in Fez about one-fifth of the city's school children attended them, and in Rabat about one-quarter of the children attended them. By 1930 André Colliez estimated that between 25,000 and 30,000 pupils were attending them throughout the empire.[16] Since these schools were unofficial, however, the French had no authority or power of supervision over them.

b) Écoles de Fils de Notables.—Schools were established in February, 1916, for the sons of the upper classes of Morocco and the boys accepted for them were carefully selected.[17] The purpose of these schools was to prepare their pupils for admission to the Collèges Musulmans. They were fee-paying schools, although some scholarships were available.[18]

The course of studies lasted four years and included the following subjects: (1) study of the Koran (taught by a faqih according to the traditional methods of the Koranic schools); (2) Arabic (taught by a Moroccan); (3) moral Islamic religious studies (taught by a faqih); and (4) French culture (taught by a Frenchman). This course was to be a

[12] Colliez, p. 271.

[13] Paul Marty, "L'enseignment primaire et professionnel des indigènes à Fez," *RC*, No. 3 (March, 1925), p. 75. Cf. Paul Bernard's "L'enseignement primaire des indigènes musulmans de l'Algérie," *RMM*, I, No. 1 (1906), 5–21.

[14] "L'enseignement primaire et professionnel des indigènes à Fez," p. 78; Colliez, p. 271.

[15] "L'enseignement primaire et professionnel des indigènes à Fez," p. 75.

[16] *Notre Protectorat marocain*, p. 270.

[17] Dahir of Feb. 18, 1916, Art. 2, *BO*, 175 (Feb. 28, 1916), 219. Marty reports that approximately 100 pupils were registered in Fez early in 1925 ("L'enseignement primaire et professionnel des indigènes à Fez," p. 77). By Dec. 31, 1926, there were five such schools in Morocco; Colliez, p. 275.

[18] Dahir of Feb. 18, 1916, Art. 4.

means "of entering into relationship with the French in general and facilitating the development of business between them." It included the study of language, spelling, reading, recitation, French composition, general humanities, mathematics, rudiments of the history and civilization of North Africa and France, elementary geography, and drawing.[19] At the end of the four-year course each student who successfully completed his studies was given a certificate and became eligible to enter one of the two Collèges Musulmans.[20]

2. Technical Education

The technical schools developed from the vocational training units added to the urban primary schools. Out of the fourteen technical schools established by the late 1920's, ten were concerned principally with apprenticeship in European trades, such as metalwork and woodwork, and the other four emphasized native arts, especially cabinet work, leather work, and ceramics.[21]

By the late 1920's the technical schools were training about 550 students. The most obvious deficiency was the lack of instruction in agriculture, for agricultural instruction of any importance was only given at one school for Muslims, located at Fez.[22] For a primarily agricultural country such as Morocco, this was a surprising oversight, but governmental expenditure could not permit any more allocations for agricultural study at that stage in the Protectorate's development. Also, craftsmen, rather than farmers, were needed in the vast building program being inaugurated by the French, and there was a belief that, for the time being, the newly established French colons could supply all necessary food requirements.

a) École Professionnelle of Fez.—The Muslim technical school is illustrated by the curriculum of the Bou Djeloud École Professionnelle at Fez.[23] Although this school was for boys only, there were also special schools for Moroccan girls at Casablanca, Rabat, Salé, Marrakesh, and Mogador, where the girls were taught traditional crafts such as carpet weaving and embroidery.[24]

The curriculum of the École Professionnelle in Fez was divided into four parts: (1) joinery with plenty of equipment (work benches, benchvices, lathes, millstones, forges, planing-machines, molding machines, bandsaws), power being supplied by two electric motors; (2) locksmith-

[19] Marty, *op. cit.*, p. 72.

[20] Dahir of Feb. 18, 1916, Arts. 5–7.

[21] Colliez, p. 272. These four were located at Salé, Mogador, Marrakesh, and Safi.

[22] The French also had a very small agricultural school, with no experimental farm, attached to the École Professionnelle of Casablanca in 1924. Colliez, p. 265.

[23] Marty, *op. cit.*, pp. 78–79.

[24] *Ibid.*, p. 79. In 1925 there were 250 girl students.

ing, ironwork, and machine repair work (including farm machinery); (3) pottery and ceramics; and (4) copper and metalwork, provided with lathes, etc. The first three parts were supervised by French master craftsmen, the fourth by a Moroccan. Students usually began their studies at twelve years of age, and by 1925 there were 78 students attending the courses in Fez. Theoretical work was also taught, by the school's director, and every day each section received instruction in French in a technological subject, drawing, and mathematics. Students were also taken on tours of nearby European factories.

The successful graduates from Fez went on to attend the École Industrielle et Commerciale at Casablanca,[25] where they were trained as electricians, mechanics, foremen, and draftsmen. They could also receive preparation for the French *école d'arts et métiers,* for the various *instituts électro-techniques,* and the École Centrale.

b) *École Indigène d'Agriculture.*—In view of the basic importance of agriculture in the Moroccan economy, it is important to examine the type of training young Moroccans received at the École Indigène d'Agriculture, at Fez, which was first planned in January, 1923, and was opened one year later.[26] This school offered a two-year course intended to provide a general and technical education and included studies in the following subjects: botany, agriculture, horticulture and fruit arboriculture, general and agricultural physics and chemistry, mechanical equipment, animal anatomy and physiology and hygiene, and veterinary medicine, as well as courses in French, mathematics, economic geography, and human hygiene.

One-half day per week was set aside for demonstrations at the experimental farm, which covered 700 hectares. At times of important seasonal work the students participated in practical farmwork, such as planting, hoeing, trimming, harvesting, grape harvesting, reaping, mowing, and fruit picking. They learned how to use various types of farm machinery, and they also did practical work in the nursery garden.

The program of the École Indigène d'Agriculture was a broad one, and one of the most important instituted by the French. The numbers enrolled, however, were very limited. Twenty-five students attended courses the first year, and this figure had nearly doubled in the second year.[27]

3. Secondary Education: the Collèges Musulmans

Originally secondary education was given to only a select few at the two Collèges Musulmans, one at Fez, opened in 1914, and one at

---

[25] The École Industrielle et Commerciale was opened primarily in order to train French colons; by 1929 it had over 380 students. Colliez, p. 266.

[26] Marty, *op. cit.,* pp. 81–82.

[27] *Ibid.,* p. 83.

Rabat, opened in 1916.[28] In 1923 the colleges were renamed the Collège Moulay Idriss, at Fez, and the Collège Moulay Youssef, at Rabat.[29]

All students applying for admission to either of these two colleges (or to the École de Fils de Notables) had to be examined and screened by the autorité locale de contrôle in order to restrict the number of candidates, because acceptance of too many might "lead to the formation of déclassés." [30] These colleges were meant to receive for the most part only the cream of Moroccan society, boys from cultured, educated, upper-class Moroccan families; the French realized that a leadership class of Moroccans was necessary for Morocco. The boys usually entered the colleges between the ages of twelve and fourteen.[31]

The Écoles de Fils de Notables were to the Collèges Musulmans what the elementary schools of France were to the lycées and collèges, except that those in Morocco trained their students mainly for commercial or government work and rarely for professional careers. The Collèges Musulmans were also on a lower academic level than the lycées and collèges in France. The course of studies lasted for six years, divided fairly evenly between French and Arabic, and included both modern sciences and Islamic studies. In the last two years of the six-year cycle, administrative or commercial specialization was introduced. By December, 1926, there were five Écoles de Fils de Notables and two Collèges Musulmans, with a total of 802 pupils.[32]

Each Collège Musulman was under the supervision of a Conseil de Perfectionnement,[33] the primary purpose of which was to follow the progress of the students, give advice on the drawing up and application of syllabuses, supervise the students, and make suggestions regarding the organization of the colleges.[34] At every level in the pro-

[28] See Alfred Bel, "A propos de l'enseignement des indigènes à Fez," RC, No. 5 (May, 1925), p. 147. The college at Rabat was created by Dahir of Feb. 18, 1916, BO, 175 (Feb. 28, 1916), 219; also Dahir of Oct. 31, 1921, Art. 1, BO, 474 (Nov. 22, 1921), 1793 (modified by Dahir of Mar. 13, 1923, BO, 544 [Mar. 27, 1923], p. 394).

[29] Vizirial Decree of Mar. 14, 1923, BO, 544 (Mar. 27, 1923), 399.

[30] Colliez, p. 274.

[31] Paul Marty, "Le Collège musulman, Moulay Idris," RC, No. 1 (January, 1925), p. 5.

[32] Colliez, p. 275. In 1925 there were 70 students at the Collège Moulay Idris at Fez. Marty, "Le Collège musulman, Moulay Idris," p. 5.

[33] Dahir of Feb. 17, 1916, Art. 5, BO, 175 (Feb. 28, 1916), 218. The Conseil consisted of: the Grand Vizir's Délégué to the Direction Générale de l'Instruction Publique, as president; the Directeur Général de l'Instruction Publique, or his representative, as vice-president; the pacha of the city (Fez or Rabat), or his representative; the cadi of the city; the autorité locale de contrôle; three Moroccan notables (appointed by the Grand Vizir); and the director of the Collège, as secretary. See Dahir of Oct. 31, 1921, Art. 3 (modified by Dahir of Mar. 13, 1923). The three notables were selected from among the parents of the students at the Collège.

[34] Dahir of Oct. 31, 1921, Art. 4 (modified by Art. 2 of Dahir of Mar. 13, 1923).

gram of Franco-Muslim education there was coordination between the French authorities, represented by the Directeur Général de l'Instruction Publique, and the Makhzen, represented by the Grand Vizir's Délégué to the Direction Générale de l'Instruction Publique. For instance, the Délégué headed the Conseil de Perfectionnement.

The courses in the two Collèges Musulmans led to a Certificat d'Études Secondaires Musulmanes, after four years, and then after two more years to a Diplôme d'Études Secondaires Musulmanes,[35] the requirements being prescribed by law. For the Certificat d'Études Secondaires Musulmanes,[36] students were required to pass a series of final written examinations, varying in length from three to four hours each, which included two compositions, one in Arabic and one in French, a problem in mathematics and a problem in science, and a composition and its translation. They also had to pass an oral examination which included an explanation in Arabic of an Arabic text and an explanation in French of a French text; questions, in Arabic, on Muslim law; and questions, in French, on the sciences, mathematics, history, geography, and commerce.

The examination for the Diplôme d'Études Secondaires Musulmanes contained two sections, one general, and one on economics, each of which was divided into written and oral parts.[37] The written examination for the general section consisted of a literary Arabic composition, a French composition, mathematics and science problems, and a composition and its translation. The oral examination for the same section consisted of a literary and grammatical explanation in Arabic of an Arabic text, followed by questions on Arabic literature; an explanation in French of a French text; questions in French on history, geography, science, and the administrative organization of Morocco; and questions in Arabic on Muslim law. The written examination for the section on economics was similar to the written general exam, with a composition in French on economic studies (e.g., commerce, agriculture, or industry); a composition in Arabic on a similar subject; mathematics and science problems; and an Arabic-French translation of a composition and one from French to Arabic. The oral examination in economics consisted of a problem in French on accountancy and another on commercial technology; explanations in both Arabic and French of an economics problem; questions in French on economic geography and on general knowledge of European industry and agriculture; and questions in Arabic on Muslim law. As the examinations indicate, the French language was stressed through-

---

[35] Dahir of Feb. 17, 1916, Art. 4.

[36] Vizirial Decree of Sept. 4, 1920, Arts. 1 & 2, BO, 416 (Oct. 12, 1920), 1730. It modified all previous programs; e.g., Muslim law had previously been omitted in the oral examination for the Certificat.

[37] Vizirial Decree of May 21, 1919, Arts. 6–10, BO, 345 (June 2, 1919), p. 543.

out the courses, and a serious attempt was made to introduce the Moroccans to the twentieth century while maintaining Arabic and some traditional Islamic studies.

Since the Collèges Musulmans were usually the highest institutions of education attended by most of the upper-class Moroccans, it is important to go into more detail concerning the courses offered, so as to indicate something of the outlook and abilities of the pupils as a result of their new education.

The purpose of the French in setting up these two schools is shown in the following quotation from the Vizirial Decree of September 4, 1920:

> Secondary education designed for the Muslims must prepare the young Moroccans for a general cultural background which, without turning them away from their traditions, prepares them to accept, and become interested in, the various aspects of modern life.
>
> This educational program is prepared for an elite whom it must improve from the moral, intellectual, and material viewpoint and adapt to the new conditions of Moroccan life The motto, "L'École pour la Vie," must especially become theirs. It is not a question of giving to the young Moroccans in the Collèges a bookish education foreign to their social milieu, to their intellectual tastes, to the needs of their country, to the interests of the students themselves, or to their future. On the contrary, it is necessary to form in the young people of these establishments a good Muslim background, and to touch sufficiently upon European civilization in order that they may contribute to the normal development of their country towards its new destiny. . . .
>
> In consequence, the fundamental formula of the Collèges Musulmans is reduced to this: Muslim culture and French education. Muslim culture is taught by Moroccan Muslim teachers and is based on the study of Arabic language and literature, moral studies, and religious law; French education is taught by French teachers, and includes the study of the French language, etc.

The first four years of the six-year period of studies concentrated on general studies, leading to the examination for the Certificat d'Études Secondaires Musulmanes. In the final two years the students specialized in commerce or in a general section which prepared them for administrative work in the Makhzen, after which they were examined for the Diplôme d'Études.

Each cycle included the following subjects over a thirty-eight-hour class-week: Arabic and Islamic studies (in grammar, literature, composition, and law) and French studies (grammar and composition), in addition to translations, mathematics, science, French and Moroccan history, geography, cartography, commerce, typing, drawing, writing, and physical education.

In 1921 a badly needed department for student-teacher training was set up at the Collège Musulman of Rabat, called the Section Normale d'Élèves-Maîtres Musulmans.[38] Students with a Certificat d'Études Primaires Musulmanes were selected for the course and studied at the college for at least three years, after which they worked as assistant teachers for at least another five years.[39]

4. Higher Education

The French were dissatisfied with the teaching at the Qaraouiyne University at Fez. Its methods were completely out of date, and the curriculum was little more than a study of grammar and canon law. Being unable to reorganize this university themselves, since it was a religious institution, the French did the next best thing and created their own institutions of higher learning: the Institut des Hautes Études Marocaines and the Institut Scientifique Chérifien. The former offered a three-year course of study that would prepare students for administrative, judicial, academic, and commercial careers in Morocco; the Institut Scientifique made up for the serious deficiency in scientific studies.

The two institutions were supplemented, at a lower level, by the French lycées and collèges in Morocco, which Moroccans could also attend. By 1929, however, only forty-one Muslims were registered at the Lycée in Casablanca.[40]

a) *Qaraouiyne University.*—The Qaraouiyne University taught more or less the same subjects as it had before the Protectorate. It specialized in canon law (Chrâa) and Arabic literature and grammar. In 1938, F. Jabre bitterly complained about the great change since 1924 which had resulted in the loss of its traditional religious character.[41]

The Qaraouiyne during Lyautey's regime was still old-fashioned in its teaching methods. The academic day was usually divided into six periods, each lasting from one to one and a half hours. The curricu-

[38] Vizirial Decree of Mar. 19, 1921, Art. 1, *BO,* 442 (Apr. 12, 1921), 634. So popular did the education prove at the Collèges Musulmans that special adult courses were also given by the Collège Moulay Idris. Four to five courses were given weekly in the following subjects: (1) French and Arabic literature and grammar, and explanation of the works and authors; (2) contemporary history and current events; (3) Moroccan legislation and administration; and (4) a monthly course on hygiene, prophylaxis, and simple scientific explanations. See Paul Marty, "La nouvelle jeunesse intellectuelle du Maroc," *RC,* No. 5 (May, 1925), pp. 133–146.

[39] Decree of Mar. 19, 1921, Arts. 2 & 5. A Section Française was also opened for student-teachers interested in teaching in native primary schools in Morocco, at the École Normale d'Instituteurs de l'Enseignement des Indigènes d'Alger-Bouzaréa. Established by Vizirial Decree of Aug. 31, 1921, *BO,* 464 (Sept. 13, 1921), 1425.

[40] Colliez, p. 262.

[41] F. Jabre, "Dans le Maroc nouveau: le rôle d'une université islamique," *AHES,* X, No. 51 (May 31, 1938), 193–207.

lum consisted of courses in canon law and the principles of law, inheritance, theology, Prophetic tradition, mysticism, encomium of the Prophet, grammar and syntax, philosophy of grammar, prosody and poetry, logic and rhetoric.[42]

At the time of Lyautey's retirement the Qaraouiyne had a staff of 172 teachers, and an enrollment of about 700 students, 419 of whom were living in the various *medersas* (colleges); the remainder were Fassis, who lived at home.

b) Institut des Hautes Études.—An École Supérieure de Langue et Littérature Arabes et d'Études Dialectales Berbères was founded at Rabat as early as 1912; it was reorganized in 1920 and became the Institut des Hautes Études Marocaines in 1921.[43] The new objectives were intended to make the Institut a strong institution of higher learning, which the Qaraouiyne so clearly was not. These objectives were: (1) the development and maintenance of scientific research on Morocco and her people; (2) specialization in, and propagation of, a practical knowledge of the Arabic and Berber languages, and the geography, history, ethnography, and civilization of Morocco; (3) the preparation of Moroccan students for examinations necessary for higher or professional education.[44]

The École Supérieure was administered by a director, in conjunction with a Conseil de Direction which met once a month and was made up of the various directors of studies of the École, presided over by the director. When the École Supérieure was reorganized and became the Institut des Hautes Études Marocaines, the Conseil de Direction was replaced by a Conseil d'Administration, consisting of: the Directeur Général de l'Instruction Publique, des Beaux-Arts et des Antiquités, as its president; the Grand Vizir's Délégué à l'Enseignement, as vice-president; the Directeur of the Institut; the Directeur Adjoint of the Institut; the Directeur d'Études; and the Inspecteur de l'Enseignement Secondaire (Adjoint au Directeur Général de l'Instruction Publique), as its secretary.[45] The teachers themselves were to meet together once a term.

The Institut was divided into four sections: (1) Arabic language and Berber dialects, (2) Higher Moroccan studies, for senior students,

---

[42] Paul Marty, "L'université de Qaraouiyne," *RC*, No. 11 (November, 1924), pp. 329–353, esp. pp. 334 *et seq*. See also Michaux-Bellaire's "L'enseignement indigène au Maroc," in which the courses taught in 1911 are listed. They are very similar, with a few variations in texts and authors, though mathematics was taught at that time, but not by 1924.

[43] Residential Decree of Nov. 15, 1912, *BO*, 4 (Nov. 23, 1912), 22; Vizirial Decree of Sept. 18, 1921, *BO*, 469 (Oct. 18, 1921), 1633. See also Ismaël Hamet, "L'école supérieure de langue arabe," *F-M*, V, No. 26 (1921), 121–124.

[44] Vizirial Decree of Sept. 5, 1920, Art. 1, *BO*, 412 (Sept. 14, 1920), 1588.

[45] Vizirial Decree of Sept. 18, 1921, Arts. 1, 11, 12.

(3) Moroccan judicial and administrative studies, and (4) a school for interpreters. Courses were carefully stipulated by law. In the Department of Arabic, and Berber Dialects, examinations in Arabic and Berber dialects followed the traditional French pattern of written and oral work, and the students then sat for three degrees of examinations: the *certificat,* the *brevet,* and finally the *diplôme.*[46] The examinations covered the following material:

(*a*) Written examinations in Arabic:
   1) Certificat d'Arabe: an essay and a translation.
   2) Brevet d'Arabe: an essay in classical Arabic, a translation into classical Arabic, and an administrative Arabic translation.
   3) Diplôme d'Arabe: an essay in classical Arabic and a translation into classical Arabic.
(*b*) Written examinations in Berber Dialects:
   1) Certificat de Berbère: an essay in a Moroccan dialect (to be selected by the Institut) and a translation into the same dialect as the essay.
   2) Brevet de Berbère: an essay in a Moroccan Berber dialect (one selected by the Institut), a translation into the same dialect, with an analysis of Berber roots, and a translation of a colloquial Arabic text.
   3) Diplôme de Dialectes Berbères: an essay in each of two Moroccan Berber dialects (chosen by the Institut), a problem on comparative lexicography or on Berber grammar, and a classical Arabic translation.
(*c*) Oral examinations in Arabic:
   1) Certificat d'Arabe Parlé: the reading and translating at sight of a text in the Moroccan dialect of Arabic, and an exercise in oral interpretation.
   2) Brevet d'Arabe: an explanation of a literary text with an analysis of the grammatical forms, an explanation of an administrative text, and an exercise in oral interpretation.
   3) Diplôme d'Arabe: an explanation of, and commentary on, a prose text of a literary poem in classical Arabic; an explanation of, and commentary on, a Moroccan (Arabic) literary text; questions on Arabic dialects; and questions on the history and geography of North Africa, especially Morocco.
(*d*) Oral examinations in Berber Dialects:
   1) Certificat de Berbère Parlé: the reading and translating of a Moroccan Berber text, and an exercise in interpreting.
   2) Brevet de Berbère: an explanation of a Berber text, with questions on grammar; an oral composition including the translation of a French text into a Moroccan Berber dialect (chosen by the Institut); an exercise in interpreting; and a conversation in colloquial Moroccan Arabic.
   3) Diplôme de Dialectes Berbères: an explanation of a Berber text

[46] Vizirial Decree of July 23, 1921, Art. 2, *BO,* 459 (Aug. 9, 1921), 1240.

with a comparison of dialects, exercises in translating into various dialects, questions on the history and customs of the Moroccan Berbers, and a conversation in colloquial Arabic.

The Department of Higher Moroccan Studies, for senior students who had already been awarded their Brevet d'Arabe or Brevet de Berbère, prepared for the Diplôme Supérieur d'Études Marocaines.[47] The course of studies included Arabic dialects and classical and literary Arabic, Moroccan Berber dialects, Moroccan ethnography, Moroccan history and geography, and Berber and Muslim law.[48] To complete the course of studies and obtain the Diplôme Supérieur the student had to fulfill the following requirements: (1) the submission of a thesis on Morocco, agreed to by the Conseil; (2) an oral examination on the subject of the thesis; (3) an oral examination on one of the Arab authors taught in the department, chosen by the candidate, or else an examination on comparative Berber grammar (an oral examination in Arabic was required of candidates of Arabic literature or of Moroccan history and geography, and an oral examination in Berber was required of candidates of Berber dialects; candidates of ethnography could choose either Arabic or Berber); and (4) an oral examination on a subject taught in the department (chosen by the candidate).[49]

The courses in the Department of Moroccan Administrative and Judicial Studies covered a two-year period, and a Certificat d'Études Juridiques et Administratives Marocaines was awarded on completion.[50] In the first year courses were given in civil law (the first and second years of the Licence en Droit), administrative law, commercial or criminal law (at the candidate's choice), and colonial economy and legislation. The students had to pass examinations in these courses before they proceeded to the second-year studies. The curriculum of the second year comprised Moroccan civil legislation (personal status, obligations and contracts, judicial organization, and civil procedure), Moroccan administrative law, Muslim law (including Muslim judicial organization in Morocco), Berber customary law, and the history, geography, and ethnography of Morocco.

The course of study in the Department of Interpreter Training lasted two years, at the end of which students were given written

---

[47] Vizirial Decree of Sept. 5, 1920, *Annexe* II, Art. 1 and Art. 4 (added by Vizirial Decree of Apr. 9, 1921).

[48] Vizirial Decree of Sept. 5, 1920, *Annexe* II, Art. 1; Moroccan history and geography were added by Vizirial Decree of Apr. 9, 1921, Art. 1.

[49] Vizirial Decree of Sept. 5, 1920, *Annexe* II, Art. 2

[50] *Ibid.*, *Annexe* III (added by Vizirial Decree of May 24, 1922, *BO*, 501 [May 30, 1922], 893 and Arts. 2 & 3.

examinations, including a paper written in literary Arabic, a literary translation, an essay on administration, a Berber translation, and an essay in Berber. The oral examination consisted of an explanation of a classical Arabic text, an explanation of a modern Moroccan Arabic text, an Arabic translation, an explanation of a Berber text, a Berber translation, and questions on Moroccan history and geography.[51] If the student successfully passed both parts of the final examination, he was awarded a Certificat d'Aptitude à l'Interprétariat and was eligible for a job as official interpreter for the Civil Service.

c) *Institut Scientifique Chérifien.*—In 1920 the groundwork was prepared for another institution of higher learning to deal solely with secular, scientific subjects, none of which had been included in the curriculum of any other institution then existing in Morocco.[52] The Institut Scientific Chérifien, under the Direction Générale de l'Instruction Publique, was established in 1921 at Rabat.[53] It offered courses of study in comparative anatomy, anthropolgy, parasitology, botany, phytopathology, geology, mineralogy, astronomy, meteorology, physical geography, oceanography, applied physics, and chemistry. In January, 1925, a Comité de Direction et de Perfectionnement was set up, meeting monthly to draw up plans for research projects, in coordination with the Directeur of the Institut, and to supervise the results.[54]

d) *The École Militaire d'Élèves-Officiers Marocains.*—At the close of the First World War a special military academy was created for Moroccans called the École Militaire d'Élèves-Officiers Marocains. This institution was approved in September, 1918, and began functioning in July, 1919, in the Dar el-Beïda at Meknes.[55] It was responsible to the Direction des Affaires Indigènes et du Service des Renseignements. Its courses lasted two years, and the age of entry was between eighteen and twenty. Perhaps more than any other European or Muslim institution in Morocco, the École Militaire was highly exclusive. Its applicants were carefully screened; in the first year only fourteen candidates were admitted, and in the second year only ten of the thirty applicants were accepted.

[51] *Ibid.*, Annex IV, Art. 3.

[52] Vizirial Decree of Jan. 24, 1920, *BO*, 380 (Feb. 3, 1920), 182.

[53] Vizirial Decree of Mar. 6, 1921, *BO*, 437 (Mar. 8, 1921), 400 and Art. 2.

[54] Vizirial Decree of Jan. 10, 1925, *BO*, 640 (Jan. 27, 1925), 117. The Comité consisted of: the Directeur Général de l'Instruction Publique, des Beaux-Arts et des Antiquités, as its president; the Directeur Général de l'Agriculture, du Commerce et de la Colonisation, as its vice-president; the Directeur de l'Institut Scientifique Chérifien, as its secretary; the Inspecteur Adjoint au Directeur Général de l'Instruction Publique, as the Rapporteur des Travaux de l'Institut Scientifique; the Directeur Général des Travaux Publics, or his delegate; the Directeur Général des Services de Santé, or his delegate; the Présidents des Chambres d'Agriculture de Rabat et Casablanca; and a representative of the Conseil Supérieur du Commerce.

[55] Created by Vizirial Decree of Sept. 3, 1918. See Askri, "L'école militaire d'élvès-officiers marocains de Meknès," *AF*, No. 4 (Apr. 4, 1921), p. 109.

The course of studies, which included trips throughout Morocco, was divided into three sections, consisting of the French language, the history and geography of Morocco, France, and the colonies, and military studies.[56] Candidates passing the examinations at the end of the second year were commissioned as second lieutenants.

[56] *Ibid.* Cf. Eugène Guernier's assessment of French education in *La Berbérie, l'Islam et la France,* Vol. II (Paris, 1950), pp. 120–124.

5

JUDICIAL ORGANIZATION
OF MOROCCO

I. BEFORE THE PROTECTORATE

A. INTRODUCTION

The French Protectorate established in 1912 was to change radically the judicial organization of Morocco. To understand the significance of the French changes, it is first necessary to study the judicial system prior to 1912 in its traditional composition and role.

There were three distinct judicial organizations in the Sherifian Empire before the Protectorate: consular courts, rabbinical courts, and religious and customary Muslim courts. The consular courts exercised jurisdiction over the nationals and protégés of foreign states having consulates in Morocco. Their powers were regulated by the Convention of Madrid of 1880 and the Act of Algeciras of 1906.[1] The rabbinical courts were a traditional prerogative of the Jews in Morocco, who had been in the country since at least the third century A.D.[2] Civil and criminal matters concerning members of the Jewish population were handled by the Jewish judicial authorities. The French were to alter this in certain respects. The Muslim courts (a somewhat misleading term) included Muslim religious courts and Muslim courts of customary or secular law, as well as the tribal courts of Moroccans living beyond the reach of the Sultan's authority.

---

[1] Before 1912 Austria, Belgium, Italy, Portugal, Russia, and the United States each had one consular court in Morocco; England, France, and Germany had two consular courts each, one at Tangier, another at Casablanca; Spain had six, at Tangier, Larache, Rabat, Casablanca, Safi, and Mogador. Louis Holtz, *Traité de législation marocaine—droit public et droit privé du Protectorat* (Paris, 1914), p. 166.

[2] Nahum Slouschz, "Étude sur l'histoire des juifs et du Judaisme au Maroc," *AM*, IV, No. 2-3 (1905), 381.

B. TRADITIONAL MUSLIM JUDICIAL ORGANIZATION
IN MOROCCO BEFORE 1912

If a wealthy man steals, they say that he forgot (that the thing did not belong to him), and if a poor man forgets, they say he stole.

A MOROCCAN PROVERB

At the head of the Muslim community of Morocco was the Imam, or religious leader, who was considered the lieutenant of the Prophet and his representative on earth.[3] As the Imam, the Sultan administered the properties and protected the interests of the people. He was also the temporal sovereign of the community.[4] Theoretically, he was the absolute master of his subjects and could dispose of their persons or property at will so long as he did not violate Muslim law.[5] Because of his position as spiritual and temporal sovereign in the Sherifian Empire, the Sultan was also the highest "court" of appeals.

In principle, the *cadi* (pl. *coudat*) was the only religious judge. Throughout the centuries, however, his powers had been encroached upon by the Sultan's governors, or *oummal* (sing. *amel*), and by 1912 the cadi's authority was limited to certain civil matters.[6] The cadi, who was, technically speaking, the head of the local judicial organization, could in practice only judge criminal cases when requested to do so by the amel (pacha or caïd).[7] Before the Protectorate the cadi dealt with cases arising from inheritance, property, family matters, joint ownership, and at times with creditors' claims.[8] Such crimes as theft and murder were judged by the Makhzen, that is by the pacha or caïd of the city or locality where the crime had been committed, al-

---

[3] The Imam was the only supreme authority recognized by the Chrâa; see E. I. J. Rosenthal, *Political Thought in Medieval Islam* (Cambridge, 1962), pp. 22–23; see also Ibn Khaldoun, *Prolégomènes d'Ibn Khaldoun*, trans. de Slane (Paris, 1863), 1st Part, p. 468; and A. Péretié, "Organisation judiciaire au Maroc," *RMM*, XIII, No. 3 (1911), 510.

[4] For, ". . . there are no two swords, a spiritual and a temporal, in Islam"; ". . . there is of course no separation between Church and State." Rosenthal, p. 23.

[5] E. Michaux-Bellaire, "L'islam et l'état marocain," *RMM*, VIII, No. 7–8 (1909), 313.

[6] Péretié, p. 511. In principle the cadi remained competent in all matters; Holtz, p. 163.

[7] L. Mercier, "L'administration marocaine à Rabat," *AM*, VII (1906), 393–394. See also Holtz, p. 164. For a full study of the qualifications required of the cadi and other judicial officials, as well as the historical background of these offices see *Prolégomènes d'Ibn Khaldoun*. Émile Tyan discusses the religious and judicial status of the cadi in detail in his excellent work, *Histoire de l'organisation judiciaire en pays d'Islam* (Leiden, 1960), ch. 2.

[8] Péretié, p. 516. The Makhzen usually withdrew such claims from the cadi's competence.

though other matters were referred to the cadi when complications arose over a religious point. Formerly, the cadis were appointed by the High Cadi of Fez (the Cadi el-Djemaa), but by the turn of the twentieth century, the High Cadi's role was limited to proposing to the Sultan the nomination of the cadis of the large cities and ports, whom the Sultan appointed by dahir.[9]

The cadis of the smaller towns and localities in the Bled el-Makhzen were appointed by the Sultan after nomination by the local governor.[10] The governor would send his nominee to the Dar el-Makhzen (Government House, the main administrative office) at Fez, the nominee accompanying his request for the office with a small sum of money for the Sultan's entourage; the Sultan would confirm the appointment. The cadis of the interior were thus more or less responsible to the local governor, which further weakened their independence. Another weakening factor was that, although in theory the cadis were to be paid from the income from Habous property, in reality this was rarely so and they were often forced to accept gifts from litigants. Legally, cadis had no right to remuneration from the parties to a lawsuit, except when acting as executor of an estate.[11]

In the areas outside the Bled el-Makhzen, where the Sultan's authority was not recognized, or was recognized only in part, the position was different. In the Djebala region, where the Sultan still had some vestiges of his once considerable power, the tribal assembly of notables (the djemaa) nominated the cadi, although the nomination was publicly announced by the tribe's caïd; and the djemaa had the power to execute the cadi's judgments.[12]

In the Bled es-Siba the Berber tribes had greater independence than any other group within the Sherifian Empire. Here not only was the Sultan's temporal authority completely ignored, but also

[9] *Ibid.* This was true of Meknes and Rabat, e.g. the nomination for the cadi-ship of a city, however, was made by the pacha or caïd of that city, who forwarded his nomination to the High Cadi of Fez, who in turn forwarded it to the Sultan. The High Cadi was also known as the Cadi el-Coudat. G. Salmon, "L'administration marocaine à Tanger," *AM*, I (1904), 3. See also Michaux-Bellaire and G. Salmon, "El-Qçar El-Kebir: une ville de province au Maroc septentrional," *AM*, II, No. 2 (1904), 36 *et seq;* Tyan, pp. 128 *et seq.* The applicant for the cadi-ship had to be (1) male, (2) intelligent, (3) free (not a slave), (4) a Muslim, (5) an honorable person, (6) mentally competent, and (7) qualified in jurisprudence. Tyan, pp. 160–170.

[10] Péretié, pp. 516–517. This happened in El Kçar El Kebir. According to Péretié, the man nominated to the cadi-ship by the governor was often a relative who obtained the governor's favorable mention by giving him a *hediya* (gift).

[11] Mercier, p. 395. Usually 2 percent of the entire value of the estate went to him; the two adoul who assisted in the inventory were also paid from the same source.

[12] The Sultan could still nominate the caïd or sheikh of a Djebala tribe, but these officials held very little power. See Péretié, p. 527.

his spiritual authority.[13] These tribes often had cadis, but the complete Muslim jurisdiction of the cadis was far from effective, the tribal assemblies dealing more or less with any judicial matter, as well as punishments.[14] A special meeting of tribal notables heard all complaints and claims made by tribal members. These notables worked on a circuit basis, traveling from area to area, to mete out justice. In some cases there was also a special official called the *caïd er-rebi* who saw that pasturage rights were respected.[15] Business disputes, murders, and other crimes were settled through mutually agreed upon *azref*, or arbitration, by one judge.[16]

In the Bled el-Makhzen every community of any size had at least one mufti to help the cadi reach his verdict. As the head of the local judicial organization, the cadi appointed his adoul and the mufti.[17] In the Ottoman Empire, however, official muftis were appointed by a high-ranking official in the central government, the Sehü 'l-Islâm.[18]

C. MUSLIM JUDICIAL PROCEDURE [19]

The procedure in cases heard before the cadi in the Chrâa Court was as follows:

A complaint was lodged with the cadi,[20] and if the defendant wished to avoid imprisonment he had to deposit a sum of money analogous to bail bond (or *damen oudjouh*) as a guarantee that he would remain

---

[13] In these areas the Sultan was only recognized in his titular capacity as Imam; see Mohamed Lahbabi's interesting discussion in *Le gouvernement marocain à l'aube du XXe siècle* (Rabat, 1958), pp. 41–45.

[14] Péretié, p. 529. Some tribes had no cadi and followed local customary law as opposed to the Chrâa; the French were later to make much of this indigenous Berber characteristic.

[15] E. Michaux-Bellaire, "Les coutumes berbères dans les tribus arabes," *RMM*, IX, No. 10 (1909), 234.

[16] An anonymous article translated by G. Salmon, "Les institutions berbères," *AM*, I, No. 1 (1904), 127 *et seq*. In cases of murder, the arbiter handled the matter as follows: the family of the victim and that of the murderer were summoned before the arbiter. The latter debated with them in order to establish a *diyyah*, or blood price, which was to be paid to the victims. After agreement as to the amount, the sum was handed over to the victim's family and the opposing parties left amicably. Péretié, however, noted that among certain Rif Berbers, e.g., the Zenata, the murderer was usually executed, and interminable vendettas often resulted. In an *azref* settlement, the relatives of the victim, having accepted the diyyah, sometimes also took revenge and killed the murderer, whereupon the entire amount of the diyyah had to be returned, as opposed to the position in Arab tribes where the diyyah would have been kept.

[17] Mercier, p. 394.

[18] H. A. R. Gibb and Harold Bowen, *Islamic Society and the West*, Vol. I (London, 1957), Part 2, ch. 10, p. iii.

[19] For a study of this, see Péretié, pp. 517–523.

[20] Traditionally in the Middle East the cadi held his court in a mosque or *medersa* (school). Tyan, p. 279.

in the vicinity in which the trial was taking place. The plaintiff could refuse to grant this type of bail; if this happened, the defendant might pay a second amount and if it too was refused, a third and still higher amount was paid, which the plaintiff had to accept. A second type of bail was the *damen mouadjaba* which the defendant also had to pay to guarantee execution of the sentence; as in the case of the former bail, the third or highest amount offered might only be accepted. The cadi could excuse the defendant from payment of these two bails if he felt that the defendant's character alone presented sufficient guarantee. The defendant could also present a counterclaim and require that the plaintiff present him with a damen oudjouh and a damen mouadjaba.

The plaintiff, like the defendant, could defend himself before the cadi, or else hire a lawyer, or *oukil*, to do this.[21] The plaintiff and his lawyer then went before two notaries (*adoul*) to present his case, the lawyer repeating his client's claims and supplying the necessary judicial forms. This procedure was called the *taqyid el-maqal*. After the adoul had recorded all the facts they affixed their signatures to the document they had just recorded.

The defendant then asked the cadi for a copy, or *neskha*, of the taqyid el-maqal and could also ask the cadi for a recess in which he might consult a mufti, so as to discover the best means of answering the charges while conforming with the Chrâa. Later he, with his oukil, went before the adoul to answer the charges and to have his side of the story officially recorded. The plaintiff could now ask for a copy of the defendant's reply, and so this process would be repeated, the defendant continuing to answer the charges brought before him until one of the parties could no longer afford to go on; for each taqyid el-maqal required immediate payment of a fee to the adoul, and the mufti had to be paid for every *fetoua*, or legal opinion, that he drew up.

When these preliminary steps and documents had been completed, the cadi was ready to pronounce judgment. After judgment had been pronounced the condemned party could ask for a copy of the sentence, and again consult a mufti and return with yet another fetoua and present it to the cadi.[22] The cadi could either reply to the mufti's fetoua and stand by the original sentence, or find the arguments of the fetoua valid and pass a new sentence. In either case, depending on who was placed in the defensive position, that party could then

[21] The *oukil* was not a lawyer in the Western sense of the word, but only a type of high-ranking clerk, familiar with certain judicial formalities. He had more power than one possessing a power of attorney, but far less than a European or American advocate. See Tyan, p. 262.

[22] Émile Tyan discusses the position of the mufti in detail. Tyan, pp. 219 *et seq.*

request a copy of the latest judgment and again consult a mufti. This would continue until the cadi eventually agreed that the mufti's arguments conformed with the Chrâa. One of the parties could renounce any further action because he felt that the matter was not worth any further expenditure or because he could not afford to continue. Muslim justice in such a case far too often meant a triumph of wealth rather than of justice, although the ability of being able to appeal one's case immediately after the verdict had been given certainly had its advantages over lengthy Western procedures.

When an important case was heard—for example, concerning real estate—the cadi could, before giving his final verdict, request the Sultan (or at Tangier, his naïb) to summon a *medjlis*, or council, which was usually made up of four oulama; the cadi would then pronounce judgment according to the opinion of the medjlis. In this case, an appeal against the sentence could only be made by laying the case before the representative of the Sultan, which was usually what happened (at Tangier) when Europeans were involved in a lawsuit.[23]

II. FRENCH JUDICIAL ORGANIZATION, 1912–1925

> Permit me to draw your attention to the urgency of the proposed [judicial] reform. It is, in my opinion, the first reform that we must make in Morocco; in fact it is the basic condition necessary in order to abolish the capitulations regime and, therefore, the basic step necessary for the administrative reorganization of Morocco, the care and responsibility for which the Government has entrusted me.
>
> LYAUTEY, TO THE MINISTER OF FOREIGN AFFAIRS,
> *March 19, 1913*

> Already your red robes are following in the path of our victorious arms.
> —LYAUTEY, *Rabat, October 15, 1913*

A. Problems Faced by the French

A fairly thorough reform of Muslim and Jewish court systems was desperately needed and Lyautey and his officials had to face the usual problem of weaning the Moroccans away from traditional ideas and institutions; this was accomplished, however, with less trouble than one might have expected, in part by keeping many old institutions and titles. In addition the French had to set up a vast new French judicial system with laws, regulations, and policies specifically for Morocco, and Lyautey had to find well-qualified lawyers and judges. French courts were, of course, entirely under French control, but Muslims held the major and minor posts (even at the ministerial level) in both

[23] This conformed to Art. XI of the Convention of Madrid.

Moroccan religious and secular courts, although they were subject to French control in varying degrees.

In 1913, a year after Morocco became a French Protectorate, the first machinery for the judicial reorganization of Morocco was put into operation (See fig. 13).[24] Under the Protectorate consular jurisdictions, with two exceptions, were done away with; the competence of the Muslim courts was redefined and their procedure was reformed; a totally new judicial organization was introduced for Europeans; and even the rabbinical courts were altered to some extent.[25]

FIGURE 13

JUDICIAL ORGANIZATION UNDER THE PROTECTORATE,
1912–1925

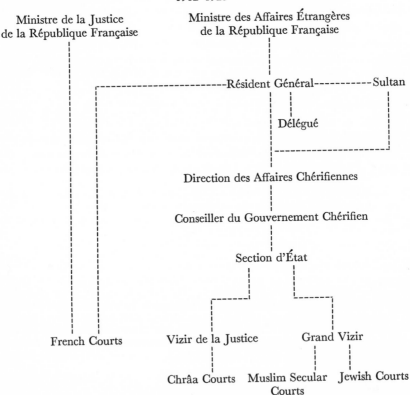

[24] For a detailed study of the entire organization, see Stéphane Berge, *La justice française au Maroc—organisation et pratique* (Paris, 1917); see also J. Caillé, *L'organisation judiciaire au Maroc* (Paris, 1948). For the original outlines of the organization, see Général Lyautey (ed.), *Rapport général sur la situation du Protectorat au Maroc au 31 juillet 1914* (Rabat, 1916), Part 3, ch. 1.

[25] E. de Viguera Franco briefly discusses the French, Spanish, and Moroccan judicial organizations in "Sistemas orgánico-judiciales en Marruecos," *CEA*, No. 8 (1949), pp. 9–54. See also Tomás García Figueras' work, *España y su protectorado en Marruecos (1912–1956)* (Madrid, 1957), esp. Part II, Ch. A, "Justicia."

B. French Judicial Organization, Jurisdiction, and Competence

French courts were set up in the Protectorate for the first time in August, 1913.[26] Three types of courts were created: Tribunaux de Paix, Tribunaux de Première Instance, and a Cour d'Appel.[27] These courts were to deal with French nationals or "justiciables," and had no power over Moroccans unless a French national was involved. When French courts (Tribunaux de Première Instance and the Cour d'Appel) heard real estate cases involving French and Moroccan nationals, two Muslim assessors could be added to the court, but they had a consultative voice only.[28]

Article 4 of the Dahir of August, 1913, reserved for Moroccan Muslim or Jewish courts cases pertaining to personal status and inheritance. French courts were declared competent to judge Moroccans in the following circumstances: (1) when crimes were committed by Moroccan subjects against Frenchmen, Europeans, or protégés of the various European powers;[29] or (2) when crimes committed within French jurisdictions by Moroccan subjects, with Frenchmen or protégés as accomplices. Article 4 was made all-inclusive so as to qualify any Moroccan acting against any Frenchman, French law, or French institution. Nationals of countries that had renounced their former consular jurisdictions in Morocco, or had never had consular jurisdiction in Morocco, were now also under French jurisdiction.[30]

[26] Established by Dahir of Aug. 12, 1913, *BO,* 46 (Sept. 12, 1913), 9. Lyautey considered judicial reform to be of primary importance. M. Landry, the Public Prosecutor for the French Republic at Oran, was given the task of outlining the entire judicial organization in French Morocco. This was accomplished early in 1913, and was based mostly on experience in French colonies. On March 19, 1913, Lyautey sent a report to the Foreign Minister in which he presented the plans drawn up by Landry and asked that a commission of jurisconsults be set up to examine and elaborate on Landry's outline. The above-mentioned Dahir of 1913 was the first result of their achievement. The Commission, which was drawn up by the Foreign Minister, consisted of MM. L. Renault, Hebraux, Romieu, Boulloche, S. Berge, Grünebaum-Ballin, Geuffre de Lapradelle, Chardenet, G. Teissier, Cruchon-Dupeyrat, Jean Labbé, Gauthier, Collavet, and Kammerer. Also taking part were MM. de Saint-Aulaire (Délégué à la Résidence) and Paul Tirard (Secrétaire Général du Proctectorat). They met for the first time on May 7, 1913. Lyautey, *Rapport général,* p. 220.

[27] Dahir of Aug. 12, 1913, Art. 1.

[28] *Ibid.,* Art. 3.

[29] This was modified by Art. 6 of Dahir of May 16, 1930 (the Berber Dahir), which gave French courts full jurisdiction for all crimes committed in *"pays berbères."*

[30] Only Great Britain and the United States maintained consular jurisdictions in Morocco after 1912. The position with regard to company law in Morocco should also be clarified. French courts alone were competent to handle civil and commercial cases by or against companies, notably the *sociétés anonymes* and the *sociétés à responsabilité limitée,* whether they were French, Moroccan, or foreign. (See Art. 4 of Dahir of Aug. 11, 1922, and Art. 7 of Dahir of Sept. 1, 1926.) This

1. Tribunaux de Paix

The first three Tribunaux de Paix were opened in 1914 and by 1925 their number had increased to twelve. These courts were competent to handle the following: (1) lawsuits and cases relating to (chattel) property, civil and commercial, involving up to 500 francs in value without right of appeal, and up to 1,000 francs in value with right of appeal (to a Tribunal de Première Instance); (2) cases involving up to 500 francs without right of appeal, and up to 3,000 francs with right of appeal in the following: travel and transport, leases and repairs, disputes involving civil damages to property regarding work, property, taxes, etc; (3) authorization of married women, or minors, to enter into a litigation when necessary; (4) criminal cases relating to (a) minor offenses dealt with in France by summary courts, (b) offenses punishable by fine only, such as vagrancy or mendicity, (c) an offense punishable by up to two years' imprisonment.[31] In criminal cases the Tribunaux de Paix added assessors to the bench who had a deliberate voice in the verdict and sentence.[32]

The Tribunaux de Paix consisted of: a Juge de Paix, one or more Juges Suppléants Rétribués, and a Juge Suppléant (or if this was not possible, a member of the judicial police appointed by the Procureur Général, to act as public prosecutor).[33] During Lyautey's administration there were twelve of these courts—two in Casablanca, two in Rabat, and one each in Oujda, Safi, Fez, Mazagan, Mogador, Marrakesh, Meknes, and Kenitra.[34] Circuit sessions of these courts in the neighboring areas within their jurisdiction were also provided for in 1920,[35]

---

was the case even when both parties were Moroccans. In penal matters, however, infractions against companies were held by French or Moroccan jurisdictions according to the general regulation of penal competence in Morocco. In principle, Moroccans were to be tried by Makhzen courts, Frenchmen and foreigners by French courts, regardless of the nationality of the victim. But Art. 6 of the Dahir on judicial organization quoted above conflicted with this. See Paul Decroux, *Les sociétés au Maroc, zone française—zone tangéroise: statut juridique et fiscal* (Paris, 1950), e.g., pp. 123–125.

[31] See Art. 9, Dahir of Aug. 12, 1913; S. Berge, pp. 137–144; J. Goulven, *Traité d'économie et de législation marocaines* (Paris, 1921), II, 66–68.

[32] Art. 9, Dahir of Aug. 12, 1913.

[33] Dahir of Nov. 20, 1922.

[34] The first five Tribunaux de Paix listed (by city) were established by Art. 18 of Dahir of Aug. 12, 1913; the next three by Dahir of Feb. 1, 1914, *BO,* 70 (Feb. 27, 1914); and the last two plus two additional ones at Casablanca and Rabat by Dahir of Nov. 20, 1922. The Tribunal de Paix at Casablanca was at least twice as busy as any of the others; in the calendar year 1913–1914 it heard 2,327 cases, and by 1915–1916 the number had increased to 4,327 cases, as compared with only 216 and 454 for the same years at Marrakesh. By 1915–1916 most of the cases in most areas were criminal. See Berge, pp. 797–802.

[35] Art. 3 of Dahir of Sept. 1, 1920, *BO,* 421 (Nov. 16, 1920), 1929. The precise jurisdiction of each of the twelve Tribunaux was announced in December, 1920, Art. 1 of Dahir of Dec. 29, 1920, *BO, 429* (Jan. 11, 1921), 35.

and each of the Tribunaux de Paix was placed under the jurisdiction of one of three Tribunaux de Première Instance, at Casablanca, Rabat, and Oujda.[36]

Under the Tribunal de Première Instance of Casablanca were the Tribunaux de Paix of Casablanca, Mazagan, Safi, Mogador, and Marrakesh; of Rabat, the Tribunaux de Paix of Rabat, Meknes, Fez, and Kenitra; the Tribunal de Première Instance of Oujda had only the Oujda Tribunal de Paix under its jurisdiction.

2 . Tribunaux de Première Instance

The three Tribunaux de Première Instance established under Lyautey between 1913 and 1917 were authorized to handle (1) appeals from the Tribunaux de Paix; (2) lawsuits and appeals (including chattel property) involving from 1,000 to 3,000 francs in value, and real estate cases when up to 120 francs in income was concerned; (3) appeals (and with no further appeal) taken against decisions of consular courts; suits or cases involving public administrators or public administration; and also any cases involving the personal status of Algerian Muslims; and (4) serious criminal cases involving imprisonment of more than two years. In criminal cases six assessors were added to the bench, all having a deliberative voice in the verdict and punishment.[37] The Tribunal de Première Instance of Casablanca was divided into three chambers and made up of the following members: a president, two vice-presidents, eight Juges (two of whom were Juges d'Instruction, or examining magistrates), three Juges Suppléants, a Procureur Commissaire du Gouvernement (i.e., public prosecutor), and two Substituts (i.e., for the Procureur).[38] The Tribunal de Première Instance of Rabat was divided into two chambers, consisting of: a president, five Juges (one of whom was the Juge d'Instruction), two Juges Suppléants, a Procureur, and a Substitut. The Tribunal de Première Instance of Oujda was composed of: a president, three Juges (one acting as Juge

[36] Art. 3, Dahir of Dec. 29, 1920, as modified by Art. 2 of Dahir of Mar. 3, 1923, BO, 543 (Mar. 20, 1923), 367.

[37] Art. 17 of Dahir of Aug. 12, 1913. This article was modified and added to by Dahir of June 10, 1924, BO, 613 (July 22, 1924), 1133. The Tribunal of Rabat was established by Dahir of Dec. 22, 1916, BO, 228–229 (Mar. 5 and 12, 1917), 266. The Tribunaux of Casablanca and Oujda were created by Art. 17 of Dahir of Aug. 12, 1913; the Tribunal de Première Instance of Marrakesh was not created until 1926 (by Dahir of July 2, 1926). Two more were created later. The Tribunal de Première Instance at Casablanca was always much the busiest, with a total of 809 cases heard in 1913–1914, as compared with only 273 at Oujda. Most of the cases heard at both Tribunaux were commercial. See Berge, pp. 144–145, 794–797; Goulven, II, 68–69.

[38] As modified by Dahir of June 10, 1924. (Originally in Art. 17 of Dahir of Aug. 12, 1913.) The third chamber dealt with real property matters only and is discussed later in this chapter. Dahir of June 10, 1924, as it modifies Art. 11 of Dahir of Sept. 1, 1920.

d'Instruction), a Juge Suppléant, a Procureur, and a Substitut. The three Tribunaux de Première Instance were under the jurisdiction of the Cour d'Appel.[39]

3. Cour d'Appel

The Cour d'Appel sat at Rabat and was established in 1913.[40] As the highest court of the land it heard all appeals taken against decisions on civil and criminal cases by the Tribunaux de Première Instance. It was composed of: a Premier Président, a Président de Chambre, four Conseillers, the Procureur Général, and a Substitut.[41] The court could be divided into chambers at the request of the Premier Président, and decisions were reached by three judges.[42]

All judges for the three types of courts were appointed by the President of the French Republic and were nominated by the French Ministers of Justice and Foreign Affairs.[43] The French judicial organization of the Protectorate was under the dual authority of the French Ministries of Justice (directly) and Foreign Affairs (indirectly, via Lyautey).

4. Circuit Courts

Circuit sessions during Lyautey's administration were begun in 1914 and extended to seven localities by the time of his resignation in 1925. These circuit sessions were Tribunaux de Paix and heard civil, commercial, and criminal cases.[44]

The first session was authorized in 1914 for Kenitra and was a circuit session originating from Rabat and sitting on the last Friday of each month. A circuit session was authorized for Ber-Rechid in 1918;[45] it was held by a Tribunal de Paix from Casablanca once each month. The Tribunal de Paix from Oujda held sessions in Berkane from 1919, once a month.[46] A circuit was authorized for Meknes in the summer of 1920 by the Tribunal de Paix of Fez and was convened

[39] Art. 3, Dahir of Mar. 3, 1923.

[40] Art. 1, Dahir of Aug. 12, 1913; see Berge, p. 145.

[41] Art. 16, Dahir of Aug. 12, 1913. During its first year (1913–1914) the Cour d'Appel heard 73 cases, the majority of which were criminal, and it was the criminal category that tended to predominate in the years to follow; Berge, p. 793. The number of Conseillers gradually increased (see Dahirs of July 23, 1926, and July 23, 1927) so that by 1927 there were six Conseillers and also an Avocat Général; Arthur Girault, *Principes de colonisation et de législation coloniale*, Vol. V (Paris, 1928), p. 311.

[42] Art. 16, Dahir of Aug. 12, 1913.

[43] Decree and Dahir of Sept. 7, 1913, Art. 2, *BO*, 46 (Sept. 12, 1913), 8.

[44] Ordonnance of the Premier Président of the Cour d'Appel of July 4, 1914.

[45] Ordonnance of Mar. 27, 1918, *BO*, 285 (Apr. 8, 1918), 346.

[46] Ordonnance of Nov. 7, 1919, *BO*, 369 (Nov. 17, 1919), 1317.

once a week.[47] In 1921 the circuit held at Ber-Rechid was extended to Settat, and likewise the hearings at Kenitra were extended.[48] In 1922 a circuit for Taza, originating from Fez, was set up, and the same year a circuit from Oujda reached Taourirt.[49] In 1924 a circuit from Casablanca was set up for Oued-Zem, thereby completing the development of the circuit court system under Lyautey's administration.[50]

5. Assessors

Judicial assessors (assesseurs) were employed under two circumstances: when property cases were heard by a Tribunal de Première Instance or the Cour d'Appel, and when criminal cases were tried in a Tribunal de Première Instance.

When a case arose involving real estate and was in the jurisdiction of a Tribunal de Première Instance or the Cour d'Appel, these courts added two Muslim assessors, although they held a consultative voice only.[51]

In criminal cases six assessors were added to the Tribunal de Première Instance.[52] If the accused were all of foreign nationality, three French assessors and three foreign assessors were added to the bench. If the accused was a native, three Frenchmen and three Moroccan assessors would be called to sit in on the case. If the accused were foreigners and natives, three French assessors, two foreign assessors, and one native assessor were called in. These six assessors held a deciding voice in the verdict and sentence.

6. Administration of the Judicial Organization

The Premier Président of the Cour d'Appel of Rabat was the administrative head of the entire French judicial organization in Morocco, with the exception of the public prosecutors. His status was roughly equivalent to that of a Directeur Général in the civil administration.[53] He had a dual function as judge and administrator. All other judges ranked beneath him, regardless of the court over which they presided. The Premier Président discussed his work and all questions pertaining to the French judicial organization of Morocco with the Procureur Général, or Attorney General, and acted in accordance with the latter's advice. The Premier Président supervised all

[47] Ordonnance of June 15, 1920, BO, 402 (July 6, 1920), 1130.
[48] Dahir of July 25, 1921, BO, 459 (Aug. 9, 1921), 1226, and Ordonnance of Sept. 20, 1921, BO, 466 (Sept. 27, 1921), 1507.
[49] Ordonnance of Oct. 9, 1922, BO, 521 (Oct. 17, 1922), 1522.
[50] Ordonnance of Mar. 6, 1924, BO, 596 (Mar. 25, 1924), 562.
[51] Dahir of Aug. 12, 1913 (BO, 46 [Sept. 12, 1913], 9), §1, Art. 3 (modified by Art. 2 of Dahir of Sept. 1, 1920).
[52] Ibid., §3 (modified by Dahirs of Aug. 22, 1923, and Feb. 17, 1923), Arts. 7 & 8.
[53] Dahir of Sept. 1, 1920, BO, 421 (Nov. 16, 1920), 1927. Arts. 2, 3, 6.

the other judges, regardless of their rank or seniority. The Procureur Général was in charge of all public prosecution throughout the French Zone of the Protectorate, and both he and the Premier Président had to notify each other if they discovered irregularities in the other's jurisdiction. Thus the French judicial organization was subject to a sort of dual control by the Premier Président and the Procureur Général. Both officials also had to supervise the recruitment and discipline of the Secretariats and Interpretariats.[54] The Premier Président and the Procureur Général sent regular reports to the French Minister of Justice as well as to the Resident General.[55]

7. Chambre du Contentieux de l'Immatriculation

The Chambre du Contentieux de l'Immatriculation, the third chamber of the Tribunal de Première Instance of Casablanca, had a very exclusive role to play in the judicial organization of the Protectorate.[56] It dealt with matters relating to real property and its registration, confiscation, and the like, and was closely linked with the Conservation de la Propriété Foncière (see ch. 3).[57] It was made up of a vice-president and four Juges. These members were chosen from among the members of the Tribunal de Premiére Instance by the Premier Président of the Cour d'Appel.

In the Tribunaux de Première Instance other than that at Casablanca, the Premier Président could, if necessary—usually at the suggestion of the president of the Tribunal in question and on the advice of the Procureur Général—order one or more judges to examine certain real estate matters for that locality.

8. Special Courts

There were other special French courts which were convened when necessary but did not form normal components of the judicial system.[58] The Conseils de Guerre, or Courts-Martial, had jurisdiction over the military personnel, Frenchmen of civil status, natives of the Moroccan auxiliary corps of the French Army, and more or less anyone else within an unpacified area.[59] A Commission Arbitrale des Litiges

---

[54] *Ibid.*, Art. 4. See below.

[55] *Ibid.*, Art. 7.

[56] *Ibid.*, Art. 11, as modified by Dahir of June 10, 1924.

[57] Dahir of June 10, 1924.

[58] It should be pointed out that, unlike the Conseils de Préfecture and the Conseil d'État of France, the French courts in Morocco could not censure or annul the acts of the administrative authority in the Protectorate (Art. 8, Dahir of Aug. 12, 1913). See also P.-Louis Rivière, *Traités, codes et lois du Maroc* (Paris, 1925), II, 473.

[59] By the early 1920's there were Courts-Martial at Casablanca, Fez, Rabat, Meknes, and Oujda (each consisting of five judges and a reporting government commissioner). See Holtz, *Traité de législation marocaine*, p. 176, and especially Goulven, II, 487–491, where the subject is covered in some detail.

Miniers was set up in January, 1914, and a Tribunal des Pensions was created in 1923.[60]

9. Secretariats, Lawyers, Interpreters, and Experts

A Secretariat was set up with each French court of the empire.[61] It supplied each court with its clerks, notaries, accountants, and so on, who carried out various clerical duties, including summoning, executing orders, and collecting court fees. The Secretariats of the public prosecutor of each court were an entirely different organization, under the ultimate authority of the Procureur Général.[62]

A professional organization for lawyers, the Ordre des Avocats, was founded in January, 1924.[63] It acted as the bar association of the Protectorate, though on a governmental basis. This Ordre was established with the Cour d'Appel and a branch of it was maintained with each of the Tribunaux de Première Instance, except that of Rabat. The purpose of this association was to enroll lawyers whose ethics and qualifications were approved by the government, and to maintain the moral standards demanded in the legal profession. The Ordre listed the activities to which the lawyers were restricted, if they wished to practice law in Morocco. Each local bar was administered by a Conseil de l'Ordre des Avocats, consisting of from five to fifteen members (depending upon the number of lawyers in each organization).

The Organic Dahir of August 12, 1913, also drew up lists of judicial interpreters, working with the Cour d'Appel and the other courts, and made arrangements for providing judicial experts when needed.[64] The organization of the corps of interpreters was only fully established in 1920 and was administered by the Chef du Service de l'Interprétariat Judiciare.[65]

III. MUSLIM COURTS UNDER THE PROTECTORATE, 1912–1925

The term "Muslim" is applied in this section both to the Moroccan Muslim religious courts and to the Moroccan secular courts. The religious courts in Morocco were not solely Muslim, because the Moroccan Jews continued to have their rabbinical courts.

Muslim courts were mentioned only indirectly in the Sherifian

[60] Dahirs of Jan. 19, 1914, *BO*, 66 (Jan. 30, 1914), 63, and Jan. 16, 1923. There was also a Cour de Pensions at Rabat for appeals; see Art. 1.
[61] Art. 26 of §V of Dahir of Aug. 12, 1913.
[62] Dahir of Mar. 18, 1921, *BO*, 440 (Mar. 29, 1921).
[63] Dahir of Jan. 10, 1924, *BO*, 586 (Jan. 15, 1924), 48, Arts. 1, 9, 10.
[64] Arts. 45 & 46 of Dahir of Aug. 12, 1913.
[65] Dahir of Feb. 20, 1920, *BO*, 384 (Mar. 2, 1924), 348 and Art. 2.

Firman (Edict) of October, 1912, by which the Makhzen ministries were organized.[66] A Moroccan Vizir de la Justice was appointed who was to be under the authority of the Conseiller du Gouvernement Chérifien (see fig. 14); in 1920 he automatically came under the authority of the Direction des Affaires Chérifiennes.[67]

The Muslim religious courts were under the Vizirat de la Justice, and the secular courts were placed under the Grand Vizir.[68]

FIGURE 14

MUSLIM JUDICIAL ORGANIZATION IN 1925

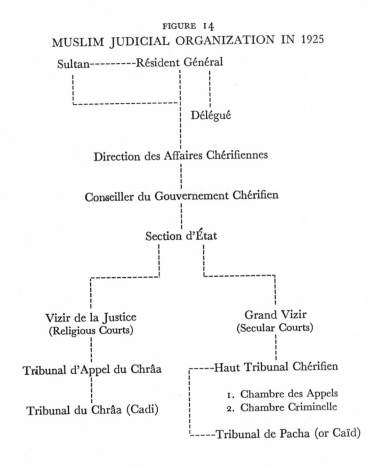

[66] Sherifian Firman of Oct. 31, 1912, *BO*, 3 (Nov. 15, 1912), 17.

[67] *Ibid.*, Arts. 1 & 5; Dahir of July 24, 1920, *BO*, 407 (Aug. 10, 1920), 1366. The term Vizir is used so as to disinguish the Moroccan Minister of Justice from the Minister of Justice of the French Republic. The Vizir de la Justice was one of the four vizirs under the Direction des Affaires Chérifiennes. See ch. 2; also André de Laubadère, *Les réformes des pouvoirs publics au Maroc—le gouvernement, l'administration, la justice* (Paris, 1949), pp. 29 and 74 *et seq.*; Goulven, *Traité d'économic* II, §I.

[68] Résidence Générale de la République Française au Maroc, *Renaissance du Maroc: dix ans du Protectorat, 1912–1922* (Rabat, n.d. [1922]), p. 117.

A. RELIGIOUS COURTS

The position of religious courts in Muslim life was in no way challenged during Lyautey's régime.[69] The cadi was kept as the judge in matters of Muslim family law, inheritance, and the like, and his decisions were still to be based on the Chrâa, interpreted if necessary with the aid of the mufti's fetoua, as had been the case throughout the centuries. The French authorities defined, rather than changed—they defined the number of persons holding office, their qualifications, and the means of carrying out their work.

1. Judicial Personnel of Chrâa Courts (excepting the Cadi)

The *muftis* remained in their traditional position as judical consultants, although their number was now limited.[70] A list of specially authorized muftis was drawn up for each city by the Vizir de la Justice, and posted at the cadi's *mahakma*, or court, in a place accessible to the public. After 1914 only fetouas of these recognized muftis were accepted in the French Zone of Morocco.

The *oukils* were to the Chrâa courts what the defense counsels, or *défenseurs agréés*, were to the Makhzen courts.[71] Regulations con-

---

[69] Dahir of July 7, 1914, Part 2, *BO*, 90 (July 17, 1914), p. 579. Since the French distinguished between the Berbers and Arabs, politically, from the very outset, it is not surprising that they also did so in law. Many Berber tribes were regulated by customary law, not by the Chrâa, and the French maintained their independent legal system; see Dahir of Sept. 11, 1914, *BO*, 100 (Sept. 21, 1914), 742. See also Girault, p. 345. Most of the Berber tribes were "resolutely Muslim"—to use Jacques Berque's phrase, but at the same time they followed their own customary law, and to quote Berque again, "Many Berber tribes of the Maghreb remain independent of [Muslim] canon law to this day." Jacques Berque, *Le Maghreb entre deux guerres* (Paris, 1962), p. 227. See also Roger Le Tourneau, *Évolution politique de l'Afrique du Nord musulmane, 1920–1961* (Paris, 1962), p. 182. In 1928 a fairly complete list of Berber tribes adhering to Berber customary law was published (Vizirial Decree of Apr. 16, 1928, *BO*, 811 [May 8, 1928], 1273). (See ch. 2, §IV.) It was not until 1930, however (i.e., the "Berber Dahir" of May 16, 1930, *BO*, 918 [May 30, 1930]), that the fully independent Berber judicial organization was set up, recognizing the judicial competence of the djemaas and creating Tribunaux Coutumiers de Notables charged with applying local custom to all civil or commercial actions, and also to matters involving personal status and inheritance. Tribunaux Coutumiers d'Appel were also created at that time. All penal matters, however, were under the sole competence of French courts. See Ch.-André Julien, *L'Afrique du Nord en march—nationalismes musulmans et souveraineté française* (2d ed; Paris, 1953), p. 146. In 1934 all penal cases were transferred to caïds and pachas (for lesser crimes) and the Haut Tribunal Chérifien (for more serious ones), but to keep to the principle of customary law, a Section Pénale Coutumière was created where two notables could inform the Tribunal of the nature of the customary laws involved. See Dahir of Apr. 8, 1934, *BO*, 1120 (Apr. 13, 1934), 306.

[70] Art. 1, Dahir of July 7, 1914.

[71] See §III, B below.

cerning oukils were fairly complete by 1925, when they were granted
the monopoly of acting as defense counsels before the Tribunal d'Appel
du Chrâa and the Tribunaux du Chrâa of the cadis; at the same time
rigid rules were drawn up governing the eligibility of candidates for
the post of oukil.[72]

Cadis were henceforth required to choose a number of candidates
for the post of oukil from among persons previously performing this
function (i.e., before the new regulations went into effect), or from
persons of known integrity.[73] The cadi drew up a list of candidates
and their qualifications and sent it to the Vizir de la Justice who made
the final choice. The Vizir's authorized list of oukils was then posted
by each cadi in his mahakma.

Every *adel* (notary public or legal clerk) was chosen for his post by
the cadi who was usually assisted by the oulama of the city, and the
Vizir de la Justice issued a decree authorizing his nomination.[74] There
were two categories of *adoul:* one was to draw up all acts or contracts,
and the other was to draw up only contracts concerning commercial
transactions, debts, marriage, divorce, and the like, but nothing having
to do with property, Habous, wills, inheritances, or sentences and
writs for the Chrâa Tribunaux.

Every notarized document had to be drawn up by two adoul, just
as before the establishment of the Protectorate, although these acts
now had to be more definitive, with the specific date of the contract
and the names and domiciles of the adoul and of the contracting
parties. In real estate matters, the acts had to define all boundaries
involved. Latitude was given the interpreter, if one was assisting the
parties, to mention in the margins of the document that he had read
it to his proxies in the dialect that they could understand; and he
was to assist in affixing their signatures to the act upon its completion
(i.e., when it had been executed). The act had to be confirmed, signed,
and sealed, and recorded in the registers of the mahakma within three
days of its being drawn up. The only time that the aduol could ever
draw up an act without prior authorization of the cadi was in the
extreme case when a dying person wished to make a declaration.

2. *Registers*

Each mahakma now had to keep registers in its archives for the
following: (1) acts pertaining to real estate transactions; (2) marriages,
divorces, etc.; (3) matters concerning inheritance and guardianship;
(4) acts concerning procedure and sentences; (5) requests to begin

[72] Art. 1, Dahir of Sept. 7, 1925, *BO,* 675 (Sept. 29, 1925), 1569. See also Girault,
p. 343.
[73] Art. 2, Dahir of July 7, 1914.
[74] *Ibid.,* Arts. 3–5.

legal proceedings or requests to draw up contracts; (6) requests for appeals; and (7) summonses to appear in court.[75] Whenever any matter was brought before the cadi, it now had to be recorded immediately in a register.

3. Supervision by the Vizirat de la Justice

The Vizir de la Justice had to appoint an agent for mahakmas of the cities and ports who was to act as an inspector, ensuring that regulations concerning Sherifian civil justice were kept and the necessary fees paid.[76] Each month the agent inspected the registers of the mahakma assigned to him. He also had to examine all complaints or claims made against any cadi, mufti, adel, oukil, aoun, or other official of the Sherifian judicial services within his jurisdiction.

4. Procedure

A complaint was brought to the attention of the cadi. If the defendant was not present at that time the cadi sent him notice to appear at a specific time and date with fifteen days in which to reply.[77] If both parties agreed to appear in a shorter period of time, this was allowed.

When the defendant duly appeared, the case would follow its normal course, the plaintiff giving evidence in support of his allegation or action. In inheritance or real property cases, the plaintiff had to make known all evidence; the defendant was then able, in the fifteen days allowed him, to obtain a copy of the case against him in order to know how to argue his defense. Once the defendant had replied, the plaintiff in turn had fifteen days in which to counter the defendant's statement. If the evidence presented by the plaintiff was reversed by evidence presented by the defendant, the cadi then gave a verdict. If, however, the cadi thought that the plaintiff had made a convincing case for himself, he summoned the defendant to present his counter-arguments. These arguments were made known during the session itself, or else during the recess, and so the process went on. The recess granted in order to rebut the latest evidence by the opposing party was always a period of fifteen days.

A copy of the plaintiff's final case was given to the defendant at his request. The last recess granted to the defendant for preparation of his final defense could be extended by an additional three days. The final summons to appear before the cadi also mentioned that judgment would be pronounced on the date announced.

[75] *Ibid.*, Arts. 6–8.

[76] Dahir of July 7, 1914, Part III, Arts. 1–3.

[77] All information on the procedure of the cadi's court is found in Arts. 8–10 of Dahir of July 7, 1914 (Part II).

At the last session the cadi assembled all documents and exhibits and studied them in order to rule on the case without any further delay, although a special recess could be ordered if the cadi felt this necessary.

In the event, however, that parties were summoned to a Tribunal du Chrâa and failed to reply or appear after three summonses, the cadi on the strength of his examination of the evidence could pass judgment by default. The defaulting party was always notified by the cadi before the sentence was pronounced. Judgment by default was an innovation introduced by the French.

When a case required the aid of experts, the two parties were invited to agree on a choice of experts. Failing this, the cadi would officially appoint the experts himself from the list supplied by the Ministry of Justice.

Every judgment pronounced by a cadi contained the following information: (1) names, occupation, and domiciles of the parties; (2) the charge(s); (3) statements and evidence given by the parties; (4) position of the law on the point(s) in question; (5) verdict and penalty; (6) date of sentence; and (7) methods by which the parties were to meet the costs.

5. Appeals

If a party wished to appeal against the cadi's decision, he could, in two months' time, notify the Makhzen either directly or through the local authorities. Ultimately the appeal reached the Vizir de la Justice who reached a decision after he had consulted the Conseil Supérieur d'Ouléma.[78] If the Vizir thought it advisable, he could have the case returned for retrial to its original jurisdiction, or else to some other venue. If the case was returned for retrial, appeal could then be made within a month of the retrial, and the Vizir de la Justice would give the final decision.[79]

6. Tribunal d'Appel du Chrâa

In February, 1921, the Conseil Supérieur d'Ouléma was raised in status and renamed the Tribunal d'Appel du Chrâa.[80] The Tribunal d'Appel consisted of two chambers and was made up of the following persons for each chamber (in addition to one president): two Juges, two Juges Suppléants, a clerk, and a secretary. As just explained,

[78] Art. 12, Part II, Dahir of July 7, 1914. This Conseil was abolished in 1921; see below.

[79] Dahir of July 7, 1914. See also Louis Milliot, Recueil de jurisprudence chérifienne —tribunal du ministre chérifien de la justice et conseil supérieur d'ouléma (medjlès al-istindf), Vol. I (Paris, 1920), p. 10.

[80] Arts. 1–3, Dahir of Feb. 7, 1921, BO, 437 (Mar. 8, 1921), 396.

the Tribunal dealt with appeals against judgments pronounced by cadis.

B. SECULAR COURTS

1. Competence of the Pacha's or Caïd's Court

In August, 1918, the Makhzen or secular courts and jurisdictions were officially reorganized.[81] The pacha or caïd was kept in his position as judge, but changes were made in court procedure: (a) judgment by default was added, (b) a systematized right of appeal was introduced, and (c) commissaires du gouvernement were appointed.

The pacha or caïd judged all offenses by Moroccans of the common law, with the following exceptions: (1) infractions that came under French jurisdictions; (2) infractions of a very serious nature, reserved for the Chambre Criminelle of the Haut Tribunal Chérifien (see below). The pacha or caïd could pronounce penalties of up to two years' imprisonment and impose fines of up to 2,000 P.H.[82] The Haut Tribunal Chérifien tried cases involving heavier penalties.

The pacha or caïd was competent to judge any civil or commercial case submitted to him, with the exception of the following:[83] (1) persons under the jurisdiction of French courts;[84] (2) questions concerning real property, which were either the responsibility of the Tribunaux du Chrâa or of the French courts;[85] (3) disputes regarding the personal status or inheritances of Muslim subjects, which were under the exclusive jurisdiction of the Tribunaux du Chrâa;[86] (4) disputes regarding the personal status and inheritances of Jewish subjects, which were under the exclusive jurisdiction of Tribunaux Rabbiniques.[87] The secular magistrate could refer the matter to a *cadi* if a point

---

[81] Another Dahir of Aug. 4, 1918, *BO,* 306 (Sept. 2, 1918), 838, Art. 2. It was modified by Dahirs of Dec. 25, 1918, *BO,* 327 (Jan. 27, 1919), 54, and Mar. 24, 1920, *BO,* 390 (Apr. 13, 1920), 623.

[82] Dahir of Aug. 4, 1918, Art. 1. The Vizirial Circular of Jan. 8, 1913, limited the competence of the caïd's or pacha's court to penalties of one year's imprisonment and 1,000 P.H. fine. All criminal cases of a more serious nature were submitted to the Conseil des Affaires Criminelles (created by Dahir of Nov. 11, 1913), which existed until August 4, 1918, when it was suppressed and replaced by the Haut Tribunal Chérifien. In 1918 the competence of the caïd's or pacha's court was also increased, to hear cases involving penalties of up to two years' imprisonment and fines of up to 2,000 pesetas.

[83] Art. 2, Dahir of Aug. 4, 1918.

[84] See Arts. 2 & 7 of Dahir of Aug. 12, 1913.

[85] See Art. 3 of the Organic Dahir of Aug. 12, 1913, and also the Dahir on Property Registration of Aug. 12, 1913 (*BO,* 46 [Sept. 12, 1913], 206).

[86] Art. 4 of Organic Dahir of Aug. 12, 1913 (*BO,* 46 [Sept. 12, 1913], 9).

[87] This conformed to Dahir of Aug. 12, 1913, and Dahir of May 22, 1918 (*BO,* 292 [May 27, 1918], 523); see below.

of religious law was involved, and could call in experts for advice
on technical aspects of a case.[88]

If any serious matter came to the attention of the caïd or pacha, he
sent all relevant information to the Chambre Criminelle of the Haut
Tribunal Chérifien. Before doing so, however, he heard all witnesses,
proceeded with the confirmation of facts, examined and arrested sus-
pects, verified allegations, confronted the accused with the plaintiff's
witnesses, ordered medical experts when necessary, and so on. If no
serious criminal charge had been brought against the suspect, the
pacha or caïd could order his provisional release. It was only after the
above-mentioned examination of the case that all documents were
immediately forwarded to the Chambre Criminelle.[89]

2. Commissaire du Gouvernement

The commissaire du gouvernement differed from the agent appointed
by the Vizir de la Justice to supervise the Tribunaux du Chrâa, for
each court of a pacha or caïd functioned with the assistance of one
of these commissaires, who performed the functions of a type of public
prosecutor and had to ensure that justice was carried out effectively
according to regulations.[90] Thus his powers were greater than those of
the agent of the Tribunaux du Chrâa. The commissaires du gouvernement came under the immediate authority of the Grand Vizir, whom
they had to notify of any irregularity in the judicial administration
within their jurisdiction.

The commissaire left his findings with the court in every case concerning public welfare, and he could intervene in all civil or commercial cases, as well as in penal cases about whose classification
(as to the type and seriousness of the alleged offense) he made a ruling.
The commissaire du gouvernement assisted in the sessions held by the
caïd or pacha; he did not, however, intervene directly in the actual
proceedings or in the sentencing, although he could request an appeal
against a sentence within one month after pronouncement, regardless
of the penalty or degree of seriousness of the case.

Another important aspect of the commissaire's supervisory powers
was that he authorized all summonses to appear before the court,
sentence to and release from prison, notifications and extracts of
sentences, receipts of fines, and any other orders issued by the pacha
or caïd. In addition he inspected the registers of the sentences and
appeals and sent all appeals and inquiries to the Haut Tribunal
Chérifien.

[88] Arts. 2 & 3 of Dahir of Aug. 4, 1918.
[89] This was done by the commissaire du gouvernement, discussed in the next
section.
[90] Arts. 21–26, Dahir of Aug. 4, 1918.

3. Procedure

No party could be condemned or sent before the Chambre Criminelle of the Haut Tribunal Chérifien without a hearing by a lower court, and anyone arrested now had to be examined (and this recorded) within twenty-four hours of the time of his arrest.[91] The remand of a suspect was brief, long enough only to complete any necessary inquiries. It could not exceed a period of forty-eight hours when the penalty was less than a fortnight's imprisonment or a fine of 50 P.H. The pacha or caïd could of course order provisional release on bail.

In civil and commercial cases, request for proceedings was sent in writing to the pacha or caïd, who ordered the request to be recorded in a register and then summoned the parties to appear before him, at which time he proceeded with the hearing. In civil and commercial cases the parties could request the aid of an expert; if both agreed on the choice of an expert, the pacha or caïd authorized it; if, however, the litigants could not come to a mutual agreement on their choice, the magistrate chose the expert.

The hearings of the Tribunaux de Pacha (or Caïd) were open to the public, and were held in his court, at fixed days and hours, at least four times a week. All interested parties had to be heard. If the judge thought that a public hearing was not appropriate, (as a danger to public morals, e.g.) he could order a hearing *in camera,* but the sentence was always pronounced in public.[92]

Every judgment given by the pacha or caïd had to contain the same information as given by the cadi (discussed above, p. 180) and likewise had to be signed by the pacha or caïd who had pronounced it, and recorded within three days of its pronouncement, with the exception that now it had to be submitted to the commissaire du gouvernement.[93]

In civil, commercial, and penal cases alike, judgment could now be pronounced by default when the defendant failed to appear after two summonses without a valid excuse. The defaulting party had to be notified by the commissaire du gouvernement within eight days after sentence had been given.

4. Défenseurs Agréés

Défenseurs agréés, or defense counsels, were also created under Lyautey, although not until 1924.[94] They were accredited to Makhzen (secular) jurisdictions only, and were equivalent to the oukils of the Tribunaux du Chrâa, though their training and qualifications were

[91] *Ibid.,* Arts. 4–8.
[92] Art. 8, Dahir of Aug. 4, 1918.
[93] *Ibid.,* Arts. 9–12, 15.
[94] Dahir of Jan. 10, 1924, *BO,* 586 (Jan. 15, 1924), 54, Arts. 1 & 2.

different. The défenseur agréé had to be Moroccan or French or a justiciable to French courts, and he was required to hold either the Certificat d'Études Juridiques et Administratives Marocaines awarded by the Institut des Hautes Études Marocaines of Rabat (see p. 159), or the Certificat de Droit Musulman et de Coutumes Indigènes awarded by the Faculté de Droit of Algiers. He also had to produce a Diplôme d'Arabe given by one of the following: the Institut des Hautes Études Marocaines of Rabat, the Faculté des Lettres of Algiers, the École Nationale des Langues Orientales Vivantes of Paris, or the École Supérieure de Langue et de Littérature Arabes of Tunis.[95] A candidate with a French Licence en Droit could, however, dispense with the certificates concerning Islamic law. Non-Moroccan lawyers practicing in Makhzen courts had to be capable of defending their clients in both written and oral Arabic. An interesting restriction for the défenseurs agréés was that they could not exercise any administrative or judicial function in the Protectorate, or be a member of the French Bar. A commissaire du gouvernement involved in a civil or criminal case could order a défenseur agréé to defend anyone who could not afford a legal defense. In this case the défenseur agréé supplied by the state was paid entirely by the state.

5. Appeals

Appeals could be made within eight days against sentences passed by default. A person, however, who defaulted a second time could no longer lodge an appeal.[96]

Appeals could not in general be made against verdicts of the courts of the pacha or caïd in the following cases: (1) in civil and commercial cases when the object in dispute did not exceed 1,000 francs in value; (2) in criminal cases when the penalty did not exceed three months' imprisonment or a fine of 300 francs (or in specifically designated cases dealt with by special legislation).[97] In all other cases appeals could be lodged within fifteen days with the Haut Tribunal Chérifien—the Chambre Criminelle for criminal cases, or the Chambre des Appels for civil cases. In criminal cases, appeal could also be lodged within the same period by the civil party whose claim was rejected in part or whole when more than 1,000 francs was involved. In both civil and criminal cases appeals could be lodged during the same session, with the commissaire du gouvernement, with the Haut Tribunal Chérifien, or even with the warden of the prison where the appellant was imprisoned.[98]

[95] Dahir of Jan. 10, 1924, Arts. 4, 5, 9, 19.
[96] Art. 16, Dahir of Aug. 4, 1918.
[97] Ibid., Art. 17 (as modified by Dahir of Mar. 24, 1920).
[98] Ibid., Art. 18 (as modified by Dahir of Mar. 24, 1920), and Arts. 19 & 20.

When the pacha or caïd received notification that an appeal had been made against one of his judgments within the time limit, he forwarded all documents of the appellant's file to the commissaire du gouvernement, who in turn sent them to the Haut Tribunal Chérifien. If the sentence had not already been carried out, it was suspended, or if the appellant had already been imprisoned he was released provisionally.

6. Haut Tribunal Chérifien

One of the most important reforms made by Lyautey's administration was the creation of a special secular court of appeals (for Muslims) at Rabat in August, 1918, called the Haut Tribunal Chérifien. This court, which was responsible to the Grand Vizir, consisted of two chambers: a Chambre Criminelle and a Chambre des Appels.[99]

The Chambre Criminelle (which replaced the earlier Conseil des Affaires Criminelles) dealt with the following: (1) rebellion, or incitement to rebellion; (2) willful or involuntary homicide; wounding when the cause of death or mutilation, infirmity, or permanent illness; infanticide; miscarriage of justice; (3) rape; (4) abduction of a minor; (5) theft, under extenuating circumstances; (6) misappropriation of public funds, embezzlement, corruption by officials; (7) forgery; (8) manufacture and circulation of conterfeit monies; fraudulence or misuse of labels; fraudulent use of weights and measures; (9) arson; (10) all offenses specified in Sherifian dahirs promulgated since March 30, 1912, and punishable by penalties exceeding two years' imprisonment and fines of 2,000 P.H.[100] The Chambre des Appels heard appeals against civil and commercial sentences pronounced by pachas or caïds.

The Haut Tribunal Chérifien had one president sitting in the two chambers and was made up of: two Juges, one Juge Suppléant, one secretary, two clerks, and an interpreter. The two chambers of the Haut Tribunal worked with the assistance of a commissaire du gouvernement who had the same powers (except for the right of appeal) as the commissaires who assisted the pacha or caïd.

When the president of the Haut Tribunal received the file of an appeal, he forwarded it to the appropriate chamber and appointed one of the members of that chamber to examine and report on it. The examining judge could order further inquiry by the qualified authority; he could summon parties and witnesses before the Haut Tribunal, appoint experts, and proceed with any examination which

[99] Another Dahir of Aug. 4, 1918, *BO*, 306 (Sept. 2, 1918), 840 and Art. 1. Years later this was enlarged to include four Chambers: Chambre Criminelle, Chambre d'Appels Correctionnels, Chambre des Appels Civils et Commerciaux, and Chambre d'Appel (for judgments rendered by Tribunaux Coutumiers).

[100] Art. 1, Dahir of Aug. 4, 1918. See also Arts. 2–12.

he thought necessary. Persons summoned to appear before the judge were notified by the commissaire du gouvernement.

As with other native courts, the period of pre-trial detention had to be kept as brief as possible, and was always deducted from the final sentence. The president of the Haut Tribunal could always order provisional release on bail.

The case was heard during the first subsequent session of the Haut Tribunal. The president examined all parties himself and the commissaire du gouvernement made known his conclusions. Sentence was pronounced during the same session.

In civil or commercial cases judgment was pronounced by default when the summoned party had not appeared, just as in other secular courts. In criminal cases, a provisionally released party who did not appear was judged by default. Every judgment had to contain the same classifications of information as in judgments of lower religious or secular courts.[101] An appeal could be lodged within eight days against a judgment pronounced by default. If a new fact was revealed, or previously unknown documents came to light, of such a nature as to establish the innocence of the condemned party, the sentence of the Chambre Criminelle was revised at the request of either the condemned party or the commissaire du gouvernement.

7. Supervision of Native Justice

It should be mentioned that the Sherifian Judicial Services supervised native justice until 1920 when supervision of Muslim justice (religious and secular) came under the Section d'État of the newly organized Direction des Affaires Chérifiennes.[102]

IV. JEWISH COURTS UNDER THE PROTECTORATE

Rabbinical courts were as indigenous to the Jewish population of Morocco as Muslim courts to the Muslims, and though the French authorities began to reorganize Muslim courts almost immediately upon the establishment of the Protectorate, they did not reorganize Jewish courts until 1918 (see fig. 15).[103] This was because the Jewish population formed a small minority within the empire, and because

---

[101] *Ibid.*, Art. 9; see p. 180 above.
[102] By Dahir of July 24, 1920.
[103] They were mentioned only briefly in the Dahir of Aug. 12, 1913. They were dealt with specifically by the Dahir of May 22, 1918, *BO*, 292 (May 27, 1918), 523. Large Jewish colonies had appeared in North Africa from about 320 B.C. See Slouschz, "Étude sur l'histoire des juifs et du Judaisme au Maroc," p. 347.

the First World War delayed many of the administrative reforms planned by the Protectorate authorities.

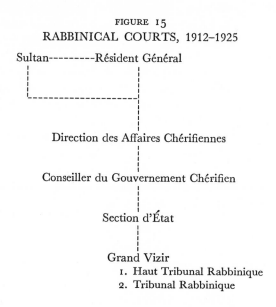

FIGURE 15
RABBINICAL COURTS, 1912–1925

Sultan---------Résident Général

Direction des Affaires Chérifiennes

Conseiller du Gouvernement Chérifien

Section d'État

Grand Vizir
1. Haut Tribunal Rabbinique
2. Tribunal Rabbinique

A. TRIBUNAUX RABBINIQUES

1. *Composition*

In 1918 Tribunaux Rabbiniques were authorized by the French in the cities and ports of the Sherifian Empire.[104] Every Tribunal Rabbinique was made up of a rabbi, as president; two rabbis, as judges (*dayyanim*); and a clerk.[105] These officials were nominated by vizirial decree. Since the Jewish population was often too small in many communities to support a Tribunal Rabbinique, a rabbi could be specially appointed by vizirial decree to supervise all notarized transactions and the like within the jurisdiction. In this latter case if the parties involved in a dispute voluntarily presented themselves before this special rabbi, his ruling was final and could not be appealed against.

2. *Jurisdiction*

When the French officially organized the Jewish judicial organization they deviated greatly from the past, especially in jurisdiction. Unlike

---

[104] Art. 1, Dahir of May 22, 1918. The traditional Rabbinical court was called the Beth Din (House of Justice) and was composed of three judges; it heard all cases except criminal matters, which were heard by the *gardien de l'ordre*. See André Chouraqui, *La condition juridique de l'israélite marocain* (Paris, 1950), p. 119.

[105] Art. 2, Dahir of May 22, 1918, and Arts. 1 & 3.

the traditional Beth Din, the Tribunal Rabbinique was only competent
to hear cases involving personal status and inheritance (i.e., marriage,
divorce, adoption, legacies, etc.); any case involving a civil or commercial matter (even if between Jews only) had to be submitted to a
Muslim secular court (of the *caïd* or *pacha*).[106] Furthermore, when a
litigation pertaining to personal status occurred involving a Jewish
subject and a Muslim, the case automatically had to be heard before
a Tribunal du Chrâa only, and all cases relating to real estate which
were not registered with the Conservation de la Propriété Foncière
(and those under French jurisdiction) were also eligible to be heard
before a Tribunal du Chrâa alone.[107] Any criminal matter was heard by
a special Jewish magistrate.

3. Procedure Before Tribunaux Rabbiniques

Proceedings were started by a written request addressed to the president of the Tribunal Rabbinique. The president ordered the subject
of the request to be recorded, summoned the parties to appear before
the Tribunal, and examined the case.[108] They could appear either in
person or through a legal representative, though the personal appearance of a party could be ordered.[109] The hearings were public
and held at fixed times and dates. As in the case of Muslim courts,
however, the president could order hearings *in camera* if he deemed
it necessary. Judgment was always pronounced in public.

Every judgment contained the following information: (1) names,
professions, and domiciles of the parties; (2) subject of the dispute or
case; (3) statements and evidence given by the parties and witnesses;
(4) grounds for the verdict; (5) sentence; and (6) date of judgment,
according to the Hebrew and Gregorian calendars. All judgments of
these courts were given in Hebrew, and within twenty-four hours of
their pronouncement they were recorded in special registers which were
then signed by the three judges.

Judgment was pronounced by default if the party, who had been
summoned twice—each summons separated by an interval of fifteen
days—was absent without a valid excuse.

Every person who had been a party to the proceedings was able to
obtain a complete copy and French translation of the minutes. The
copy was certified by the clerk, countersigned by the president, and
stamped with the court's seal; it was now considered an authentic
document, although it had no executory value.

[106] *Ibid.*, Art. 1. Chouraqui, p. 128. This was only really enforced by a Residential
Circular of General Noguès, of Feb. 15, 1938, which caused much ill-will in Jewish
communities.

[107] See Chouraqui, who discusses this in detail.

[108] Art. 4, Dahir of May 22, 1918.

[109] *Ibid.*, Arts. 5–11, 21–23. There were no traditional lawyers.

An account of the sentences given in the Tribunal Rabbinique was drawn up by the clerk at the end of every month and sent to the president, who forwarded it to the Grand Vizir.

4. The Jewish Notariate

The *sofer,* or notary (pl. *sofrim*), resembled the adel of Muslim courts. He was appointed by vizirial decree on the proposal of the president of the local Tribunal Rabbinique. As in the Muslim courts, all notarized documents were drawn up and signed by two notaries, and contained the date, names, and domiciles of the sofrim and the parties. All documents requiring notarial authentication were recorded in special registers by the sofrim within three days' of notarization, and were examined and initialled by the president of the local court. The acts of the Jewish notaries, however, were not considered valid before Makhzen Muslim courts.[110]

5. Peremptory Challenges

An interesting right granted to persons involved in a case before a rabbinical jurisdiction was that of peremptory challenge. This right was instituted in 1919.[111] The party could now challenge a judge's competence to hear the case. This right was based on the idea that the judge might be in some manner connected with, or related to, the party (because of the smallness of the Jewish community) and consequently be prejudiced for or against him. Once a challenge had been made, it had to be accepted, and when the challenge concerned a member of a Tribunal Rabbinique, the *dayyan,* or rabbinical judge, objected to was replaced by another rabbi appointed by the Grand Vizir. When the peremptory challenge concerned a member of the Haut Tribunal Rabbinique, the judge was again appointed by the Grand Vizir but he always had to be a president of one of the Tribunaux Rabbiniques.

B. HAUT TRIBUNAL RABBINIQUE

At the same time as the Tribunaux Rabbiniques were created, a Haut Tribunal Rabbinique was established at Rabat to act as a high court of appeals against decisions of the Tribunaux Rabbiniques.[112]

The Haut Tribunal Rabbinique was made up of a rabbi, as president; two rabbis, as judges; and a clerk. These officials were appointed by decree of the Grand Vizir.

[110] Chouraqui, p. 129.

[111] Dahir of May 17, 1919, *BO,* 343 (May 19, 1919), 457, Arts. 2–4.

[112] Dahir of May 22, 1918, Arts. 1–5, 8. (There were two dahirs of this date pertaining to Jewish courts.)

Summonses to appear before the court were issued in the normal way. As in other Jewish and Muslim courts, judgment was pronounced by default when a party who had been twice summoned failed to appear. Final verdicts pronounced by this court contained all particulars required by other rabbinical and Muslim courts, and sentences were recorded in a special register and were examined and initialled by the president of the Haut Tribunal.

Similarly a report of the sentences pronounced every month was drawn up by the clerk of the Haut Tribunal at the end of each month and given to the president of the Haut Tribunal, who forwarded the report to the Grand Vizir.[113]

[113] André Chouraqui has best summarized the criticisms of the French changes (*La condition juridique de l'israélite marocaine*, pp. 129–130):

"This [new] judicial organization, which might seem satisfactory were there also a competent secular jurisdiction alongside it, in reality sanctifies inequalty between Moroccan Muslims and Jews. This discrimination is easily seen in five specific aspects. . . .

"1. Jewish law courts are absolutely forbidden to hear suits of a civil or commercial character, even if in these cases all the parties are Moroccan Jews, and even if the parties wish to go before these [rabbinical] courts of their own accord.

"Now the *cadi*, apart from his competence in matters of inheritance and personal status, has maintained the right to hear civil and commercial cases, provided that all parties are Moroccan Muslims. In these latter cases, he judges concurrently with the *caïds* and *pachas*.

"2. When, in a case regarding personal status, the two litigants are made up of one Muslim and one Jew, the affair must be brought before the jurisdiction of the Chrâa.

"3. The Muslim Chrâa court is competent *ratione personae* to rule in all proceedings against Muslims, whether the other party is a Muslim or not. In complete contrast to this, rabbinical jurisdictions must refer the parties to the French or American courts, according to the case, if one of them is Jewish, though not of Moroccan nationality.

"4. A Muslim never appears before a rabbinical jurisdiction; and yet in real property matters, if a property is involved which has not been registered [with the Conservation], the only competent court is that of the *cadi*. Thus the Jew in such a case has to appear before a court of Muslim canon law.

"5. The acts of the *sofrim* are not considered valid before Makhzen jurisdictions, but those of the *adoul* attached to each *mahakma* of the local *cadi* are considered valid and authentic.

"These measures are all the more resented as nothing justifies their existence. While, in fact, the judgments of rabbis usually leaves all parties contented, and while the judges of rabbinical courts always prove to be men of integrity, such cannot usually be said in Chrâa jurisdictions.

"Procedure is long and consequently expensive; *cadis* are often ignorant of the law; their venality has frequently caused the Government to recall them from office.

"There we have a situation of injustice which it is important to redress by a complete reorganization of the judicial system in Morocco."

6

A CRITICAL ASSESSMENT
OF LYAUTEY'S ADMINISTRATION

The foregoing chapters have surveyed some of Lyautey's achievements in the administration of the Moroccan Protectorate. In this chapter an attempt is made to assess their significance.

The choice of criteria for such an assessment is by no means easy. After the Second World War and the establishment of the United Nations Organization, colonialism got a bad name, and colonial regimes, so far as they continued to exist, came to be regarded as temporary trusteeships responsible for guidance of non-self-governing peoples to earliest possible independence. Although this concept was first formulated in the mandates set up by the League of Nations after the First World War, the colonial powers did not then regard it as generally applicable to their overseas territories. The French were still confident of the inherent superiority of their own civilization and had not begun to contemplate a future dissolution of their empire. They considered Algeria to be a part of France, and expected their dominant influence in Tunisia and Morocco to be long-lasting or even perpetual. In Morocco itself, nationalism in the modern sense did not begin to become important until the 1930's, when Moroccan graduates of French colleges made their way into active life and ideas of Islamic reform emanating from Egypt began to gain ground. It would therefore be historically anachronistic to try to assess Lyautey's work from the standpoints of modern trusteeship theory or modern Moroccan nationalism.

Morocco, unlike Turkey, Egypt, and Tunisia, had not undergone any significant modernization during the nineteenth century, and until 1912 had remained an essentially medieval society. Lyautey was thus called upon both to consolidate the French Protectorate and to lead Morocco into the twentieth century. For both purposes pacification of the tribes was a necessary first step. Lyautey endeavored to do this with a minimum of bloodshed and ill-will in most parts of the country and he achieved a large measure of success, though the task was not fully accomplished until 1934. At the same time he laid the foundations of most of Morocco's modern institutional structure and shaped the development of its cities, ports, and lines of communication. The successful achievement of all these tasks was the more remarkable because Lyautey was handicapped by a shortage of military, financial, and personnel resources, especially during the Great War. To a very great extent this success must be attributed to his personal force of character and wisdom.

All these tasks would of course have been incumbent on the first French Resident General and Commander-in-chief in Morocco, whoever he might have been. Lyautey's distinction, aside from his exceptional force of character, was that, unlike most contemporary French colonial officials, he was not an "assimilationist." He felt a sincere respect for Moroccan civilization, and did not think it either possible or desirable simply to Frenchify the Moroccans. He hoped that Frenchmen and Moroccans would be able to collaborate in the necessary modernization of Morocco without destroying intrinsically valuable Moroccan traditions and characteristics. He wanted the Protectorate to be a genuine protectorate, not a disguised colonial administration.

Lyautey's own declared principles would seem to be the best criteria by which his work may be assessed. How far did he, and his subordinates, actually put them into practice? To what extent did his successors maintain or reverse them?

As has been stated, it was a matter of primary importance to Lyautey that Moroccans and Frenchmen should cooperate closely. On many occasions he declared that he hoped for such an association. In reality, apart from his personal contacts, he does not appear to have done as much as he might have to bring this about. The French tended to hold themselves more aloof from the Moroccans than did their counterparts in the Spanish Zone. This was probably the result of an inbred haughtiness or of a feeling of the superiority of French civilization. Lyautey himself was responsible for the practice whereby the French in Morocco (unlike those in Algeria) built their own cities outside Arab cities; he wished to preserve the character and charm of the Arab cities. But this separation also accentuated the French tendency to look upon the Moroccans as the "natives," holding a lower position in the social and class structure. In practice, French officials failed to work closely with the Moroccans at most of the higher levels of government. In his report of December, 1920, to the French government, Lyautey stated that he was very disappointed over the degree of collaboration so far established between high-ranking French officials and the Sultan and the vizirs. He frankly described the Sultan as a figurehead with no real authority, and he was well aware that this state of affairs ought to be remedied; more responsibility could certainly have been given to Moulay Youssef, who was an intelligent man. But Lyautey made no attempt to strengthen the authority of this Sultan, and left him with insufficient knowledge of developments in the Neo-Sherifian and Residential (i.e., French) Directorates, about which his primary informants were supposed to be the Conseiller du Gouvernement Chérifien and the Resident General himself.

Another most important field where collaboration should not have been too difficult was between the Moroccan vizirs and the French chefs de service. Yet as Lyautey had to admit in his 1920 report:

> There is almost no collaboration between the *chefs de service* and the *vizirs.* Nothing galvanizes the Makhzen, which in turn is slipping into a gentle lethargy.
> Below the Makhzen level, the participation of the native element in affairs is still far too insufficient.

Although at the beginning of the Protectorate, Lyautey had requested that the chefs de service and the vizirs meet weekly to discuss civil and military matters, the practice gradually fell into disuse; the Directeur des Renseignements, for example, sent a lower official to represent him. Lyautey could have solved this problem either by making such top-level meetings mandatory, or by forming a joint Conseil des Vizirs and Conseil des Directeurs; but as André de Laubadère pointed out,[1] Lyautey was opposed to such a scheme, though it is not clear why. Such a council had been set up in the Tunisian Regency, where the vizirs and directeurs met jointly as the Conseil des Ministres et des Chefs de Service. Eventually a similar council was established in Morocco, but not until 1947 under General Juin.

Various factors may partly explain this situation. At the beginning of the Protectorate, Lyautey may have considered participation impossible because the Moroccans had not been sufficiently trained nor their loyalty proved; but since he drew a fairly sharp line of distinction between Moroccans and Frenchmen in nearly all spheres of activity, this may have been just an extension of his general policy. In the final analysis the blame appears to rest fully on Lyautey, for he was the one man strong enough to enforce a policy of collaboration, and could foresee more clearly than anyone else the negative results of the lack of such a policy. What actually happened was that Lyautey allowed an unnecessary and harmful cleavage to arise between Moroccans and Frenchmen at the higher levels, those of policy-making and execution.

[1] André de Laubadère, "Les réformes des pouvoirs publics au Maroc," RJPUF, II (1948), 2–25.

It is a remarkable fact that although Lyautey always stated that the French were in Morocco to "supervise" and not to "administer directly," to uphold the existence of a single government and not to organize two totally separate ones, in practice this is just what he seemed to foster by his failure to bridge the gap between Moroccans and Frenchmen, between the Makhzen and the Protectorate administration. When the French policy at the highest level was so clearly inclined toward segregation, it could hardly be expected that integration would proceed smoothly at the lower level, as, for example, in the training of young Moroccans for posts in the various Residential Directions. When Moroccan officials were not permitted to collaborate with French officials at the top, it is not surprising that the natives were denied any other voice in government policy, except to a small extent through municipal commissions and various local assemblies. Perhaps during the first years of the Protectorate, when the French still had to subdue most of the country militarily, they had grounds for thinking that direct collaboration with the Moroccans was not feasible. They may also have thought that if they associated Moroccans with them from the outset, the latter would demand and perhaps obtain administrative powers which French officials would be reluctant to part with. It may be mentioned here that Lyautey was constantly fighting strong political pressure for a more direct type of administration, which would make of Morocco another Algeria.

Lyautey was a French aristocrat, and of the old school; although he accepted the French Republic, he was not at heart a republican. This background was reflected in his attitudes to governmental problems. Moreover, since the French had only just entered Morocco and hoped to remain there a long time, most of them probably thought that immediate collaboration with the Moroccans would not be compatible with French interests. Nationalism was a word that frightened colonists, and Lyautey himself feared a "Young Turk" movement in Morocco, as he several times admitted during his term of office as Resident General.

The French Protectorate has been criticized for overprotecting Moroccans and their institutions, and above all for overprotecting tribal institutions. Before the Protectorate, tribal assemblies had skillfully managed tribal business, property, and funds; but their powers were taken over by the French and tribal government became a Protectorate responsibility. The French gave several reasons for this move: they feared that Moroccan tribesmen might squander or mismanage their tribal patrimony; that they might simply slip out of the Protectorate administration's control; and that if tribal affairs throughout the country were not coordinated by French officials, no effective planning could take place on a national level.

The results of this French protection of the tribes were partly beneficial, but also, for several reasons, partly harmful. (1) The central Protectorate authorities—all French—took all major initiatives in tribal matters, and the tribal leaders became mere dependents; (2) Moroccan tribesmen lost their former "grass roots" ability to administer their own affairs and take direct responsibility; (3) the members of the tribes consequently ceased to look with respect upon their own assemblies, thereby breaking down the strength and place of the tribes in Moroccan society. This contributed to the growth of a feeling of inferiority among the Moroccans about their own administrative abilities and their position in society in general.

Overprotection was also applied at the municipal level. Frenchmen administered all major cities, despite the maintained figurehead position of the caïd or pacha, and made all major decisions on budgetary matters, sanitation, engineering, and public works. Thus the Moroccan Muslims, apart from certain traditional figures, were not introduced to the administration of the modern world even at the local level. Although expert supervision was probably more needed in the cities than elsewhere, with the introduction of modern installations (sewage, water, electricity), taxation, and accountancy procedures, the municipalities could have been proving grounds for young Moroccan administrators if they had been allowed better opportunities to work their way up—for example, in public works (at the local level), municipal engineering, or accounting.

At the central level of administration, the main opportunity for Moroccans was within the structure of the Moroccan (Makhzen) civil service. They were more or less excluded from the vast areas covered by the Residential Directorates—areas admittedly beyond their traditional experience, but holding the keys to their country's future. Thus they were kept out of the main business of administering the country in native administration, agriculture, commerce and industry, public health, public works, public instruction, and communications. How could Moroccans be expected to run the country at some later date when at least 75 percent of the present business of its administration and management was kept out of their hands at almost every important level? Their feelings about this matter were reflected by Moroccan nationalists in 1934 when they presented a request to the Residency for specific reforms, including a reorganization of the Moroccan government so as to include new ministries and vizirs for Public Instruction, Finance, Economy, the Interior, Communications, and Public Health, with subordinate French advisers when necessary. At the same time they demanded that the Moroccans should have a

"deliberative voice" (i.e., a right to be consulted) in various governmental councils.

The main excuses given by the French for this policy of excluding
Moroccans even from local responsibilities were that the Moroccans,
through their own ignorance and maladministration in the past (i.e.,
before the Protectorate) had shown themselves incapable of handling
such matters, and that the younger generations first had to be trained
in modern French schools before being capable of taking over. These
were the same reasons that they gave for excluding Moroccans from
higher positions in the central administration. Yet the same French
policy tended to discourage the young Moroccan from acquiring or
even seeking a modern education or training; for why should he go
to all the work of becoming well educated when in the end his talents
would remain unused?

Thus in practice at all levels—tribal, municipal, and central—native talents were on the whole neither searched for nor tapped. This
neglect led to a stunting of Moroccan abilities—abilities that were
sorely needed by both the French and the Moroccan administrations
for both the present and the future. The failure of the French to
integrate Moroccans gradually into modern, technical fields at all
levels was their worst shortcoming, and all the more remarkable because Lyautey was forever commending Moroccan loyalty, intelligence, and hard work. Inability to obtain satisfactory employment under the French was the greatest grievance of the Moroccan *jeunesse
évoluée* throughout the history of the Protectorate.

Another sphere of French policy under Lyautey is also open to
criticism—namely, colonization. France came to Morocco with various
aims and prerogatives. As the conqueror she saw herself as possessing
certain rights (perhaps not considered ethically valid today, but traditionally regarded through the centuries as belonging to conquerors).
Among these were the right to make the Moroccans pay the costs of
the French administration, armed forces, military operations, buildings, and construction projects; and the right to treat Morocco as a
special field for French trade, investment, and banking and for French
colonization.

As seen earlier in this work, the French did not colonize Morocco
to the same extent as Algeria or Tunisia. Vast areas were not just
taken and given away to settlers (as was done in Algeria). Nonetheless, the Moroccans lost much land, including a large portion of their
richest soil. Against this, the Moroccans were to a certain extent compensated for their losses. A discussion of the ethics of this transfer of
rich soil from natives to Frenchmen must take into account the realities of the contemporary situation. (What, after all, had happened in

Spain during the Muslim conquest?) In addition to the fact that they paid for expropriated land, the French could also claim that they were bringing two important benefits—namely, the introduction of modern farming methods, and the provision of work for Moroccans. Basically, the last point was not valid, in so far as the Moroccans concerned would have had some sort of work on the same land if it had remained theirs. The first point was basically true, and the French agricultural colonists provided rising tax revenues and export earnings; but the government might itself have purchased modern equipment and appointed agricultural advisers to train Moroccan tribesmen—as Mohammed V later did—so that they might acquire technical knowledge while still remaining the owners of their land. This last course, however, was probably not feasible in the circumstances of Lyautey's time. There are good grounds for recognizing that the French agricultural colonization produced some good results for Morocco, and that its harmful effects to some degree were mitigated.

Another ethical aspect of this problem concerns the transfer to French colonists of lands that had formerly belonged to Moroccan tribes. This had several consequences. (1) The tribesmen lost much of their land, and with it all or part of their traditional livelihood—whether in farming, or in sheep-breeding and transhumance. (2) This led to the break-up of the tribal structure, as members of the tribe were forced to leave their ancestral abodes and go elsewhere in search of a livelihood. Most went to the cities, thereby adding to the pool of unskilled and often unemployed labor in the slums (bidonvilles). This caused a great upheaval in Moroccan traditional life, the effects of which are still felt today. (3) Indirectly another result was a break-up of the concept of a communal property and a changeover to private property in former tribal territories. French agricultural colonization, along with other French policies, thus led to detribalization and a crumbling of much of the essence of Moroccan society, something which the British in Muslim territories under their rule generally tried to avoid. All the same it must be recognized that tribalism has everywhere been decaying under the pressure of economic forces.

The French authorities wanted to establish French influence throughout Morocco, and they regarded colonization as one of the most important instruments for this purpose. Aside from the question of principle, they may be criticized because they imposed no system of control over the number of colonists entering the country. Immigration might at least have been restricted to persons qualified in various fields or possessing adequate capital so that they would not have to depend on the Moroccan government for financial help. The only check on French agricultural colonization was in fact the price and the amount of land available for acquisition by them after their arrival in the country. Control would have been far wiser, not only because of the land factor but also because the influx of colonists made it necessary to provide amenities and medical and educational facilities for them at the government's expense. Despite the logic of such considerations, any suggestion of immigration restrictions would certainly have been countered by political pressure from France, since the average Frenchman felt that it was his right to live in Morocco if he so chose.

Closely linked to the problem of colonization was that of property registration. Before the establishment of the Protectorate, property holdings had fallen into classes which were defined for the most part in different and sometimes conflicting ways. Most property matters had been dealt with by Chrâa (Muslim religious) courts. Agreements had in many cases only been concluded orally, and because of the lack of written documentation it had often been difficult and sometimes impossible to trace a property back through successive ownerships and prove title to it. No title deed was automatically valid before a court. The French instituted their property registration system in order to untangle past claims to titles and ensure the validity of future title deeds, especially though not solely for the benefit of French colonists. As soon as the title to a property was registered with the French authorities, all future changes of title and other matters pertaining to it passed into the exclusive jurisdiction of the French courts and out of the competence of the Chrâa.

In all the Muslim countries during the nineteenth and twentieth centuries, governments, whether independent or imperial, found it necessary to introduce land and property registration systems; and all learned that the task was very difficult and very slow. The French Protectorate in Morocco was no exception. Registration, when accomplished, would mean that established titles (i.e., those established under the new system) would be guaranteed before the courts (in Morocco, before the French courts). The system would also eventually produce an inventory of property holdings in the territory, which would facilitate taxation, and at the same time prevent usurpation of public and waqf (Habous) properties, which in the past had too easily disappeared from the public records.

These advantages of property registration have everywhere been accompanied by disadvantages. In Morocco natives might lose their legally held property if they did not see or hear of official notifications concerning it which had been posted in the court or market. According to the rules, such notifications were to be communicated both in Arabic and in French and both in writing and orally; but in practice this system, even when conscientiously and diligently applied, sometimes resulted in loss of property by native owners without their knowing what was in the wind. On religious grounds also, Moroccans could object that the sphere of the Chrâa courts was being progressively diminished as more and more property was registered and transferred to the jurisdiction of the French courts. All the Muslim states, however, have sooner or later transferred property jurisdiction to modern secular courts. The French claimed that their system was fair to all and ensured equal treatment to Moroccans and Frenchmen alike, whereas the traditional Muslim system had been unsatisfactory, ineffective, and often corrupt. The fees charged in the French system, though seemingly light, were possibly heavy enough to weigh on poor Moroccans who might otherwise have taken advantage of it. In most cases, however, property registration was not mandatory; and thus the French could claim, on the whole rightly, that Moroccans could freely choose which jurisdiction to accept.

In the field of civil engineering and transport, the French achieved great things and only deserve criticism for their falure to train and employ more competent Moroccans. In 1912 no modern transport systems had been developed in Morocco, not even a primitive road system, let alone railways (such as the Ottoman Empire possessed). Immediately after their arrival the French started drawing up plans for a modern highway network linking the cities; and almost all of it was brought into being before the end of Lyautey's term in Morocco. Railway development—apart from some narrow-gauge military lines —was delayed for the first several years by difficulties arising from international conventions and the European War; but by the time of Lyautey's departure this, too, was well on the way to becoming a reality. New cities, schools, hospitals, dams, and other important projects were completed. Probably the most important advance was in the ports—a matter particularly dear to Lyautey—and especially in the vast and complex new port of Casablanca, which Lyautey decided to develop as the country's principal outlet.

Morocco today still owes much of its infrastructural equipment to those opening years of the French Protectorate. The Spaniards achieved nothing comparable in their admittedly much poorer zone.

The judicial organization set up in Morocco under Lyautey was also well founded. Generally speaking, the French, Muslim, Berber, and Jewish legal systems worked satisfactorily, with only a few exceptions such as the removal of Jewish civil and commercial cases from rabbinical courts to the jurisdiction of Muslim secular courts. Although strict Muslims feared innovations, the new legal measures enforced by the French, such as the introduction of appellate jurisdictions, were a great improvement over the old system. Moroccans benefited in that they were allowed to maintain and reform their traditional courts, whereas in Algeria the natives were judged by French courts in all criminal cases.

The French also introduced major educational reforms in Morocco, while taking care not to disturb traditional Muslim institutions. They set up schools for two types of pupils: those of the lower classes, and those of the upper. The French schools of the former type aimed at introducing the French language and training artisans such as carpenters, plumbers, and electricians for the needs of everyday life. The schools of the second type, forming what was called the Franco-Muslim educational system, provided education at every level for a small number of Moroccan pupils from the more cultured classes. This system is to be criticized on two main grounds. In the first place its output of trained pupils was extremely low. Second, the curriculum was almost wholly restricted to commerce, government, law, and the humanities. Little or no preparation was given to pupils who might otherwise have wished to proceed to further training as teachers or medical doctors. Even today Morocco suffers from a shocking shortage of doctors and teachers, two professions that are essential to the welfare of any society and particularly of a developing nation.[2] Lyautey has been rightly blamed for negligence in these two fields. He also failed to provide for the training of enough engineers, and even worse of enough agricultural experts, although a modest start was made in agricultural training before his resignation to encourage young men to train in agriculture. It was on Lyautey's suggestion, however, that a Military Academy was created to train Moroccan officers; but again only a pitifully small handful was admitted.

For the medium of instruction in the new schools, Lyautey chose French and not Arabic. In this he followed the precedents of French policy in Algeria and Tunisia. This policy had been partly determined by the traditional French colonist aim of cultural assimilation. Other factors had been the gap between written Arabic and the spoken Maghribi dialects, and the weak state of written Arabic. The modern renaissance of written Arabic in Syria and Egypt had scarcely begun by 1881, though it had progressed a long way by 1912. Whatever its motives, the French educational policy meant that the modern

[2] By October, 1954, there was a total of only 530 Moroccans with high school diplomas in Morocco; in addition there were 625 Jews. In the professions there were only 36 Moroccan doctors (17 of whom were Jewish) in the country, 5 dentists (including 3 Jews) and surprisingly only 48 lawyers (including 21 Jews). There were approximately 30 Moroccan engineers. Georges Spillmann, *Du Protectorat à l'independance: Maroc, 1912–1955* (Paris, 1967), pp. 153–154.

world was presented to the youth of Morocco, as of Algeria and Tunisia, through French and not Arabic. Moreover, Frenchmen in Morocco, with the exception of a few experts, took little interest in traditional Moroccan or other Arabic literary culture. All this tended to demean the traditional culture in the eyes of the future elite, who grew up with a far better knowledge of French than of their mother tongue. This cultural cleavage is still one of the gravest problems facing Morocco and the other Maghreb countries.

Various reasons may explain the failure of Lyautey and the French administration to do more for Moroccan education. Lyautey himself came from an environment of traditional class barriers, and perhaps for this reason leaned instinctively toward the principle of priority in education for a small but elite group. Another reason for the relative neglect of education was financial stringency. There were even some French colons who could not afford to send their children to the new lycées because fees were beyond their means. The French government in Paris expected the Moroccan Protectorate to pay its own way, apart from loans and from contributions to military expenses; and in any case France was heavily burdened by the cost of the First World War and its aftermath, and by the cost of maintaining troops in Syria, Tunisia, Algeria, and other territories as well as Morocco. Lyautey was obliged to spend a large part of the Moroccan revenues on military pacification of the tribes; and he evidently considered expenditure on communications and public works more important than expenditure on education. Even so, there was probably a more significant underlying reason. French officials feared the growth of nationalism, and foresaw that the development of education and professional training for Moroccans would do more than anything else to stimulate it.

It has been alleged that Lyautey sought to separate the Berbers from the Arabs, and to isolate the Moroccans from the rest of the Muslim world. In point of fact the divisions between Berber-speaking tribes, Arabic-speaking tribes, and Arabic-speaking sedentary Moors had existed for centuries, and none of the Moroccan sultans had been able to overcome them. Lyautey only accepted existing facts when he confirmed the administrative rights and customary laws of the various tribes including the Berber tribes. Had he not done this, he would have been criticized for overriding long-established rights and customs. It could be argued that in the interest of Moroccan unity he ought to have promoted Arabic at the expense of the Berber languages through tribal schools, and to have substituted the Chrâa for customary law in the tribal courts; but any such measures would have been censured as unfair anti-Berber discrimination. The evidence indicates that Lyautey did not seek either to separate or to unite the Berbers and Arabs, but saw the division between them as a normal aspect of the Sherifian Empire. In the task of pacifying the tribes, Lyautey certainly used "divide and rule" tactics, and may well have taken advantage of Arab-Berber frictions, although this is denied by Georges Spillmann,[3] but even if so, such conduct on Lyautey's part was temporary and tactical, and did not reflect any permanent policy of creating Arab-Berber disunity.

As for the charge that Lyautey sought to isolate Morocco from the Muslim world,[4] history shows that under the independent sultans Morocco had led a self-contained existence since the French conquest, and indeed since the Turkish conquest, of Algeria. Only with Mecca, and at times with Muslim West Africa, did Morocco have close contacts. In the early years there was a possible danger that dissident politically minded Moroccans might look to the Pan-Islamic Ottoman Empire and its ally Germany. After the First World War, young Moroccans receiving educations in Paris and also Muslim theologians of the Qaraouiyne University at Fez began to learn of the Egyptian and Syrian nationalist movements and of the "Salafiya" Islamic reform movement in Egypt. Lyautey feared that these influences, together with the impact of modern European civilization, might bring into being a group of Young Moroccans comparable with the Young Turks, whose presence would disturb France's work in Morocco. There can be little doubt that for this reason he did in fact try to discourage Moroccans from contact with other Muslims and to prevent Morocco's tenuous relations with other Muslim countries from becoming any closer.

An important question that must be asked is how the French Protectorate in Morocco compared with other French colonial enterprises in North Africa and the Middle East.

The mandates of Syria and Lebanon were given to France in 1920 by the League of Nations, in accordance with the trusteeship principle, which did not apply to the French colonies and protectorates. The two territories were allowed to choose their own Presidents and parliaments, which was a big step ahead of anything allowed in North Africa. On the other hand, the French High Commissioners could dissolve these parliaments and veto their decisions. In practice the parliaments were at most times either powerless or nonexistent, when the French High Commissioner exercised virtually dictatorial powers.

Algeria was a different case altogether. There was no native parlia-

---

[3] *Du Protectorat à l'Indépendance.*
[4] Sidi Mohammed (V) only openly pleaded for closer ties with the rest of the Muslim countries for the first time during the regime of Erik Labonne in 1947.

ment. The Governor General did not have military powers, his post being purely civil. Every important appointment made by him had to be authorized by the metropolitan government, and his civil powers were thus not nearly so great as those of the High Commissioners at Beirut and the Residents General at Tunis and Rabat. The northern section of Algeria was legally part of France and was divided into three départements. The desert territory in the south was separately administered. The population was classified into French citizens and French subjects. Only persons willing to submit to French law in all fields (including family law) could become French citizens; almost all the Muslims clung to Muslim law and remained French subjects. As part of France, northern Algeria was represented in the French Chamber of Deputies at Paris; but in practice only the Christians (mostly French colons) possessed the right to vote.

Tunisia resembled Morocco, in that it was also a protectorate, with a native government under the Bey and fairly similar French Directions. The Resident General, however, held only civil powers over the country, and the natives possessed more extensive rights of collaboration at the highest levels after the creation in 1922 of a joint council consisting of Tunisian ministers (one-third) and French chefs de service (two-thirds).

The Moroccan Protectorate would have benefited through the introduction of at least two of the institutions set up in these other territories, if only in modified forms. A joint council of vizirs and chefs de service could have been set up, as in Tunisia; this was not done in Morocco until 1947. Second, some sort of elected parliament, with at least a consultative voice, might have been set up, as in Syria; and the legal status of the Sultan might have been changed from that of an absolute monarch to that of a constitutional monarch.

The above discussions have been concerned with what the French did or might have done in Morocco during Lyautey's term of office. The question arises, to what extent was he personally able to shape the new Protectorate regime and its institutions?

Lyautey has sometimes been said to have had almost dictatorial powers: he could personally select the members of his government; he was empowered to initiate laws and programs, such as the setting up of new types of schools (e.g., the Military Academy); and being at the same time Commander-in-chief, he personally planned military campaigns (which were removed from the competence of his successor, Steeg). Besides all this, Lyautey could give a moral impetus to his policies, through his character and personality. There were many factors, however, that he could not control. The French Parliament had the last word in matters of general policy and in matters of finance, more particularly on the tricky question of loans. The Ministry of Foreign Affairs in Paris handled Morocco's foreign relations. In military matters, Lyautey was sometimes restricted by the metropolitan government; for instance during the First World War and during the Rif War when his requests for additional troops and supplies were not met. Another curb on Lyautey's authority was the presence of French colonists. He was not able to control the type or influx of colons, nor the activities of large Paris-based corporations which planted deep roots in Moroccan finance, agriculture, and mining. After the First World War, when the colons were dissatisfied with economic conditions and wanted a more direct voice in the administration of the Protectorate, they nearly succeeded in ousting Lyautey, who was saved by the intervention of the Prime Minister of the French Republic. During his last years of office, the growing power of the socialists in the French Parliament made it difficult for Lyautey to act decisively in Morocco. Finally, it must be said that French officials and officers had (and still have) their own long-established bureaucratic, legalistic, and military traditions. Those who worked under Lyautey served him well, but not even he could have fundamentally changed their ingrained attitudes and ways of doing things. Nevertheless Lyautey, through his personal zeal, charm, and idealism, impressed both the French and the Moroccans themselves as a great leader.

In conclusion it may be fitting to quote a tribute, albeit a rather highly colored one, which the young monarch Mohammed V paid to Lyautey in a speech at the Colonial Exhibition at Vincennes in 1931:

> Coming to admire the Colonial Exhibition, which is a wonderful achievement of your [French] genius, it is Our special pleasure on this occasion to convey Our greeting to the great Frenchman who was able to safeguard Morocco's ancient traditions, morals, and customs, while at the same time introducing the spirit of modern organization, without which no country could exist today.
>
> Can we in fact forget that upon your arrival in Morocco, the Sherifian Empire was threatened with ultimate ruin? Her institutions, her arts, her faltering administration—all were calling for an organizer, a renovator of your ability to put her back on the right path, to direct her toward her destiny. By taking into consideration the susceptibilities of her inhabitants, by respecting their beliefs and customs, you have drawn them to *la France protectrice* by your noble qualities of heart and by the grandeur of your soul.
>
> In less than fifteen years, new cities have been erected without our old cities losing any of their character in the process. Highways facilitating commerce have been quickly laid out across the entire extent of Our Empire. Ports that excite the administration of everyone have been opened to allow for the development of Moroccan commerce. Schools built with most artistic taste and in a most practical way have brought to Our subjects the

science indispensable to understand modern life and to enter onto the path of progress. Everywhere dispensaries and hospitals have appeared, while France, being compassionate for those who suffer, has made possible, without counting the costs of struggling against illness.

All your work cannot be mentioned in one speech alone.

It would take a book to say what Morocco owes you. You have remembered, Monsieur le Maréchal, the solid friendship which you promised Our noble and lamented Father [the former Sultan Moulay Youssef]. By his attitude to you, by family ties which We cherish as a precious memory, We know that he always considered you as the most faithful and deeply cherished of his friends.

When he left this ephemeral world, he left us with a legacy of sacred duty to maintain that friendship. You know with what joy We convey to you in addition the expression of Our gratitude assuring you that, throughout all of Morocco, the name of Marshal Lyautey will remain engraved in all our hearts and will be the symbol of the finest qualities of the French race, being synonymous of magnanimous grandeur and everlasting glory.

REFERENCE MATERIAL

Appendix 1
TREATY OF FEZ,
MARCH 30, 1912

The Government of the French Republic and the Government of His Sherifian Majesty, anxious to establish a stable Government in Morocco, founded on order and security, which will allow the introduction of reforms and the economic development of the country, are agreed on the following provisions:

ARTICLE I

The Government of the French Republic and of His Majesty, the Sultan, have agreed to the creation in Morocco of a new regime involving administrative, judiciary, scholastic, economic, financial, and military reforms which the French Government will judge useful to introduce in Moroccan territory.

This regime will safeguard the religious position, the traditional respect and prestige of the Sultan, the practice of the Muslim religion and its religious institutions, viz. those of the Habous. It will allow the organization of a reformed Sherifian Makhzen.

The Republican Government will act with the Spanish Government regarding the interests which that Government have as a result of their geographical situation and their territorial possessions on the Moroccan coast.

Similarly, the town of Tangier will keep the special character which has been recognized to it and which will determine its municipal organization.

ARTICLE II

His Majesty, the Sultan, will henceforth permit the French Government, after having told the Makhzen, to proceed with the military

occupation of Moroccan territory which they judge necessary in order
to maintain law and order for commercial transactions and to exercise all police action on Moroccan land and waters.

ARTICLE III

The Government of the Republic assumes the responsibility of always
supporting His Sherifian Majesty against all dangers which may
threaten his person or throne or which may compromise the tran-
quillity of his States. The same support will be lent to the heir to the
throne and to his successors.

ARTICLE IV

The measures which the new regime of the Protectorate will necessitate will be decreed, on the proposal of the French Government, by
His Sherifian Majesty or by the authorities to which he will have delegated power. There will also be new regulations and changes in those
already existing.

ARTICLE V

The French Government will be represented at the Court of His
Sherifian Majesty by a Resident Commissioner General, as the depository of all the powers of the Republic in Morocco, who will ensure the
execution of the present Agreement.

The Resident Commissioner General will be the sole intermediary
of the Sultan with foreign representatives with the Moroccan Government. He will in particular be put in charge of all questions involving
foreigners in the Sherifian Empire. He will have the power to approve
and promulgate, in the name of the French Government, all decrees
pronounced by His Sherifian Majesty.

ARTICLE VI

The diplomatic and consular agents of France will be put in charge
of the representation and protection of Moroccan subjects and interests abroad.

His Majesty, the Sultan, undertakes not to conclude any act of an
international character without first receiving the consent of the
Government of the French Republic.

ARTICLE VII

The Government of the French Republic and that of His Sherifian Majesty reserve for themselves the right to establish, by common accord, the bases of a financial reorganization which, by respecting the rights conferred to the holders of titles of Moroccan public loans, permits the guarantee of the engagements of the Sherifian Treasury and the regular collection of the revenues of the Empire.

ARTICLE VIII

His Sherifian Majesty is forbidden to contract in the future, directly or indirectly, any public or private loans, and to grant concessions, under any form, without the permission of the French Government.

ARTICLE IX

The present Convention will be submitted for ratification by the Government of the French Republic and the instrument of the said ratification will be given to His Majesty, the Sultan, as soon as possible.

In witness whereof the undersigned have drawn up the present Act and have affixed thereto their seals.

Done at Fez, the 30th day of March, 1912 (11 Rebiah 1330).

REGNAULT
MOULAY ABD-EL-HAFID

Appendix 2
DECREE ANNOUNCING
LYAUTEY'S APPOINTMENT

DÉCRET

Le Président de la République Française,

Sur la proposition du Président du Conseil, Ministre des Affaires Étrangères,

Décrète:

ART. 1er. Le Général de division Lyautey est nommé Commissaire Résident Général de la République Française au Maroc.

ART. 2. Le Président du Conseil, Ministre des Affaires Étrangères, est chargé de l'exécution du présent décret.

Fait à Rambouillet, le 28 Avril 1912.

A. FALLIÈRES

Par le Président de la République:
Le Président du Conseil,
Ministre des Affaires Étrangères,

R. POINCARÉ

Appendix 3
CHRONOLOGY OF RESIDENTS
GENERAL OF MOROCCO, 1912–1956

Marshal Hubert Lyautey .... April, 1912   –October,1925
Théodore Steeg .... October, 1925   –January, 1929
Lucien Saint .... January, 1929   –August, 1933
Henri Ponsot .... August, 1933   –March, 1936
Marcel Peyrouton .... March, 1936   –September, 1936
General Auguste Noguès .... September, 1936–June, 1943
Gabriel Puaux .... June, 1943   –March, 1946
Erik Labonne .... March, 1946   –May, 1947
Marshal Alphonse Juin .... May, 1947   –July, 1951
General Augustin Guillaume .... July, 1951   –June, 1954
Francis Lacoste .... June, 1954   –June, 1955
Gilbert Grandval .... June, 1955   –August, 1955
Boyer de Latour .... August, 1955   –November, 1955
André Dubois .... November, 1955–March, 1956
    "   " .... March, 1956   –June, 1956
   (as *Haut Commissaire*)

Appendix 4

PREFACE TO
RAPPORT GÉNÉRAL SUR LA SITUATION DU PROTECTORAT DU MAROC AU 31 JUILLET 1914

Ce rapport a été préparé par les Services du Protectorat pendant la période de juin-juillet 1914. Il était presque terminé et quelques chapitres imprimés déjà, lorsque la guerre a éclaté. On conçoit aisément que cette oeuvre ait été, à ce moment, quelque peu délaissée: d'autres préoccupations dominaient les esprits, d'autres affaires, plus urgentes et plus graves, accaparaient les efforts d'un personnel réduit. Il n'était nullement question, pourtant, de l'abandonner. Et l'on gardait l'idée de publier un jour ou l'autre ce document,—non pas seulement pour conserver le fruit d'un gros travail, pour éviter l'impression décevante du gaspillage—mais surtout la conception de la guerre était telle à cette époque, qu'il semblait qu'elle dût marquer nécessairement pour le Maroc un temps d'arrêt dans son évolution, peut-être même un régression; ce rapport fixerait donc le tableau de l'oeuvre accomplie par le Protectorat au jour même de son arrêt; il marquerait le coup; il serait, pour ainsi dire, le testament du Maroc en paix.

Cette conception s'est vite modifiée. En raison de la durée encore indéterminée de la guerre, de son étendue, de l'universalité de ses moyens, il est vite apparu qu'un arrêt prolongé dans le développement du Maroc ne serait plus, comme on l'avait pensé, un temps de sommeil nécessaire, mais d'inaction malheureuse, et qu'à l'inverse, son réveil économique jetterait une force de plus dans la lutte générale. L'activité du Maroc, dès lors, a été intense. Cette activité même devait rejeter au second plan l'impression de ce travail et de sa publication. Les yeux n'étaient plus tournés vers le passé, mais vers l'avenir, l'avenir immédiat, toujours renouvelé.

Et pourtant, après 18 mois de guerre, après 18 mois de travail et de progrès, cette publication est apparue de nouveau nécessaire,—non plus cette fois comme un testament, mais plutôt comme un compte de raison,—pour marquer un *stade* d'une évolution qui s'est poursuivie et accélérée. En le rapprochant d'un autre document, dont la publication va être entreprise: *Les Conférences de l'Exposition franco-marocaine,* on aura sous les yeux l'image des deux échelons principaux de cette évolution: *avant* et *pendant* la guerre.

Il est donc essentiel, en lisant ce rapport aujourd'hui, en 1916, de ne jamais perdre de vue qu'il a été écrit avant la guerre et qu'il porte la date du 31 juillet 1914. Nous n'en sommes pas moins en 1916, et il faut être actuel. Or, depuis la guerre, beaucoup de progrès matériels ont été réalisés, beaucoup de réformes ou de créations, annoncées par ce rapport ou déjà amorcées en 1914, ont été accomplies. On doit signaler brièvement ces progrès, dans les grandes lignes. D'autre part, l'expérience même a provoqué des modifications à certaines idées de principe. On ne peut les passer sous silence.

Au moment où la guerre a éclaté, le sentiment de tous, au Maroc comme en France, était que tout ce qui n'était pas la guerre d'Europe allait être suspendu. Dans ces premières heures, c'est tout au plus si l'on envisageait la possibilité de maintenir notre occupation militaire du Maroc dans les limites déjà acquises. Non seulement il n'était pas question de l'étendre, mais le développement administratif, la vie économique apparaissaient comme devant être totalement paralysés, les travaux publics, les entreprises commerciales et industrielles, les mesures en cours dans l'ordre de l'évolution sociale et politique du pays comme devant y être mis au cran d'arrêt. Si le Maroc ne nous échappait pas totalement ou partiellement, du moins semblait-il, dans le cas le plus favorable, devoir être "mis en sommeil" jusqu'à la paix.

Les circonstances en ont décidé autrement. La guerre s'est prolongée et se prolonge encore bien au delà du terme qu'on avait pu prévoir. Au Maroc après avoir pris les mesures militaires qui, malgré le prélèvement des deux tiers de l'effectif des troupes actives et grâce à l'appoint des bataillons de territoriaux envoyés de France, ont permis le maintien intégral de notre occupation et de notre situation militaire, on fut amené à reconnaître qu'une des conditions, la condition essentielle même, du maintien de notre situation consistait à indigènes la confiance la plus entière dans notre foi dans le succès, dans notre force, dans notre richesse, dans notre sérénité, bref, à leur donner l'impression tangible, comme on l'a dit, que "la séance continuait."

On fut donc amené rapidement, non seulement à laisser la vie

administrative suivre son cours, mais encore à chercher par tous les
moyens à rendre toute son activité à la vie économique, à l'intensifier
même et à reprendre, à développer l'exécution du programme des
travaux publics, condition première de la vie économique.

Dans l'ordre militaire, la décision de maintenir intacts les fronts
intérieurs de notre occupation, "l'armature," comportait forcément
l'obligation de maintenir une certaine activité à notre effort militaire.
Il ne s'agissait plus, bien entendu, de réaliser l'achèvement intégral
de notre occupation, de conquérir les difficiles régions encore dissidentes
qu'il nous restait à aborder au moment de l'ouverture des hostilités:
il s'agissait en principe de s'y maintenir sur les positions acquises,
c'est-à-dire d'une action défensive par définition. Mais là nous étions
à deux de jeu. Il ne suffisait pas de dire: "Nous nous arrêtons ici," il
fallait que ceux d'en face y consentissent. Or, ils n'y étaient nullement
disposés. Le fait seul d'arrêter notre progression, ininterrompue au
Maroc depuis les premiers jours de l'occupation, était l'aveu d'une
situation nouvelle et critique. Nos adversaires étaient d'ailleurs trop
avertis des événements extérieurs pour s'y tromper, les agents de nos
ennemis ne manquaient pas de leur donner tous motifs de reprendre
confiance et tous moyens de mener avantageusement la lutte. Dès lors
que nous n'attaquions plus, c'est eux qui attaqueraient et, dès les
premiers jours, ils ne s'en firent pas faute. Notre défensive ne pouvait
donc être une défensive passive et inerte, mais devait être une défensive
active, c'est-à-dire que, dans bien des cas, et dans toute la mesure
où il était indispensable, elle devait être une offensive hardie qui
prévient au lieu de se laisser prévenir. C'est ainsi que notre action
militaire sur toute la périphérie, tout en écartant jusqu'à la fin des
hostilités les opérations de grande envergure, tout en réservant jusqu'à
ce moment la conquête des objectifs exigeant des moyens matériels
dont nous ne disposions plus, conserva néanmoins une activité incessante qui, sur certains points, par le fait seul de la riposte aux
attaques, étendit encore d'une manière sensible le champ de notre
occupation.

Depuis dix-huit mois, le Maroc a donc continué à vivre et à évoluer
aussi bien dans l'ordre militaire et politique que dans l'ordre administratif et économique.

Cette préface est donc une simple mise au point du rapport qui
va suivre. Il n'a plus valeur *actuelle,* mais *historique,* il doit donc
être mis à sa place dans le temps.

*   *   *

Il ne s'agit pas d'entrer dans le détail de l'oeuvre nouvelle réalisée
dans chaque service depuis le 1er août 1914, mais simplement d'y
indiquer les points sur lesquels d'importantes modifications sont sur-

venues, les prévisions données comme immédiates ou prochaines que la guerre n'a pas permis de réaliser, parfois même les doctrines, les conceptions que les leçons d'une expérience continue ont fait évoluer.

* * *

La première partie de ce rapport (La Pacification) se termine ainsi (page 37): "Il serait prématuré d'établir des prévisions pour l'avenir, notre occupation va-t-elle continuer à s'étendre et marcher rapidement dans le massif berbère? Son développement est intimement lié aux conséquences politiques de la jonction Taza-Fez et de la conquête du pays Zaïan qui ne peuvent être pleinement escomptés avant la fin de 1914. Il est également subordonné aux intentions du Gouvernement de la République *et aussi à la situation internationale européenne.*"

Ce qu'est devenue, au lendemain du jour où ces lignes ont été écrites, *la situation internationale européenne,* on le sait, et c'est elle qui est venue peser de tout son poids sur les prévisions qui avaient été envisagées dans ce chapitre comme devant découler moralement des opérations qui venaient d'être terminées ou qui étaient encore en cours.

1° COULOIR DE TAZA

En juillet 1914, on prévoyait que la résistance des Riata, éstablis au sud de Taza, étant définitivement brisée et l'extension de notre établissement, au nord de cette ville, chez les Branès, devant se faire par simple action politique sans opérations militaires, la route de Taza à Fez serait complètement dégagée, et la liberté de communications entre le Maroc et l'Algérie assurée avant la fin de 1914. C'est sur ce point que la guerre d'Europe apporta le plus sérieux mécompte.

Notre occupation était encore trop récente, notre installation trop fragile, pour ne pas subir le contre-coup immédiat des importants prélèvements d'effectifs effectués dans cette région, ainsi que de la disparition des chefs (général Gouraud, général Baumgarten) qui y étaient en plein travail. Les Riata, battus mais non soumis, appuyés sur les irréductibles Beni Ouaraïn, reprirent immédiatement confiance, et les tribus de soumission récente, telles que les Branès, changèrent d'attitude. Une série d'agressions de plus en plus audacieuses et d'importance croissante, auxquelles nos effectifs ne permettaient plus de répondre avec efficacité, dirigées contre nos convois, nos lignes télégraphiques, nos travaux de chemin de fer, nos postes même, interceptèrent de fait la communication entre Oued Amelil et Mçoun, sur laquelle il ne fut plus possible de circuler qu'avec les convois périodiques escortés de tous les bataillons disponibles. Chacun de ces mouvements était marqué par de vifs engagements où nous subissions des pertes sensibles. Taza était virtuellement bloquée, et la question se posa même si nous ne serions pas forcés d'abandonner momentanément ce point et de renoncer jusqu'à des jours meilleurs à cette communication entre le Maroc occidental et le Maroc oriental devenue si précaire. Déjà il avait fallu renoncer à y poursuivre les travaux de routes et à y maintenir la liaison télégraphique. Il se formait là un consortium de nos principaux adversaires, les chefs des Beni Ouaraïn et des Riata au sud, le Chenguiti au nord en liaison permanente avec Melilla où, sous l'action intense d'agents allemands, se créait un foyer des plus actifs grossi progressivement de légionnaires déserteurs, de prisonniers politiques évadés et de personnalités venues de l'extérieur. Plus tard, en mars 1915, vint s'y ajouter Abd el Malek, neveu de l'Emir Abd el Kader, transfuge de Tanger, dont le prestige personnel, les ressources financières et les relations avec les agents turcs et allemands apportèrent un appoint notable à ce noyau hostile.

Mais, dès septembre 1914, le général Henrys, commandant la région de Meknès, avait été mis à la tête d'un nouveau groupement dit "Commandement général du Nord," comprenant les régions de Fez, de Meknès et du Tadla-Zaïan, puis, ultérieurement, le territoire de Taza et enfin toute la zone du Gharb limitrophe de la zone espagnole. Il eut ainsi sous ses ordres, y assurant d'une façon absolue l'unité de direction, tous nos fronts de combat, au nord face à la frontière espagnole, au sud face aux Beni Ouaraïn, aux Riata, aux Zaïan et aux Berbères du Moyen Atlas. Les mesures énergiques qu'il prit sans retard et sans répit, l'articulation qu'il donna à l'ensemble des moyens réduits dont il disposait, dégagèrent progressivement la situation et écartèrent une fois pour toutes l'éventualité de toute mesure extrême, telle que l'abandon d'une de nos positions ou d'une de nos lignes de communications. La ligne télégraphique fut rétablie: les travaux de chemins de fer continués amenèrent la locomotive de Mçoun à Taza même (le 15 juillet 1915). Une série d'opérations vigoureuses, sanctionnées par l'établissement du poste de Bab Moroudj, en plein pays Branès, ramenèrent cette tribu dans l'obéissance et dégagèrent le nord de Taza. Au sud, la création des deux postes de Djebla à l'est du pays Riata, et d'Oued Matmata à l'ouest et au pied du massif Beni Ouaraïn, tint en respect les Riata, fit réfléchir les Beni Ouaraïn et, sans nous donner encore un libre champ d'action au sud, où nous nous heurtons de suite aux grands massifs montagneux occupés par les dissidents, assura du moins la sécurité immédiate du poste de Taza. La communication entre le Maroc occidental et l'oriental, c'est-à-dire avec l'Algérie, est ainsi restée ouverte, et sans être praticable aux isolés, l'est du moins en temps normal avec de faibles escortes. Néanmoins, ce point reste toujours le plus précaire de notre occupation parce que, tant que nous n'aurons pas abordé le massif Beni Ouaraïn, ce qui ne peut s'envisager qu'après la guerre et avec des effectifs importants, cet étroit couloir formera un véritable isthme entre les dissidents du nord et les dissidents du sud en communication par une infiltration constante. Abd el Malek, établi sur notre flanc nord, appuyé à la zone espagnole, où il a, à Melilla, sa base d'opérations, en communication avec un foyer allemand qui ne cesse de grossir, reste pour nous une menace constante et même croissante. Par les Riata et les Beni Ouaraïn, il est en relations suivies avec les grands chefs dissidents du Moyen Atlas auxquels il prodigue les encouragements, leur assurant l'appui allemand, leur faisant parvenir les appels de Constantinople à la guerre sainte, les factums les plus hostiles et enfin de l'argent qu'il a en abondance.

2° FRONTIÈRE DE LA ZONE ESPAGNOLE

Il existe en bordure de cette zone, depuis Ouezzan jusqu'au nord de Taza, dans un pays des plus difficiles, un glacis que nous n'occupions pas encore. Jusqu'à la guerre, sauf au nord de Taza et au nord-est de Fez, il ne nous avait causé aucun souci. Nous vivions dans la meilleure intelligence avec les tribus qui le peuplaient, et nous n'avions à y envisager aucune opération militaire. A partir du début des hostilités, la situation s'y modifia progressivement. Des groupements s'y formèrent, alimentés par les tribus turbulentes de la partie espagnole du Rif, non encore occupée par nos voisins. Ils trouvèrent des chefs, Ali ben Abdesselam, Kacem ben Salah, protégés allemands ou autrichiens, et surtout subirent l'excitation violente de Raissouli qui, malgré ses relations avec les autorités espagnoles, n'en passe pas moins, aux yeux des Marocains, comme l'agent le plus actif de l'action allemande contre nous. Cette effervescence toujours croissante aboutit, en mai et juin 1915, à une action d'ensemble, à une violente poussée contre les tribus soumises et contre nos postes qui nous causèrent les plus sérieuses préoccupations jusqu'aux abords même de Fez. Une action militaire des plus vigoureuses, dirigée par le général Henrys, qui dut momentanément dégarnir le front berbère, disloqua le bloc de nos adversaires. Ali ben Abdesselam fit même sa soumission. De nouveaux postes de surveillance furent établis le long et au nord de l'Ouergha, reliant Kelaa des Sless à Arbaoua, dans une zone que nous n'avions pas occupée jusque-là et, depuis août 1915, nous avons établi sur ces confins une tranquillité relative.

3° FRONT BERBÈRE

Le premier prélèvement d'effectifs en pays Zaïan, au mois d'août 1914, et la dislocation du groupe mobile de Khenifra réduit à sa seule garnison, eurent comme conséquence immédiate la rentrée en campagne des Zaïan, qui se ruèrent sur ce poste et sur nos communications, et le décrochage des unités renvoyées en France se fit difficilement et avec des pertes sérieuses. Une vigoureuse riposte les rejeta dans leurs montagnes et, peu à peu, sous l'influence de la misère dans laquelle ils y vivaient, devant l'approche de l'hiver et la constatation que nous maintenions intacte notre armature, se fit une détente dont on pouvait espérer le développement. Un incident des plus regrettables vint out remettre en question. Malgré les instructions contraires formelles, le commandant du poste de Khenifra crut devoir profiter du voisinage de Moha ou Hamou, chef des Zaïan, venu camper sans méfiance à El Herri, à quelques kilomètres du poste, pour le surprendre (13 novembre 1914). Cette initiative aboutit à un échec complet, à une perte d'hommes et de matériel importante qui eut un retentissement immédiat dans le Maroc entier. Une rapide et remarquable intervention du colonel Garnier-Duplessis, commandant la région du Tadla, et du général Henrys rétablit la situation et assura, une fois de plus, l'intégrité de notre front d'occupation. Mais la détente commencée ne se retrouva plus et, depuis lors, les Zaïan sont restés dans leurs montagnes, face à nous, dans une attitude jusqu'ici irréductible. Ce grave incident n'empêcha heureusement pas des progrès de se réealiser sur d'autres points. Un très habile travail politique pratiqué chez les Beni Mguild de la vallée du Guigou aboutit, en 1915, à l'occupation de ce nouveau couloir, parallèle à notre front, au sud de la ligne Anoceur-Azrou. L'installation des postes de Timhadit et d'Almis étendit ainsi la protection sud des régions de Meknès et de Fez ainsi que la sécurité des tribus soumises et nous mit en relations avec de nouvelles tribus avec lesquelles nous prîmes un contact pacifique. Enfin, il nous assure un gain d'une étape dans la direction de la Haute-Moulouya dont nous ne sommes plus séparés que par deux jours de marche. A cette progression correspondait un travail intéressant de nos troupes du Haut-Ouir qui, sous l'habile direction du colonel Bertrand, poursuivaient, au nord de Gourrama, une progression pacifique continue, prenant de jour en jour contact avec de nouveaux groupements, et poussant des reconnaissances jusqu'en vue de Kasba el Makhzen. Aujourd'hui nos postes du Guigou sont déjà en relations par émissaires avec nos postes du Haut-Ouir, préparant ainsi une liaison future sur la Moulouya, qui ne pourra être envisagée que lorsque l'issue de la guerre nous aura rendu des effectifs.

4° FRONT TADLA

De ce côté, on s'est borné à maintenir en principe les positions acquises: nous, sur l'Oum er Rebia; les Chleuh, dans leurs montagnes. Toutefois, le général Garnier-Duplessis, par une activité incessante et une série de coups de main heureux, a réussi, en dégageant le glacis sud de l'Oum er Rebia, à donner de l'air à ses postes de Kasba Tadla et de Dar ould Zidouh. Il vient même (décembre 1915) de donner pour la première fois la main, au nord de Demnat, aux troupes de Marrakech venues y établir le poste de Tanant.

5° FRONT SUD.—MARRAKECH.—SOUS

De ce côté a été menée, depuis la guerre et malgré la guerre, une action des plus intéressantes par les seuls moyens indigènes, dirigée par le Service des Renseignements sous l'impulsion constante du commandant de le région de Marrakech, le colonel de Lemothe.

Le rapport arrêté au 31 juillet 1914 signalait les progrès de notre influence dans le Sous, où commande Haïda ou Mouis, pacha de Taroudant.

Dès le début des hostilités, le prétendant Hiba, en relations suivies avec les agents allemands par la côte atlantique et ravitaillé par la zone de Rio de Oro, reprenait confiance et rentrait en campagne. Il exerçait une forte pression sur le sud du Sous, coupait les communications entre Tiznit, où commandait un pacha fidèle au Makhzen, et Agadir. Tiznit était investie étroitement, bloquée et mise dans le plus sérieux péril. Une vigoureuse offensive d'Haïda ou Mouis et de ses contingents, secondée par une intervention efficace de la Division navale, dégageait Tiznit (septembre-octobre 1914). Puis, se retournant à l'est, Haïda ou Mouis infligeait un sérieux échec aux partisans d'Hiba dans les montagnes qui bordent le Sous au sud de Taroudant (janvier 1915). Depuis lors, l'autorité du Makhzen n'a fait que s'affermir dans cette région où les efforts d'Hiba sont restés impuissants. Le Grand Atlas restait absolument indemne sous l'autorité des grands caïds Glaoua, Mtougui et Goundafi, dont la fidélité à notre cause n'a pas eu de défaillance depuis le début de la guerre. A l'est de Marrakech seulement, une certaine effervescence se manifestait dans les massifs montagneux à l'est de Demnat, et c'est pour en prévenir le développement que le colonel de Lamothe proposait et recevait l'autorisation d'étendre notre occupation de ce côté en y créant le poste de Tanant (décembre 1915), au débouché des couloirs qui mènent sur le revers du massif Chleuh. Ce poste, actuellement sentinelle avancée, forme ainsi une excellente base d'opérations pour le jour où, après la guerre, avec des effectifs reconstitués, nous pourrons régler la question Chleuh par une action concentrique partant de Tanant, Tadla et Khenifra.

En résumé, si la guerre d'Europe, la réduction de nos effects et l'obligation où nous nous trouvions de n'engager aucune opération risquée et de nous abstenir de tout engrenage, ne nous ont pas permis de poursuivre et peut-être d'achever la réduction totals du Maroc dissident, du moins avons-nous maintenu intactes les limites de notre occupation. Nous les avons même étudues sur certains points.

Si notre communication avec l'Algérie par le couloir de Taza reste toujours précaire, du moins avons-nous étendu au nord la zone de sécurité de cette ville. En face de la zone espagnole, les ripostes aux agressions dirigées contre nous ont étendu notre occupation portée sur certains points jusqu'à frontière espagnole même.

Sur le front berbère, nous avons pu poursuivre, dans une certaine mesure, notre avance sur la Moulouya, à laquelle a correspondu une progression symétrique du Haut-Guir. Enfin, à l'est de Marrakech et dans le Sous, nous avons réalisé des gains sensibles et acquis une supériorité politique et morale incontestable. *La carte placée à la fin de cette préface les fait ressortir clairement.*

Il ne faut néanmoins pas perdre de vue que ces résultats ne pourront être maintenus jusqu'à la fin des hostilités que par une vigilance toujours en éveil, une activité incessante et une action politique intensive. Non seulement, les foyers de dissidence existent toujours, mais ils sont attisés par une action extérieure qui dispose de moyens puissants, que rien ne lasse et qui a ses bases d'opérations hors de notre portée. Enfin, notre situation militaire au Maroc reste toujours, de toute évidence, fonction de la situation militaire générale. Les événements d'orient, notamment, par leur répercussion dans cette caisse sonore qu'est l'Islam, y exigent la plus sérieuse attention. Si détachés du Khalifat de Constantinople que soient les Marocains, dont le chef religieux est leur Sultan, ils ne sauraient être indifférentes à rien de ce qui atteint les Musulmans à l'est du côté de la Tripolitaine, de l'Egypte, de la Syrie et de Stamboul, et il importe, pour ce qui concerne le Maroc, de garder l'oeil et l'oreille ouverts à tous les incidents, à tous les bruits, à tous les symptômes.

* * *

Au point de vue de l'organisation régionale, la guerre n'a apporté de modification à ce qui est exposé dans le rapport du 31 juillet 1914 que sur un point essentiel.

Du fait de l'état de guerre, les commandements régionaux sont passés provisoirement aux mains de l'autorité militaire. Il n'y a donc plus, jusqu'à la fin des hostilités, à distinguer entre les régions, les commandements militaires et l'administration civile, ainsi qu'il était spécifié au chapitre V. Le Maroc occidental est aujourd'hui divisé en six subdivisions militaires (Fez, Meknès, Rabat, Tadla, Casablanca, Marrakech) commandées chacune par un officier général ou supérieur. Chacune de ces subdivisions forme en même temps une région politique et administrative, où l'unité de commandement militaire, politique, administrative est assurée dans les mains du commandant de subdivision.

Les circonscriptions qui étaient passées à l'administration civile ont néanmoins gardé, pour la plupart, leurs contrôleurs, mais ceux-ci, au lieu d'être autonomes et de relever directement de la Résidence générale, sont placés sous l'autorité du commandant de la région.

Comme il a été dit plus haut, trois de ces régions: Fez, Meknès, Tadla, et une partie de celle de Rabat, le Cercle du Gharb, ont été réunies temporairement, pour des motifs militaires et politiques, en un groupement nommé Commandement Général du Nord.

POLITIQUE INDIGÈNE.—MAKHZEN.—MEDJLESS

Notre situation, au Maroc, ne pouvait être maintenue par des moyens purement militaires. L'envoi en France de la majorité des troupes actives aurait rendu impossible le maintien, pourtant si nécessaire, de l'"armature" et, par suite, de la paix au Maroc, si d'autres éléments de force n'étaient venus compenser cet affaiblissment considérable des moyens militaires. C'est, en effet, grâce à une politique indigène et à une politique économique intenses, incessantes, que le pays a pu se garder lui-même, à l'abri des postes avancés du front.

Politique indigène et politique économique, ce sont aussi les deux facteurs essentiels des progrès réalisés au Maroc depuis dix-huit mois. L'heure était bonne pour marcher de l'avant, et il fallait marcher de l'avant pour devancer en quelque sorte l'avenir.

Sauvegarder le Maroc dans la lutte actuelle et l'armer par avance pour la grande lutte économique qui suivra la guerre: tel a été le double objectif poursuivi depuis dix-huit mois, par les mêmes moyens.

* * *

Le Maroc est un Protectorat. Mais ce mot, qui contient pourtant une doctrine coloniale grande et simple, est regardé le plus souvent comme une étiquette et non comme une vérité: on y voit, sinon un mensonge, du moins une formule théorique, une formule de transition, destinée à disparaître après des modalités successives. C'est là le résultat de la plupart de nos expériences coloniales. Et ce sentiment est tellement fort, qu'au Maroc comme ailleurs, avant la guerre, on résistait avec peine, et déjà presque sans conviction, à cette poussée, que beaucoup croient *fatale,* vers le gouvernement direct, vers l'annexion de fait précédent l'annexion légale. La guerre nous a fait une nécessité politique absolue de changer de voie; et cette expérience nouvelle, commencée dans un sentiment de prudence, a pleinement réussi. Le Protectorat apparaît ainsi, non pas comme une formule théorique et de transition, non pas même comme une formule, mais comme un réalité durable; la pénétration économique et morale d'un peuple, non par l'asservissement à notre force ou même à nos libertés, mais par une association étroite, dans laquelle nous l'administrons dans la paix par ses propres organes de gouvernement suivant ses coutumes et ses libertés à lui.

C'est dans ce sens que s'est orientée franchement et définitivement notre politique. On s'est attaché d'abord à rehausser le prestige personnel du Sultan, en faisant revivre autour de lui les anciennes traditions et le vieux cérémonial de la cour, à garantir scrupuleusement l'autonomie de son pouvoir religieux, à raffermir sa confiance et son autorité en l'associant à nos projets, en sollicitant ses réflexions et ses avis. Le Makhzen a été associé plus étroitement chaque jour au gouvernement. Son rôle, avant la guerre, s'était réduit insensiblement, et par la force même de nos habitudes administratives, à un simple droit de veto sur les projets qui lui étaient communiqués. Il possède aujourd'hui, en fait, un véritable droit d'examen; et son initiative même est sollicitée dans bien des cas. Le Conseil des Vizirs est devenu une institution vivante, un organe normal de l'Administration. Tous nos projets y sont exposés, expliqués, dans leur esprit et dans leur tendance. L'administration des biens habous s'exerce de même sous le contrôle effectif d'un Conseil, dont une réunion particulièrement importante, ayant le caractère d'un véritable Congrès religieux, s'est tenue pendant la guerre.

Enfin partout, dans les provinces, on s'est efforcé de donner aux indigènes, non pas un pouvoir de façade, mais une part effective dans l'administration et une véritable autorité pour la garantie de leurs coutumes et de leurs "libertés." Il est donc inexact de dire que l'institution du medjless musulman de Fez ne correspond plus aux besoins actuels et que cette organisation doit être rapprochée du type municipal créé dans les autres villes. Car c'est dans le sens inverse que nous sommes orientés; et le medjless de Fez doit plutôt nous servir de modèle. Dans cette assemblée, en effet, les indigènes sont *entre eux;* les décisions qu'ils prennent, les avis qu'il émettent après discussion représentent vraiment leur opinion, et ils savent qu'il est impossible de n'en pas tenir compte. Dans les assemblées municipales des autres villes, les indigènes, noyés au milieu des Européens, incapables de suivre la discussion qui se poursuit en français et dont on leur donne de loin en loin un résumé hâtif, ont le sentiment d'être des figurants, et ils votent d'autant plus volontiers avec la majorité que leur vote ne signifie rien pour eux. La formule à laquelle il faut tendre est celle d'assemblées *distinctes* pour les Européens et pour les indigènes (ou peut-être de sections distinctes, siégeant séparément, dans une même assemblée). Cette formule seule, à l'heure actuelle, peut nous assurer une représentation sincère des indigènes, et une indépendance complète de leur avis.

ENSEIGNEMENT

C'est dans le même esprit que des réformes importantes ont été apportées dans l'enseignement indigène. La réussite du Protectorat, avec ses deux administrations associées qui s'aident mutuellement et se complètent, dépend de la valeur du personnel indigène autant que de la valeur du personnel français. Il faut donc songer dès maintenant à fonder une pépinière d'administrateurs indigènes, profondément instruits de leur législation et de leur civilisation propre, ouverts en même temps aux questions modernes, capables de comprendre nos intérêts comme nous comprenons les leurs et de se rendre compte en quoi ils se concilient. Ces éléments existent au Maroc: il suffit de les recueillir et de les instruire.

Une sorte d'enseignement secondaire musulman sera donc créé au Maroc: à l'échelon inférieur, dans chaque centre, des écoles payantes pour les fils de notables; au-dessus, à Rabat et à Fez, des collèges musulmans. L'enseignement donné comportera nécessairement l'étude de la langue française, car c'est par la communauté de langue que commence la communauté de pensée, mais cet enseignement, destiné à doter le pays d'administrateurs indigènes et non de fonctionnaires français, n'en sera pas moins essentiellement musulman; il formera des lettrés, et des lettrés modernes. Un Comité consultatif à Rabat et dans chaque centre un Comité de perfectionnement local, tous composés de personnalités indigènes, assureront la direction de cet enseignement.

En attendant ces résultats forcément loitains, il est créé auprès du Makhzen des postes de "stagiaires." Ces stagiaires, choisis après examen parmi les jeunes fils de notables les mieux doués, acquerront peu à peu la pratique du gouvernement des tribus et la connaissance de nos méthodes administratives.

Cette lacune importante devait être comblée.

Une réorganisation de l'École supérieure arabo-berbère de Rabat, une organisation encore rudimentaire de l'enseignement professionnel, ont complété cette réforme.

ASSISTANCE INDIGÈNE

Les efforts devaient porter également sur le développement de l'assistance indigène, déjà en si bonne voie au début de la guerre. (L'instituteur et le médecin ont toujours été les deux agents essentiels de notre politique indigène au Maroc.) Et de grands progrès matériels ont été réalisés. Mais l'organisation même du Service de la Santé et de l'Assistance médicale a été l'objet d'une importante réforme.

Comme on le voit dans le rapport, l'organisation de ce service avait déjà subi, de 1912 à 1914, plusieurs transformations provenant aussi bien de la progression des besoins que des tâtonnements de l'expérience dans un pays nouveau. Ces tâtonnements avaient leur cause essentielle dans la coexistence de deux services distincts, l'un exclusivement militaire, le Service de Santé du corps d'occupation; l'autre d'un caractère plutôt civil, le Service de l'assistance indigène, deux services distincts mais dont les agents devaient être nécessairement confondus. Dans la plupart des postes, en effet, il n'y a qu'un seul médecin; il ne peut y avoir qu'un médecin; et c'est ce même médecin qui exerce à la fois les fonctions administratives et militaires de médecin-major auprès des troupes et l'apostolat médical auprès des populations indigènes. Ce médecin dépendait ainsi, au début, de deux chefs distincts.

La réforme de 1914, en réunissant dans les mêmes mains sous les ordres d'un directeur général, les deux Services de Santé militaire et de l'Assistance publique, avait remédié en partie aux conflits et aux chevauchements qui résultaient nécessairement de l'organisation précédente. Cette centralisation était nécessaire. Par contre, la création de deux zones distinctes, la zone des villes et territoires civils, et la zone dite d'occupation, dirigées, pour tout le Maroc, par deux chefs distincts, mais ayant les mêmes attributions, et où prédominaient un personnel et un esprit différents, a donné de mauvais résultats. Ces deux centralisations parallèles étaient mauvaises.

Le Service a été réorganisé récemment sur des bases différentes.

Au centre, distinction entre les deux services. Ils sont toujours réunis entre les mains du médecin inspecteur, directeur général. Mais un médecin chef de service, placé sous ses ordres, a la direction et la responsabilité de l'Assistance médicale.

Dans chaque région, centralisation de tous les pouvoirs médicaux (santé, assistance, hygiène) entre les mains d'un médecin, directeur de la Santé et de l'Assistance publique de la région, seul responsable vis-à-vis de l'Administration centrale.

Ce système paraît tout concilier. Tous les médecins, dans chaque région, qu'ils soient médecins militaires ou médecins de l'assistance médicale, ou qu'ils cumulent les deux fonctions, sont sous les ordres directs d'un même chef local. Ainsi les chevauchements et les conflits sont évités.

Ce chef local dépend directament du médecin inspecteur, directeur général, véritable "ministre de la Santé et de l'Hygiène publiques" pour l'ensemble du Maroc, mais auprès et sous la direction duquel le directeur de l'Assistance publique centralise et suit spécialement out ce qui concerne l'assistance indigène.

DÉVELOPPEMENT ÉCONOMIQUE

Nous venons de faire une mise au point, aussi succincte que possible, du raport d'ensemble en matière indigène. Mais c'est dans le domaine économique, au sens le plus large du mot, que l'oeuvre du Protectorat a été la plus importante pendant la guerre. Là, plus que partout ailleurs, le rapport est en retard. La mise au point rapide qui va suivre intéresse particulièrement les 4e et 5e parties du rapport (organisation financière et organisation économique).

L'effort aporté, en premier lieu, sur l'outillage du Maroc.

Les Ports.—Le programme général des travaux n'est pas modifié; un grand port moderne à Casablanca, des ports secondaires à Safi, Mazagan, Rabat et Kénitra. Mais le port de Kénitra, dont le développement s'est considérablement accru depuis la guerre et qui tend à devenir le débouché naturel de la région du Gharb et de Fez, mérite une mention spéciale. Les travaux ont avancé à Casablanca. Après un arrêt provoqué par la guerre, des nouveaux chantiers ont été constitués, permettant la reprise des travaux de la grande jetée.

La concession des ports de Kénitra et de Rabat avait été décidée, et les bases du régime de concession à peu près arrêtées avant la guerre. Les circonstances actuelles ne permettent pas de donner suite à ce projet. Les travaux d'un appontement à Kénitra sont néanmoins en voie d'exécution.

A la question des ports se lie celle du transbordement des marchandises. Le monopole de l'aconage est maintenu en principe, mais l'exploitation par l'État de ce service commercial a présenté de telles difficultés dans la pratique, par suite de l'insuffisance des taxes et du manque de souplesse d'une gestion trop administrative, que la concession de ce service a été envisagée et étudiée. Ce projet vient d'aboutir, en ce qui concerne Casablanca, à un contrat de concession entre l'État chérifien et la Société "L'Entreprise maritime et commerciale."

Les routes.—La création d'un réseau de routes est une question urgente et vitale pour le Maroc, pays essentiellement agricole et qui manque de débouchés vers la mer. L'activité a été portée surtout sur ce point.

Le programme est sensiblement élargi. Il comprenait, dans ses grandes lignes, avant la guerre, un réseau d'environ 1.440 kilomètres, ainsi constitué: une route côtière allant de Mogador à Arbaous, trois route côtière allant de Mogador à Arbaous, trois routes intérieures sur Marrakech (venant de Casablanca, Mazagan et Mogador); deux routes sur Fez (venant de Kénitra et d'Arbaoua). Il comprend aujourd'hui en outre:

1° La grande voie de jonction de l'Algérie au Maroc: Oudja–Taza–Fez;

2° Une grande voie de pénétration vers le Tadla: Casablanca-Boujad;

3° Enfin, tout un réseau secondaire de routes destinées à servir d'affluents aux routes principales et desservant les régions agricoles: Gharb, Chaouïa, Doukkala, Abda.

L'exécution de ce programme a été entreprise avec une activité telle qu'au jour où nous sommes plus de 300 kilomètres de routes sont contruits et livrés à la circulation; une centaine de kilomètres de tronçons sont également construits; plus de 800 kilomètres sont en pleine voie d'exécution. Dès la fin de 1916 ou les premiers jours de 1917 le réseau principal sera terminé.

Les Chemins de fer.—Malgré les difficultés de l'heure présente, le programme établi en 1914 a été poursuivi dans toute la mesure possible.

Les études du chemin de fer de Tanger à Fez sont presque terminées pour tout le tracé Fez–Mechra bel Ksiri. La Compagnie générale du Maroc, en raison de l'état du marché financier, a obtenu, par une convention nouvelle, l'élévation du taux de la garantie d'intérêt à la condition que l'exécution des premiers travaux soit entreprise dans les six mois.

Sur les autres lignes, les brigades d'études, appartenant tant au P.-L.-M. qu'à la Compagnie d'Orléans, opèrent activement, sous la Direction des Travaux publics, sur les signes suivantes: Casablanca–Rabat, en partant de Casablanca; Kénitra–Sidi Kacem.

La question du régime à adopter pour les chemins de fer du Maroc, posée dès le mois de janvier 1914 et sur laquelle une Commission spéciale avait donné son avis, est restée toujours en suspens.

Les travaux urbains.—Le "problème des villes," si l'on peut dire, est l'un des plus délicats qui se soit présenté à nous au Maroc, dès le début de l'occupation. Il avait été laissé dans l'ombre dans ce repport.

L'immigration européenne, poussée subitement sur les côtes du Maroc, s'est trouvée en présence de villes indigènes compactes, malpropres, malsaines, et, autour de ces villes, de terrains déjà accaparés et dont la spéculation rendait les prix inabordables. On s'est installé n'importe où, on a bâti en toute hâte. Des constructions éparses, sans plan ni voirie quelconque, s'égaillaient au hasard sur un immense espace.

Trois objectifs s'impossient à nous:

Protéger les villes indigènes, impropres à toute vie moderne et dont la plus complète indépendance morale et le pittoresque physique méritent à la fois d'être sauvegardés;

Orienter, diriger l'établissement des villes modernes, suivant un plan logique; prévoyant l'avenir et tenant compte du présent;

Assainir l'ensemble par des travaux de voirie appropriés.

Le premier programme a été réalisé. Le contrôle des constructions dans les villes indigènes est confié à la Direction des Beaux-Arts, qui a mission d'en sauvegarder le caractère. Les villes européennes, d'autre part, sont attirées en dehors de leurs murs.

Une mission spéciale est chargée, au Maroc, de l'établissement des plans de villes. Ce travail, à peine entrepris au moment de la mobilisation, est aujourd'hui très avancé, surtout en ce qui concerne Casablanca, Rabat et Marrakech. Par le choix judicieux des emplacements d'immeubles administratifs, par les abandons de terrains provoqués et gracieusements consentis, par la constitution de *réserves* prélevées sur les terrains domaniaux, on est arrivé à mettre un peu d'ordre dans les constructions, dans le tracé des voies, et à dresser, pour un long avenir, un programme d'ensemble qu'il suffira de suivre. A Casablanca, un échange important conclu entre l'État français et l'État chérifien met à notre disposition un lot considérable de terrains absolument nécessaire au développement de la ville.

Quant aux travaux d'assainissement ou de voirie (construction de chaussées, de trottoirs, d'égouts), ils ont été menés avec une activité particulière.

L'éclairage électrique de Casablanca va pouvoir être assuré à bref délai, à la suite d'un contrat passé avec la Société du port.

Un projet d'adduction d'eaux à Rabat a été dressé par les Travaux Publics.

Autres projets figurant au programme des Travaux publics.—Les constructions scolaires sont très avancées: deux grandes écoles modernes ont été terminées à Casablanca: la troisième sort de terre. Des améliorations notables ont été apportées, dans chaque ville, à l'installation des écoles françaises et indigènes. A Rabat, la construction de l'Ecole supérieure arabo-berbère est aujourd'hui presque terminée.

Les hôpitaux s'organisent en même temps et de nouvelles formations surgissent de terre: hôpital de Marrakech, de Mazagan, infirmeries indigènes, etc. . . .

Signalons, enfin, comme un élément important de l'outillage du

Maroc, l'établissement d'une relation télégraphique sous-marine directe entre la France et le Maroc. Le câble Brest–Casablanca vient d'être livré à l'exploitation.

L'accélération apportée dans l'exécution du programme des travaux et l'extension même de ce programme ont profondément modifié la situation financière du Protectorat.

Au moment où la guerre a éclaté, un emprunt de 170 millions venait d'être autorisé. Cet emprunt était déjà insuffisant pour assurer la première mise en valeur d'un pays comme le Maroc, dont l'avenir agricole est si vaste, dont les ressources futures constituent un gage si sûr, et, d'autre part, il devait être consommé lentement.

Aussi le budget, déjà si lourd, supportait-il la charge d'un certain nombre de dépenses de premier établissement indispensables et que les crédits d'emprunt ne pouvaient englober.

La guerre survient. Elle nous impose, pour des nécessités politiques de tout ordre, l'exécution rapide, urgente, simultanée, de tous les travaux de premier établissement prévus. Le programme est élargi. Il en résulte des dépenses nouvelles, qu'il est nécessaire de liquider et de prévoir. Un examen de conscience complet de la situation financière du Maroc nous a conduits alors à une demande d'emprunt supplémentaire de 71 millions, actuellement soumise à la Chambre. Ces 71 millions, joints aux 170 millions autorisés en 1914, représentent la dépense véritable et sincère de la mise en valeur du Maroc.

La situation est désormais plus claire. Nous sommes assurés de pouvoir continuer jusqu'au bout cette politique de travaux, à laquelle nous devons, pour une large part, la sécurité complète du Maroc pendant la guerre, et qui nous vaudra, la guerre finie, la possession d'un empire outillé et armé pour la lutte économique. Le budget, d'autre part, dégagé d'un certain nombre d'impediments et ne représentant désormais en toute réalité que les dépenses d'exploitation du pays, peut espérer atteindre l'équilibre.

Mais, dans toute affaire importante et sérieuse à ses débuts, les bénéfices ne sauraient couvrir du premier coup ni suivre même de loin les charges grandissantes d'un capital qui s'accroît. Il convient d'en tenir compte. Au Maroc, quelle que soit l'augmentation des recettes pendant les premières années, la charge de l'emprunt, que les nécessités politiques, économiques, militaires même, forcent à consommer si rapidement, sera de beaucoup supérieur, pendant les premières années, à l'importance de ces bénéfices.

On l'avait si bien compris que, d'après la loi de 1914, la charge de l'emprunt n'incombait au Protectorat qu'à partir d'un certain chiffre de recettes de son budget. Mais, ce chiffre étant trop bas, la réserve était illusoire. Un système plus logique est proposé dans le nouveau projet du Gouvernement: il consiste à ne faire peser la charge de l'emprunt sur le budget du Protectorat qu'à partir d'une certaine date et ensuite progressivement pendant quelques années.

L'augmentation des charges budgétaires résultant, dans quelques années, de l'augmentation de la Dette, et dans un avenir immédiat, de l'entretien seul des travaux exécutés sur l'emprunt, impose dès maintenant une politique fiscale destinée à nous créer des ressources.

L'impôt foncier, le Tertib, dont l'assiette, la tarification, la perception étaient également arbitraires, a été remanié cette année et codifié. La réforme, expérimentée pour la première fois cet été, a donné d'excellents résultats. Elle ne donnera son plein que lorsque des agents spéciaux seront chargés du recouvrement de l'impôt; ce personnel ne pourra être recruté qu'après la guerre.

L'impôt sur l'enregistrement, dont la première application, entreprise pendant la guerre, avait soulevé quelques difficultés dans la pratique, particulièrement dans les milieux indigènes, a été également remanié par un texte nouveau. Les explications données au rapport ne sont plus exactes.

Enfin, d'autres impôts vont être établis. La création de patentes fera l'objet d'une étude immédiate.

* * *

L'outillage économique du Maroc, qui fait l'objet de tout notre effort, a pour but essentiel le développement de l'agriculture et du commerce, en un mot, de la colonisation au Maroc. Mais ce n'est là que l'outil. Il convient d'en tirer le meilleur parti possible, et de seconder, d'organiser, d'orienter les initiatives privées en vue d'un développement agricole et commercial intense du Protectorat.

Cette tâche ne pouvait être menée à bien que si elle était centralisée dans les mêmes mains. Les questions de toute nature intéressant la colonisation en général étaient jusqu'ici dispersée entre plusieurs services: Secrétariat général chérifien, Service économique, Service de l'Agriculture, Service des Forêts. Le Secrétariat général du Protectorat, dont relèvent tous les services civils, ne pouvait assurer à lui seul une centralisation suffisante. L'étude de toutes les questions et la responsabilité de toute cette organisation sont confiées désormais à un directeur de l'Agriculture, du Commerce et de la Colonisation, dont relève le Service des Études économiques.

Le programme envisagé ne saurait être exposé dans ses détails. Mais c'est un article essentiel de notre politique au Maroc, sur lequel a porté toute notre attention, et il convient d'en donner une idée.

Ce programme comporte, à l'heure actuelle, deux grands chapitres:
Développement de la colonisation agricole;
Organisation commerciale.
Les difficultés du problème de la colonisation au Maroc proviennent

de ce qu'elle a suivi de près, quelquefois même devancé, la conquête militaire et que ses espoirs étaient prématurés. Tant que la pacification n'a pas été complète, tant que le pays n'a pu être outillé, si succincte-ment soit-il, il était impossible à un gouvernement prudent d'encour-ager la colonisation, destinée fatalement à une faillite. La situation n'est plus la même aujourd'hui; elle aura surtout changé après la guerre. Et il convient dès maintenant de préparer le terrain; et, pour acquérir l'expérience nécessaire, de tenter en temps utile les premiers essais.

Une des plus grosses entraves apportées au développement agricole du pays était la complexité, l'embarras, l'insécurité du régime foncier. Elle est levée aujourd'hui. Le régime de l'immatriculation des terres fonctionne, en fait, depuis le mois de mai dernier, et le nombre des réquisitions déposées est une preuve du besoin urgent auquel répondait cette institution. Dans le Gharb, où la situation est particulièrement difficile, une Commission arbitrale est offerte aux intéressés pour le règlement de leurs litiges, avant immatriculation.

Quant à la colonisation officielle, de premiers essais vont être tentés dans la banlieue de certaines villes, pour diminuer les risques et favoriser, d'autre part, la culture maraîchère. La reconstitution du patrimoine makhzen permettra d'aborder, dès la fin de la guerre, des essais plus importants: l'emprunt nouveau comporte un crédit spécial réservé à l'achat de terrains pour cet objet.

L'agriculture doit être, en outre, encouragée et aidée: réformes apportées dans le régime fiscal, directions et conseils à donner aux agriculteurs, toutes ces mesures ont été envisagées et étudiées. L'Expo-sition de Casablanca, en nous donnant la première documentation concrète, vivante, sur l'agriculture au Maroc, a marqué un progrès important. Nous possédons désormais les bases de toutes nos recherches, et nous pouvons nous orienter en connaissance de cause.

L'organisation du commerce et de la lutte économique est le complément nécessaire de ce programme. Dans ce domaine, toute l'activité du Protectorat a été tendue, depuis la guerre, vers un seul but: la main-mise par la France sur les places occupées par le commerce austro-allemand, et, dans un sens plus général, l'établissement d'une association commerciale étroite entre la Métropole et le Maroc. Cette activité a abouti, après les études, les enquêtes et les mesures pré-liminaires, à l'Exposition franco-marocaine de Casablanca.

Mais cette Exposition n'est que l'origine d'une mouvement. Elle est un départ et non une fin. L'oeuvre qu'elle a fondée continue par l'organisation de musées commerciaux permanents, par la création d'organes de relation permanents entre La Métropole et le Maroc, par une direction unique au centre.

Dans toute cette oeuvre, l'Administration devait être éclairée et secondée. La conception primitive, qui a présidé à la création des

Chambres de Commerce et d'Agriculture, a paru, à ce point de vue, trop étroite. Tous les problèmes nouveaux et urgents créés par l'état de guerre et par la politique économique intense qu'elle a provoquée, nécessitaient une consultation très générale, très approfondie, très sérieuse, des intérêts particuliers. A cette préoccupation a répondu l'institution des Comités d'Études économiques, organes qui se sont superposés aux Chambres de Commerce et qui comprennent l'ensemble des notabilités commerciales, industrielles ou agricoles de chaque région. L'oeuvre de ces Comités, le secours et l'appui qu'ils ont apportés au gouvernement dans une tâche écrasante lui ont été précieux. D'une réunion générale de tous les Comités tenue à Casablanca à l'occasion de l'Exposition, est sortie l'élaboration commune, établie d'accord entre tous les intérêts particuliers et les intérêts généraux que représente l'Administration, d'un vaste programme d'ensemble, financier, commercial et agricole.

Ce n'est pourtant pas là la formule définitive, et il faut prévoir la création d'organismes à la fois plus restreints, plus souples et plus forts, ayant la personnalité civile et budgétaire. La réorganisation des Chambres de Commerce, fondée sur l'élection, suivra nécessairement l'institution des patentes.

* * *

Le cadre de cette préface m'empêche de signaler encore toutes les autres mises au point nécessaires; le détail importe peu. Néanmoins, je dois noter, en terminant, comme devant être réservées les idées exprimées dans ce rapport au sujet du personnel. Il a été reconnu, à l'expérience, que le statut du personnel administratif, trop rigide et étroit, devait être à la fois élargi et assoupli. Une réorganisation complète de ce statut est en voie d'élaboration.

* * *

Tels sont, d'une manière très rapide et très générale, les idées et les faite *actuels* qu'il faut connaître, avant de lire un rapport qui a déjà 18 mois de date. Dix-huit mois représentent déjà, pour une colonie en crise de croissance, une période de développement. Dix-huit mois de guerre représentent beaucoup plus encore pour le Maroc: un développement et une avance, une évolution et une anticipation. Il était impossible que le lecteur l'ignorât.

LYAUTEY

Janvier 1916.

Appendix 5
CHRONOLOGY OF SULTANS, *1873–1970*

Moulay el-Hassan	1873–1894
Moulay Abd el-Aziz	1894–1908
Moulay Abd el-Hafid	1908–1912
Moulay Youssef	1912–1927
Sidi Mohammed (V) ben Youssef	1927–1953
Sidi Mohammed ben Moulay Arfa	1953–1955
Sidi Mohammed ben Youssef	1955–1961
Hassan II	1961–

REPORT OF MARCH 19, 1913,
ON JUDICIAL ORGANIZATION

Marrakech, le 19 Mars 1913.

Le Général de Division Lyautey,
Commissaire Résident Général de France
au Maroc,

à Monsieur le Ministre des Affaires Etrangères,
Paris

J'ai l'honneur de vous adresser ci-joint le projet d'organisation de la Justice française au Maroc. Élaboré dans des conditions rendues particulièrement difficiles par l'absence des ouvrages de droit et de jurisprudence les plus indispensables, ceux que j'ai commandés en France ne m'étant pas encore parvenus, ce projet contient sans doute bien des imperfections; je me suis efforcé d'établir, dès mon retour au Maroc, un texte aussi complet que possible que je soumets aujourd'hui à votre bienveillante approbation: une commission de jurisconsultes, ainsi que je vous le propose à la fin de la présente lettre, pourra rapidement mettre au point notre projet et en combler les lacunes.

Je me permets d'attirer toute votre attention sur l'urgence de la réforme proposée: c'est, à mon sens, la première que nous devions réaliser au Maroc; elle est en effet la condition nécessaire de l'abrogation du régime des capitulations et, par suite, la condition même de la réorganisation administrative du Maroc dont le Gouvernement m'a confié le soin et remis la responsabilité.

Je me suis efforcé, dans l'élaboration du projet qui vous est soumis, de réaliser une organe judiciaire entièrement moderne. J'ai tenu à écarter tout ce que le mécanisme judiciaire français a de suranné, toutes les complications d'une procédure justement critiquée par les meilleurs de nos jurisconsultes et par les politiques les plus avertis des choses de droit. Par contre, pour des motifs tant diplomatiques que politiques, j'ai voulu qu'aucune des règles proposées n'apparût comme une innovation qui n'aurait pas subi l'épreuve de l'expérience; les organismes et les procédures dont je demande l'adoption, s'ils s'écartent parfois du droit commun, sont exactement tirés de textes actuellement en vigueur en France, en Algérie, en Tunisie ou aux Colonies; je me suis attaché, en outre, à mettre en oeuvre dès aujourd'hui diverses réformes actuellement soumises aux Chambres par le Gouvernement.

Le projet d'organisation judiciaire étant accompagné d'un commentaire par article du texte proposé, je me bornerai ici à en retracer les grandes lignes.

* * *

La première question qui se pose est celle de savoir quelle est l'autorité compétente pour organiser les tribuneaux français au Maroc.

Il m'est apparu qu'il est conforme à la fois à l'esprit et à la lettre du Traité du Protectorat du 30 Mars 1912 de confier à S.M. le Sultan, sous la forme d'un dahir revêtu de mon visa, le soin de réorganiser la justice de son empire. Le texte précité dispose, en effet, que la réforme sera effectuée, sur la proposition du Gouvernement français, par Sa Majesté Chérifienne.

J'estime donc, les traités de protectorat devant être interprétés *stricto sensu,* que nous ne saurions, sans porter une atteinte imprévue par le texte à la souveraineté du Sultan, instaurer par une loi ou un décret des tribuneaux français au Maroc. Cette doctrine est entièrement confirmée par la consultation que j'ai demandée à M. Jean Labbé, avocat au Conseil d'État et à la Cour de Cassation, dont vous trouverez ci-joint copie. Il résulte de l'étude de ce jurisconsulte que la Cour de Cassation a constamment reconnu la compétence et la légalité des décisions des tribuneaux institués en exécution des dispositions d'un traité de protectorat approuvé par une loi et conformément à ces dispositions: s'il appartient généralement au Président de la République, statuant par voie de décret, de procéder à la réorganisation judiciaire dans nos pays de protectorat, il résulte des dispositions ci-dessus rappelées du traité du 30 Mars 1912, que ce soin a été laissé au Maroc à Sa Majesté Chérifienne, sous le contrôle du Gouvernement français.

II

L'organisation des tribuneaux français au Maroc comportera des Justices de Paix à compétence étendue, deux Tribunaux de première instance, une Cour d'Appel.

Les Juges de Paix à compétence étendue siégeront dans les mêmes conditions et auront les mêmes attributions qu'en Algérie. Des Juges de Paix titulaires seront institués dans toutes les villes de quelque importance, dans ces mêmes villes des juges de paix suppléants pourront être nommés. En outre, les fonctions de Juge de Paix pourront être confiées, le cas échéant, à des officiers.

Deux Tribunaux de première instance sont prévus, l'un à Casablanca, l'autre à Oudjda.

Enfin une Cour d'Appel est instituée à Rabat. Il m'a paru préférable de ne pas envoyer à Alger ou à Aix l'appel des décisions de première instance prises par les jurisdictions duc Maroc; outre qu'une telle solution eût en pour conséquence de retarder considérablement le règlement des affaires, elle eût nécessité l'intervention d'une loi pour établir a compétence de l'une de ces cours.

Au criminel, les Justices de Paix et les Tribunaux Correctionnels auront la même compétence qu'en Algérie. Le Tribunal, avec l'adjonction d'assesseurs jurés, aura, comme en Tunisie, la compétence de la Cour d'Assises. Le Jury délibérera, avec les magistrats, sur la culpabilité et sur l'application de la peine.

La question a été examinée de savoir s'il ne conviendrait pas de donner à la Cour de Rabat les pourvoirs de juge de Cassation. Cette solution offrait l'avantage d'une grande rapidité dans le règlement définitif des litiges; elle s'inspirait, d'autre part, de l'exemple de la juridiction du Conseil d'État. Il m'a semblé par contre qu'un grand avantage s'attachait au contrôle suprême de la Cour de Cassation sur les décisions rendues par les juridictions marocaines; les plaideurs français et étrangers y trouveront une garantie qui ne manquera pas d'accroître le prestige de notre organisation judiciaire et qui facilitera les négociations ouvertes en vue du retrait des capitulations. Aucune disposition spéciale, d'après M. Jean Labbé, n'est nécessaire pour donner compétence à la Cour de Cassation qui trouve son droit de contrôle dans le texte même du Protectorat et dans la loi approbative de ce traité. Il m'a paru toutefois que les Tribunaux marocaine devant statuer au nom de S.M. le Sultan, il était nécessaire qu'un accord intervînt entre les deux Gouvernements pour soumettre les décisions des juridictions nouvelles à la censure de la Cour suprême. Cet accord donners en même temps, force exécutoire, en France, aux décisions et actes de procédure émanant des autorités judiciaires chérifiennes, et réciproquement.

En ce qui concerne la composition des juridictions instituées, je me suis attaché, d'une part, à réduire le nombre des magistrats appelés à siéger, d'autre part, à faciliter les remplacements en cas d'absence. A cet effet, la Cour pourra siéger valablement à trois membres, conformément aux projets déposés à la Chambre par M. le Garde des Sceaux

Cruppi. En outre les Juges de Paix pourront être appelés à monter au siège, conformément au projet déposé par M. le Garde des Sceaux Briand.

Des dispositions sont prévues qui tendent à éviter les abus auxquels ont parfois donné lieu les remplacement des magistrats dans nos colonies.

III

Le personnel des Tribunaux français au Maroc doit, dans ma pensée, être celui des Cours et Tribunaux de France et d'Algérie. Seul un cadre unique permet d'assurer un jeu nécessaire au développement de carrières normales et à une bonne administration de la justice.

Mais une loi serait, je crois, nécessaire pour autoriser les magistrats français à siéger en service régulier au Maroc et réciproquement. Devant l'urgence absolue qui s'attache au fonctionnement de nos tribunaux, j'ai l'honneur de vous prier instamment de solliciter de M. le Garde des Sceaux et de M. le Ministre des Finances l'envoi provisoire de magistrats français qui conserveraient leurs droits à la retraite, et seraient autorisés à ramplir les fonctions judiciaires au Maroc, conformément au précédent établi pour M. Landry. Un projet de loi serait incessamment déposé qui règlementerait définitivement la situation des magistrats français au Maroc.

Je me suis donc borné dans le projet qui vous est soumis, à préciser, pour donner toute garantie aux justiciables, que pourront seuls siéger dans les tribunaux marocains, des magistrats français ou des personnes légalement aptes à remplir les fonctions judiciaires en France. Un statut réglant l'avancement et la discipline de ces magistrats est, en outre, institué en conformité des textes français ou des projets actuellement soumis aux Chambres.

IV

L'une des innovations les plus notables du projet d'organisation judiciaire est celle qui concerne les auxiliaires de la Justice.

Il m'a paru désirable d'éviter au Maroc l'établissement d'Officiers ministériels qui constituent une lourde charge pour les justiciables et dont l'institution en France a soulevé de nombreuses critiques. Aux Colonies et en Algérie, des plaintes se sont également élevées relatives aux abus qu'occasionnent les Offices d'Avocats-Défenseurs, les charges d'Officiers publics ou ministériels. Le Gouvernement général de l'Algérie a même récemment soumis à la Chancellerie un projet tendant à transformer les notaires en fonctionnaires et à les recruter au concours. On sait enfin quels regrettables scandales ont été récemment soulevés en France par la gestion de certains liquidateurs judiciaires.

Je n'hésite donc pas à vous proposer de confier l'ensemble des attributions dévolues en France aux divers auxiliaires de la justice; notaires, greffiers, avoués, liquidateurs judiciaires de sociétés, syndics de faillites, curateurs, etc., à un corps de fonctionnaires, divisés en classe et recevant, en principe, un traitement fixe. Ce corps de fonctionnaires est, d'ailleurs, destiné à devenir ultérieurement l'Administration de l'Enregistrement.

Cette solution, au reste, n'est pas nouvelle, elle est précisément celle qui a été adoptée par le Parlement à la suite des incidents précités et qui a consisté dans la remise à l'Administration de l'Enregistrement de la liquidation des biens des congrégations religieuses. (Loi du 29 Mars 1910.)

Des dispositions spéciales tendent à réglementer le recrutement et la discipline du Barreau. Celle-ci est confiée au Tribunal, solution nécessaire dans un pays où l'intervention des avocats étrangers pourra être ultérieurement envisagée.

Enfin, en ce qui concerne le personnel des experts près les tribunaux, je me suis inspiré, pour les garanties à exiger des hommes de l'art, des dispositions du projet déposé au Sénat par M. le Garde des Sceaux Barthou.

V

Les Tribunaux français au Maroc seront compétents pour le règlement des affaires entre Français; entre Européens, lorsque les Capitulations auront été abrogées en matière immobilière ou mobilière; entre Indigènes, en toutes matières lorsque les deux parties accepteront cette juridiction; en matière mobilière, dans les affaires entre Européens et Indigènes. Je n'ai pas cru devoir, quant à présent imposer la compétence de la Juridiction française, c'est-à-dire dessaisir le Tribunal indigène, dans les causes immobilières entre Européens et Indigènes. D'une part, le caractère spécial des questions immobilières au point de vue indigène, d'autre part, l'absence d'un régime foncier régulier m'ont amené à penser qu'il est préférable de surseoir, jusqu'à la promulgation d'une règlementation immobilière, pour étendre aux Indigènes la compétence des Tribunaux français. Cette réglementation est, dès à présent, mise à l'étude. Au cas où vous estimeriez qu'il convient de généraliser immédiatement la compétence des nouvelles juridictions, il me paraît nécessaire d'adjoindre pour le jugement de ces affaires, deux Assesseurs indigènes au Tribunal et à la Cour.

VI

Comme en Tunisie, les tribunaux français seront juges des affaires civiles, commerciales et administratives. Le contentieux administratif est soumis à une réglementation spéciale qui s'inspire des dispositions du Décret tunisien du 27 Novembre 1888. Il m'est apparu, en effet, qu'il convient dans l'état politique actuel du Maroc, de ne soumettre à la censure des Tribunaux judiciaires que le contentieux de pleine juridiction à l'exclusion du contentieux de l'excès de pouvoir. Cette solution n'ayant pas, à ma connaissance, soulevé de réclamations en Tunisie, j'ai l'honneur de vous proposer de l'étendre au Maroc, sous réserve toutefois de quelques modifications.

VII

Désireux avant tout d'instaurer au Maroc une justice rapide et peu coûteuse, j'estime inopportun de promulguer le Code de Procédure civile et le Code d'Instruction criminelle français. Le premier de ces textes surtout a soulevé de nombreuses critiques à raison des complications de procédure et des retards qu'il permet de susciter dans le règlement des litiges. J'ai pensé qu'il convenait plutôt de faire appel à une loi de procédure qui, expérimentée depuis plus de 20 ans, est unanimement reconnue comme excellente, la loi du 22 Juillet 1889 sur la procédure devant les Conseils de Préfecture.

C'est de ce texte que s'inspire le Code de Procédure civile dont j'ai l'honneur de vous proposer l'adoption. Je me suis attaché toutefois à y introduire toutes les procédures spéciales qui, en raison de leur simplicité, justifient la faveur dont elles sont l'objet de la part des plaideurs et des hommes de loi; c'est ainsi que la procédure des référés, complétée conformément aux dispositions du projet de loi déposé par M. le Garde des Sceaux Cruppi, a été insérée dans le nouveau Code chérifien. Je me suis également efforcé de simplifier, tant au civil qau'au criminel, la procédure du recours en cassation, par des dispositions qui trouvent leur force exécutoire dans la loi approbative du Traité de Protectorat, ou, le cas échéant, dans un décret du Président de la République à intervenir. Les recours en cassation sur les incidents seront joints au recours sur le fonds, et, d'autre part, l'arrêté de cassation ayant pour effet le renvoi de l'affaire devant la Cour de Rabat ou devant une juridiction marocaine, la juridiction du renvoi sera liés, sur l'interprétation du droit, par l'arrêt de la Cour Suprême, procédure conforme à celle qui est suivie devant le Conseil d'État et qui permettra de limiter la durée et les frais de recours en cassation.

VIII

Au criminel, la procédure suivie, qui s'inspirera de celle de notre Code d'instruction criminelle, se rapprochera sensiblement néanmoins de celle qui est pratiquée devant les tribunaux institués en Algérie par le décret du 9 Août 1903. Il m'est apparu qu'il importait tout d'abord dans l'état d'insécurité du Maroc, que la justice criminelle fût rapide et que, tout en assurant les droits de la défense, l'exercice de l'action publique ne fût pas entravé par des incidents de procédure. J'ai estimé notamment que l'instruction des affaires devait pouvoir être conduite avec la plus grande célérité.

Enfin, m'inspirant du décret du 15 Septembre 1896 sur l'organisation judiciaire en Indo-Chine, j'ai prévu la constitution d'une Commission criminelle spéciale destinée à assurer la répression des crimes et délits intéressant la sûreté du Protectorat et des Colonies européennes; en cas de sédition une action judiciaire rapide peut devenir nécessaire et il m'a paru préférable de prévoir dès aujourd'hui, à toutes éventualités, une procédure légale offrant un minimum de garanties, procédure dont il a d'ailleurs été fait usage, en 1908, en Indo-Chine.

IX

Vous trouverez, enfin, annexé à la présente lettre, un tarif des frais de justice au Maroc. Ce tarif s'inspire de dispositions relatives aux droits de Chancellerie actuellement perçus devant les juridictions consulaires. J'ai désiré en outre que les frais de justice fussent, dans la mesure du possible, proportionnels à l'importance du litige. Cette règle est, en effet, celle dont s'inspirait le tarif des avoués élaboré, il y a quelques années, par le Conseil d'État sur le désir qui en avait été exprimé par le Parlement.

Ces frais sont perçus, par suite de l'absence d'Officiers ministériels, au profit du Trésor; ils constituent, en fait, des taxes destinées à compenser les charges du service judiciaire; ils sont payés, en principe, par le plaideur qui succombe ou répartis par le Tribunal entre les parties selon les circonstances de l'affaire. Les droits taxés pourront, dans certains cas, atteindre un chiffre assez élevé: l'assistance judiciaire, organisée comme en Algérie, en dispensera les justiciables peu fortunés.

X

Les Tribunaux français au Maroc statueront au civil conformément aux règles du droit international privé. Au criminel, ils appliqueront les dispositions du Code pénal français. Je me réserve de constituer auprès du Secrétariat Général du Protectorat un service d'études législatives qui mettra au point et adaptera aux besoins locaux les lois et décrets qu'il y aura lieu par la suite de promulguer au Maroc.

XI

Telles sont les grandes lignes du projet que j'ai l'honneur de soumettre à votre approbation, avant d'en proposer l'adoption à S.M. le Sultan. Ainsi que je l'ai indiqué au débat de la présente dépêche, il me paraît nécessaire de le faire préalablement examiner par une Commission de jurisconsultes qui en corrigerait utilement les imperfections. Il conviendrait toutefois que cet examen fût conduit dans les conditions de la plus grande célérité afin de ne pas retarder la constitution des Tribunaux français au Maroc. A cet effet, j'ai fait établir, du projet organique, des projets de codes, des tarifs, de la consultation de M. Jean Labbé et de la présente lettre un nombre d'exemplaires suffisant. Sous réserve de votre haute approbation, je me permets de vous signaler tout le prix que j'attacherai à la collaboration, au sein de la commission, des personnalités suivantes:

MM. Herbaux, Conseiller à la Cour de Cassation,
     Berge, Conseiller à la Cour d'Appel,
     Georges Teissier, Professeur à l'École des Sciences politiques,
     Romieu, Conseiller d'État,
     Jean Labbé, Avocat au Conseil d'État et à la Cour de Cassation,
     Paul Grünebaum-Ballin, Président du Conseil de Préfecture de
       la Seine,
     Chardenet, Maître des Requêtes au Conseil d'État,
     X . . . , représentant de votre Département,
     Paul Boulloche, Directeur des Affaires civiles à la Chancellerie,
     Collavet, Chef-Adjoint du Cabinet du Garde des Sceaux.

Dès que la Commission sera constituée et les Rapporteurs désignés, je me tiendrai à votre disposition pour déléguer un fonctionnaire du Protectorat qui pourra fournir à la Commission toutes explications utiles et qui se mettra d'accord avec votre Département et avec la Chancellerie pour le choix des magistrats appelés à composer les nouvelles juridictions. J'attache le plus grand prix à ce que celles-ci fonctionnent immédiatement, dès leur constitution, et je ne doute pas que vous ne consentiez à me prêter tout l'appui de votre autorité pour la réalisation d'une des plus importantes réformes que le Gouvernement m'ait chargé de poursuivre au Maroc et qui est la base nécessaire de notre oeuvre de réorganisation.

GÉNÉRAL LYAUTEY

Appendix 7
LETTERS OF RESIGNATION
24 SEPTEMBRE 1925

Le Maréchal de France Lyautey, Commissaire Résident Général
de France au Maroc, à Monsieur le Président du Conseil,
Ministre de la Guerre. Paris.
Sous couvert de M. le Ministre des Affaires Étrangères. Paris.

J'adresse, par le courrier de ce jour, deux lettres à M. le Ministre des Affaires Étrangères, de qui je relève directement en qualité de Commissaire Résident Général au Maroc, et j'ai l'honneur de vous en envoyer ci-joint copie sous son couvert.

Le rétablissement de la situation militaire qui vient d'être réalisé par les dernières opérations me permet de renouveler la demande que j'avais formulée à plusieurs reprises en vue d'être relevé de mes fonctions. Je serais reconnaissant au Gouvernement de bien vouloir pourvoir à mon remplacement dans le plus bref délai.

LYAUTEY

Le Maréchal de France Lyautey, Commissaire Résident Général
de la République Française au Maroc, à son Excellence
Monsieur le Ministre des Affaires Étrangères. Paris.

Lettre d'envoi.

Les dernières opérations militaires viennent de réaliser un redressement qui nous replace sensiblement sur les lignes que nous occupions avant l'agression riffaine.

La situation du Protectorat se trouve rétablie telle qu'elle était en avril, c'est-à-dire au point où elle avait été portée après treize ans de progression continue.

Je crois avoir le droit de dire que ma tâche, telle qu'elle m'avait été confiée en 1912, a été remplie.

Tant que le Maroc a été en péril, je ne me suis pas permis de renouveler la demande de remplacement que j'avais présentée au Gouvernement en 1923 et en 1924, demande motivée par de graves accidents de santé et par le besoin d'un repos auquel mes trente ans d'activité coloniale me donnaient légitimement droit.

Du jour où la menace riffaine, que j'avais signalée avec une inquiétude croissante, s'est réalisée à l'époque où mes rapports l'avaient fait prévoir, je n'ai plus eu d'autre pensée que de tenir le coup avec les moyens réduits dont je disposais au début et de sauver la situation.

Aujourd'hui, on peut sincèrement affirmer que le danger est écarté et que, avec l'importance des effectifs à pied d'oeuvre, l'avenir peut être envisagé avec confiance.

C'est donc en toute sécurité de conscience que je demande à être relevé de mes fonctions de Commissaire Résident Général du Maroc.

Au demeurant, la question du Riff ouvre des problèmes nouveaux, comme je l'expose dans la lettre confidentielle ci-jointe, rappelant ce qui a été réalisé depuis l'agression riffaine.

A ces problèmes nouveaux, qui demandent à être abordés et suivis avec continuité, il faut un homme nouveau, dans la force de l'âge, bénéficiant de toute la confiance du Gouvernement.

Je demande que mon successeur soit désigné sans délai.

Je me tiendrai à sa disposition pour le renseigner au cas où il estimerait que mon expérience du pays pût lui être utile.

LYAUTEY

Lettre jointe.

On peut considérer que, aujourd'hui, grâce à la vigoureuse offensive que l'arrivée de forces importantes a permis de mener depuis le début d'août sur tout notre front Nord, la situation militaire et politique du Protectorat français au Maroc est rétablie.

La récente occupation de la position de Bibane et du territoire des Beni Ouriaghel au nord de l'Ouergha, succédant au dégagement des abords d'Ouezzan et à la reprise en mains des Tsoul et des Branes sur nos deux ailes, à la progression sur le Leben et chez les Beni Zeroual, nous a reportés dans l'ensemble sur les lignes que nous occupions avant l'agression riffaine.

Nous les avons même dépassées sur un point que nous n'avions pu atteindre précédement et qui présente un importance capitale, Amjot, centre de l'action religieuse et politique des Cheurfa Derkaoua, qui avait été, en avant de nos lignes, le premier objectif d'Abd-el-Krim. Son occupation réalise un intérêt politique majeur, en raison de l'action qu'y exercent ces personnages religieux, dont l'influence a toujours été au service du Sultan et du Protectorat.

La sécurité des points vitaux, tels que Fez, Taza, la communication avec l'Algérie, sont désormais garanties, grâce à la mise en ligne de forces qui permettent d'en assurer solidement la protection et la couverture.

Dans tout le Maroc, je le constate depuis mon retour, la répercussion de ce rétablissement, a, dès maintenant, rendu toute confiance dans notre force et dans l'avenir du Protectorat.

C'est donc en toute sécurité de conscience que je puis aujourd'hui demander au Gouvernement de me remplacer comme Commissaire Résident Général au Maroc.

Cette demande, je l'avais présentée dès la fin de 1923, à la suite des graves accidents de santé que je venais de subir.

Je l'ai formulée de nouveau en octobre 1924, avec la plus vive instance, auprès de M. le Président du Conseil, Ministre des Affaires Étrangères, et de M. le Ministre de la Guerre, en invoquant le besoin d'un repos auquel mon âge et trente années d'activité coloniale me donnaient légitimement droit.

Il m'a été opposé une fin de non-recevoir fondée sur la situation créée par la meance d'Abd-el-Krim, signalée par moi-même avec une anxiété croissante, et sur les services qu'on jugeait, avec exagération à mon avis, que ma présence rendait au Maroc.

Je n'ai pu que m'incliner devant ces pressants appels à mon devoir envers le Pays, mais en précisant que ma succession devait être regardée comme ouverte, et que, si je faisais le sacrifice de rejoindre encore mon poste, c'était sous la réserve que mon remplacement serait envisagé dans un délai aussi rapproché que possible.

Cette demande, je ne me suis pas permis de la renouveler cette année.

On ne demande plus à quitter son poste quand le péril est là; on n'a qu'a y tenir ferme.

C'est ce que je crois avoir fait.

D'abord en "tenant le coup" avec les moyens si réduits dont je disposais au début. Grâce à la vaillance et à l'énergie de troupes admirables, luttant pied à pied pendant trois mois, nous avons réussi, au prix de plus rude effort, à nous maintenir au Nord de l'Ourgha sur les deux bastions de Taounat et de Tafrant, qui ont pu servir ainsi de bases à la reprise d'offensive qui vient de rétablir la situation. Nous avons pu nous maintenir à Taza et à son poste avancé de Kifane, d'où partira l'offensive de demain, et sans qu'un seul jour la communication avec l'Algérie ait été coupée, laissant ainsi le temps d'arriver aux renforts importants dont le Gouvernement a décidé l'envoi. Je ne rendrai jamais assez complètement hommage au dévouement et à l'énergie des Chefs, à la vaillance et à l'endurance des troupes, qui ont soutenu un tel effort pendant cette dure période. Tous ont bien mérité du Pays.

Les Français du Maroc, fonctionnaires, colons, commerçants, artisans, dont le dévouement et le confiance n'ont pas fléchi un seul instant, ont le droit d'être associés à cet éloge.

Le même témoignange est dû à la population marocaine, au loyalisme des villes, à la fidélité des tribus dont, à l'exception de celles au contact immédiat des Riffains, pas une n'a bougé, là même où elles étaient le plus récemment soumises et le plus douteuses. Leurs chefs ont fait preuve d'une loyauté absolue, à commencer par le plus haut de tous, Sa Majesté le Sultan, qui nous a apporté sans répit un appui dont la France doit lui garder une profonde reconnaissance.

Enfin, depuis la venue des renforts et l'arrivée du général Naulin, nous avons pu préparer et commencer le redressement qui, dès la fin d'août, dégageait nos deux ailes, au Nord d'Ouezzan d'une part, chez les Tsoul et les Branès d'autre part, et nous rétablissait au centre sur la ligne de l'Ouergha.

Aujourd'hui on peut sincérement affirmer que l'heure du péril est passée, que le rétablissement de la situation antérieure à l'agression riffaine est réalisé et que, avec l'importance des effectifs amenés à pied d'oeuvre et la fort organisation du commandement, des résultats plus importants encore sont désormais assurés.

Si l'on objectait qu'il m'appartient d'assurer et d'exploiter les résultats politiques des opérations, je répondrais que les modifications apportées à mes attributions enlèvent toute efficacité à l'action politique inséparable de l'action militaire qu'elle doit déterminer, et que, de ce fait, ma présence ici, comme je le constate chaque jour depuis mon retour, est devenue inutile.

J'estime par ailleurs qu'il y a, pour le Gouvernement, pour le Maroc, pour la France, un intérêt de premier ordre à procéder à mon remplacement dans le plus bref délai.

Si, en effet, je crois pouvoir affirmer, comme j'ai dit plus haut, que la situation se trouve aujourd'hui dans le Protectorat sensiblement telle qu'elle était avant l'agression riffaine, il s'est posé à la frontière Nord de la zone française, du fait de l'évolution de la conception de l'Espagne dans sa zone, un problème nouveau.

Le Protectorat français au Maroc, tel que j'en ai reçu la charge en 1912, ne comportait pas de "Front Nord," en prenant ce terme, non seulement au sens militaire, mais dans son sens politique et géographique le plus général. Ce front était constitué par la zone espagnole dont l'occupation devait se réaliser intégralement et se réalisait en effet sans discontinuité. De ce côté, nous nous tenions avec soin en deçà de nos limites, ne nous avançant qu'à mesure que les Espagnols avançaient, en jumelant nos postes avec leurs, de façon à ne nous mettre sur les bras aucune difficulté avec le Riff et le Djebel, dont la charge revenait entièrement à l'Espagne et où nous n'avions pas le droit d'intervenir.

Or, depuis un an, la conception de l'Espagne a évolué. Elle considère qu'il ne lui est pas indispensable d'occuper tout le pays pour exercer son action dans le cadre des traités.

Nous avons donc là, désormais, sur la frontière Nord du Protectorat, une zone qui n'est pas de notre ressort, mais que nous ne pouvons plus ignorer ni négliger. Elle est habitée par une population guerrière qu'a constamment attirée la zone voisine la nôtre, riche et pacifique, laquelle a toujours, historiquement, subi ses agression. Avec les forces et les moyens dont nous disposons actuellement, et sous l'énergique direction du maréchal Pétain, il n'y a pas à douter du succès militaire final sur Abd-el-Krim. Mais, qu'il s'agisse d'Abd-el-Krim ou d'un autre, le Riff n'en existera pas moins, et il y a là une question nouvelle à envisager, l'organisation politique, administrative aussi bien que militaire à prévoir et à réaliser pour mettre le Protectorat français à l'abri de toute menace ultérieure.

C'est un problème qui se pose dès maintenant et qui exige d'être abordé, puis suivi avec continuité. Il y faut donc un homme nouveau, dans la force de l'âge, ayant du temps devant lui, pénétré des vues du Gouvernement, bénéficiant de toute sa confiance et de celle de la majorité du Parlement. Il y a donc intérêt évident à ce que ce soit cet homme, mon successeur, qui aborde ce problème dès le début.

LYAUTEY

Appendix 8

DECREE OF JUNE 11, 1912, ASSIGNING THE POWERS OF THE RESIDENT GENERAL

Décret.

Le Président de la République Française,

Sur la proposition du Président du Conseil, Ministre des Affaires Étrangères,

Décrète:

ART. 1er. Le Représentant de la République Française au Maroc porte le titre de Commissaire Résident Général et relève du Ministre des Affaires Étrangères.

ART. 2. Le Commissaire Résident Général est le dépositaire de tous les pouvoirs de la République dans l'Empire Chérifien.

Il est le seul intermédiaire du Sultan auprès des représentants des puissances étrangères.

Il approuve et promulgue, au nom du Gouvernement de la République, les décrets rendus par Sa Majesté Chérifienne.

Il dirige tous les services administratifs; il a le commandement en chef des forces de terre et la disposition des forces navales.

ART. 3. Le Commissaire Résident Général communique par l'entremise du Ministre des Affaires Étrangères avec les divers membres du Gouvernement de la République; il les saisit, sans délai, des questions qui intéressent leurs départements.

ART. 4. Le Commissaire Résident Général est assisté d'un Délégué à la Résidence Générale, destiné à le remplacer, en cas d'absence ou d'empêchement.

Art. 5. Le Président du Conseil, Ministre des Affaires Étrangères, est chargé de l'exécution du présent décret.

Fait à Paris, le 11 juin 1912

A. FALLIÈRES

Par le Président de la République:
Le Président du Conseil,
Ministre des Affaires Étrangères,

R. POINCARÉ

Appendix 9

THE PROTECTORATE STRUCTURE, 1912–1925

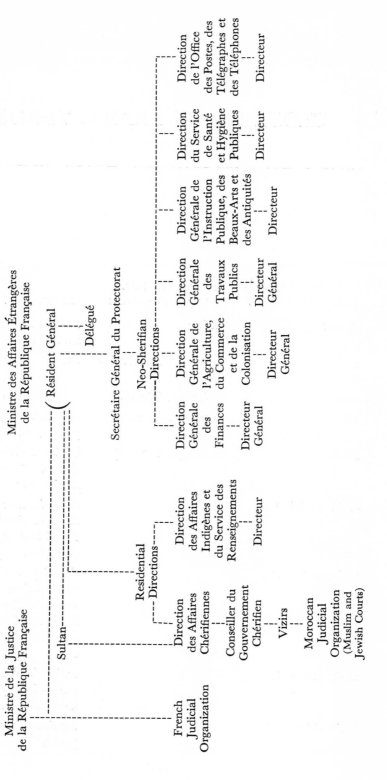

GLOSSARY OF ARABIC TERMS

FRENCH TRANSLITERATION	INTERNATIONAL TRANSLITERATION	DEFINITION
achour	ʿus͟hūr	traditional Islamic harvest tax
adel	ʿādel (pl. adoul = ʿudūl)	notary
alem	ʿalim (pl. ʿulamā)	learned doctor of law
amel	ʿamīl (pl. ʿummā)	tax collector, agent prefect, or governor
amin	amīn (pl. oumana)	holder of various positions of "trust"; administrator
amin ed-dakhl		administrator of all funds received by the Bit el-Mal el-Mouslimin (Treasury)
amin ed-diouana		the city official who auctioned off the privilege of collecting the market and gate taxes each year to tax-farmers
amin el-hassab		senior bookkeeper of the Ministry of Finance (before 1912)
amin el-kharadj		administrator of expenses

amin el-moustafad		city tax collector
amin el-oumana		supervisor of administrators (e.g., in Ministry of Finance)
amin es-sagar		administrator of expenditures of the Bit el-Mal
amir	amīr	commander, governor, prince
Amir el-Moumenin		Commander of the Faithful; one of the traditional titles of the Moroccan Sultan
azref	azraf	arbitration, i.e., of legal disputes
Berber	Barbar	Berbers are the non-Arab native white population of Morocco and North Africa. They speak their own Berber language, which has several different dialects, even within the Moroccan borders.
Bit el-Mal ed-Dakhli	Bait al-Māl al-Dākhili	Sultan's Private Treasury
Bit el-Mal el-Mouslimin	Bait al-Māl al-Muslimīn	Moroccan Public Treasury (before 1912)
Bled el-Makhzen	Bilād al-Makhzan	that territory under real or theoretical government control
Bled es-Siba	Bilād al-Sibāh	literally, "land of dissidence," i.e., territory outside government control
bou maouarith	abu 'l-mawārīth	city official in charge of protecting the interests and property of widows and orphans

cadi	qāḍī (pl. quḍāt)	judge of Muslim religious (Chrâa) courts
caïd	qāʾid (pl. qāda)	title given the town administrator who was also judge of a Makhzen court; same title was often given tribal chiefs
chérif	sharīf (pl. ashrāf or shurafāʾ)	Muslim noble
Chrâa	Sharīʿah	Muslim law, e.g., Chrâa courts
dahir	ẓāhir	Imperial Decree issued by Sultan
damen mouadjabah	ḍāmin al-murwājabah	a type of bail bond
damen oudjou	ḍāmin al-wujūh	a type of bail bond
Djebala	Jabalah	a mountainous area of Morocco stretching from the River Sebou to the Mediterranean, inhabited by Berber tribes
djemaa	jamāʿah	tribal council
djezya	jizyah	traditional Islamic capitation tax
faqih	faqīh	Muslim theologian
fetoua	faṭwā	legal opinion rendered by mufti and presented in a court case
frida	faridah	an arbitrary tax levied by the Sultan on the rural populations whenever he was short of funds
guich	jaysh	those tribes which supplied troops for the Makhzen in lieu of taxes (cf. naïba)

Habous	Ḥubūs	Waqf, or property constituted as a special religious trust
hedya	hadiyah	the only direct tax paid by Moroccans before the Protectorate was established
imam	imām	religious leaders (e.g., a title given the Sultan)
khalifa	k͟halīfah	assistant or lieutenant; in Morocco it applied to various officials at various levels
kharadj	k͟haraj	traditional Islamic property tax
khatib	k͟haṭīb	leader of the prayers in a mosque
mahakma	maḥkamah	courtroom or building
Makhzen	Mak͟hzan	the Moroccan Government
m'dris	mudarris	professor
mechâoury	mus͟hāwiri	chief constable
medjlis	majlis	council
meks	maks (pl. mukūs)	market tax
melk	milk	private property
mohtaseb	muḥtasib	market inspector
moulkiya	milkiyah	private ownership of property
mufti	muftī	jurisconsult
nadir	nāẓir	the administrator of Habous property
naïb	nāʾib	the Sultan's special diplomatic agent at Tangier before the Protectorate
naïba	naʾibah	those tribes in Morocco which had to pay taxes (cf. guich)

neshka	nushkah	a copy (of a legal document)
orf	ʿurf	custom
oukil	wakīl	a type of modified lawyer, being more concerned with the presenting of forms and papers in court than anything else; the closest equivalent to a lawyer in Muslim law
Ouzir ech-Chikayat	al-Wazīr al-Shikāyat	Minister of Administrative Appeals
Ouzir el-A'dham	al-Wazīr al-A'ẓam	Grand Vizir
Ouzir el-Bahr	al-Wazīr el-Baḥr	Foreign Minister
Ouzir el-Harb	al-Wazīr al-Ḥarb	Minister of War
Ouzir el-Malis	al-Wazīr al-Malīyah	Minister of Finance
pacha	bāshā	title of a town or city administrator, used interchangeably sometimes with caïd; like the caïd, he also acted as a judge in the Makhzen courts
sheikh	shaykh	chief, head
taleb	tālib (pl. ṭalabah or ṭullāb)	student, e.g., one who successfully memorized the Koran
zaouïa	zāwiya	a Muslim brotherhood, and a combination of a private school and monastery
zekkat	zakāt	alms

BIBLIOGRAPHY

I. OFFICIAL SOURCES

Trattati e Convenzioni fra il regno d'Italia e gli altri Stati. Vol. XXII: *Atti conchiusi dal 1° gennaio 1912 al 31 dicembre 1913.* Roma: Tipografia del R. Ministero degli Affari Esteri, 1930.

British and Foreign State Papers. Vols. XCI-CVI: 1898–1913. London: H.M. Stationery Office, 1902–1916.

Gooch, G. P., and Temperley, Harold. *British Documents on the Origins of the War, 1898–1914.* London: H.M. Stationery Office, 1927–1932.

    Vol. I: *The End of British Isolation.*

    Vol. II: *The Anglo-Japanese Alliance and the Franco-British Entente.*

    Vol. III: *The Testing of the Entente, 1904–6.*

    Vol. VII: *The Agadir Crisis.*

Public Record Office. *Confidential Prints: Morocco.* F.O. 413, Nos. 32–58 (1900–1913).

Ministère des Affaires Étrangères. *Documents diplomatiques. Affaires du Maroc (1901–1912).* 6 vols. Paris: Imprimerie Nationale, 1914.

————. *Documents diplomatiques français (1871–1914).* Paris: Imprimerie Nationale, 1930–1959.

1ʳᵉ Série (1871–1900), Vols. XIV-XV.

2ᵉ Série (1901–1911), Vols. I-XIV.

3ᵉ Série (1911–1914), Vols. I-V.

Lyautey, Général (ed.). *Rapport général sur la situation du Protectorat au Maroc au 31 juillet 1914.* Rabat: Imprimerie Officielle, 1916.

————. *Principes fondamentaux de l'organisation gouvernementale du Protectorat marocain.* Rabat: Imprimerie Officielle, 1918.

Résidence Générale. *Renaissance du Maroc: dix ans du Protectorat, 1912–1922.* Rabat: Imprimerie Officielle, n.d. [1922].

Bulletin Officiel du Protectorat de la République Française au Maroc. Rabat: Imprimerie Officielle.

    Nos. 1 (Nov. 1, 1912), 2 (Nov. 8, 1912), 3 (Nov. 15, 1912), 4 (Nov. 23, 1912), 5 (Nov. 29, 1912), 13 (Jan. 24, 1913), 14 (Jan. 31, 1913), 28 (May 9, 1913), 34 (June 20, 1913), 37 (July 11, 1913), 43 (Aug. 22, 1913), 46 (Sept. 12, 1913), 47 (Sept. 19, 1913), 50 (Oct. 10, 1913), 51 (Oct. 17, 1913), 66 (Jan. 30, 1914), 70 (Feb. 27, 1914), 71 (Mar. 6, 1914), 74 (Mar.

27, 1914), 83 (May 29, 1914), 89 (July 10, 1914), 90 (July 17, 1914),
96 (Aug. 21, 1914), 100 (Sept. 21, 1914), 101 (Sept. 28, 1914), 108
(Nov. 16, 1914), 129 (Apr. 12, 1915), 137 (June 7, 1915), 148 (Aug. 23,
1915), 168 (Jan. 10, 1916), 175 (Feb. 28, 1916), 196 (July 24, 1916), 214
(Nov. 27, 1916), 217 (Dec. 18, 1916), 228–229 (Mar. 5 and 12, 1917), 233
(Apr. 9, 1917), 236 (Apr. 30, 1917), 241 (June 4, 1917), 242 (June 11,
1917), 274 (Jan. 21, 1918), 306 (Sept. 2, 1918), 326 (Jan. 20, 1919), 327
(Jan. 27, 1919), 335 (Mar. 24, 1919), 345 (June 2, 1919), 368 (Nov. 10,
1919), 378 (Jan. 19, 1920), 380 (Feb. 3, 1920), 384 (Mar. 2, 1920), 386
(Mar. 16, 1920), 389 (Apr. 6, 1920), 390 (Apr. 13, 1920), 402 (July 6, 1920),
404 (July 20, 1920), 406 (Aug. 3, 1920), 407 (Aug. 10, 1920), 408 (Aug.
17, 1920), 409 (Aug. 24, 1920), 410 (Aug. 31, 1920), 412 (Sept. 14, 1920),
418 (Oct. 26, 1920), 419–420 (Nov. 2 and 9, 1920), 421 (Nov. 16, 1920),
426 (Dec. 21, 1920), 429 (Jan. 11, 1921), 430 (Jan. 18, 1921), 437 (Mar.
8, 1921), 440 (Mar. 29, 1921), 442 (Apr. 12, 1921), 447 (May 17, 1921),
459 (Aug. 9, 1921), 464 (Sept. 13, 1921), 466 (Sept. 27, 1921), 469 (Oct.
18, 1921), 474 (Nov. 22, 1921), 482 (Jan. 17, 1922), 499 (May 16, 1922),
501 (May 30, 1922), 502 (June 6, 1922), 505 (June 27, 1922), 521 (Oct.
17, 1922), 544 (Mar. 27, 1923), 547 (Apr. 17, 1923), 553 (May 29, 1923),
556 (June 19, 1923), 572 (Oct. 9, 1923), 586 (Jan. 15, 1924), 596 (Mar.
25, 1924), 599 (Apr. 15, 1924), 606 (June 3, 1924), 607 (June 10, 1924),
618 (Aug. 26, 1924), 640 (Jan. 27, 1925), 675 (Sept. 29, 1925), 679 (Oct.
27, 1925).

II. PRINCIPLE WORKS BY LYAUTEY (SEE ALSO "Official Sources")

"Du rôle social de l'officier dans le service militaire universel," in Maréchal
Lyautey, *Du rôle social de l'officier.* Paris: René Julliard, 1946 (First pub-
lished in *Revue des Deux Mondes,* March 15, 1891.)
Lettres de jeunesse: Italie (1883). Danube, Grèce, Italie (1893). Paris: B.
Grasset, 1931.
Lettres du Tonkin et de Madagascar (1894–1899). 2 vols. Paris: Armand
Colin, 1920, 1921.
Lettres du Tonkin. 2 vols. Paris: Éditions Nationales, 1928.
"Du rôle colonial de l'armée," in Maréchal Lyautey, *Du rôle social de
l'officier.* Paris: René Julliard, 1946. (First published in *Revue des Deux
Mondes,* January 15, 1900.)
*Dans le sud de Madagascar: pénétration militaire—situation politique et
économique (1900–1902).* Paris: Lavauzelle, 1903.
Paroles d'action—Madagascar, Sud-Oranais, Oran, Maroc (1900–1926). 3d
ed. Paris: Armand Colin, 1938. (First published in 1927.)
Vers le Maroc. Lettres du Sud-Oranais (1903–1906). Paris: Armand Colin,
1937.
Choix de lettres, 1882–1919. Ed. Lt.-Col. de Ponton d'Amécourt. Paris: Armand
Colin, 1947.
Lyautey l'Africain—textes et lettres du maréchal Lyautey. 4 vols. Ed. Pierre
Lyautey. Paris: Plon, 1953, 1954, 1956, 1957. Vol. I: 1912–1913; Vol. II:
1913–1915; Vol. III: 1915–1918; Vol. IV: 1919–1925.
Les plus belles lettres de Lyautey. Ed. Pierre Lyautey. Paris: Calmann-Lévy,
1962. (These letters cover the period from 1880 to 1934.)

III. PRINCIPAL WORKS ON LYAUTEY

Barthou, Louis. *Lyautey et le Maroc*. Paris: Éditions du "Petit Parisien," 1931.

Bègue, Léon. *Le secret d'une conquête: au Maroc avec Lyautey*. Paris: Taillandier, 1929.

Boisboissel, Général Yves de. *Dans l'ombre de Lyautey*. Paris: André Bonne Éditeur, 1954.

Britsch, Amédée. *Le maréchal Lyautey: le soldat, l'écrivain, le politique*. Paris: Renaissance du Livre, 1921.

Catroux, Général Georges. *Lyautey le Marocain*. Paris: Hachette, 1952.

Dubly, Henry-Louis. *Lyautey-le-magicien*. Lille: Mercure de Flandre, 1931.

Espèrandieu, P. *Lyautey et le Protectorat*. Paris: Pichon et Durand-Auzias, 1947.

Garric, Robert. *Le message de Lyautey*. Paris: Éditions Spes, 1935.

Gaulis, B.-G. *La France au Maroc: l'oeuvre du général Lyautey*. Paris: Armand Colin, 1919.

Goulven, Joseph. *Lyautey l'Africain*. Nancy: Humblot, 1935.

Gouraud, Général Henri-Joseph-Eugène. *Lyautey*. Paris: Hachette, 1938.

Hardy, Georges. *Portrait de Lyautey*. 10th ed. Mayenne: Bloud & Gay, 1949.

Heidsieck, Patrick. *Rayonnement de Lyautey*. Paris: Gallimard, 1941.

Howe, Sonia Elizabeth. *Lyautey of Morocco—An Authorized Life*. London: Hodder and Stoughton, Ltd., 1931.

Leclerc, Max. *Au Maroc avec Lyautey*. Paris: Armand Colin, 1927.

Maurois, André. *Lyautey*. Paris: Plon, 1931.

d'. Ormesson, Wladimir. *Auprès de Lyautey*. Paris: Flammarion, 1963.

Postal, Raymond. *Présence de Lyautey*. 4th ed. Paris: Éditions "Alsatia," 1944.

Tarde, Guillaume de. *Lyautey—le chef en action*. 5th ed. Paris: Gallimard, 1959.

Usborne, Vice Admiral Cecil Vivian. *The Conquest of Morocco*. London: S. Paul & Co., Ltd., 1936.

Vanlande, René. *Au Maroc, sous les ordres de Lyautey*. Paris: Peyronnet, 1926.

IV. BOOKS AND OTHER WORKS

Adam, André. *La maison et le village dans quelques tribus de l'Anti-Atlas*. Paris: Collection Hespéris, 1951.

Amar, Émile. *L'organisation de la propriété foncière au Maroc: étude théorique et pratique*. Paris: Paul Geuthner, 1913.

Andersen, Eugene N. *The First Moroccan Crisis, 1904–1906*. Hamden, Conn.: Archon Books, 1966.

Aubin, Eugène. *Le Maroc d'aujourd'hui*. Paris: Armand Colin, 1904.

Ayache, Albert. *Le Maroc—bilan d'une colonisation*. Paris: Éditions Sociales, 1956.

Barbour, Nevill. *Morocco*. London: Thames and Hudson, 1965.

———— (ed.). *A Survey of North West Africa (The Maghrib)*. London: Oxford University Press, 1959.

Barlow, Ima Christina. *The Agadir Crisis*. Chapel Hill, N.C.: University of North Carolina Press, 1940.

Becker y Gonzales, Jerónimo (ed.). *Tratados, convenios y acuerdos referentes a Marruecos y la Guinea española*. Madrid: Imprenta del Patronato de Hérfanos de Intendencia a Intervencion Militares, 1918.

Belal, Abdel Aziz. *L'investissement au Maroc (1912–1964) et ses enseignements en matière de développement économique*. Paris and La Haye: Mouton, 1968.

Berge, Stéphane. *La justice française au Maroc—organisation et pratique*. Paris: Leroux Éditeur, 1917.

Bernard, Augustin. *Le Maroc*. Paris: Félix Alcan, 1913.

Bernard, Stéphane. *Le conflit franco-marocain, 1943–1956*. 3 vols. Brussels: Éditions de l'Institut de Sociologie de l'Université Libre de Bruxelles, 1963.

Berque, Jacques. *Le Maghreb entre deux guerres*. Paris: Éditions du Seuil, 1962.

Betts, Raymond F. *Assimilation and Association in French Colonial Theory, 1890–1914*. New York: Columbia University Press, 1961.

Blondel, Georges. *Pétain, 1856–1951*. Paris: Presses de la Cité, 1966.

Bourgeois, Émile. *Manuel historique de politique étrangère*, Vol. IV: *La politique mondiale (1878–1919), empires et nations*. 4th ed. Paris: Librairie Classique Eugène Belin, 1925.

Brémard, Frédéric. *Les droits publics et politiques des français au Maroc*. Paris: R. Pichon & R. Durand-Auzias, 1950.

———. *L'organisation régionale du Maroc*. Paris: R. Pichon & R. Durand-Auzias, 1949.

Bülow, Bernhard Fürst von. *Denkwürdigkeiten*, Vols. I and II. Berlin: Verlag Ullstein, 1931.

Cagigas, Isidro de las. *Tratados y convenios referentes a Marruecos*. Madrid: Instituto de Estudios Africanos, 1952.

Caillé, J. *L'organisation judiciaire au Maroc*. Paris: Librairie Générale de Droit et de Jurisprudence, 1948.

Castre, Charles. *The Ideals of France*. New York: The Abingdon Press, 1922.

Célérier, Jean. *Le Maroc*. Paris: Armand Colin, 1953.

Charles-Roux, François, and Caillé, Jacques. *Missions diplomatiques françaises à Fès*. Paris: Éditions Larose, 1955.

Chastenet, Jacques. *Histoire de la troisième république*, Vol. III: *La république triomphante, 1893–1906;* Vol. IV: *Jours inquiets et jours sanglants, 1906–1918;* Vol. V: *Les années d'illusions, 1918–1931*. Paris: Hachette, 1955, 1957, 1960.

Chouraqui, André. *La condition juridique de l'israélite marocain*. Paris: Presses du Livre Français, 1950.

Colliez, André. *Notre Protectorat marocain: la 1ère étape, 1912–1930*. Paris: Librairie des Sciences Politiques et Sociales, 1930.

Cordero Torres, José-Maria. *Organización del protectorado español en Marruecos*. 2 vols. Madrid, 1943.

Decroux, Paul. *Les sociétés au Maroc, zone française—zone tangéroise: statut juridique et fiscal*. Paris: R. Pichon & R. Durand-Auzias, 1950.

Despois, Jean. *La Tunisie orientale—Sahel et basse steppe: étude géographique*. Paris: Presses Universitaires de France, 1955.

Drummond Hay, Sir John. *A Memoir of Sir John Drummond Hay*. London: John Murray, 1896.

Famchon, Yves. *Le Maroc—d'Algésiras à la souveraineté économique*. Paris: Éditions des Relations Internationales, 1957.

Fouillée, Alfred. *Psychologie du peuple français*. Paris: Félix Alcan, 1914.

Fumey, Eugène. *Choix de correspondances marocaines.* Paris: J. Maisonneuve, 1903.

Fyzee, Asaf A. A. A. *Outlines of Muhammadan Law.* London: Oxford University Press, 1955.

Gallissot, René. *Le patronat européen au Maroc—action sociale, action politique (1931–1942).* Rabat: Éditions Techniques Nord-Africaines, 1964.

García Figueras, Tomás. *España y su protectorado en Marruecos (1912–1956).* Madrid: Instituto de Estudios Africanos, 1957.

García Figueras, Tomás, and Llebrés, Fernández. *Manuales del Africa española.* Madrid: Instituto de Estudios Africanos, 1955.

Gibb, H. A. R., and Bowen, Harold. *Islamic Society and the West,* Vol. I, Part 2. London: Oxford University Press, 1957.

Girault, Arthur. *Principes de colonisation et de législation coloniale,* Vol. V. Paris: Recueil Sirey, 1928.

Gordon, David C. *North Africa's French Legacy, 1954–1962.* Cambridge, Mass.: Harvard University Press, 1964.

Goulven, J. *Traité d'économie et de législation marocaines.* 2 vols. Paris: Librairie des Sciences Économiques et Sociales, 1921.

Guennoun, Saïd. *La montagne berbère—les Aït Oumalou et les pays Zaïan.* Rabat: Éditions Omnia, 1933.

Guernier, Eugène. *Le Berbérie, l'Islam et la France,* Vol. II. Paris: Éditions de l'Union Française, 1950.

Guillaume, Albert. *La propriété collective au Maroc.* Paris: Librairie de Médicis, 1960.

El-Hajoui, Mohamed Omar. *Histoire diplomatique du Maroc (1900–1912).* Paris: G. P. Maisonneuve, 1937.

Halstead, John P. *Rebirth of a Nation. The Origins and Rise of Moroccan Nationalism, 1912–1944.* Cambridge, Mass.: Harvard University Press, 1967.

Hanotax, Gabriel. *L'énergie française.* Paris: Flammarion, 1902.

Hardy, Georges, de Caix, Robert and Dehérain, Henri. *Le Maroc—la Tunisie, la Syrie, l'oeuvre scientifique française en Syrie et en Perse.* Vol. III of *Histoire des colonies françaises et de l'expansion de la France dans le monde,* ed. Gabriel Hanotaux and Alfred Martineau. Paris: Société de l'Histoire Nationale—Librairie Plon, 1931.

Henderson, W. O. *Studies in German Colonial History.* London: Frank Cass & Co., Ltd., 1962.

Holtz, Louis. *Traité de législation marocaine—droit public et droit privé du Protectorat.* Paris: Édition des Juris-Classeurs, 1914.

Hopkins, J. F. P. *Medieval Muslim Government in Barbary, until the Sixth Century of the Hijra.* London: Luzac & Co., Ltd., 1958.

Israël, Gérard. *L'alliance israélite universelle: 1860–1960.* Numéro Spécial. *Cahiers de l'Alliance Israélite Universelle,* Vol. CXXVII (February, 1960).

Julien, Ch.-André. *L'Afrique du Nord en marche—nationalismes musulmans et souveraineté française.* 2d. ed. Paris: René Julliard, 1953.

———. *Histoire de l'Afrique du Nord—Tunisie, Algérie, Maroc,* Vol. II: *De la conquête arabe à 1830.* Paris: Payot, 1956.

———. *Histoire de l'Algérie contemporaine,* Vol. I: *La conquête et les débuts de la colonisation (1827–1871).* Paris: Presses Universitaires de France, 1964.

Kann, Réginald. *Le Protectorat marocain.* Paris: Berger-Levrault, 1921.

Khaldoun, Ibn. *Prolégomènes d'Ibn Khaldoun.* Trans. de Slane. Paris, 1863.

Labour Survey of North Africa. Geneva: International Labour Office, 1960.

Lahbabi, Mohamed. *Le gouvernement marocain à l'aube du XXe siècle*. Rabat: Éditions Techniques Nord-Africaines, 1958.

Lambton, Ann S. K. *Landlord and Peasant in Persia*. London: Oxford University Press, 1953.

Landau, Rom. *Moroccan Drama, 1900–1955*. London: Robert Hale, Ltd., 1956.

Landes, David S. *Bankers and Pashas*. London: Heinemann, 1958.

Laubadère, André de. *Les réformes des pouvoirs publics au Maroc—le governement, l'administration, la justice*. Paris: Librairie Générale de Droit et de Justice, 1949.

Le Tourneau, Roger. *Évolution politique de l'Afrique du Nord musulmane, 1920–1961*. Paris: Armand Colin, 1962.

——. *Fès avant le Protectorat: étude économique et sociale d'une ville de l'occident musulman*. Casablanca: Société Marocaine de Librairie et d'Édition, 1949.

Løkkegaard, Frede. *Islamic Taxation in the Classic Period*. Copenhagen: Branner Og Korch, 1950.

Luccioni, J. *Le habous ou wakf (rites malékite et hanéfite)*. Casablanca: Imprimeries de la Vigie Marocaine, et du Petit Marocain, n.d.

Lucien-Graux, Docteur. *Le Maroc économique*. Paris: Librairie Ancienne Honoré Champion, 1928.

Lyautey, Pierre. *Gallieni*. Paris: Gallimard, 1959.

Maroc. Encyclopédie Coloniale et Maritime. Ed. Eugène Guernier. Paris: Éditions de l'Empire Français, 1948.

Martin, Claude. *Histoire de l'Algérie français, 1830–1962*. Paris: Édition des 4 Fils Aymon, 1963.

Maxwell, Gavin. *Lords of the Atlas: The Rise and Fall of the House of Glaoua, 1893–1956*. London: Longmans, 1966.

Michaux-Bellaire, E. *Conférences*, Vol. XXVII of *Archives Marocaines* (1927).

——. *Le Gharb*, Vol. XX of *Archives Marocaines* (1913).

——. *Les habous de Tanger—registre officiel d'actes et de documents*, Vols. XXII and XXIII of *Archives Marocaines* (1914).

——. *Quelques tribus de montagnes de la région du Habt*, Vol. XVII of *Archives Marocaines* (1911).

Miège, Jean-Louis. *Le Maroc et l'Europe (1830–1894)*, Vol. IV: *Vers la crise*. Paris: Presses Universitaires de France, 1963.

Milliot, Louis. *Démembrement du habous—menfa'â, gzâ, zînâ, istighraq*. Paris: Ernest Leroux, 1918.

——. *Recueil de jurisprudence chérifienne—tribunal du ministre chérifien de la justice et conseil supérieur d'ouléma (medjlès al-istinâf)*, Vol. I. Paris: Éditions E. Leroux, 1920.

——. *Les terres collectives (blâd djemâ'a)—étude de législation marocaine*. Paris: Éditions E. Leroux, 1922.

Montagne, Robert. *Les Berbères et le makhzen dans le sud du Maroc: essai sur la transformation politique des Berbères sédentaires (groupe Chleuh)*. Paris: Félix Alcan, 1930.

——. *Villages et kasbas berbères: tableu de la vie sociale des Berbères sédentaires dans le sud du Maroc*. Paris: Félix Alcan, 1930.

Ennâṣiri Esslâoui, Aḥmed ben Khâled. *Kitâb Elistiqsa Li-Akhbâri Doual Elmagrib Elagsâ. Chronique de la dynastie alaouite du Maroc*. Trans. Eugène Fumey. Vol. X of *Archives Marocaines* (1907).

Naval Intelligence Division. *Morocco.* 2 vols. Oxford: H.M. Stationery Office, 1941, 1942. (Geographical Handbook Series, B.R. 506A.)

Passeron, René. *Les grandes sociétés et la colonisation dans l'Afrique du Nord.* Algiers: Typo-Litho, 1925.

Peyrouton, Marcel. *Histoire générale du Maghreb—Maroc, Algérie, Tunisie: des origines à nos jours.* Paris: Albin Michel, 1966.

Piquet, Victor. *Le Maroc: géographie et histoire—mise en valeur.* Paris: Armand Colin, 1917.

Poncet, Jean. *La colonisation et l'agriculture européennes en Tunisie depuis 1881—étude géographique, historique et économique.* Paris: Mouton & Co., 1962.

Pourquier, René, and Chagneau, Roger. *Cours élémentaire d'organisation administrative marocaine.* Rabat: Éditions "La Porte," 1949, 1950, 1951. (Released in mimeographed form in 10 parts.)

Revelière, Comte de la. *Les énergies françaises au Maroc: études économiques et sociales.* 2d ed. Paris: Plon, 1917.

Rivière, P.-Louis. *Traités, codes et lois du Maroc.* 3 vols. Paris: Recueil Sirey, 1924.

Robert-Raynaud. *En marge du "livre jaune"—Le Maroc.* Paris: Plon, 1923.

Roberts, Stephen H. *The History of French Colonial Policy, 1870–1925.* London: Frank Cass & Co., Ltd., 1963.

Rosenthal, E. I. J. *Political Thought in Medieval Islam.* Cambridge: Cambridge University Press, 1962.

Sautayra, and Cherbonneau, Eugène. *Droit musulman—statut personnel et des successions,* Vol. II: *Des successions.* Paris: Maisonneuve, 1874.

Selous, G. H. *Appointment to Fez.* London: The Richards Press, 1956.

Simsar, Muhammed Ahmed. *The Waqfiyah of 'Ahmed Pāšā.* Philadelphia: University of Pennsylvania Press, 1940.

Spillmann, Georges. *Les Aït Atta du Sahara et la pacification du Haut Dra.* Rabat: Félix Moncho, 1936.

———. *Du Protectorat à l'Indépendance: Maroc, 1912–1955.* Paris: Plon, 1967.

Stewart, Charles F. *The Economy of Morocco, 1912–1962.* Cambridge, Mass.: Harvard University Press, 1964.

Stuart, Graham Henry. *The International City of Tangier.* 2d ed. Stanford: Stanford University Press, 1955.

Tabouis, Geneviève. *The Life of Jules Cambon.* Trans. C. F. Atkinson. London: Jonathan Cape, 1938.

Taillandier, G. Saint-René. *Les origines du Maroc français—récit d'une mission (1901–1906).* Paris: Librairie Plon, 1930.

Tardieu, André. *La conférence d'Algésiras: histoire diplomatique de la crise marocaine (15 janvier–7 avril 1906).* 3d ed. Paris: Félix Alcan, 1909.

Tyan, Émile. *Histoire de l'organisation judiciaire en pays d'Islam.* Leiden: E. J. Brill, 1960.

———. *Institutions du droit public musulman.* 2 vols. Paris: Recueil Sirey, 1954, 1956.

Warringer, Doreen. *Land Reform and Development in the Middle East.* London: Oxford University Press, 1962.

Westermarck, E. *Ritual and Belief in Morocco.* 2 vols. London: Macmillan, 1926.

———. *Wit and Wisdom in Morocco: A Study of Native Proverbs.* London: George Routledge & Sons, Ltd., 1930.

V. ARTICLES

Agwani, M. S. "Morocco: from Protectorate to Independence," *International Studies,* I (1959–1960), 51–70.

Askri. "L'école militaire d'élèves-officiers marocains de Meknès," *Bulletin du Comité de l'Afrique Française,* No. 4 (April 4, 1912), pp. 107–110.

Bel, Alfred. "A propos de l'enseignement des indigènes à Fez," *Renseignements Coloniaux,* No. 5 (May, 1925), pp. 146–148.

Bernard, Général. "La conquête et l'organisation du Maroc, 1912–1919: l'oeuvre du général Lyautey," *La Géographie,* XXXIV (June–December, 1920), 337–360 and 458–478.

Bernard, Paul. "L'enseignement primaire des indigènes musulmans de l'Algérie," *Revue du Monde Musulman,* I, No. 1 (1906), 5–21.

Bousquet, G. H. "Le droit coutumier des Aït Haddidou des Assit Melloul et Isselatena (Confédération des Aït Yafelmanes): notes et réflexions," *Annales de l'Institut d'Études Orientales,* XII (1954), 113–229.

Chapelle, F. de la. "Les tribus de haute montagne de l'Atlas occidental: organisation sociale et évolution politique," *Revue des Études Islamiques,* II, No. 3 (1938), 339–360.

———. "Une cité de l'oued Dra' sous le protectorat des nomades: Nesrat," *Hespéris,* IX, No. 1 (1929), 29–42.

Durand, E. "La réforme politique et administrative du gouvernement chérifien depuis 1912," *Revue Juridique et Politique de l'Union Française,* IX (1955), 83–122.

Al Fasi, Abou-Zeid Sidi Abderrahman. "Commentaire de Sidi Mohammed ben Qasim as-Sidjilmasi ar-Rabati" (trans. E. Michaux-Bellaire), *Revue du Monde Musulman,* XIII, No. 2 (1911), 216–238.

Gardet, Louis. "La propriété en Islam," *Revue de l'Institut des Belles Lettres Arabes,* XXXVIII, No. 2 (1947), 109–134.

Gromand, Roger. "La coutume de la 'Bezra' dans les ksour de Figuig," *Revue des Études Islamiques,* V, No. 3 (1931), 277–312.

Hamet, Ismaël. "L'école supérieure de langue arabe," *France-Maroc,* V, No. 26 (July 1, 1921), 121–124.

Hardy, Georges. "L'education française au Maroc," *La Revue de Paris,* No. 8 (April 15, 1921), pp. 773–788.

Heffenig, W. "Waḵf," *Encyclopaedia of Islam,* IV (1934), 1906.

"In memorium, général J.-B. Marchand," *Académie des Sciences Coloniales,* XXI (1934), 37–51.

"Les institutions berbères" (trans. G. Salmon), *Archives Marocaines,* I, No. 1 (1904), 127–148.

Jabre, F. "Dans le Maroc nouveau: le rôle d'une université islamique," *Annales d'Histoire Économique et Sociale,* X, No. 51 (May 31, 1938), 193–207.

Jacqueton, G. "La colonisation française au Maroc," *Annales de Géographie,* XXXIII (1924), 307–312.

Joly, A. (in collaboration with MM. Xigluna and L. Mercier). "Tétouan. Deuxième partie: historique," *Archives Marocaines,* V, Nos. 2 & 3 (1905), 161–264 and 311–430.

Laubadère, André de. "La réforme de l'organisation judiciaire marocaine," *Revue Juridique et Politique de l'Union Française,* II (1948), 443–465.

————. "Les réformes des pouvoirs publics au Maroc," *Revue Juridique et Politique de l'Union Française,* II (1948), 1–28 and 137–174.

Lyautey, Pierre. "La politique du protectorat en Afrique marocaine. Ses origines de 1905 à 1918," *Convegno di Scienzi Morali e Storiche,* II (1938), 987–1002.

Marty, Paul. "Le collège musulman, Moulay Idris," *Renseignements Coloniaux,* No. 1 (January, 1925), pp. 1–16.

————. "L'enseignement primarie et professionnel des indigènes à Fez," *Renseignements Coloniaux,* No. 3 (March, 1925), pp. 73–84.

————. "La justice civile musulmane au Maroc," *Revue des Études Islamiques,* Vol. V, No. 4 (1931).

————. "La nouvelle jeunesse intellectuelle du Maroc," *Renseignements Coloniaux,* No. 5 (May, 1925), pp. 133–146.

————. "L'université de Qaraouiyne," *Renseignements Coloniaux,* No. 11 (November, 1924), pp. 329–353.

Maudit, René. "Le makhzen marocain," *Renseignements Coloniaux,* No. 3 (1903), pp. 290–299.

Al Medjaci, Mohammed ben Al Hasan. "Naouzil" (trans. E. Michaux-Ballaire), *Revue du Monde Musulman,* XIII, No. 2 (1911), 239–241.

Mercier, L. "L'administration marocaine à Rabat," *Archives Marocaines,* VII (1906), 350–401.

Michaux-Bellaire, E. "Les biens habous et les biens du makhzen, au point de vue de leur location et de leur aliénation," *Revue du Monde Musulman,* V, No. 7 (1908), 436–457.

————. "Les coutumes berbères dans les tribus arabes," *Revue du Monde Musulman,* IX, No. 10 (1909), 224–234.

————. "Le droit d'intervention du nadir des habous de l'amin el moustafad et du pacha, dans les transmissions d'immeubles," *Revue du Monde Musulman,* XIII, No. 3 (1911), 487–492.

————. "L'enseignement indigène au Maroc," *Revue du Monde Musulman,* XV, No. 10 (1911), 422–452.

————. "La guelsa et le gza," *Revue du Monde Musulman,* XIII, No. 2 (1911), 197–248.

————. "L'impôt de la naïba et la loi musulmane," *Revue du Monde Musulman,* XI, No. 8 (1910), 396–404.

————. "Les impôts marocains," *Archives Marocaines,* I (1904), 56–96.

————. "L'Islam et l'état marocain," *Revue du Monde Musulman,* VIII, No. 7–8 (1909), 313–342.

————. "L'organisation des finances au Maroc," *Archives Marocaines,* XI, No. 2 (1907), 171–251.

————. "La propriété et les habous," *Archives Marocaines,* Vol. XX (1913).

Michaux-Bellaire, E., and Aubin, Paul. "Le régime immobilier," *Revue du Monde Musulman,* XVIII, No. 1 (1912), 1–105.

Michaux-Bellaire, E., and Salmon, G. "El-Qçar El-Kebir: une ville de province au Maroc septentrional," *Archives Marocaines,* II, No. 2 (1904), 1–228.

Al-Motabassir. "Les habous de Tanger," *Revue du Monde Musulman,* I, No. 3 (1907), 325–342.

Péretié, A. "Organisation judiciaire au Maroc," *Revue du Monde Musulman,* XIII, No. 3 (1911), 509–531.

Rezzouk, A. "Notes sur l'organisation politique et administrative du Rif," *Archives Marocaines,* V, No. 2 (1905), 265–275.

Salmon, G. "L'administration marocaine à Tanger," *Archives Marocaines,*
   I (1904), 1–37.
Slouschz, Nahum. "Étude sur l'histoire des juifs et du Judaisme au Maroc,"
   Archives Marocaines, IV, No. 2–3 (1905), 345–411; VI, No. 1–2 (1906),
   1–167.
Viguera Franco, E. de. "Sistemas orgánico-judiciales en Marruecos," *Cuadernos
   de Estudios Africanos,* No. 8 (1949), pp. 9–54.

INDEX